Competencies for Teaching:
Classroom Instruction

Competencies for Teaching

A competency-based teacher education system in four volumes:

1. Individual Instruction
2. Classroom Instruction
3. Therapeutic Instruction
4. Teacher Education

Competencies for Teaching: Classroom Instruction

Laurence J. Peter

Wadsworth Publishing Company, Inc.
Belmont, California

Education Editor: Dick Greenberg

Designer: Gary A. Head

Editor: Victoria Pasternack

Technical Illustrator: John Foster

ISBN 0-534-00387-7

L. C. Cat. Card No. 74-28638

Printed in the United States of America

1 2 3 4 5 6 7 8 9 10—79 78 77 76 75

Preface

Competencies for Teaching: Classroom Instruction consists
of three books bound in one volume: Classroom Instruction
Textbook, Classroom Instruction Workbook, and Classroom
Instruction Record. This volume briefly reviews the basic
elements of the first volume of the Competencies for
Teaching system, *Individual Instruction*, so that it can be
used independently of the first volume. However, the
knowledge and skills acquired during the individual instruction phase are components of the more complex process
of classroom instruction. Therefore, to derive the maximum value from systematically acquiring complex teaching
skills, the first phase of the system, individual instruction, should be completed before beginning the classroom
instruction phase.

Each volume of Competencies for Teaching—*Individual
Instruction, Classroom Instruction*, and *Therapeutic Instruction*—consists of self-instructional programs that
can be studied by the student independently. The topics
treated within these three phases of the system correspond
directly to the decisions teachers must make during the
process of instruction. Although each of the three volumes of the system is a self-contained unit, each should
be thought of as a component of the total Competencies for
Teaching system.

A college of education can use *Individual Instruction, Classroom Instruction*, and *Therapeutic Instruction*
to implement a program for preservice or inservice teachers, which integrates educational psychology, general
methods, and practice teaching, permitting the student to
systematically acquire educational theory and practical
teaching skills. The Competencies for Teaching system
provides competency-based texts for teacher education programs, including a system of accountability for each component of knowledge and skill.

The competencies acquired from *Classroom Instruction*
are valuable to individuals preparing for a teaching
career at any level of instruction—from kindergarten

through college. The book is called *Classroom Instruction* rather than "classroom teaching" because *instruction* refers to a more specific process. Instruction is the process of planning, presenting, and evaluating the outcomes of certain educational interventions, or strategies. Although the specifics and content vary, the instructional process is essentially the same at all levels. *Teaching* is a more inclusive term frequently used to describe non-professional, unsystematic, and unplanned activity. Examples of the general use of the word *teacher* are, "Parents are the child's first teachers"; "Experience is the best teacher"; and "He is a natural teacher." The term *instruction* has been used to designate the specific functions described in the first three volumes of the Competencies for Teaching system, and *teaching* has been used to refer to the more general or inclusive Competencies for Teaching system.

The systematic approach to instructional decision making brings intellectual rigor to the instructional process. In spite of the research evidence provided by behavioral scientists in support of the effectiveness of the application of learning principles, in far too many cases, educators are still either defending traditional unscientific teaching practices or adopting new methods that are inconsistent with sound learning principles. Within *Classroom Instruction*, relevant areas of educational psychology—including learning principles, child growth and development, individual differences, perception, and evaluation—are incorporated into instructional practice. Integrating learning principles and instructional procedures provides a sound basis for the instructional process.

The student who completes the exercises in the textbook, workbook, and record will acquire a repertoire of tangible competencies for planning and implementing instructional activities that promote pupil achievement. Mastering the instructional process is essential to efficient classroom instruction but does not replace other important acquisitions or qualities of the classroom teacher. For example, the teacher must be a competent scholar or subject matter expert. That is, the effective teacher must know not only *how* to teach but also *what* to teach. Other qualities that are essential to maximum effectiveness and satisfaction in teaching have to do with general behavioral characteristics, or the teacher's personality. Ideally, the teacher should like to teach and be enthusiastic about the content of instruction. He or she should be a person who derives satisfaction from learning and who maintains a high level of intellectual curiosity. The teacher should view his vocation as a highly skilled profession and one in which he enjoys perfecting his skill. Every teacher should be interested in pupils as individuals. Assuming these desirable personal characteristics as given, *Classroom Instruction* will provide the student in education with the means of achieving an effective and satisfying professional role.

Note to the Teacher Education Instructor

Because this volume is a self-instructional package, it can be used as a text in a variety of ways. It can be assigned for independent study by the students, and class sessions can either follow the outline of the text or present content not directly related to the text. Volume IV, *Teacher Education*, provides a detailed discussion of various ways that a competency-based course in classroom instruction can be conducted. It describes how to use *Classroom Instruction* as a text for courses independent of the other phases of Competencies for Teaching, as well as suggesting how to implement the total system with accountability for each component of theory, methods, simulation, and practicum.

Note to the Student Teacher

The three books contained in this volume—Classroom Instruction Textbook, Classroom Instruction Workbook, and Classroom Instruction Record—integrate theory and practice into a self-instructional program of ten major components for developing your competencies as a classroom teacher. The classroom instruction course differs in two substantial ways from that of individual instruction. First, in individual instruction you acquire a conceptual model of the instructional process, in the classroom instruction phase, you will apply this model. Because you do not have to go through the systematic development of the model again in order to apply it, the practice teaching in this phase can be much more flexible. This flexibility is desirable because in classroom practicum, you will have to perform the teaching functions appropriate to the time and place of your particular situation. In the practicum classroom or school, many variables beyond your control—for example, special events, emergencies, and other problems—may make it impractical for you to implement the content of classroom instruction in a precisely ordered sequence.

Second, it is more important in classroom instruction than it was in individual instruction that you experience teaching success from the beginning. Ineffective instruction can create difficulties in the classroom which could make further instruction with that class problematic. The Competencies for Teaching system prepares you for classroom instruction by providing you with individual instruction as a prerequisite and by presenting learning principles and other aspects of educational psychology through practical examples that can be applied directly during classroom instruction. If you are beginning classroom instruction without having first completed individual instruction, the student teacher should, if possible, study the textbook and workbook in *Individual Instruction*.

The Classroom Instruction Textbook and Classroom Instruction Workbook present theory, methods, programed instruction, and simulated experiences to prepare you for practice teaching. Each chapter in the Classroom Instruction Textbook should be studied first, followed by completing the parallel chapter in the Classroom Instruction Workbook. In the concurrent practicum, you will use the Classroom Instruction Record. This record provides instruction for practicum activities and convenient forms for recording observations, lessons, and evaluations of your students.

Contents

Classroom Instruction Textbook

Classroom Instruction Workbook

Classroom Instruction Textbook

Laurence J. Peter

One

Introduction

Objectives: After completing your study of this chapter,
you will be able to (1) define the purposes of classroom
instruction, (2) explain the need for classroom instruction, (3) describe cybernetic feedback and the cycle of
the instructional process, (4) follow the instructions
regarding the use of this book, and (5) complete the exercises in Chapter One of the Classroom Instruction Workbook.

The classroom is intended to be an environment in
which every child is treated as a unique--working,
playing, and growing--partner with his teacher
and his classmates in the cooperative process of
learning. It is a place in which each child should be
progressing at his capacity while participating in group
activities or in independent learning. The classroom
activities should create in him a desire to attend school
each day to experience the joy of learning. The modern
classroom must be an environment that eliminates the traditional barriers to the learning process—the group-
paced, lockstep organization that forces the able child to
limit his achievement and causes the less able child to
become frustrated through fear of failure.

Effective classroom instruction must unleash each
child's potential for learning and add new and creative
dimensions to childhood experience. It must ensure that
each child proceeds through his courses, confident in the
knowledge that he will meet with frequent and rewarding
success. Classroom instruction can foster achievement
that will develop independent, self-managed students.
Systematically applying sound learning principles to
classroom organization and management plays a major role
in achieving effective classroom instruction.

Purposes of Classroom Instruction

The *classroom instruction* phase of the Competencies for
Teaching system is designed to follow the individual instruction phase, during which the student teacher acquired
the skills of tutoring an individual pupil and became familiar with the conceptual model of the process of instruction. Pupils in the classroom frequently need the
individual assistance which the graduate of the first
phase is equipped to provide. In addition, effective
classroom strategies are achieved through applying the
same conceptual model of the process of instruction as was
employed during individual instruction. In other words,

effective classroom instruction is achieved by applying to teaching groups the same skills and concepts that were acquired during the individual instruction phase of the system.

Applying scientifically established principles of learning to classroom management and instruction can create an environment wherein each strategy contributes to achieving educational objectives. The classroom instruction phase offers the teacher experiences that develop his skills in (1) instructing groups, (2) implementing learning principles to solve instructional problems, and (3) managing the group experience. Classroom instruction does not deal directly with the *content* of instruction. The teacher must already have mastered the subject matter to be taught. The Competencies for Teaching system will develop skills essential to teaching the subject matter efficiently, but the system is in no way a substitute for the teacher's competence in the subject matter.

With the exception of educational psychology, the Competencies for Teaching system does not replace general education and foundation courses in education. Sociological and philosophical studies may provide a useful background for understanding cultural differences and educational values. The Competencies for Teaching system is a means of employing that understanding in educating children from different social or cultural backgrounds and a method of translating philosophical values into attainable educational and instructional objectives. Competencies for Teaching is primarily concerned with *how* to teach. The examples of content presented in this text and the other books in this series are meant only to illustrate the instructional process.

Classroom instruction and the other phases of the Competencies for Teaching system discuss principles of learning as well as other areas included in educational psychology, such as theories of child development, transfer and generalization of learning, perception, motivation, retention, individual differences, intelligence, testing, evaluation, and statistics. The Competencies for Teaching system, however, integrates educational psychology into the process of instruction, as one component of the total system.

Classroom Instruction, the second volume in the series of the Competencies for Teaching system, has multiple purposes: (1) to apply the skills acquired during the first phase, individual instruction, to a classroom, (2) to put into practice the model of the instructional process in organizing and managing the classroom, (3) to apply scientifically established learning principles in planning group instruction, (4) to employ the teacher's experiential and academic background in classroom instruction, (5) to translate social and philosophical values into practical achievements, and (6) to acquire relevant knowledge of educational psychology.

The Need for Classroom Instruction

In the past, one function of public education was to select from the mass of students the small group of superior students who could advance into such professions as medicine and law. A high school diploma was neither necessary for nor the goal of the majority of students. Simple literacy and perhaps some basic knowledge of arithmetic were usually adequate for the world of work and everyday living. When school lost its holding power for a student, he left to join the labor force wherever his level of competence or opportunity permitted. In these earlier times, a high school graduation rate of ten to fifteen percent suited the needs of society and probably the needs of the students.

Today, if a student does not complete high school, he or she is excluded from many possibilities of employment and is stigmatized as a dropout. Contemporary civilized society recognizes education as the one legitimate route to maturity. Society requires the majority of students to graduate from high school or to receive an equivalent vocational training. The former high rate of educational failure is no longer acceptable.

This change in the expectations of public education, from educating the select few to educating nearly all children, in addition to many technological and social changes, requires the educational system to be much more effective than it was in the past. These changes require that education receive augmented financial support, dynamic leadership, better communication with the public, that it implement technological advances, and create a more relevant curriculum. *But all of these improvements will be of little value unless the teacher is highly skilled in instructional methods*. It is essential for the teacher to know the subject matter, and it is desirable for him or her to have appropriate instructional materials. If, however, the teacher lacks the necessary skills to use his knowledge and materials effectively, the outcome may be inadequate. To successfully employ such technological achievements as schools with central-core libraries, closed-circuit television, programed, automated, and computer-assisted instruction, the teacher must master the process of instruction. Otherwise, the result could be a vast technology incompetently managed.

These new demands on education require that teachers for today and tomorrow have competencies that greatly exceed those demanded of teachers in the past. These competencies go far beyond the traditional list of such desirable characteristics as wholesome attitude, healthy personality, love of learning, and so forth, because these attributes do not of themselves yield the precise skills required to meet contemporary educational needs. Yet the traditional characteristics of sound personal philosophy, love and understanding of children, motivation to teach, and social awareness are directly related to the development of precise instructional skills. The teacher who systematically acquires a precise methodology through the Competencies for Teaching system and consequently has effective interactions with children improves his or her understanding of children, motivation to teach, and other desirable qualities at the same time that these qualities support his or her effectiveness and motivation to master the precise skills.

For classrooms to be lively centers of successful learning for all concerned, teachers must be skilled in operationally sound techniques for engaging students in the rewarding pursuit of learning. This requires that schools and school boards employ effective methods of recruitment, training, and retention of teachers. By providing high-quality teacher training, the classroom instruction phase of the Competencies for Teaching system indirectly influences recruitment and retention of teachers by raising the prestige of the profession and providing greater fulfillment for the teacher.

Although the process of instruction is similar for preschool, elementary, secondary, and higher education, the specifics vary according to the grade level and the subject matter. The current emphasis on early childhood education, focusing on compensatory education for children from various ethnic, social, and cultural backgrounds, demands greater precision in teaching than did the middle-class kindergarten of the past, in which socialization was the primary objective.

The child's elementary school classroom experience must prepare him to deal with a rapid and constant increase in human knowledge. Fact-finding skills and instruction in how to use information have become more important than memorizing collections of facts. In addition, the child's constant exposure to mass media makes the acquisition of well-developed thought processes and skill in critical judgment imperative. This vast fund of information as well as improved methods of teaching traditional academic skills are now the responsibility of elementary education.

The secondary school classroom must provide relevant experiences for the student. Science and technology have unleased forces whose long-range effects on the social and physical environment are unpredictable. Compartmentalized education that fails to integrate current information with traditional academic skills will not safeguard the future of mankind. Today's adolescents face an age different from any other. They will have to possess both the courage to defend what they determine is right and the ability to bring about change. Secondary education should offer students the opportunity to become actively involved in understanding and solving real and pressing problems concerning themselves and their world.

The preschool, elementary, and secondary classrooms that will provide these experiences may come in many shapes and sizes. They might sometimes be the traditional four walls accommodating a teacher and a class. At other times they may be "open" classrooms, classrooms employing team teaching, classrooms consisting of learning centers that have teachers and aides, classrooms linked electronically to instructional centers, classrooms consisting of community resources, laboratories, libraries, or shops. Improved learning may take place in classrooms within or without walls.

Cybernetic Feedback

The Competencies for Teaching system is based on a feedback-control process called cybernetics. The term *cybernetics* is derived from the Greek word for "steersman" or "helmsman." It is based on the concept of man using information from the world around him, such as wind direction, water movement, and star positions, to guide his ship. Man's skill in controlling his own behavior in relation to what he observes in his environment determines his success or failure in reaching his destination.

Before we explore the application of cybernetics to teaching, let us examine the role of feedback in the learning process. Most children have the experience of learning to ride a bicycle. The child sees other children riding bicycles, having fun, and achieving speeds unattainable on foot. The child becomes motivated to learn to ride a bicycle. Riding a bicycle requires balancing, pedaling, braking, steering, and successfully integrating all of these actions into controlling the operation of the bicycle.

Learning to balance involves trial and error. The child may begin by using training wheels or having someone run alongside to keep him from falling. While this is happening, he is experimenting with the effects of his body movements on the balance of the bicycle. Through feedback from his nervous system, the child discovers that when the bicycle begins to lean toward the right, he can move it back toward the upright position by shifting his body weight to the left. At first he overcompensates and makes the bicycle lean too far to the left. He then shifts his body back to the right to correct the error. Through practice he becomes sensitive to the overcompensation errors made in balancing and eventually learns to keep the bicycle in an upright position using subtle and unconscious movements of his body. While he is learning to balance, he is also going through the same process of trial and error in learning the other components of successful bicycle riding. He finally learns to coordinate all the component skills so that it becomes necessary for him to be conscious only of his destination and the conditions enroute. The complex behaviors constituting the process of bicycling become automatic responses.

The inexperienced bicycle rider has difficulty balancing and steering so that he deviates in both directions from his line of travel. By focusing on his objective, feedback information of the deviations from the intended line of travel produces successively finer adjustments so that the final result is balance and steering in which the adjustments are barely perceptible.

The process of learning to ride a bicycle is similar to many other learning experiences. You know what you want to accomplish, you attempt to do it, and you evaluate the discrepancy between your attempt and what you wished to accomplish. You modify your next attempt by using this feedback.

Similarly, the student driver tends to oversteer or overcompensate in attempting to control the automobile. At first, the task of driving seems very complex, but the experienced driver acquires so many coordinated automatic responses that he may direct his attention to his destination, the route he is taking, to traffic signals, and road conditions. The complex behaviors required for operating the vehicle become integrated automatic responses.

Man has such a finely adaptive nervous system that, through practice in successively more precise or complicated tasks, he can acquire the skills required for miniature engraving, neurosurgery, athletic competition, or playing a five-manual pipe organ. He can compose and conduct symphonies and operas, and he can design and operate complex mechanical systems.

Learning to teach is as much a process of learning as is learning any other complex skill. It depends in large measure on feedback that modifies the teacher's behavior in the direction of greater precision and effectiveness. Ultimately, as in the examples above, once the teacher learns to identify an instructional objective, many of the complex procedures required to achieve it will be produced almost automatically. Through the carefully designed activities of the Competencies for Teaching system, the teacher acquires sensitivity to effective interactions with pupils so that feedback continually modifies the teacher's performance.

Smith and Smith (1966) reduced the process illustrated above to three primary functions of a cybernetic system.

1. *Movement toward a target or objective is initiated.*
    In the example given earlier, the objective was to ride a bicycle. Getting on the bicycle was a movement toward that target.

2. *Comparison is made of the effects of the initial actions with the desired objective.*
   In learning to balance the bicycle, the child learned that by moving his body to the left when the bicycle leaned to the right, he could regain balance. The corrections in the early attempts were not precise.

3. *Utilize the detected error in redirecting succeeding behaviors.*
   When the child leaned too far or too long to one side, he learned to compensate by leaning to the other side. Succeeding shifts of his body became more refined until only slight, automatic movements maintained his balance.

The Cycle of the Instructional Process

Feedback is used in the Competencies for Teaching system to continually refine and redirect teacher behavior in the direction of optimal effectiveness. This is illustrated in the diagram, "Cycle of the Instructional Process."

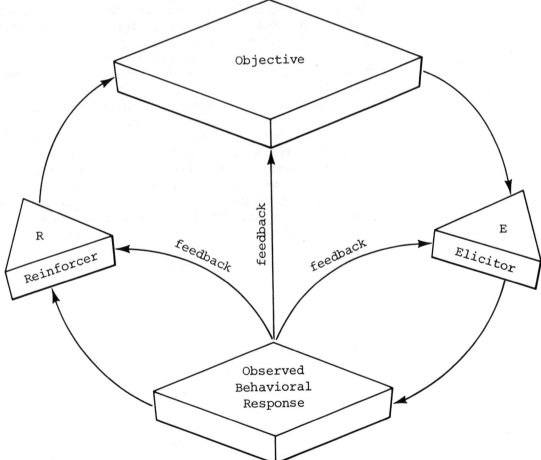

The elements of the process of instruction are objectives, elicitors, behavioral responses, and reinforcers. Objectives direct the process and identify the appropriate behavioral responses. Elicitors and reinforcers are the means of achieving progressive changes toward the objectives. These progressive changes are represented in the diagram by the circle and arrows connecting the elements.

The cycle begins with the teacher's identifying an objective for the learner, represented by the rectangle at the top of the cycle. The teacher then provides an elicitor (E) to bring forth the desired behavioral response stated in the objective. When the behavioral response (B) occurs, it is immediately reinforced (R). It is then possible to identify the next objective. This cycle represents the ongoing process of teaching and learning.

The earlier illustrations of cybernetic feedback describe learning as a complex skill requiring practice that is goal oriented. In learning to teach, errors of judgment about objectives, elicitors, and reinforcers are inevitable. These errors are detectable only in the pupil's behavioral response. If the pupil fails to respond to an attention cue, the teacher must modify the attention cue so that the pupil responds by attending. If the pupil fails to respond to a task cue, the teacher must modify either the method of presentation or the instructional material so that the pupil engages in the appropriate task behavior. This is illustrated in the diagram by feedback travelling from the observed behavioral response to the elicitor.

Similarly, the observed behavioral response sends feedback to the reinforcer. That is, throughout the instructional process, the observation of pupil response provides information about the effectiveness of the current reinforcers and either supports their continuance or indicates a need for their modification.

In situations in which the intended elicitors and reinforcers are not effective, the teacher may decide that the objective was beyond the pupil's present capability. The most common error is adopting an objective that represents too large an increment of learning for the pupil or pupils. In this case, the feedback from the observed behavioral response would result in an analysis of the learning task and then presenting it in a sequence of enroute objectives based on smaller increments of learning.

When an objective is identified and the observed behavioral response indicates that the behavior appeared spontaneously, then feedback indicates a need only to reinforce the behavior. The teacher can then move on to the next objective.

It is not necessary at this point to explore the great range of possible observations and modifications that are involved in learning to teach effectively. If you completed Phase One of Competencies for Teaching, you were involved in this process throughout individual instruction. The Individual Instruction Record required you to state enroute objectives. You then attempted to provide elicitors and reinforcers that would bring forth the desired responses. When the behavior occurred it was reinforced. Your decisions about elicitors and reinforcers were based on your observation of the pupil's responses. Finally you decided whether the behavioral responses indicated that you should move on to the next objective, repeat the objective in the next lesson, or reduce the size of the learning task. The Individual Instruction Record provided you with feedback with which to analyze this process.

Now that you are entering a more complex phase, classroom instruction, it is essential that you become aware of the precise function of feedback. Your success in the classroom will depend in large measure on your continuing observation of your pupils and on how your observations influence your own behavior. If you modify your interventions in a positive and constructive way, your teaching skills will be continually improved and refined.

Feedback from careful observation develops sensitivity to students' needs in relation to the learning process. If you follow the plan for using this book—reading the text, completing the exercises in the workbook, and then teaching in the practicum (student teaching), you will be provided with simulated and actual experiences in which feedback will help you develop precise control of the process of instruction.

Assignment

Complete the exercises in Chapter One of the Classroom Instruction Workbook.

References

Smith, Karl U., and Margaret Foltz Smith. *Cybernetic Principles of Learning and Educational Design*. New York: Holt, Rinehart and Winston, 1966.

Two

Competencies for Classroom Instruction

Objectives: After completing your study of this chapter, you will be able to (1) identify and define the components of the conceptual model (elicitors, behaviors, reinforcers, entering behavior, terminal objectives, and enroute objectives) and relate these to the process of classroom instruction, (2) describe classroom instruction as practiced by a competent teacher, (3) describe contingency management in the classroom, (4) describe token economy as used in the classroom, and (5) complete the practice items in Chapter Two of the Classroom Instruction Workbook.

This chapter presents an overview of the process of classroom instruction. In doing this, it omits describing many of the subtleties and complexities of the classroom environment, since these will be described in considerable detail in succeeding chapters. This overview is provided so that you will be able to relate the conceptual model to the process of classroom or group instruction before you analyze in detail each component of the model. The most important skill that can be learned during the classroom instruction phase is effective teacher behavior. A teacher who systematically acquires the competencies described in this phase of the Competencies for Teaching system will be effective in a variety of teaching situations.

Once you have achieved the competency objectives of the first two phases of the Competencies for Teaching system—individual instruction and classroom instruction—you will be effective in teaching children who range widely in abilities, interests, and degrees of readiness. You will be able to teach them either individually or in groups, and you will be able to teach children who were not willing or eager learners initially. You will even be able to teach in classrooms that have inadequate or badly organized facilities. You will also be able to help remedy the inequalities in traditional public education, which favors the child who starts school earlier, is healthier, or is better prepared to learn as a result of his socioeconomic environment.

The Conceptual Model

The Competencies for Teaching system bases the process of effective classroom instruction on the same conceptual model as was introduced in *Individual Instruction*. The conceptual model visually represents the structure of the instructional process used for classroom management and teaching procedures, whose purpose is to optimize learning. The following is a brief review of the conceptual model.

ELEMENTS OF THE CONCEPTUAL MODEL

The conceptual model is composed of three elements: *elicitors* (E), *behaviors* (B), and *reinforcers* (R).

An elicitor (E) is an event that precedes and brings forth a behavior. It can be an instructional material, such as a toy, game, book, test, paints, or crayons. It can be a command, a request, a demonstration, or a set of instructions. It can be a person or a human behavior, such as a smile or a frown. An elicitor can be one or a combination of these variables.

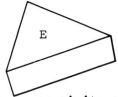

A behavior (B) is an *activity* of the child. It is something he does, such as running, walking, speaking, writing, assembling a formboard, reading, answering questions, or sitting in his seat.

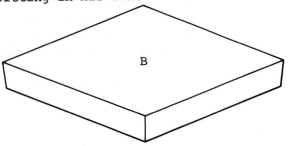

A reinforcer (R) is an event that follows a behavior and strengthens subsequent behavior. Reinforcers that are satisfying increase the frequency of that behavior in the future. Stimuli that follow a behavior and are not satisfying or are discomforting are not reinforcers.

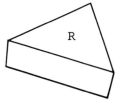

ENTERING BEHAVIOR

Before you begin to teach an individual, a group, or a class, it is essential that you know where or at what level you should begin instruction. What are the academic tasks and study-related behaviors (*entering behaviors*) that the pupils in your class are capable of performing upon entering this particular learning situation? A complete answer to this question includes a description of the elicitors to which the pupils can respond, the behaviors the pupils can produce, and the reinforcers that will strengthen appropriate responses.

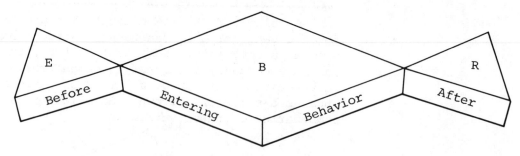

TERMINAL OBJECTIVES

Any instructional program—a lesson, a unit, or a course—should produce some change or outcome. A terminal can be an end or it can be what connects one thing to the next. Any segment of instruction—a lesson, a unit, or a course—can be conceptualized as beginning with entering behavior and concluding with a terminal objective. The *terminal objective* describes the intended performance of the class at the conclusion of the instructional sequence. The terminal objective describes the elicitors that the class will respond to, their behavioral response, and the reinforcement required to maintain their behavior.

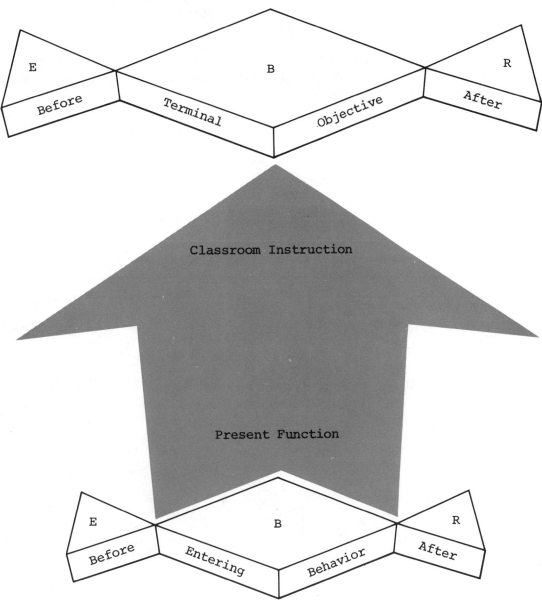

Future Behavior
(Intended achievement at termination of program)

ENROUTE OBJECTIVES

The space between entering behavior and terminal objective is the distance that must be covered by the
instructional sequence. The route from entering behavior
to terminal objective is usually divided into steps or
enroute objectives. Each enroute objective describes the
achievement that the class must attain before moving on to
the next enroute objective.

The conceptual model visually represents the process
of instruction, providing the teacher with a structure for

identifying (1) the academic or social performance level of the class, (2) the goal and direction of instruction, and (3) the steps required to achieve the goal. The model of the instructional process provides the teacher with a system of accountability with which he can identify, at any point, where the class is in relation to the entering behavior, the enroute objective, and the terminal objective.

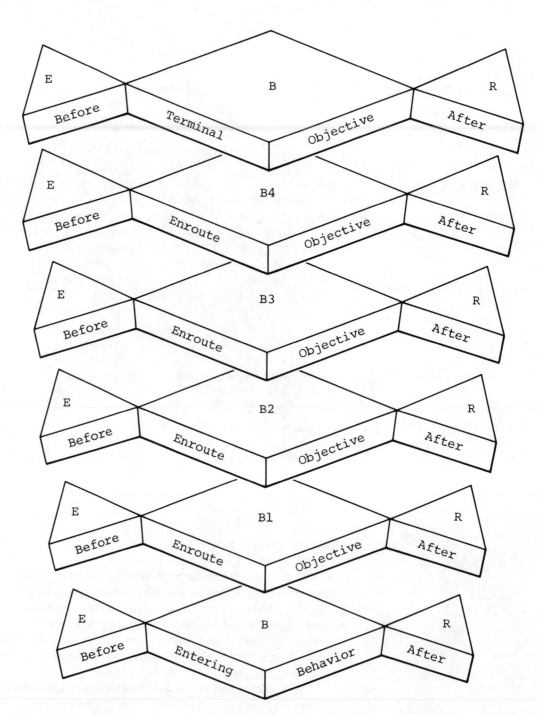

Classroom Instruction

Successful classroom instruction is a complex process involving subtle interactions between the teacher and the pupils as well as interactions among the pupils. Competencies for Teaching creates classroom environments in which these interactions are used to facilitate learning. A description of the potential complexity of classroom instruction is beyond the scope of this chapter. The fundamental skills required for effective classroom teaching are systematically acquired through performing the activities included in this phase and studying the total system. This chapter presents only brief descriptions of the conceptual model employed (1) by the classroom teacher, (2) in contingency management, and (3) for token economies. It is not intended to provide a model of how to teach in all situations or how to organize all classes but only to illustrate classroom instruction based on sound learning principles.

The Classroom Teacher

The teacher's function is to behave so as to elicit and reinforce progressive changes in the academic and social behaviors of the pupils in the class. The ability to motivate the members of a class to move toward higher levels of performance is the most important component in the total complex of teacher skills. It is the basis of effective teaching in nursery school, kindergarten, elementary, secondary, and university classes.

The teacher who has acquired the basic components of these complex skills can elicit the attention of the class and ask a question, present a task, or demonstrate a procedure so that the pupils will respond with answers, task completion, or performance of the demonstrated procedures. The teacher who can then indicate with words, gestures, or symbols the appropriateness of the pupils' performance has acquired optimal control of the learning process. To do this effectively the teacher must provide elicitors to which the class can make appropriate responses and reinforcements suited to the developmental level of the pupils in the class. The following example illustrates a teacher's behavior in instructing a class.

TEACHING AN INTERMEDIATE CLASS

Mrs. Adams taught a regular class of twenty-seven fifth-grade students. The children lived in the central area of an industrial city of 125,000 people. The students had normal interest in school and an average intelligence level. The following is a brief description of a mathematics lesson Mrs. Adams taught.

Entering Behavior. The class had completed the review section on addition and subtraction of common fractions and could add mixed fractions and rename improper fractions into their simplest forms.

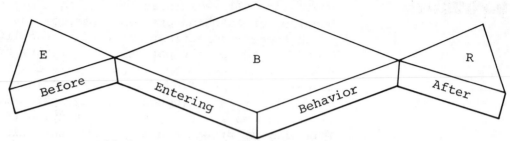

Elicitors. During the previous class period, Mrs. Adams had distributed a worksheet of ten mixed fraction addition problems as a review quiz. She had instructed the class to find the sum of each problem and to reduce each answer to its simplest form.

Behavior. The students calculated the sum of each problem and reduced it to its simplest form. After completing the assignment, each student raised his hand to indicate he had finished.

Reinforcers. Mrs. Adams responded to each raised hand by going to the student and praising him for completing the assignment. She then placed a correct mark beside each right answer while saying "very good" or "that's right." Finally she wrote the number of correct answers at the top of each child's quiz paper and recorded the score in her grade book.

Mrs. Adams observed that the number of correct responses ranged from six to ten, the majority of her pupils achieving ten correct answers. She was satisfied that the students' performances were adequate to permit her to proceed to the next lesson.

Terminal Objective. Mrs. Adams wrote terminal objectives that described the performance she expected from her pupils at the termination of the lesson.

The terminal objective was: "Given a worksheet of twenty mixed fraction subtraction problems, each student will calculate and write at least ten correct answers while receiving only regular teacher praise and attention."

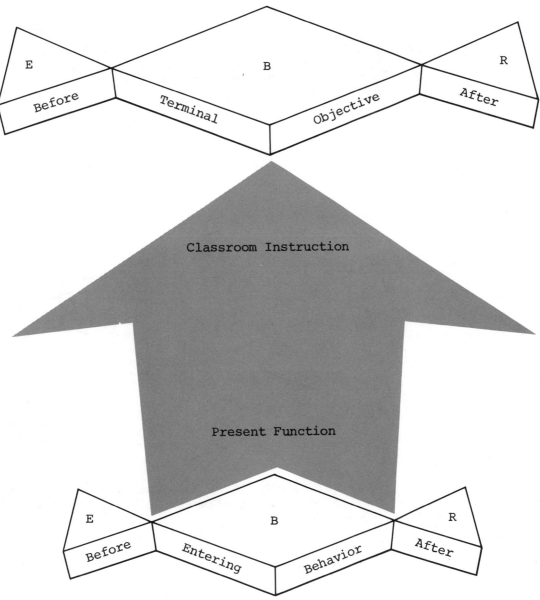

Future Behavior
(Intended achievement at termination of program)

Classroom Instruction

Present Function

<u>Enroute Objectives</u>. Now that Mrs. Adams had observed and assessed her students' entering behavior and had identified a terminal objective, she was ready to develop a plan to move from entering behavior to the terminal objective.

Mrs. Adams' lesson plan included three enroute objectives.

<u>Enroute Objective 1</u>. The class will subtract simple mixed fractions.

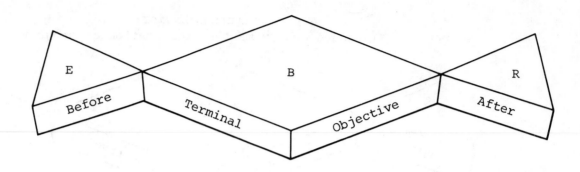

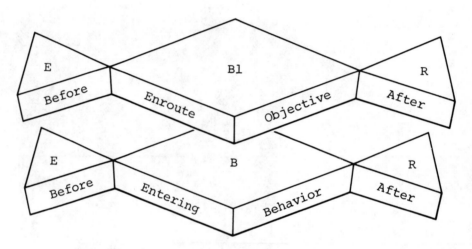

Elicitors. Mrs. Adams began the lesson by demonstrating on the chalkboard solutions to the following problems.

2 7/8	2 3/4	9 1/2
- 1 1/8	- 1 3/8	- 3 1/4

She demonstrated the procedures for simple subtraction of mixed fractions and the methods for finding common denominators. Mrs. Adams then wrote a similar problem on the chalkboard and told the students to find the answer.

Behavior. Each student worked the problem and then raised his hand.

Reinforcer. When most of the students had raised their hands, Mrs. Adams called on one student to give his answer. She said, "Thank you. Now, class, how many of you agree with that answer?" If a majority of the class agreed and the answer was correct, she praised the student who had given the answer and said, "That is very good, class. You are all doing very well."

Enroute Objective 2. The class will rename mixed fractions into equivalent forms.

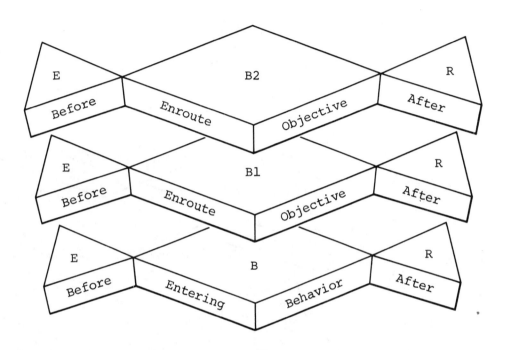

Elicitors. Mrs. Adams reviewed the fact that the numeral *1* can be stated as a fraction. Using the flannelboard and fractional parts of circles, she demonstrated that three-thirds and eight-eighths are equal to one. She wrote mixed fractions on the chalkboard and instructed the students to rename them. She made them progressively more difficult, such as:

$$1\ 3/8 = \underline{?/8} \qquad\qquad 1\ 1/6 = \underline{\hspace{1.5em}} \qquad\qquad 5\ 1/2 = \underline{\hspace{1.5em}}$$

Behavior. As each problem was written on the chalkboard, each student calculated the equivalent form. When he had found the answer he raised his hand.

Reinforcer. Mrs. Adams waited until most of the students had raised their hands before she asked one student to give the answer. She reinforced each correct answer with such praises as, "Fine!" or "You're doing very well."

   <u>Enroute Objective 3</u>. The class will subtract mixed fractions requiring renaming of the minuend.

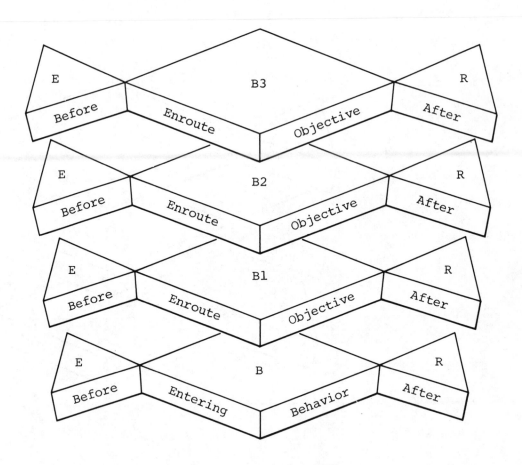

   Elicitor. Mrs. Adams directed ten students at a time to go to the chalkboard. She read the following problems aloud and instructed the students to find the answers.

$$\begin{array}{cccc} 5\ 2/5 & 2\ 1/3 & 9\ 2/9 & 11\ 1/8 \\ -\ 2\ 4/5 & -\ 1\ 2/3 & -\ 3\ 4/9 & -\ 6\ 3/4 \end{array}$$

   Behavior. The students renamed the minuends and then found the remainders. When they had finished they turned their backs to the chalkboard and faced the class.

   Reinforcer. As each student completed the problem, Mrs. Adams said, "Sue has finished; John has finished," and so on until all the students were finished. She looked at the work and complimented each student by name for the correct answer.

Evaluation

Mrs. Adams gave the students a worksheet of twenty mixed fraction subtraction problems. She instructed them to work the problems, write the answers in the simplest form, and bring the completed worksheet to her desk, one at a time.

After correcting the worksheets, Mrs. Adams observed that the range of scores was from thirteen to twenty correct answers, the majority of her students correctly answering sixteen or more. By comparing this terminal behavior with the stated terminal objective, Mrs. Adams concluded that the students had achieved the terminal objective.

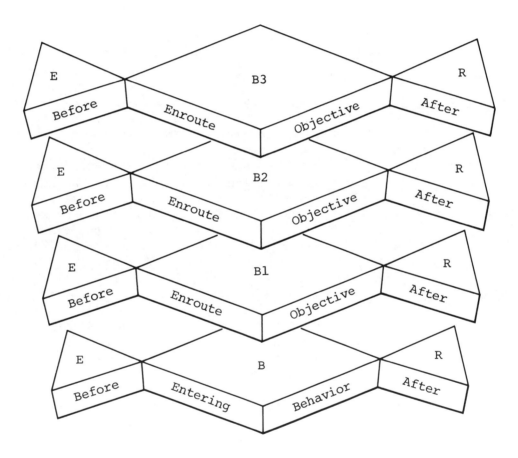

COMPETENT TEACHERS

Mr. Shaw, a junior college art teacher, watched as his students completed a still-life subject they were painting in water colors. During the period, Mr. Shaw moved from student to student pointing out good points of each student's work and suggesting how certain difficulties might be overcome.

When all students had finished, Mr. Shaw selected a few of the paintings to show the entire class. He selected those that had been particularly successful in using various techniques and in the total execution of the project. These paintings were discussed and then placed on display for the students to examine more closely.

Miss Moore is a successful teacher. Her questioning techniques are a model of effectiveness. She almost always receives responses from her students when she asks a question. She has attained this level of response by reacting positively to every answer a student offers. If the answer is correct she may say: "Yes, that is correct, John"; "Very good, May, you've done your homework"; or "Good thinking, Mark, you are correct." If an answer is incorrect or not exactly the one Miss Moore is looking for, she may say: "Thank you, Jack. Let us consider some other possibilities"; "That is a very interesting answer, Sue. Can you be more specific?"; or "That is very logical, Barry." By responding in these ways to her students' answers, Miss Moore increased the probability that her students will attend and respond to her questions in the future.

The students in a ninth-grade general science class were working on experiments. The teacher, Mrs. Golden, moved about the room talking, smiling, and praising each student for certain appropriate behaviors. She smiled and complimented June for being the first to prepare for the experiment. She made a note on Bert's lab book that his description of the experimental procedures was excellent. Cathy was complimented on how well she was working. David was praised for explaining one of the experimental procedures to Evelyn. Mrs. Golden continued this kind of interaction with each of her students.

Mr. Sector had the attention of his physical education class. To demonstrate the correct way to serve in tennis, he broke the serving process down into individual steps. As he demonstrated each step he explained its relationship to the total serve. By asking questions and observing the students' execution of each step, Mr. Sector was assured that the students were learning to serve.

The classroom teacher acquires a conceptual model that consistently focuses his or her expectation on positive outcomes for each intervention or teaching act. Mrs. Adams' formally planned lesson began with her pupils' observed entering behavior. Next she identified a positive expectation, or terminal objective, to be achieved through intermediate positive expectations, or enroute objectives. The model also helped her identify the elicitors and reinforcers that were effective in achieving these objectives.

If a question she asked did not elicit an appropriate response from her pupils, this feedback indicated that she should change the working of her question or provide more cues. Feedback gave her the information necessary for continual monitoring of her teaching performance so that her effectiveness was continually enhanced.

Mr. Shaw employed his pupils' creative use of watercolor techniques to elicit attention to their artistic effectiveness, and provided social reinforcement for specific applications of good technique. He employed higher-level reinforcement by encouraging self-evaluation.

Miss Moore asked questions that were based on positive expectations. Her objective sought to ensure that each response would (1) strengthen the pupil's recall, (2) advance the pupil's knowledge, understanding, application, or evaluation, (3) encourage transfer of training, or (4) support any other progress in academic or social learning. Her effective questioning technique was the result of ongoing sensitivity to the feedback she received from her pupils' responses. She elicited and reinforced responses from all of her pupils. When pupils offered incorrect responses, she did not reprimand or give the answer but instead encouraged alternate responses or provided additional cues.

Mrs. Golden reinforced her pupils' efforts in the direction of her positive expectations by praising in-task behavior, achievement, and cooperative social interaction toward these objectives.

Mr. Sector provided effective attention and task cues so that his demonstration was successful in eliciting modeling behavior.

Each of these teachers employed the model effectively by identifying positive expectations that were consistent with the educational objectives and that brought about changes in their pupils' progress toward those objectives. Not employing the conceptual model of instruction might have made the teachers less sensitive to the feedback and less constructive and precise in their interventions. Frustration on the part of both students and teacher could have led to negative expectations and counterproductive teaching performance. For example, when a pupil fails to produce an acceptable response, the teacher's frustration might sometimes be expressed in statements indicating that little was expected of that pupil anyway. Such negative teacher performance can develop if the teacher lacks a conceptual model of the process being employed and is deficient in the skills or behaviors that define professional competence. Mastery of subject matter and curriculum along with mastery of the instructional process are the most important elements of professional competence, because these can be employed in any teaching situation.

Competencies for Classroom Instruction -- Contingency Management and Token Economies

Although creating a competent classroom teacher is the ultimate aim of this phase of the system, the organization of the classroom and the arrangement of its physical facilities contribute significantly to the effectiveness of the learning environment. Only for purposes of description and explanation have we separated instructional materials and classroom organization from teacher performance. Selecting materials and organizing the classroom are aspects of the teacher's responsibility and behavior. Unfortunately, the competent teacher cannot always have sufficient control of these factors to create an ideal classroom environment or provide ideal instructional materials.

Remember, however, that effective teaching can take place in a room, in the school yard, during field trips, under a tree, or in classrooms arranged by other teachers whose ideas may be different from yours. It is especially useful to keep this in mind during student teaching, substitute teaching, relief teaching, or in situations that require you to move from room to room.

Classrooms can be arranged so that one part of the room is used as a task area and another part as a reinforcement area. In such an arrangement, admittance to the reinforcement area is contingent on the student's completing an assignment in the task area. This contingency management classroom is called a *separate task and reinforcement area classroom*. Contingency management classrooms in which the task and reinforcement occur in the same area are called *combined area classrooms*.

SEPARATE TASK AND REINFORCEMENT AREA CLASSROOMS

A class was composed of fifteen pupils, all of whom had a history of underachievement. Because the pupils had little previous success with academic subjects, they had been placed in Mr. Tate's remedial class. They came from a large agricultural community in which the families had varying socioeconomic backgrounds. All the pupils were seven or eight years old and had failed to pass from the first to the second grade.

Because the pupils were underachievers who had experienced considerable failure in school, the teacher, Mr. Tate, organized his classroom so that each child received reinforcement for completing assigned tasks many times throughout the school day. He accomplished this by employing contingency management as the basis for classroom organization. His purpose was to present assignments and to follow their completion immediately with a reinforcing experience. This ensured that every child in the class would experience success and feel satisfied.

A diagram of Mr. Tate's classroom follows. As the students enter the room, they hang up their coats and proceed to their desks in a section of the room called the "task area." This area contains the students' and teacher's desks, a worktable, chalkboards, shelves of worksheets and workbooks, and other instructional materials. In this area the students receive instruction and carry out assigned learning tasks.

```
┌─────────┬──┬────┬───┬─────┬───────────────┬──────────────┐
│         │  │    │   │     │   Teacher's   │  Coats and   │
│ Animal Cages │ Chairs   │      Desk      │  Lunchboxes  │
│                                                          │
│  ┌───────┐                        Task Area             │
│  │ Arts  │ Reinforcement Area                           │
│  │ and   │                                              │
│  │ Crafts│          ┌──────┐  ┌─┐ ┌─┐ ┌─┐ ┌─┐           │
│  └───────┘          │      │  └─┘ └─┘ └─┘ └─┘           │
│                     │      │ G                          │
│                     └──────┘ a  Students' Desks         │
│                              m                          │
│                              e ┌─┐ ┌─┐ ┌─┐ ┌─┐     C    │
│                              s └─┘ └─┘ └─┘ └─┘     h    │
│  ┌───────┐          ┌──────┐                       a    │
│  │Listen-│          │      │ P                     l    │
│  │ing    │          │      │ u ┌─┐ ┌─┐ ┌─┐ ┌─┐     k    │
│  │Table  │          └──────┘ z └─┘ └─┘ └─┘ └─┘     b    │
│  └───────┘                   z                     o    │
│                              l                     a    │
│                              e ┌─┐ ┌─┐ ┌─┐ ┌─┐     r    │
│    Play Area                 s └─┘ └─┘ └─┘ └─┘     d    │
│                              T                          │
│                              o                          │
│                              y     Materials Storage    │
│                              s                          │
└──────────────────────────────┴─────────────────────────┘
```

Dividing the room from one wall to within eight feet of the opposite wall are four-foot high bookshelves and storage cabinets. These separate the task area from the reinforcement area. In the reinforcement area, a "listening table" contains a tape recorder, a phonograph, listening posts, audio tapes, and phonograph records available for student use. At another table, paints, brushes, modeling clay, and other art materials are available.

One cabinet contains games and puzzles; another cabinet has construction toys, such as Tinker Toys, Lincoln Logs, blocks, and an Erector Set. In one corner are two cages, one containing hamsters and the other, white mice. For the more active students, the back corner is a play area with jump ropes, twist boards, and balance beams. For students who want just to sit and watch, chairs are available. Entrance to the reinforcement area is contingent on the student's completing an assignment in the task area.

Mathematics Period

The following describes a mathematics lesson in Mr. Tate's contingency management classroom.

<u>Entering Behavior</u>. All fifteen of Mr. Tate's students can count, name, and write the numbers from 1 to 20. They can also say and write the number of objects in a given set.

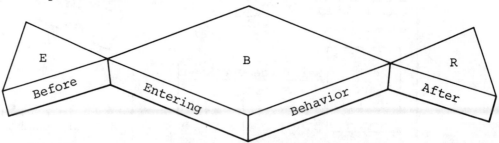

Elicitor. During the mathematics period of the previous day, Mr. Tate had distributed the following worksheet. The students were instructed to count the number of items in each set and write the total in the box beside each figure.

Behavior. Each student counted the number of items in each set, wrote the number in the box, and raised his hand to indicate to Mr. Tate that he had completed the worksheet.

Reinforcement. Mr. Tate responded to each raised hand, complimented the student for successfully completing the assignment, marked "C" by each correct response, and allowed the pupil to go to the reinforcement area.

ARITHMETIC WORKSHEET #1

NAME _____

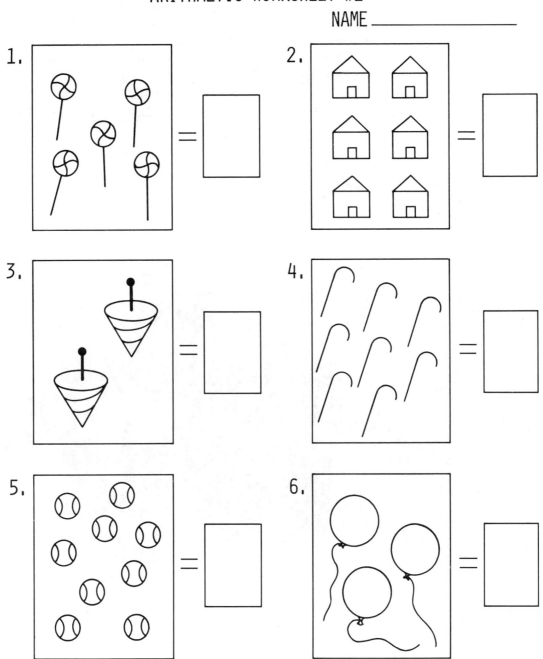

After correcting the papers, Mr. Tate observed that all students had correctly counted and written the number of objects in each set for at least five of the six problems on the worksheet. Satisfied with this performance, Mr. Tate decided to begin some basic instruction in addition during the following mathematics period.

Terminal Objective. The following is the terminal objective for the mathematics period. "Given a worksheet of eight, single-digit addition problems, the student will correctly calculate and write the sum of at least six problems and spend not less than five minutes in the reinforcement area."

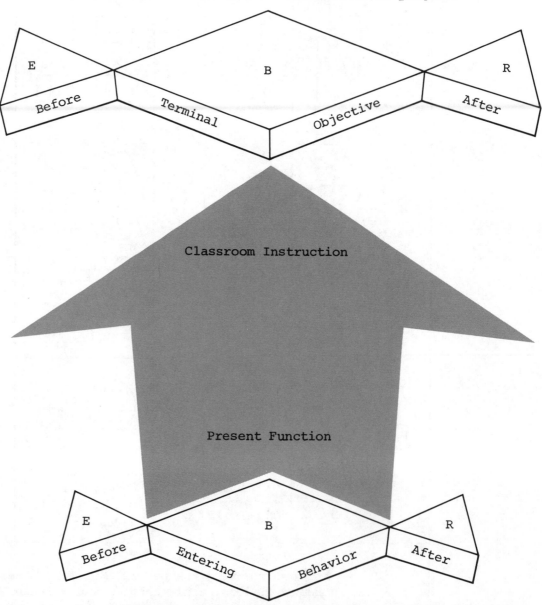

Future Behavior
(Intended achievement at termination of program)

Classroom Instruction

Present Function

Enroute Objectives. Mr. Tate identified three steps or enroute objectives essential to the achievement of the terminal objective.

Enroute Objective 1. Count and write the number of objects in two sets and then the number of objects in a set made by combining the two sets.

Elicitor. Mr. Tate demonstrated combining two sets of objects to make one set of objects having a larger number of objects than either of the first two sets. For example, he presented a set of two sheep and a set of three sheep. He then placed the sheep from these two sets into one set and counted them to show the new set contained five sheep. After working a number of similar examples and involving the students in counting the number in each set, he passed out the following worksheet. The students were instructed to count and write the number of objects in each set in the boxes provided.

ARITHMETIC WORKSHEET #2

NAME _____

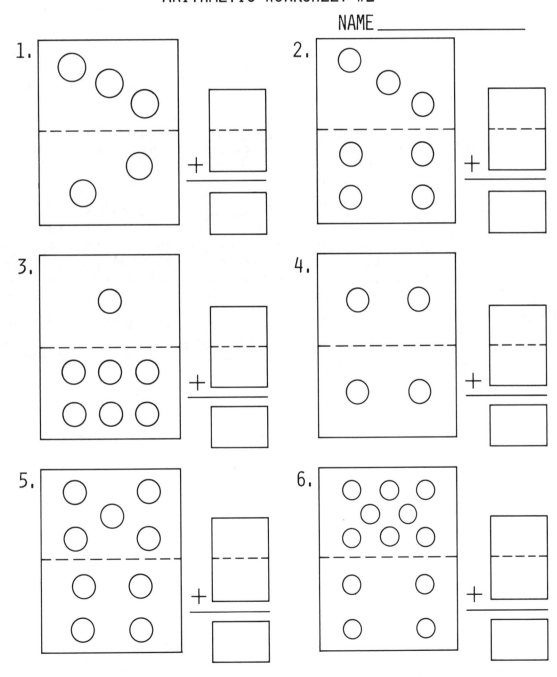

Behavior. The students counted the number of objects in each set and wrote the number in the squares. As each student completed the worksheet, he raised his hand.

Reinforcement. Mr. Tate checked each worksheet to confirm that it was completed and then marked each correct answer with a "C" while praising the child. The student was told how many answers he had correct and then was allowed to go to the reinforcement area.

From the many possible activities in the reinforcement area, the first student who had finished chose to feed and water the hamsters. Two students began a game of checkers. Some listened to records, while others engaged in art projects.

After the last student had entered the reinforcement area, Mr. Tate waited five minutes before flashing the room lights to signal the students to return to their desks in the task area.

Enroute Objective 2. Given two numerals, the students will make dot sets for each numeral and will then write the number of dots in a new set made by combining the first two sets.

Elicitor. The following worksheet was passed out to the students. Mr. Tate instructed the students to draw the correct number of dots in the two boxes. After they had done this they were to count the number of dots in both boxes and write the total in the box under the two numerals.

Behavior. Each student drew the dots in the two boxes, counted them, and wrote the total number in the appropriate box. When this was done, each student raised his hand.

Reinforcement. Mr. Tate responded to the raised hand as quickly as possible, praised the student for completing the worksheet, marked the correct answers with a "C," and told the student his number of correct answers. After filing the corrected worksheet in his mathematics folder, the student was allowed to go to the reinforcement area.

ARITHMETIC WORKSHEET #3

NAME _____

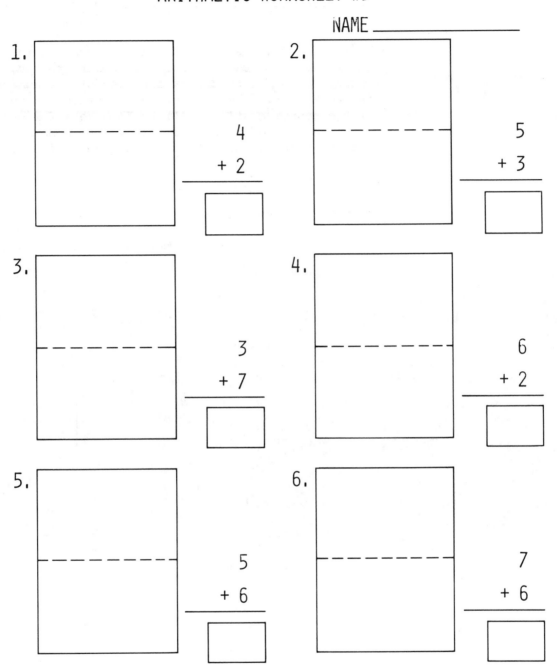

1.
$$\begin{array}{r} 4 \\ + 2 \\ \hline \end{array}$$

2.
$$\begin{array}{r} 5 \\ + 3 \\ \hline \end{array}$$

3.
$$\begin{array}{r} 3 \\ + 7 \\ \hline \end{array}$$

4.
$$\begin{array}{r} 6 \\ + 2 \\ \hline \end{array}$$

5.
$$\begin{array}{r} 5 \\ + 6 \\ \hline \end{array}$$

6.
$$\begin{array}{r} 7 \\ + 6 \\ \hline \end{array}$$

As before, each student chose the activity he found most enjoyable. Some students continued work on art projects, others played games, a few used the twist boards and balance beams while listening to music. All selected activities based on personal preferences. Five minutes after the last student had entered the reinforcement area, Mr. Tate flashed the room lights to signal that it was time to continue with the mathematics period.

Enroute Objective 3. The class will write the sums in single-digit addition problems by using counting sticks.

Elicitor. As soon as all students had returned to their seats following the reinforcement period, Mr. Tate passed out a set of twenty counting sticks and the following worksheet. The students were instructed in the use of the counting sticks: (1) to form sets for each number given in the addition problems, (2) to combine the two sets of sticks, and (3) to count them to find the number to write in the box.

ARITHMETIC WORKSHEET #4

NAME _____

1. 2
   + 1
   ⬜

2. 1
   + 5
   ⬜

3. 7
   + 2
   ⬜

4. 3
   + 5
   ⬜

5. 3
   + 4
   ⬜

6. 6
   + 2
   ⬜

7. 2
   + 3
   ⬜

8. 4
   + 7
   ⬜

Behavior. Making sets of counting sticks to represent each of the two numbers in the problem, the students combined the two sets, counted them, and wrote the number in the answer box. When a student had completed all eight problems, he again raised his hand.

Reinforcement. Each student was praised for completing the worksheet. A "C" was marked next to each correct answer and the total number of correct answers was written at the top of the page. The student recorded the number in his record book and placed the worksheet in his mathematics folder. He was then allowed to enter the re-inforcement area.

As before, each student selected an activity, either trying something new or continuing with a game or project.

Evaluation. To determine whether the students had reached the terminal objective, Mr. Tate passed out the following worksheet to each student.

ARITHMETIC WORKSHEET #5

NAME _____

1. 3
   + 3
	2. 4
	   + 2
		3. 7
		   + 1
			4. 2
			   + 3

5. 3
   + 6
	6. 8
	   + 2
		7. 5
		   + 4
			8. 6
			   + 7

After correcting the completed worksheets, Mr. Tate observed that all students in the class had answered at least six problems correctly, and four students had answered all eight correctly. Mr. Tate determined that the terminal objective had been successfully achieved.

COMBINED TASK AND REINFORCEMENT AREA CLASSROOMS

Mrs. Washington's room was not large enough for separate task and reinforcement areas. There was space at the back of the room for two tables and space for one table in the front corner. Because of the limited space, not all students could be accommodated at one time at the tables. However, some of the activities the students

```
┌──────────────────────────────────────────────┬──────────────┐
│              Chalkboard                        │  Listening   │
│  ┌──────────┐                                  │    Table     │
│  │ Teacher's│                                  ├──────────────┘
│  │   Desk   │                                  │
│  └──────────┘                                  │
│                                                │
│   ┌─┐   ┌─┐   ┌─┐   ┌─┐   ┌─┐                  │
│   └─┘   └─┘   └─┘   └─┘   └─┘                  │
│              Students' Desks                   │
│   ┌─┐   ┌─┐   ┌─┐   ┌─┐   ┌─┐                  │
│   └─┘   └─┘   └─┘   └─┘   └─┘                  │
│                                                │
│   ┌─┐   ┌─┐   ┌─┐   ┌─┐   ┌─┐                  │
│   └─┘   └─┘   └─┘   └─┘   └─┘                  │
│                                                │
│  ┌────────────┐      ┌────────────┐            │
│  │  Arts and  │      │   Games    │            │
│  │   Crafts   │      │            │            │
│  └────────────┘      └────────────┘            │
└────────────────────────────────────────────────┘
```

chose to do individually could be done at their desks. To identify who was in task time and who was in reinforcement time, Mrs. Washington placed a pass on the upper left-hand corner of each student's desk. One side was yellow and had the word *TASK* printed on it; on the other side, which was blue, was the word *REWARD*. At the beginning of each task period, all the students turned their passes to the yellow "task" side. As each student completed the assigned task and Mrs. Washington checked it, the pass was turned to the blue "reward" side. A student who did not choose to go to one of the tables remained at his desk to read, draw, work on a project, or engage in some other activity of his choice. Each student could be identified as being either in the reinforcement or the task period by his pass. After all passes had been turned to the reinforcement side, Mrs. Washington waited a specified time before ringing a bell to begin the next task period.

A senior high school American history program was developed for gifted students. It was an individualized course of study consisting of a programed text, sound filmstrips, and review tests. Four periods per week were scheduled for the self-instruction laboratory. Each student was given a guideline schedule of the amount of material to be covered each week to complete the course within the semester. The students were allowed to proceed through the prescribed material at their own pace. The only requirement was that they take and pass the final examination by the end of the semester. Any extra time, after achieving the objective for each week or after completing the program, was available for the student to use as he or she wished.

The students were able to complete the required content and accumulate earned time to use for individual research or utilization of community resources. The student was required merely to sign in at the self-instruction laboratory and, when the week's objective was achieved, to indicate where he or she would be working during the earned time.

Contingency management can be employed in such a highly structured setting as a separate task and reinforcement area classroom or it can be employed in a combined task and reinforcement area classroom. Remedial classrooms and special classes can use most effectively the highly structured separate area arrangement so that each child experiences satisfaction many times throughout the day. This arrangement ensures that each child accomplishes the required tasks and also permits individualization in the time each child needs to complete each task. In addition, it permits individualized reinforcement for each pupil, which is a virtual impossibility in classes organized along traditional lines. It is not recommended that classrooms operate indefinitely in this highly structured way. Mr. Tate's class should prepare children to return to regular classrooms, and therefore should provide only a remedial phase in the children's total educational program. If the teacher is going to retain the children in his classroom for a whole school year, he should gradually relax the highly structured program to make his classroom more like a regular class.

Contingency management in regular classrooms can successfully employ the combined task and reinforcement area arrangement. In so doing, no special physical changes in the classroom are necessary. The individual task and reinforcement passes described earlier permit each pupil and the teacher to know who is on task time or reinforcement (reward) time—a useful management device that allows for flexible programing. For example, a task can be assigned to a whole class at one time; all passes are turned "TASK" side up. As each pupil finishes his task, he turns his pass over and begins an activity of his choice. The teacher can see who has completed the assignment and can respond by collecting or checking the work. If corrections are required, the pass is turned back to "TASK" until the corrections are completed. This method can be used even more flexibly with individual assignments that do not require all pupils to start at the same time.

After students are accustomed to this procedure, the passes can be dispensed with so that the students simply finish their assigned tasks and then spend the balance of the period engaged in projects or activities of their choice.

TOKEN ECONOMY CLASSROOMS

Reinforcement in the classroom can be organized around a token economy. A token is a symbol or object that can be exchanged for something else. Commonly used tokens are trading stamps, check marks, bus or subway tokens, poker chips, score cards, and various coupons. Exchanging any of these for something of value establishes a token economy. If the token can be exchanged for something of value, it will acquire independent reinforcing value. In a classroom, a token economy is a program in which tokens may be earned at established rates for certain behaviors and later exchanged for material objects, services, privileges, or may be saved for future use.

Our economic system is organized around a token economy. We receive money from our employer for time spent on the job or for output produced. We exchange this money for clothes, groceries, rent, recreational activities, and so forth. We may invest some of the money or place it in a savings account for future use.

A Primary Class Token Economy

Mrs. Monroe established a token economy in her primary class of nineteen students. She obtained a box of play money and nineteen small notebooks to be used as bankbooks. She established that each completed assignment would be worth ten cents in play money. Each student had a bank account in which to deposit his money at the end of each day if he did not wish to spend it. Each student kept his own record of deposits, withdrawals, and balances in his bankbook.

The routine was very simple. An assignment was made. The students worked on the assigned task. As each student completed the assignment, he raised his hand and Mrs. Monroe checked his work. If the student had successfully completed the assigned task, Mrs. Monroe recorded it in her record book and gave the student a ten-cent piece of play money. This routine was repeated throughout the day for each curricular activity.

At 2:30 P.M. each day, Mrs. Monroe opened the bank and store for business. Those students who wished to deposit or withdraw money filled out the correct slip of paper and brought it along with his bankbook to the bank. The students who wished to buy something took their day's earnings or what they had withdrawn from the bank and went to the store. Small items, such as pencils, crayons, charms, and paper could be purchased with a normal day's earnings. (For example, a pencil cost one dollar; a crayon cost fifty cents.) More expensive items, such as models, records, or tickets to movies took several days' or several weeks' savings to buy. The entire procedure was carried out in the spirit of a game, and no emphasis was placed on the real value of money.

Mrs. Monroe was pleased with the results of the token economy in her class. The play money became an effective reinforcer for all her students. They attended to instructions carefully to avoid any delay in moving on to the next task that would enable them to earn more play money. From their deposit and withdrawal transactions, they also became proficient and accurate in counting and adding. For a few students, their bank accounts became particularly reinforcing, and they saved their earnings for large purchases.

Classroom Token Economies

The type of tokens used, what has to be done to earn them, and what they can be exchanged for afford sufficient variety to meet the needs and limitations of most teaching situations. The token economy has all the flexibility of the monetary system. Tokens can be dispensed immediately, contingent upon appropriate responses by the student, without interrupting his performance. The tokens can be exchanged later—at the end of the lesson, at the end of the day, or saved for a later day.

One of the most practical token systems is the work-record card. The card is divided into 100 or 200 squares or boxes and is placed on the corner of the child's desk. The teacher enters check marks in the boxes as he moves about the classroom. The schedule of check marks is usually posted so that pupils know how many can be earned. A typical schedule for elementary grades might provide for a possible score of ten check marks for each assignment:

2 checks for starting on time

3 checks for being a good worker

5 checks for completing work correctly

The teacher uses this schedule objectively to give the pupil information about his performance and provide reinforcement for appropriate academic, study-related, and social behaviors. Bonus checks can be awarded for special accomplishments. For example, when Tommy finished his paper, the teacher went to him and said, "Tommy, you took your book out and started on time. That was very good, so you get two checks. You worked well and steadily so here are three checks. You did not answer question three, and question ten was incorrect, so you have earned four out of a possible five checks for your work. You were a very good citizen when you helped Sue pick up the papers she dropped so you are going to receive a bonus check." The student can exchange completed work-record cards for toys, trinkets, or privileges.

Token economies for high school pupils would use exchange materials suitable to their interests. Records or tapes of popular music, and tickets to sports events or movies are usually quite popular. Some classes have used trading stamps with trading stamp books and catalogues so that the students made their purchases from a trading stamp store. Although these token economies based on material rewards are not necessary for all classes, they are effective for motivating students who have experienced frequent failure in school and are particularly useful in working with culturally disadvantaged students.

Combination token economy and contingency management classrooms have been effective in regular, remedial, and special classes. In these classes, a specified number of tokens or points must be earned, as described above, to gain admittance to the reinforcement area. In all of these classroom systems, *the teacher's behavior is the key to achieving the objectives*. Contingency management and token economies are effective facilitators of learning, but the teacher's and classmates' social reinforcement and the learners' self-evaluations are the stimuli that will eventually lead students to develop internalized, higher-level reinforcers. Internalized reinforcement is essential for producing motivated, self-monitoring students.

Assignment

Complete the exercises in Chapter Two of the Classroom Instruction Workbook.

References

Becker, W., S. Englemann, and D. Thomas. *Teaching: A Course in Applied Psychology*. Chicago: Science Research Associates, 1971.

Haring, N. G. *Attending and Responding*. San Rafael, Calif.: Dimension Publishing, 1968.

————, and C. L. Phillips. *Analysis and Modification of Classroom Behavior*. Englewood Cliffs, N.J.: Prentice-Hall, 1972.

Homme, L., with A. P. Csanyi, M. A. Gonzales, and J. R. Rechs. *How to Use Contingency Contracting in the Classroom*. Champaign, Ill.: Research Press, 1969.

Meacham, M. L., and A. E. Wiesen. *Changing Classroom Behavior*. Scranton, Pa.: International Textbook, 1969.

Three
Entering Behavior

Objectives: After completing your study of this chapter, you will be able to (1) explain the need for studying entering behavior, (2) identify sources of information about past performance, (3) describe standardized tests, including readiness tests, achievement tests, diagnostic tests, and intelligence tests, (4) describe the purpose of teacher-made tests, (5) apply observation methods to the classroom, (6) respond to the feedback mechanism in the cycle of the instructional process, (7) apply diagnostic teaching to classroom instruction, (8) describe individual differences in intellectual and academic ability and some variables that influence these abilities, and (9) complete the exercises in Chapter Three of the Classroom Instruction Workbook.

The main purpose of studying the entering behavior of a student or a group of students is to identify the beginning level of instruction. Because most new learning depends on prior learning, it is important to determine that the students have the prerequisite knowledge, attitudes, or skills to enable them to benefit from instruction. Every instructional sequence, whether it is an incidental intervention, a lesson, a unit, or a course of study, has a beginning. For instruction to be maximally effective, the student's performance levels or entering behavior should include the prerequisite skills.

Prerequisites

Readiness for instruction is essential for effective learning. Traditionally, children who were six years old were assumed to be ready for reading instruction and for introduction to other formal studies. Later, when experience indicated that all children who reached school age were not ready for these learning activities, various tests were devised to determine readiness. Some schools introduced readiness programs to prepare children for instruction in basic school subjects. Nursery schools and kindergartens attempted to prepare the child socially and give him other prerequisite readiness skills for first grade. Preschool programs of compensatory early childhood education for the culturally disadvantaged are part of a recent effort to ensure that children have the appropriate prerequisites for success in school. Although such programs may often raise the level of readiness, there still remain great differences in the readiness levels of children entering the first grade.

Passing children from grade to grade on the basis of overall achievement is the general principle of promotion in most elementary schools, and promotion by successful performance in a particular subject is usual in secondary schools. Although there are variations such as ungraded

primary classes and promotions based on social performance
levels, most schools employ some kind of assessment of
achievement as the basis for promotion. Even if some pupils are held back, those who are promoted may not necessarily have the prerequisite skills for success in all
subjects or all areas of development. For a wide variety
of reasons, children of approximately the same age enter
school and are promoted from grade to grade although re-
taining and developing individual differences. Children
who are generally successful may still have difficulties
in certain subjects. Some pupils who achieve adequately
and match their classmates academically may lack the emotional or social maturity of their peers.

The assessment of entering behavior of a class, even
at the beginning of a school year, should not be based on
the assumption that because these pupils were promoted
they necessarily have the prerequisites for the new curriculum. In assessing entering behavior at any time during the school year, it is desirable to obtain a measure
of the average achievement level of the class as well as
the range of achievement. This information will help you
to be aware of the individual differences that should be
accommodated by your instruction.

The terminal evaluation of a student's performance
during previous instruction establishes a basis both for
placement and for predicting success in subsequent instruction. The competent teacher begins a lesson in a
particular series using the appropriate instructional
methods and materials determined by an evaluation of the
students' previous performances. For example, an English
teacher who has just completed a unit of study on the
structure and composition of paragraphs may use the final
evaluation from that unit as the entering behavior for the
next unit on writing essays.

School records are a valuable source of information
about students' past performances, particularly when the
teacher and students are meeting for the first time. For
example, the cumulative records of the beginning fourth-
grade student usually contain a chronological record of
his past performances and achievements in kindergarten,
first, second, and third grade. This record often contains test scores, course grades, evaluations of his social development, and anecdotal information such as teachers' and other professionals' notes commenting briefly on
the child's behavior.

An accurate and useful assessment of a class's entering behavior provides information about (1) the knowledge,
attitudes, and skills of students, (2) the appropriate materials and techniques to use with these pupils, and (3)
the possible outcomes that can be expected from instruction.

Bloom (1971) states that one of the primary purposes
of assessing entering behavior is to determine placement.

He describes an imaginary continuum applicable to most subjects, along which students can be placed. Identifying students' entering behavior allows the proper placement along this continuum. Bloom's study suggests that often students' boredom and lack of interest are due to inappropriate placement. If instruction is aimed at the average student and fails to accommodate the range of individual differences in entering behavior, those students who are well beyond the beginning point of instruction will become uninterested and those who have not yet reached the beginning point will become disheartened and defeated.

Effective placement in the class may be achieved in a number of ways. For example, in a language class there may be a wide range of skills in the use and understanding of English. The teacher may organize various groups ranging from one in which students need help in reading comprehension to one in which the students use written language for creative expression through prose, poetry, and drama. In another class the teacher may individualize instruction without grouping. Some schools attempt homogeneous grouping by assigning pupils to classes on the basis of achievement.

Another purpose for determining entering behavior is to diagnose specific problems. Identifying specific problems or weaknesses, including gaps in knowledge and skills, permits early remediation and possible prevention of serious difficulties.

A third purpose for determining entering behavior is prediction. The objective of prediction is to determine the students' probability of success in a given instructional sequence and to help identify where the students can be expected to be at the end of the sequence.

The procedure for assessing an individual's entering behavior, as described in *Individual Instruction* (Peter, 1975), can be employed successfully in attempting to help a pupil who is having difficulties, but the complete procedure would be impractical for assessing each member of a standard-sized class. In a regular class, in which most students are ready and able to progress normally, the students are usually appropriately responsive to the traditional range of elicitors, including academic tasks and the classroom's social environment. Those students who do not respond adequately to written or oral instruction might require more intensive individual assessment.

A classroom teacher embarking upon an instructional sequence should have answers to a number of questions regarding his pupils. For example, what knowledge and skills do these pupils already possess? Do they have the prerequisites to pursue and profit from this instruction? What methods of presentation and instructional approaches will produce the most effective results with these students? Do some have special problems? Are some of them gifted? Are some already well beyond the entering point of instruction for the rest of the class?

This chapter will discuss the following means of answering these questions: (1) standardized tests, (2) teacher-made tests, (3) observation, and (4) diagnostic teaching.

Standardized Tests

A standardized test is one that has been developed by experts in psychological and educational test construction and has been administered to a large number of pupils over a long period of time. These tests are published commercially and are available through educational test agencies. The advantage of using standardized tests is that they provide norms, or objective measures, that can be used to compare your pupils to the larger student population. Manuals accompanying these tests describe the population used by the testmakers in obtaining the norms and the tests' validity and reliability. For example, norms described as "national averages" indicate that the test was standardized using a sample of school children presumably representative of those of the total population of the country.

The teacher who considers using any standardized test should study the test manual to be certain that the test is appropriate for his or her class. That is, if you want to test your pupils' skill in addition, subtraction, multiplication, and division, you should be assured that the test measures these four basic operations and is not a test of problem-solving or some other mathematical skill. For the scores to be valid, the characteristics of the students you are testing should closely resemble those of the students with whom the test was standardized. For example, the norms for a test standardized on an urban Anglo-Saxon population may not be valid when applied to a rural Mexican-American population. The most important consideration in selecting a standardized test is that it measure what you want it to measure. In other words, it should be valid in relation to the objectives of the course you are teaching.

There are four types of standardized tests frequently employed in determining entering behavior: (1) readiness tests, (2) achievement tests, (3) diagnostic tests, and (4) intelligence tests. Although all provide information that can be used to identify a student's level of performance, each reports specialized information.

READINESS TESTS

Readiness for learning school subjects can be determined by using readiness tests. These are administered either prior to entering first grade, or soon after, when the children have become accustomed to the teacher and the classroom. Readiness is influenced by prior nursery school or kindergarten experiences as well as by the child's social, cultural, and ethnic background. Readiness tests are closely related to general intelligence tests but are designed to predict school success with particular emphasis on reading and arithmetic. They yield scores that indicate the range of abilities the teacher must accommodate in beginning instruction in the basic school subjects.

ACHIEVEMENT TESTS

Achievement tests are available for a single academic curriculum or for a range of academic areas. Elementary school tests are usually arranged in batteries, or series, consisting of separate tests in each of the basic school subjects, such as reading, arithmetic, language, science, and social studies. For example, the Metropolitan Achievement Tests consist of separate tests for word knowledge, reading, language, spelling, mathematics computation, mathematics concepts, mathematics problem solving, science, and social studies.

The results of an achievement battery are converted into grade-equivalent scores. These scores are plotted on a graph on the test booklet, providing a profile of the pupil's status in relation to the norms for his grade placement, and his relative strengths and weaknesses. The achievement profile can alert the teacher to a student's weakness in a particular subject. For example, in a mathematics subtest, a student may score low on problem solving. This indicates that the student needs some special instruction in problem solving but it does not reveal the exact nature or cause of the difficulty. The test profile can also be used to group pupils in the class according to their educational needs. For instance, a child could be in an advanced group for reading and an intermediate group for arithmetic.

Some elementary-level tests and most secondary-level tests are constructed for single academic areas. A few of the widely used tests and test batteries for assessing achievement are: (1) California Achievement Tests, (2) Gates Reading Survey, (3) Gray Oral Reading Paragraphs, (4) Iowa Tests of Educational Development, (5) Metropolitan Achievement Tests, (6) Stanford Achievement Tests, (7) SRA Achievement Series, (8) Wide Range Achievement Test, and (9) Woody-McCall Arithmetic Fundamentals Test. Some of these tests yield subscores that identify specific areas of difficulty and, to that degree, are diagnostic. But diagnostic tests are designed specifically to yield differential subscores in a particular subject area.

DIAGNOSTIC TESTS

The scores from a diagnostic test provide a detailed analysis of particular subskills. If a particular academic area or skill has been identified as weak by a low score on an achievement test, a diagnostic test may be in order to help assess this weakness in more detail. Most diagnostic tests are for assessing language, reading, and arithmetic skills, and are used to identify areas of difficulty or developmental problems to which specific and precise remedial instruction can be applied.

Some widely used diagnostic tests are: (1) Brueckner Arithmetic Diagnostic Tests, (2) Buswell-John Diagnostic Tests of Arithmetic, (3) Durrell Analysis of Reading Difficulty, (4) Gates Reading Diagnostic Tests, (5) Monroe Diagnostic Reading Examination, and (6) Stanford Diagnostic Arithmetic Test. New tests and revised versions of established tests appear continually.

INTELLIGENCE TESTS

The concepts of mental age (M.A.) and intelligence quotients (I.Q.) are widely used by educators. A specific mental age represents the average intellectual development of that chronological age (C.A.). For example, a six-year-old child who has average intellectual development will have a mental age (M.A.) of six years. Because intellectual development varies from child to child, a bright child aged four years and a dull child aged eight years may both score at a mental age (M.A.) of six years. An up-to-date evaluation of a child's mental age represents his average level of intellectual development and can be viewed as a general indication of his ability to handle academic tasks at his level of development. A general picture of the intellectual development of the members of a class can be derived from examining the distribution of mental age scores in the class. However, this overview does not specify either learning problems or exceptional abilities.

Berelson and Steiner (1967) list seven primary mental abilities that most intelligence tests measure: (1) verbal comprehension, (2) number, (3) spatial perception, (4) memory, (5) reasoning, (6) word fluency, and (7) perceptual speed. The intelligence quotient (I.Q.) is an expression of the rate of intellectual growth and is calculated from the formula I.Q. = (M.A. + C.A.) × 100. If a ten-year-old child has a mental age of ten, then his I.Q. is 100. If he has a mental age of twelve, his I.Q. is 120. If he has a mental age of eight, his I.Q. is 80. The I.Q. indicates differences in the rate of learning. Generally, the child who has a high I.Q. has succeeded more frequently with abstract and verbal reasoning than

the child who has a low I.Q. The M.A. is an index of the
child's intellectual maturity, and the I.Q. is a measure
of the rate of growth based on the ratio of mental age to
chronological age.

Individual tests and group tests are the two main
types of intelligence tests. The individual tests are
administered to one child at a time by a psychologist
trained in psychological measurement. Group tests can be
administered by a teacher to an entire class of children.
The two most popular individual intelligence tests for
children are the Revised Stanford-Binet Intelligence Scale
and the Wechsler Intelligence Scale for Children. The
Binet Scale is based on the ratio of M.A. to C.A. as described above. The Wechsler Scale employs a standard
score in which the I.Q.'s are based on deviation from a
mean of 100. Since administering individual tests is an
expensive and specialized procedure, these tests do not
usually form a part of the testing program for most children. Instead, group tests, such as the California Test
of Mental Maturity, the Henmon-Nelson Tests of Mental
Ability, or the Otis Quick-Scoring Mental Ability Test,
are used in most schools.

Most intelligence tests measure verbal competencies
which predict school performance but do not measure all
aspects of intellectual ability (Torrance, 1965). The
measurement of intellectual ability and the use of I.Q.
scores in schools are current areas of controversy. Although there have been attempts to develop culture-free
or culture-fair I.Q. tests, most tests are biased against
certain ethnic groups and children from deprived socioeconomic backgrounds. These and other problems related
to intelligence and its measurement are discussed in the
Classroom Instruction Workbook.

Teacher-Made Tests

Teachers can construct tests that measure the pupils'
achievement of certain specific or enroute objectives of
the course being taught. These tests provide the teacher
with valuable feedback about how well the pupils are being
taught and the degree to which the objectives are being
achieved. In addition, these tests provide feedback to
the pupils, which can be used to help them plan their
studies. To some degree, standardized tests can serve
these purposes, but they are not specifically designed
for the ongoing needs in a course of study. Although
standardized tests have been continually refined and, when
properly administered, are the most valid and reliable
measures of achievement, the teacher-made test is most appropriate as an integral part of the teaching process and
a source of feedback regarding the progress of the pupils
at the time of the testing.

The teacher can construct different tests to meet
specific objectives. Teacher-made tests can be divided

into three main categories: (1) objective tests, (2) essay tests, and (3) performance tests.

An objective question is one in which the answer can be scored objectively, that is, one in which there is only one possible correct answer. This is usually achieved by carefully wording the question so that ambiguity is avoided and responses are limited to short answers. Answering an objective question usually requires writing one word or a short phrase, completing a sentence, filling in a blank, identifying a statement as true or false, selecting from a multiple choice, or matching correct pairs.

The essay test requires the pupil to write an answer of some length to a given question or problem. The pupils are not expected to produce a high degree of similarity in their responses to this kind of test. In constructing an answer to an essay question, the pupil may find it necessary to rearrange or restructure material he has learned to suit the particular demands of the question, he may be required to interpret content he has acquired, or he may be asked to draw conclusions from the information. In grading essay tests, the teacher may assign identical scores to widely varying points of view. No matter how fair the teacher tries to be in grading an essay, the result is inevitably a subjective evaluation.

The performance test is particularly appropriate for evaluating achievement of psychomotor skills. In subjects such as physical education, home economics, industrial arts, and instrumental music the teacher can test performance to be assured that the pupil has acquired the essential prerequisite skill before advancing to a more complex activity. Usually this does not have to be a formal test because the pupil has demonstrated by completing his last project or activity that he has acquired the skill for entering the next task. Formal performance tests are particularly appropriate when the student's safety is of concern. For example, a pupil may be required to demonstrate for his industrial arts teacher that he can safely operate a circular saw before he is permitted to operate it independently.

Teacher-made tests, whether objective, essay, or performance, are a means of determining achievement in one learning sequence and readiness for entering the next. This does not mean that a test must be constructed for every enroute objective. In many situations the pupils' performance of tasks and assignments provide evidence that they have achieved the prerequisites for the next learning task or sequence. Directly observing the pupils' performance gives the teacher the information necessary to assess entering behavior.

Observation

An important component of the instructional process is observing pupil behavior, not only when assessing entering behavior but also throughout instruction. Unlike group testing, which samples the performance of an entire class at a particular time, a teacher's observation is not usually equally distributed over all the class members. For example, a teacher may present an assignment and observe that all but two pupils are soon engaged in the assigned task. She or he would direct further observation toward these two pupils, and if they did not begin the assignment, might take some form of action before redirecting attention back to the class.

It is more instructionally useful to observe a class that is engaged in a specific assigned task than it is to observe when children are engaged in diverse activities. An objective provides a meaningful basis for observation. In addition, it is physically impossible to observe simultaneously all of the behaviors of all the pupils in a class, although it is usually possible to determine whether or not behaviors are oriented toward a goal. While a child or a class is performing any assignment, whether a test, a game, a research project, or a group activity, the teacher's observation of how the assignment is being carried out provides valuable information regarding the entering behaviors available for the next assignment.

Since it is impossible for a teacher to accurately study all the behaviors of a regular-sized class, it is necessary to focus on *specific behaviors* such as the number of contributions made during discussion periods or the number of questions asked during a lesson. The teacher can determine whether a particular behavior is increasing or decreasing by calculating base rates, which record the number of occurrences of a specific response during a given period of time.

Because there are so many variables that the student teacher must attend to while teaching, using audio- or videotape to record a class period and then reviewing the tape later is an especially effective method of observing behavior in a classroom. Although this method is too time-consuming and costly for continual practice, it does provide valuable feedback during practice teaching.

Observation is such a pervasive component of the total instructional process and so critical to the development of effective teaching skills that it merits a brief description here of its broader application. Observation provides most of the ongoing feedback in the process of instruction. In the Competencies for Teaching system, the "cybernetic loop" consists of first identifying an enroute objective; second, eliciting progressive changes in behavior toward the objective; third, reinforcing relevant behavior; and fourth, determining the next enroute objective. This process is maintained in dynamic balance through feedback derived from observation of pupils' behavioral responses—the most important element of effective teaching.

The same cybernetic concept is employed in industrial automation, which has been made possible through continuous feedback from the manufacturing process—thus reducing or eliminating error. In a system lacking this constant automatic feedback, a product could not be discovered to be defective until final inspection, following a complex assembly process in which possibly only one machine was slightly out of adjustment. In such an inefficient system, the entire production line might have to be shut down until the specific malfunction had been isolated and repaired, as well as necessitating the rejection of all the defective products. In contrast, when the machinery in an assembly line is provided with cybernetic feedback circuits, slight deviations are detected and the machinery adjusted immediately, making the manufacturing process continuous and self-regulatory.

Naturally, the *processes of manufacturing and the processes of teaching are extremely different*, but the principle of cybernetic feedback is appropriate for both. In teaching, feedback is derived primarily from the teacher's observations. The decisions made are the product of the teacher's observations and rational processes. The validation of the decisions comes from observing and assessing changes in the pupils' performance. Through practice, feedback increases the teacher's precision in observation and decision making. When these skills are highly developed, the teacher appears to know intuitively what to do. Observation and feedback develop the qualities described as the teacher's "sensitivity" and "intuition." During the process of eliciting and reinforcing progressive changes and identifying new objectives, observation of the pupils' responses becomes the basis for the teacher's decisions regarding modification of elicitors, reinforcers, and objectives. The quality of these decisions depends on the accuracy of the observations.

Like other complex skills, learning to teach requires practice. As in the example of bicycle riding presented earlier, practice that is goal oriented provides feedback that modifies performance in a positive direction. This applies equally to learning to play a musical instrument or learning to teach. Practice teaching that lacks precise instructional objectives is like trying to improve your accuracy in pitching a ball at a target when the target is hidden from view. The participant in this activity might develop a powerful pitching arm but little control of the pitching process. It is only when pitching practice uses a visible target, and the pitcher can observe his deviation from the target, that practice will improve his skill. Similarly, goal-oriented practice teaching that employs precise instructional objectives, including observation and feedback, gives the student

teacher a specific framework within which to assess his
skills.

Diagnostic Teaching

Diagnostic teaching in the classroom is a special type of
observation that requires analyzing the pupils' responses
to instruction. Classroom diagnostic teaching uses the
pupils' regular assignments, such as workbooks, projects,
and essays, and other classroom activities, to help diagnose skills and deficiencies. Diagnostic teaching can be
used to analyze specific difficulties by systematically
increasing the complexity of a task so as to identify the
pupil's optimal level of functioning. For example, a
teacher instructs a class to carry out a task and observes
that three children have difficulty following verbal directions. The teacher can then instruct these three children in simple one-step tasks and successively increase
the complexity of instruction to identify the number of
instructional steps these pupils can follow.

Individual Differences

Differences among pupils contribute to the challenge and
excitement of teaching, but if the teacher does not recognize individual differences and is unable to accommodate
individuality in the classroom, teaching will be frustrating and its enjoyment limited. To be effective, the
teacher must accept pupils' differences and possess adequate techniques to meet each individual's needs.

The range of intellectual ability in the general population has been estimated by large-scale studies based on
conventional individual intelligence testing. The distribution of intellectual ability by Stanford-Binet Intelligence Scale I.Q.'s is shown in the following table (Terman and Merrill, 1960).

I.Q.	Classification	Population
140-169	Gifted	1.33%
120-139	Superior	11.30%
110-119	High Average	18.10%
90-109	Normal	46.50%
80-89	Low Average	14.50%
70-79	Borderline	5.60%
30-69	Mentally Retarded	2.63%

"Gifted" children, who have I.Q.'s of 140 and higher,
are potentially the high academic achievers. Because
these pupils are capable of learning very rapidly, they
may underachieve in classrooms that fail to offer them
opportunities to work up to their potential. Gifted

pupils show superior powers of reasoning, generalizing from specific facts, dealing with higher-level abstractions, perceiving relationships, and solving problems. In addition, they usually exhibit intellectual curiosity and ability to work independently. They frequently read at an earlier age and possess a superior vocabulary.

"Superior" children, who have I.Q.'s from 120 to 139, usually experience little difficulty in public school and college, as long as they are motivated to work up to their potential. These pupils frequently attain the highest marks on achievement tests since they tend to spend less time exploring marginal possibilities than do the gifted.

The "high average," I.Q.'s 110 to 119, usually do well in high school, but at the university level may not succeed in studies requiring superior capacity for abstract reasoning.

"Normal" children, I.Q.'s 90 to 109, constitute the majority, the normal ability group that succeeds to varying degrees in the regular school program.

"Low average" children, I.Q.'s 80 to 89, frequently experience some difficulty in elementary school. Upon entering first grade at six years of age, the pupils in this group are likely to vary in mental age from under five years to five and one-half years. They lack the readiness of children in the normal group and are likely to have difficulty in dealing with abstract concepts. These pupils usually require some individualized instruction to provide extra practice with fundamentals. This individualization includes the necessity for some learning tasks to be presented in smaller increments than would otherwise be needed for the average pupil.

"Borderline" children, I.Q.'s 70 to 79, are also referred to as "slow learners." With appropriate educational preparation and social adjustment, these children usually achieve independence in adult life.

"Mentally retarded" children, I.Q.'s 30 to 69, are divided into two categories: *educable mentally retarded* (EMR) and *trainable mentally retarded* (TMR). The trainable mentally retarded are usually placed in special classes or special schools. The educable mentally retarded may be in regular, special, or integrated classes. The present trend is toward various degrees of integration— that is, the child is registered in a regular class but spends part of his time in a special class or resource room. Educators are aware of a number of factors other than I.Q. that should be taken into account in determining the educational program for mentally retarded children. Pupils having identical I.Q.'s may vary greatly in their ability to develop occupational competence and independent adult lives.

The I.Q. scores and classification system described above were derived from the standardized Stanford-Binet Intelligence Scale. It is presented here to illustrate the variability and distribution of intellectual ability. This system can generally indicate the frequency with which a teacher can expect to encounter pupils of different intellectual abilities, but it does not provide a picture of the distribution within a particular class, which may contain a wide range of abilities.

The development and wide use of the concept of I.Q. as a single index of intellectual ability has been subject to widespread criticism because it does not include all aspects of the hypothetical construct called "intelligence." Although I.Q. testing has limitations, some of which are discussed in the Classroom Instruction Workbook, a description of the variability and distribution of mental ability is valuable when considering individual differences.

Both heredity and environment contribute to individual differences. Certain genetic determinants are present at the moment of conception, at which time environment also begins to exert its influence. A distinction must be made between characteristics that are present at birth (congenital) and those that are of genetic origin. An infant's defect at birth may be the result of a pathological condition affecting the mother during pregnancy, such as virus infections or malnutrition, or it may be the result of defective genetic endowment.

Geneticists have demonstrated that such characteristics as physical build, eye color, skin color, blood type, and hair color are inherited. Some inherited physical characteristics are also influenced by environment. Height and physical development are affected by such environmental factors as nutrition and the presence or absence of disease.

Similarly, genetic inheritance partially accounts for intellectual potential but environment plays an important role in its development. Studies of culturally deprived children indicate the extent to which intellectual development is affected by lack of environmental stimulation (Riessman, 1962).

Individual differences that affect learning include the child's physical health, eyesight, and hearing. The child's social development, including his ethnic and cultural background, is also relevant to his academic success. Variations in language development, particularly those affecting the culturally disadvantaged or bilingual child, play an important role in the child's success in school. Emotional factors can help or hinder learning. For example, individual differences in motivation—the tendency that directs and maintains effort toward an objective (Smith, 1966)—greatly influence achievement. These variables along with intellectual ability are components of the child's readiness and capacity for learning.

Assignment

Complete the exercises in Chapter Three of the Classroom Instruction Workbook.

References

Berelson, B., and G. A. Steiner, *Human Behavior*. New York: Harcourt, Brace and World, 1967.

Riessman, F. *The Culturally Deprived Child*. New York: Harper & Row, 1962.

Smith, C. P. *Child Development*. Dubuque, Iowa: Wm. C. Brown, 1966.

Terman, L. M., and M. A. Merrill. *Stanford-Binet Intelligence Scale*. Boston: Houghton Mifflin, 1960.

Torrance, E. P. *Gifted Children in the Classroom*. New York: Macmillan, 1965.

Four
Terminal Objectives

Objectives: After completing your study of this chapter, you will be able to (1) define terminal objectives, (2) describe the function of general, specific, and behavioral objectives, (3) describe some of the ways in which society relates to and influences educational objectives, (4) define the domains of the *Taxonomy of Educational Objectives* and identify the categories of learning outcomes, (5) explain the function of the *Taxonomy* in identifying and writing objectives, (6) identify and write instructional objectives in the cognitive, affective, and psychomotor domains, (7) define the essential levels, (8) define creativity and developmental levels, (9) state the reasons for sharing objectives with students, and (10) complete the exercises in Chapter Four of the Classroom Instruction Workbook.

After you have assessed the entering behaviors of a class of students, the next step is to estimate what you can reasonably expect as learning outcomes at the termination of an instructional sequence. A statement of expected terminal outcomes is variously called a "goal," an "aim," or an "objective." In the Competencies for Teaching system, the phrase *terminal objectives* is used to describe meaningful, unambiguous statements about intended instructional outcomes. Terminal objectives are written for any instructional sequence —whether a lesson, a unit, or a course.

Phrasing terminal objectives as behavioral outcomes, increases the probability that the other elements in the instructional program will be designed to help achieve the objectives. Writing behavioral objectives also helps the teacher select materials and methods that will attain the desired outcomes (Gronlund, 1970).

The terminal objectives for any lesson, unit, or course should reflect general educational objectives. The purpose of this chapter is to describe procedures for identifying and writing (1) general objectives, (2) specific objectives, and (3) behavioral objectives for lessons, units, and courses.

General Objectives

General objectives are usually considered to be the province of educational philosophy rather than that of educational psychology and instructional methodology. Although classroom teaching integrates educational psychology with instructional methodology, it derives its terminal and enroute instructional objectives from general educational objectives. The following brief discussion of educational philosophy, values, and general objectives is intended only to illustrate the relationship of terminal objectives to general objectives.

Educational philosophy is in some ways different from other philosophies. In seeking explanations, most other philosophies examine the relationships between thought and reality, and for this reason are frequently described as speculative philosophies. Educational philosophy, on the other hand, is more concerned not with what is but with what ought to be. In this sense, educational philosophy is a philosophy of values.

For the most part, the aims and objectives of education reflect the values and attitudes of the society that has created the schools. These values, attitudes, and priorities are expressed through administrative, financial, curricular, and other educational policies established by national and state departments of education and by regional and local school boards. The general policies derived from these socially responsible educational bodies are interpreted and applied by school administrators and classroom teachers to the school as a whole and to the work in the classroom.

Although the individual teacher does not determine the school system's general objectives, as a citizen the teacher is entitled to share in determining society's policies regarding its schools.

Throughout the history of education, individuals, groups, and nations have held different views concerning the degree of emphasis placed on first, developing the individual to his maximum potential according to his personal needs and capabilities, and second, developing individuals who will meet society's needs for citizens, workers, leaders, and parents, whom society regards as essential to its survival.

A truly democratic society cannot exist without an informed and consenting electorate. The highest development of the individual consistent with the common good and general welfare of the state is the general objective of democratic education. This objective is subject to criticism and controversy because there is a lack of general agreement about what is a reasonable balance between the needs of the individual and the welfare of the state. Those who favor an authoritarian regime seek to promote individual development primarily to serve the state's interests. Those who favor the individual consider the state to be the servant rather than the master, and generally seek to promote a more permissive approach to education.

The extremes of these two views—separation, in which the individual must be independently himself at any cost, and recognition, in which group strength has as its price the abandonment of individualism—create a dilemma regarding general objectives for public education. This conflict between the relative values of individualism and membership has at times produced excesses in both directions.

We live in a world that must be shared with people with whom we feel different degrees of cohesion, tradition, and common meanings. The role of education is to provide the child with recognition of group membership and belonging, while at the same time recognizing the liability of excessive conformity. The more the child accepts group norms and standards the more likely he is to abandon his own. Through socialization and integration, the child loses his fear of isolation but may forfeit his right to be idiosyncratic or original.

Through membership the child gains security and commonality. Through separation the child gains individuality and originality. There are dangers to the individual, the society, and the world by following either doctrine to the point of polarization. No society whose citizens reject their membership can survive. Individualism and group cohesion can be maintained in balance only when individuals perceive themselves to be in a particular relationship to each other and share the meaning of membership in the group.

In a democratic society, controversy stems in part from the difficulty of maintaining a reasonable balance between the individual's and society's needs. Part of this controversy is the continuing dispute regarding the degree to which education should be (1) child-centered or subject-centered, (2) scholarly or vocational, and (3) promote intellectual development or social-emotional adjustment.

In the past, general objectives expressed society's wishes that education should develop the child's mental powers, provide the intellectual foundation of morality, and lead to self-sufficiency and successful living. Such general objectives were interpreted to mean that children should be adjusted to their environment and that vocational training was an important aspect of self-sufficiency. Because it is not known what the students' future environment will be (schools cannot predict where pupils will live or what social, economic, or political conditions will prevail), educators are finding it difficult to "adjust" pupils to their environment. Similarly, vocational training may not produce self-sufficiency since the shifts in technology and migration of workers may make training in one place and time useless in another.

Specific Objectives

There are no absolute criteria for differentiating between general and specific objectives, but general objectives tend to incorporate values and specific objectives tend to incorporate application. The following discussion describes some of the attempts to relate general objectives to specific application in public education.

Society expects schools to prepare children to live in the future, but opinions differ about what specific knowledge and skills an individual will need in the future and even about whether there will be a future for mankind.

A number of agencies are involved in establishing the educational objectives that teachers and schools employ in their instructional programs. State and federal agencies have been part of this process for many years. In 1918, the Commission on Reorganization of Secondary Education wrote the *Seven Cardinal Principles of Secondary Education*. This influential report described the educated individual as one who has learned the principles of (1) health, (2) command of the fundamental processes, (3) worthy home membership, (4) vocational preparation, (5) citizenship, (6) worthy use of leisure time, and (7) ethical character. These seven educational principles even today influence the curriculum of the secondary school.

In 1938, the Educational Policies Commission made the following statement concerning the relationship between society and schools:

A society which exalts force and violence will have one set of educational aims. A society which values reason, tranquility, and the paths of peace will have another and very different set. Again a society which worships its ancestors and blindly reverences the past will have and does have different educational purposes from a society which recognizes the necessity for adjustment and change. The educational objectives in each case rest on certain ideas of good and bad. Detailed purposes of education can never be developed so as to be universally applicable and perpetually enduring. Constant study and revision are required to keep them meaningful to the people, and effective in the schools.

THE EDUCATED PERSON

The Educational Policies Commission described the characteristics of an educated person.

THE OBJECTIVES OF SELF-REALIZATION

The Inquiring Mind. The educated person has an appetite for learning.

Speech. The educated person can speak the mother tongue clearly.

Reading. The educated person reads the mother tongue efficiently.

Writing. The educated person writes the mother tongue effectively.

Number.   The educated person solves his problems of counting and calculating.

Sight and Hearing.   The educated person is skilled in
listening and observing.

Health Knowledge.   The educated person understands the
basic facts concerning health and disease.

Health Habits.   The educated person protects his own
health and that of his dependents.

Public Health.   The educated person works to improve the
health of the community.

Recreation.   The educated person is participant and spec-
tator in many sports and other pastimes.

Intellectual Interests.   The educated person has mental
resources for the use of leisure.

Aesthetic Interests.   The educated person appreciates
beauty.

Character.   The educated person gives responsible direction to his own life.

THE OBJECTIVES OF HUMAN RELATIONSHIPS

Respect for Humanity.   The educated person puts human relationships first.

Friendships.   The educated person enjoys a rich, sincere,
and varied social life.

Cooperation.   The educated person can work and play with
others.

Courtesy.   The educated person observes the amenities of
social behavior.

Appreciation of the Home.   The educated person appreciates
the family as a social institution.

Conservation of the Home.   The educated person conserves
family ideals.

Homemaking.   The educated person is skilled in homemaking.

Democracy in the Home.   The educated person maintains democratic family relationships.

THE OBJECTIVES OF ECONOMIC EFFICIENCY

Work. The educated producer knows the satisfaction of good workmanship.

Occupational Information. The educated producer understands the requirements and opportunities for various jobs.

Occupational Choice. The educated producer has selected his occupation.

Occupational Efficiency. The educated producer succeeds in his chosen vocation.

Occupational Adjustment. The educated producer maintains and improves his efficiency.

Occupational Appreciation. The educated producer appreciates the social value of his work.

Personal Economics. The educated consumer plans for the economics of his own life.

Consumer Judgment. The educated consumer develops standards for guiding his expenditures.

Efficiency in Buying. The educated consumer is an informed and skillful buyer.

Consumer Protection. The educated consumer takes appropriate measures to safeguard his interests.

THE OBJECTIVES OF CIVIC RESPONSIBILITY

Social Justice. The educated citizen is sensitive to the disparities of human circumstances.

Social Activity. The educated citizen acts to correct unsatisfactory conditions.

Social Understanding. The educated citizen seeks to understand social structures and social processes.

Critical Judgment. The educated citizen has defenses against propaganda.

Tolerance. The educated citizen respects honest differences of opinion.

Conservation. The educated citizen has a regard for the nation's resources.

Social Application of Science. The educated citizen measures scientific advance by its contribution to the general welfare.

World Citizenship. The educated citizen is a cooperating member of the world community.

Law Observance. The educated citizen respects the law.

Economic Literacy. The educated citizen is economically literate.

Political Citizenship. The educated citizen accepts his civic duties.

Devotion to Democracy. The educated citizen acts upon an unswerving loyalty to democratic ideals.

This report attempted to translate the general educational objectives of self-realization, human relationships, economic efficiency, and civic responsibility into specific statements that would help guide the educational process. The complex task of identifying appropriate values and interpreting them as instructional objectives continues to receive extensive and intensive investigation by social and educational institutions. However, the diversity in the expectations of various societal factions remains a major problem.

Public opinion polls and community involvement in educational planning are two important contributions toward resolving this problem. The *CFK-Gallup Educational Surveys* (Gallup, 1972) are particularly well-conducted polls that provide a major source of information concerning the status and trends of opinion about significant school questions in the United States. In the past, most efforts to discover the public's ideas of the goals of education have produced questionable findings because researchers have failed to distinguish between ends and means. However, the *Fourth Annual Gallup Poll of Public Attitudes Toward Education* (Gallup, 1972) clearly distinguishes between them. For example, the survey included the following question intended to sample the public's ideas of the ultimate goals of education: "People have different reasons why they want their children to get an education. What are the chief reasons that come to your mind?" The response to this question indicated that the public regards education largely in a pragmatic way, heavily emphasizing material and financial objectives. Apparently, Americans believe that education is the royal road to success. The survey also sampled public opinion about methodology, school financing, curriculum, and compulsory attendance.

Since the Gallup polls have revealed shifts in public opinion from year to year, to identify society's contemporary educational values, one should study up-to-date reports.

Community involvement in educational planning is a tradition in democratic countries. Local school boards, parent-teacher organizations, and other citizen groups have significantly influenced public education. There has been a long-standing controversy over the division of authority between the public and the professional educator; arising primarily from a confusion of ends and means. From time to time, the public, through its elected representatives, has made decisions affecting curriculum and methods, and has assigned to educators responsibilities that the schools were not equipped to fulfill. On the other hand, educators have been reluctant to define adequately their areas of competence and responsibility.

There is general agreement that parents should be involved in communicating their educational aspirations for their children and that educators should be involved in planning the means of achieving any valid aspirations. This is the basis of the public's relationship to most other professional services. The public may decide that it wants a new highway or a new bridge, but it does not tell the engineer how to build it. The public may decide that it wants government sponsored medical services, but it does not tell the physician how to prescribe for the patient. Such analogies, though, are oversimplifications when applied to education. Parents feel that they have rights and responsibilities toward not only what their children will be taught but also how their children are treated in school.

A recent attempt to increase community and professional involvement in resolving these issues has been described by Lange and Rose (1972). A program for community involvement was field-tested in small and large districts in rural and urban areas, enabling the school districts to:

1. Rank goals according to priority

2. Secure community participation in goal determination and program development

3. Increase community and professional involvement, interaction, and communication

4. Involve community, professional staff, and students in assessments of perceived needs

5. Improve teacher and administrator skills in program planning

6. Enhance opportunities for educators to serve effectively in leadership roles

7. Provide effective documentation of local district needs for state and national consideration

8. Develop a defensible basis for allocating resources to achieve goals and objectives

The evidence from this study indicates that this program can provide substantial benefits to school districts. The materials for implementing such a program, *Educational Goals and Objectives: A Model Program for Community and Professional Involvement*, are available from:

> Commission on Educational Planning
> Phi Delta Kappa
> International Headquarters
> Box 789, Eighth and Union
> Bloomington, Indiana 47401

The *accountability* movement has contributed to community involvement in establishing viable educational objectives. Accountability implies identifying goals, obtaining evaluative feedback, and accepting professional responsibility for outcomes. School boards and professional personnel have always been legally accountable for such things as spending public funds, staffing schools with certificated teachers, and maintaining school buildings. But they have not been held accountable for the success or failure of students. Accountability can stimulate actively seeking community involvement in determining educational goals and policies. Sharing in the development of clearly delineated educational goals can improve communication between educators and those who feel remote from the source of educational decision making. Under ideal conditions, accountability can urge groups having specialized and sometimes diverse interest to unite in a common cause. There is potential in accountability for reducing the public's avowed unwillingness to pay for education without having visible evidence that the investment is producing an appropriate return in its children's learning—accountability programs could provide that evidence.

Behavioral Objectives

Developing specific objectives provides guidelines for writing behavioral objectives that reflect society's wishes. In some cases, specific objectives will be defined behaviorally, that is, they will describe the precise behavior that the pupil will display on completion of the educational program. Usually, though, it is the responsibility of curriculum specialists and teachers to produce the behavioral objectives.

Every educational program does in fact have behavioral objectives, whether they are only inferred or are stated explicitly. The advantages of specifying behavioral objectives for instructional purposes are manifold. They enable the teacher to (1) select appropriate evaluation procedures, (2) choose suitable learning activities for the class, (3) determine the adequacy of the instructional objectives, (4) communicate the objectives to mature students in advance of instruction, and (5) evaluate instruction on the basis of whether the pupils achieve the objectives (Popham and Baker, 1970).

Since the purpose of education is to change behavior, there are real advantages to stating objectives in behavioral terms; but simply because an objective describes the expected behavioral outcome does not mean that it is a valuable or relevant objective (Ebel, 1970). One of the means of identifying valuable and relevant educational objectives is to use the *Taxonomy of Educational Objectives* (Bloom, 1956; Krathwohl, 1964). Evaluating objectives by comparing the emphasis of one domain over another will result in objectives that express an improved balance of educational values.

Domains of the Taxonomy of Educational Objectives

The *Taxonomy of Educational Objectives* establishes helpful guidelines for identifying and defining instructional objectives. The *Taxonomy* is a classification scheme of general and specific categories of learning outcomes. The system is based on the assumption that learning outcomes should be described as changes in student behavior.

The *Taxonomy* is presented in three parts: the cognitive domain, the affective domain, and the psychomotor domain. *The Taxonomy of Educational Objectives, Handbook I: Cognitive Domain* (Bloom, 1956) includes objectives that stress *intellectual* outcomes, including knowledge, understanding, and thinking skills. The *Taxonomy of Educational Objectives, Handbook II: Affective Domain* (Krathwohl, 1964) consists of objectives that stress *feelings*, including interests, attitudes, appreciation, and methods of adjustment. The psychomotor domain consists of objectives that stress *motor skills*, such as handwriting, typing, and other physical activities. At the time of this writing, the psychomotor domain has not yet been published.

COGNITIVE DOMAIN

In the cognitive domain, objectives are subdivided into six categories, arranged in hierarchical order from the simplest to the most complex: (1) knowledge, (2) comprehension, (3) application, (4) analysis, (5) synthesis, and (6) evaluation. One should study the original text (Bloom, 1956) to use these categories most effectively in writing test items to evaluate achievement of objectives. The following brief description of the categories is meant to assist you in evaluating and identifying the levels of objectives:

1. Knowledge

   Knowledge is the retention or remembering of previously learned content. Objectives in this category include the recall of a wide range of content, from simple facts to complete theories. Knowledge is the lowest level in the cognitive domain because it requires only recall.
   Instructional objectives at the knowledge level may involve recall of (1) terms, words, dates, (2) specific facts, (3) methods and procedures, (4) basic concepts, or (5) principles. Knowledge-level objectives can be expressed behaviorally in terms such as: *describes, defines, labels, identifies, names, matches, lists, states, reproduces, selects,* and *outlines.*

2. Comprehension

   Comprehension is the ability to secure the meaning of content or information. This includes performances such as translating material from one form to another, interpreting, explaining, summarizing, and estimating future trends. These objectives go beyond simple recall and form the first level of understanding.
   Instructional objectives at the comprehension level may involve (1) understanding information and principles, (2) interpreting verbal material, (3) interpreting charts and graphs, (4) translating content from one form to another, for example, verbal material into mathematical formulas, (5) estimating consequences implied by data, and (6) justifying selection of methods and procedures. Comprehension-level objectives can be expressed behaviorally in such terms as: *differentiates, explains, translates, converts, defends, estimates, extends, generalizes, infers, paraphrases, gives examples, predicts, rewrites,* and *summarizes.*

3. Application

   Application is the ability to employ acquired content in new situations. This includes applying rules, methods, concepts, principles, laws, and theories to simulated new or real situations. Application objectives involve a higher level of understanding than does comprehension.

Instructional objectives at the application level may involve (1) implementing concepts and principles in new situations, (2) applying laws and theories to practical problems, (3) solving mathematical problems, (4) constructing charts and graphs, and (5) demonstrating application of a procedure. Application-level objectives can be expressed behaviorally in the following terms: *operates, performs, prepares, produces, changes, demonstrates, computes, solves, uses, relates, discovers,* and *shows.*

4. Analysis

Analysis is the ability to differentiate and break down material into its component parts. This includes identification of components, analysis of relationships, recognition of organizational principles, and understanding organizational structures. These require both comprehension and application in understanding the content and structural form of the learned material.

Instructional objectives at the analysis level may involve (1) identifying the relevancy of data, (2) distinguishing between facts and inferences, (3) identifying errors in reasoning, (4) recognizing unstated assumptions, and (5) analyzing the structure of a work of art, music, or literature. Analysis-level objectives can be expressed behaviorally in such terms as: *differentiates, discriminates, distinguishes, breaks down, identifies, selects, separates, subdivides, infers,* and *illustrates.*

5. Synthesis

Synthesis is the ability to put components together to form a new whole. This includes creating a unique composition, communication, speech, theme, proposal, plan, or scheme for classifying information or abstract relations. These objectives emphasize creativity and formulating new structures and organizations.

Instructional objectives at the synthesis level may involve (1) writing organized compositions, (2) presenting a well-structured speech, (3) writing creative stories, poems, or music, (4) proposing a plan of action for a project or experiment, (5) integrating content learned from different areas into a plan for solving a problem, and (6) formulating new systems for classifying things, experiences, or ideas. Synthesis-level objectives can be expressed behaviorally in such terms as: *compiles, categorizes, combines, composes, creates, devises, designs, generates, organizes, explains, rearranges, plans, reconstructs, reorganizes, revises, rewrites, summarizes,* and *writes.*

6. Evaluation

Evaluation is the ability to judge the worth of a statement, novel, poem, research report, or other material for a given purpose. Evaluations are judgments based on criteria. The pupil may produce his own criteria or the criteria may be externally imposed by the situation, another person, the problem, or the purpose of the activity. Objectives at the evaluation level are the highest in this domain because they contain elements of all of the other categories, plus conscious judgment based on clearly defined criteria.

Instructional objectives at the evaluation level may involve (1) judging the logical consistency of written material, (2) judging the adequacy with which conclusions are supported by data, (3) judging the value of a work of art, music, literature by internal criteria, and (4) judging the value of a work of art, music, literature, by external standards of excellence. Evaluation-level objectives can be expressed behaviorally in such terms as: *appraises, contrasts, compares, concludes, criticizes, describes, discriminates, justifies, explains, interprets, relates,* and *summarizes.*

Cognitive Hierarchy

Classifying objectives involving intellectual tasks places the behavioral aspect of the objective in a hierarchical framework, each category consisting of more complex learning than the previous category. These categories form a continuum from simple to complex. For some objectives the learner has only to recall and for others he must determine the essential problem and then reorder given material or combine it with previously learned ideas, methods, or procedures.

AFFECTIVE DOMAIN

The affective domain includes those objectives that emphasize feeling, emotion, and degrees of acceptance or rejection. In this domain, the objectives are subdivided into five categories arranged in hierarchical order: (1) receiving, (2) responding, (3) valuing, (4) organizing, and (5) characterizing by a value or a value complex.

1. Receiving

Receiving is willingness to attend to particular phenomena or stimuli, such as classroom activities, textbooks, music, and so on. Learning outcomes at this level range from the simple awareness that a thing exists to selective attention on the part of the learner. This includes receiving, obtaining, holding, and directing student attention.

Instructional objectives at the receiving level may involve (1) showing awareness of the importance of learning, (2) listening attentively, (3) showing sensitivity to human needs, (4) accepting differences of race and culture, and (5) attending to classroom activities. Receiving-level objectives can be expressed behaviorally in such terms as: *asks, follows, gives, holds, chooses, describes, identifies, locates, names, points to, selects,* and *replies.*

2. Responding

Responding refers to active participation. It includes not only attending to a particular phenomenon but also reacting to it. Learning outcomes range from acquiescence, such as "reads assigned pages," to interest, such as seeking out and enjoying reading materials.

Instructional objectives at the responding level may involve (1) obeying school rules, (2) completing assignments, (3) volunteering for special assignments, (4) participating in discussions, (5) completing homework, and (6) enjoying helping others. Responding-level objectives can be expressed behaviorally in such terms as: *answers, assists, conforms, complies, discusses, helps, practices, presents, reads, reports, selects,* and *writes.*

3. Valuing

Valuing is the worth a student attaches to a particular object, subject, phenomenon, or behavior. This is based on the internalization of a set of values, but the internalization is expressed in the student's overt behaviors. These objectives are commonly called "attitude" and "appreciation."

Instructional objectives at the valuing level may involve (1) appreciating good literature, art, or music, (2) demonstrating belief in the democratic process, (3) appreciating the role of science, literature, or other subjects in everyday life, (4) demonstrating problem-solving attitudes, and (5) showing concern for the welfare of others. Valuing-level objectives can be expressed behaviorally in such terms as: *completes, describes, follows, initiates, joins, invites, proposes, reads, reports, shares,* and *studies.*

4. Organizing

Organizing means bringing together different values, resolving conflicts between them, and building an internally consistent value system. The emphasis is on comparing, relating, synthesizing values, and developing a philosophy of life. Objectives in this category are concerned with recognizing each individual's responsibility for improving human relations and for developing vocational plans that satisfy individual needs for economic security and social service.

Instructional objectives at the organization level may involve (1) recognizing the need for balance between freedom and responsibility in a democracy, (2) accepting responsibility, (3) recognizing the role of systematic planning in solving problems, (4) accepting one's own strengths and limitations, and (5) formulating a life plan in harmony with one's own abilities, interests, and beliefs. Organization-level objectives can be expressed behaviorally in such terms as: *arranges, combines, adheres, compares, defends, identifies, integrates, orders, modifies, organizes, prepares, relates,* and *synthesizes.*

5. Characterization by a Value or Value Complex

At this level, the individual has a value system that has controlled behavior for a long enough time for it to become internalized to the degree that it is a pervasive, consistent, predictable life style. Objectives at this level of the affective domain are concerned with the individual's characteristic patterns of personal, social, and emotional adjustment.

Instructional objectives at this level may involve (1) displaying safety consciousness, (2) demonstrating self-reliance, (3) practicing cooperation, (4) employing an objective approach in problem solving, and (5) demonstrating industry, punctuality, self-discipline, and good health habits. Characterization by value-level objectives can be expressed behaviorally in such terms as: *acts, displays, influences, listens, modifies, practices, proposes, qualifies, serves, revises, solves, uses,* and *verifies.*

Affective Hierarchy

Classifying objectives that involve affective learning places the objectives in a hierarchical framework, each category consisting of behavior reflecting greater degrees of internalization. The continuum describes the process by which a given value progresses from a level of bare awareness through degrees of power to guide the individual's actions.

PSYCHOMOTOR DOMAIN

The psychomotor domain consists of objectives describing motor skills that are common to most school subjects—writing, speaking, drawing, and so forth. Its major emphasis is in physical education, industrial education, home economics, art, music, and commercial subjects.

Instructional objectives in the psychomotor domain may involve (1) demonstrating correct form in ball throwing, running, swimming, and so forth, (2) operating a lathe, power saw, or sander safely and skillfully, (3) operating a sewing machine correctly, (4) drawing accurate representations of still-life subjects, (5) performing skillfully on the violin, (6) typing with speed and accuracy, (7) writing smoothly and legibly, (8) setting up laboratory equipment correctly, (9) performing dance steps correctly, and (10) driving an automobile safely and skillfully. Psychomotor objectives can be expressed behaviorally in such terms as: *assembles, builds, changes, cleans, connects, constructs, creates, dismantles, drills, fastens, fixes, grinds, hammers, locates, makes, manipulates, mixes, nails, paints, sands, saws, sews, sketches, stirs, uses, weighs,* and *wraps.*

Psychomotor Hierarchy

Because the taxonomy for the psychomotor domain has not yet been published, a hierarchy of categories applicable to all subjects is not available. This should not present too great a problem to the writer of educational objectives because in the areas of greatest concern— physical education, industrial education, home economics, art, and music—the hierarchies of physical skills have already been identified. Also, curriculum followed in teaching reading and writing is based on identifying the psychomotor components involved in learning these skills.

USING THE *TAXONOMY*

The *Taxonomy* provides a three-domain scheme—cognitive, affective, and psychomotor—for classifying educational objectives. Each of the published domains is presented in a series of categories arranged hierarchically from simple to complex. These categories help in (1) identifying objectives for an instructional unit, (2) stating objectives at the proper level of difficulty, complexity, or generality, (3) defining objectives in relevant behavioral terms, (4) evaluating the comprehensiveness of a list of objectives, (5) communicating with others the nature and level of learning outcomes included in a list of objectives, and (6) evaluating the outcomes of instruction.

Most objectives contain elements of all three domains. For example, objectives in the cognitive domain require some form of psychomotor response, such as speaking, writing, or performing. In addition, there is some degree of emotion or affect in all learning. It is not necessary to identify and write all the possible objectives for a lesson, unit, or course of instruction. Instead, the taxonomies should serve as a guide in identifying the most important objectives and the relevant behavioral descriptions that will identify the desired outcome. Education is a process that helps pupils change their behavior in many ways, some intentional and others unintentional. One of the educator's main responsibilities is to determine how students are to change and what part education can play in facilitating that change. During instruction and at its conclusion, the educator must determine whether the student has changed in the desired direction.

The *Taxonomy* can be used to ensure that objectives are comprehensive and that an adequate range of categories is represented. It is impossible in most learning situations to anticipate the full range of results. During instruction, unanticipated outcomes, some positive and some negative, will occur. These unanticipated outcomes are an important part of teaching and learning. Negative outcomes provide opportunities for problem solving; incidental positive outcomes are sometimes as valuable as planned outcomes.

The *Taxonomy* can be used to translate broadly stated objectives and specify them operationally in behavioral terms. The *Taxonomy* provides test items for all categories which can be used by teachers as models for constructing or selecting similar test items. It can help the teacher write terminal objectives and construct or select tests to evaluate achievement of the objectives.

Changing Patterns in Educational Objectives

Changing social values influence educational objectives. A century ago most educators agreed that there were three main aspects of education—the intellectual, the moral, and the physical. Moral education was concerned with inculcating in the student a sense of duty and reverence (Whitehead, 1929). Most of the values and methods employed in moral education were derived from Christian teachings and accepted ideas about how to prepare children for responsible citizenship. Changes in moral values, emphasis on individual liberty, and deemphasis of religious attitudes in public education have resulted in a reduced emphasis on moral education. For the past several decades, values and morality have been included in the affective domain, which emphasizes the individual's feelings toward a democratic way of life. Recent concern about ecological disasters, increasing violence, the threat of overpopulation, and the possibility of a nuclear holocaust have caused a reexamination of the affective domain and social objectives of education (Ebel, 1972). Since scientists have begun to predict with some frequency that if man continues to degrade his natural environment—eventually resulting in an uninhabitable planet and ultimately, the destruction of the race—experts now suggest that education's primary aim should be to ensure the survival of mankind (Swan, 1969; Terry, 1971).

Although the stress on survival has not been formally adopted everywhere, it has had considerable influence. Courses on population and "reproductive responsibility" have been introduced in public schools (Dykstra, 1968); information about the environment has become a part of many courses, and some schools have introduced comprehensive programs on ecology (Boyer, 1971). The threat of the destruction of civilization and ultimately of mankind appears to be creating a new moral education, in which the survival of mankind is viewed as the chief good. The effect of imposing a moral value, such as survival, on education will cause a shift in emphasis on education's social objectives. Human relations, self-actualization, and individual feelings and values may still be important objectives, but greater emphasis will be placed on social responsibility. The general objectives of social education will not only result in healthy relationships between the individual and society but also between the individual and his environment. Students will be taught that man is not the conqueror of nature but only part of nature and responsible for environmental integrity. The need to teach responsibility for the environment and the interrelatedness of all things will have a profound influence on instructional objectives in all school subjects.

Boyer (1971) has pointed out that technology itself is not inherently evil; but when it develops without corresponding political, economic, and educational advances, a society becomes glutted with physical change unguided by integrated social planning. Schools that fail to develop students' capacity to participate intelligently in controlling their society alienate students rather than integrate them with their culture. Some traditional values, such as maximum freedom of choice, are still important, but schools must illuminate the new context in which choices must be made. Schools should help students identify trends that are suicidal or that perpetuate social injustice and exploitation. If people were less alienated from the forces of social change, more aware of the problems of common survival, and more accustomed to cooperating in directing the future, the future would not look gloomy. Schools play a crucial role. They can either continue to reinforce pathological trends, or else, by reconstructing themselves, they can help divert society from the suicidal path on which it now seems embarked.

Swan (1969) describes environmental education as being directed toward developing a citizenry aware of the opportunities for participation in environmental problem solving and motivated to take part in such activity.

Terry (1971) considers that the schools' practical goal in environmental education is to do all that is possible to improve the school's relationship with the total environment. He presents the following specific objectives: (1) awareness (sensory awareness of the environmental phenomena), (2) concern (achieving constructive involvement in solving problems), and (3) competence (a combination of responsibility, relevance, commitment, and feeling adequate to the task of solving some of the problems).

Accepting public education as an instrument of social change, whose specified objectives are to create a world civilization at once capable of preventing destruction and ensuring peace, abundance, and the survival of mankind, is the realization of a new form of moral education. This new morality is based on an awakened awareness of the consequences of advancing technology and on new concepts of social responsibility, rather than on traditional religious teachings and ideas about citizenship that were appropriate during frontier days.

This discussion has presented an example of change in rather basic educational goals, from an old morality to a new morality, brought about by an awareness of the need for a fundamental change in social values.

Writing Instructional Objectives

There are many sources of prepared objectives, so that the classroom teacher frequently selects rather than constructs objectives. Textbooks, workbooks, programed instruction, curriculum guides, and commercially prepared courses of study frequently specify their objectives. Curriculum committees and curriculum directors are involved in writing objectives. Commercial companies and nonprofit educational organizations develop and collect objectives for various curriculum areas (Popham, 1970). These organizations compile lists of objectives developed by schools throughout the nation. Using these sources, the teacher can select objectives to meet the students' needs.

A prerequisite to selecting or developing an instructional program is to define sets of tasks that the student can perform on completion of the lesson, unit, or course.

The *Taxonomy* presents classes and subclasses of objectives that are particularly valuable in constructing tests, but it does not help the classroom teacher in writing objectives or in conducting day-to-day instruction. A number of practical handbooks are available to help the teacher identify and write appropriate objectives. A small programed text, *Preparing Instructional Objectives* (Mager, 1962), presents the fundamentals of identifying appropriate terminal behaviors and stating criteria for successful achievement. A second volume, *Developing Attitude Toward Learning* (Mager, 1968), analyzes what is meant by "attitude toward learning" and illustrates a method of stating objectives that describes behavior indicating that students have learned the subject matter and will continue their interest in it. Another worthwhile volume is *Goal Analysis* (Mager, 1972), which presents a more thorough analysis of objectives. These short, easy-to-read, how-to books are practical, informative, and enjoyable, and provide a foundation of knowledge and simulated experience that helps the teacher in the actual task of writing objectives.

A practical guide to actually writing objectives is *Stating Behavioral Objectives* (Gronlund, 1970). This book gives instructions for stating general objectives and specific outcomes in behavioral terms. The author also includes excellent sections covering the use of instructional objectives in test preparation, marking students' work, and reporting pupils' progress.

IDENTIFYING OBJECTIVES

The first step in writing instructional objectives is to state the learning outcomes that your instruction is intended to produce. These objectives may refer to a generalization, such as "understands the problem of twentieth-century democracy," or a specific objective, such as "appreciates the music of Bach." An instructional objective may be abstract, such as "understands the meaning of a construct," or it may be complex, such as "understands the function and operation of a machine lathe." When an important instructional objective has been identified, the next step is to analyze it to select the performances that describe its meaning in behavioral terms (Popham, 1970). These behavioral outcomes will be adequate evidence that the instructional objective has been achieved.

The written instructional objective usually consists of two parts—a statement of the instructional objective, and a list of behavioral outcomes.

Objectives in the cognitive domain could be written as follows.

Knows number facts:

1. Recites numbers from 1 to 100

2. Counts objects

3. Adds single-digit numbers

4. Recalls multiplication tables

Understands how to find the volume of a cylinder:

1. Recalls the formula

2. Describes in own words the procedure for calculating volume

3. Explains the use of the third dimension in calculating volume

4. Measures three cylinders and calculates the volume of each

Applies a procedure for constructing a line graph:

1. Identifies the x- and y-axis

2. Explains how a given point is plotted

3. Plots six points

4. Constructs two line graphs from given data

Understands and interprets literary works:

1. Identifies the major and minor themes

2. Describes the appearance, personality, and behavior of the major characters in own words

3. Explains rationale of behavior of characters

4. Relates elements of literary work to other writings

The number of behaviors in these examples could be expanded depending on the particular requirements of the course and the class. The first example, "knows number facts," is at the knowledge level. The second, "understands how to find the volume of a cylinder," involves understanding a process. If understanding were not a requirement, the second and third behaviors would not be necessary. The third, "applies a procedure for constructing a line graph," does not involve understanding and therefore does not require an explanation of why. The fourth, "understands and interprets literary works," is an objective that could be applied to the study of many different literary works at different levels, but still it describes behaviors that are precise enough that outcomes can be observed and measured.

Instructional objectives in the affective domain are arrived at through a similar procedure to that described above. The general educational objectives cannot be achieved unless certain affective objectives are accomplished. Educators are primarily occupied with terminal objectives for the end of an instructional sequence, but the general objectives of education go far beyond the termination of instruction. Objectives are directed toward the future, so that sometime subsequent to termination of instruction, performance will be altered. The probability that instruction will affect performance at some future point after termination of instruction is influenced by the attitude, affect, or emotion associated with the students' performance at the termination of instruction. Achieving a general objective, "The students will, in adult life, appreciate, enjoy, and read literary works of merit," is facilitated by a terminal objective that describes approach behaviors to reading. The approach behaviors will vary in content for the grade or stage of development of the members of the class.

Appreciates and enjoys reading:

1. Reads during free time and after completion of assignments

2. Uses the reading center during free-time activity periods at least three times per week

3. Uses supplementary books from classroom library

4. Begins reading promptly

5. Uses the library voluntarily

6. Discusses stories and content of reading

These six behaviors describe the objective, "appreciates and enjoys reading." If these and similar approach behaviors are achieved along with the reading skills described in the cognitive objective, the probability of the student's putting his knowledge and skill to use in the future is enhanced. Affect or attitude toward other persons, the environment, or society can be similarly described as appropriate behaviors.

Appreciation of music or art can be described as an approach behavior and as making discriminations among compositions, performances, or designs of varying quality.

Instructional objectives in the psychomotor domain are handled in like fashion. A main objective is stated, followed by descriptions of the skills or tasks required to achieve it.

Essential Levels

Instructional objectives should describe the learning outcomes essential for all members of the class. Objectives at the essential level are those that can be easily achieved and that serve as prerequisites for further learning in a subject or area of social behavior. Essential-level objectives should be described in sufficient detail and with enough behavioral examples so that these minimum requirements are clearly defined.

Creativity and Developmental Levels

Many objectives describe desirable outcomes that allow for different degrees of individual achievement. The ability to be creative, to understand, to apply, to interpret, and to evaluate varies greatly among pupils. It is therefore important to include instructional objectives that go well beyond the essential level. The complete attainment of these objectives is not expected since they are intended to encourage maximum development. To encourage each student to progress as far as possible, it is desirable to write objectives that encourage understanding, originality, and creativity (Torrance, 1962, 1965).

Understanding is an internalization of meanings that cannot be observed or measured directly, as can the application of a formula, principle, or theory. In writing instructional objectives for understanding, it is important to sample a variety of behaviors from which the inference of understanding is made. The following example lists only four of the many behaviors that could be used to describe understanding a principle.

Understands scientific principle:

1. States the principle in own words

2. Provides examples of the principle

3. Identifies predictions that support the principle

4. Distinguishes between correct and incorrect application of the principle

Because originality is unpredictable, these objectives are open-ended. An objective describing rational processes or scientific method does not limit the number or quality of possible solutions. The solution may be achieved by a somewhat limited response or by great originality or creativity.

Uses scientific method:

1. Defines and delineates problem

2. Establishes criteria of acceptable solutions

3. Proposes probable solutions

4. Orders proposed solutions in a hierarchy of probability

5. Implements solutions in hierarchical order and evaluates them by criteria test

6. Adopts solution that best satisfies criteria

A creativity objective may describe an outcome in terms of alternate responses, in which achievement is measured according to the number of ways a problem can be solved rather than on the basis of the traditional, one correct answer. In written compositions, art, and music, the creativity objective calls for unique or original productions or expressions. Objectives describing behaviors, such as establishing one's own criteria, producing alternate solutions and answers, and creating original designs, compositions, and expressions, allow for the widest possible creative responses in a given area.

Eisner (1966) constructed a definition of creative behaviors, describing levels of creativity.

1. Boundary Pushing. Extension of ordinary subject matter and common forms through novel combinations or through novel elaboration

2. Inventing. Production of new subject matter or forms

3. Boundary Breaking. Production of new subject matter or utterly new forms by creating completely new forms or revising premises on which the old subject matter or forms were developed

4. Aesthetic Organizing. Ordering specific forms so as to constitute a coherent, harmonious, and balanced whole

Instructional objectives such as these maximize originality and individual expression.

Sharing Objectives

It is evident that more effective learning is likely to result when classroom experiences grow out of the students' purposes and goals. On the other hand, if planning the curriculum is put into the hands of the students, their education is likely to be fragmentary and incomplete. The objectives should be shared with the class so that the students know the intended outcomes. Mature students can be given written objectives. Young children can be shown samples of the kinds of projects they will be able to accomplish. The students should be allowed freedom to choose the particular experiences through which the objectives are to be achieved. The efficiency and effectiveness of instruction are enhanced when students know what they will be doing at the end of a unit of instruction. When students know precisely what is required of them, they are more likely to direct their efforts toward those ends and not waste time trying to guess the purpose or "psych out" the teacher.

Sharing the objective, whether it has been selected or constructed by the teacher or developed cooperatively with student participation, is an important component of good teaching at the essential-objective level. Every student should know what the essentials are that he must master. Creativity and developmental objectives also can be shared to improve communication between the teacher and the students.

Summary

Instructional objectives describe what you intend to achieve in an instructional sequence, that is, the desired level of student achievement. The Competencies for Teaching system uses two types of instructional objectives, convergent and divergent. Convergent objectives describe behaviors that are considered essential for all the members of your class. Word recognition, reading, writing, and arithmetic skills, along with the social behaviors required for participation in classroom activities, are examples of convergent objectives. Divergent objectives describe the behaviors that encourage maximization of potential resulting from individual differences in ability and creativity. Properly constructed objectives for convergent and divergent behaviors provide for the learning needs of a wide range of children, including the intellectually gifted and creative, while specifying the essential minimum requirements for all children.

A well-constructed terminal objective should:

1. *Identify an instructional objective.* This is an objective that is important because of its relationship to general educational objectives. It may be broad or quite specific. It may be a generalization, an abstraction, or a learning task. The imperative requirement is that it be worthwhile or important.

2. *Identify behaviors*. Write brief statements describing performances that, when accomplished, will indicate that the objective has been achieved. These descriptions should contain descriptions of activities such as those presented earlier in the examples from the *Taxonomy*. Analyze these performance descriptions to ensure that the behaviors describe the objective adequately. Eliminate duplications and, if necessary, rewrite the list.

3. *Estimate the criteria of acceptable performance*. Describe the nature, quality, or amount of the behaviors considered as acceptable evidence that the essential minimum requirements for progress have been met. This provides criteria for preparing and evaluating tests at the essential level. It is impractical to attempt to list all the many possible behaviors that describe the essential objectives. An instructional objective should be a tool that facilitates effective teaching. Objectives that adequately describe behaviors that give the teacher a clear picture of intended outcomes are the most effective. Meaningful descriptions are achieved by listing behaviors that constitute a representative sample.

The behaviors describing divergent outcomes should sample a wide range of performances to accommodate individual differences and provide a basis for selecting test items that sample understanding, originality, and creativity.

Assignment

Complete the exercises in Chapter Four of the Classroom Instruction Workbook.

References

Bloom, B. S. (ed). *Taxonomy of Educational Objectives, Handbook I: Cognitive Domain*. New York: David McKay, 1956.

Boyer, W. H. "Education for Survival," *Phi Delta Kappa*, 1971, 52:258-262.

Commission on Reorgranization of Secondary Education. *Seven Cardinal Principles of Secondary Education*, Bulletin No. 35, Washington, D.C.: Government Printing Office, 1918.

Dykstra, J. W. "Imperative: Education for Reproductive Responsibility," *Phi Delta Kappa*, 1968, 49:473-479.

Ebel, R. L. "Behavioral Objectives: A Close Look," *Phi Delta Kappa*, 1970, 52:171-173.

————. "What Are Schools For?" *Phi Delta Kappa*, 1972, 54:3-7.

Educational Policies Commission. *The Purposes of Education in American Democracy*. Washington, D.C.: National Education Association, 1938.

Eisner, E. W. "Typology of Creativity in the Visual Arts," in D. W. Ecker and E. W. Eisner (eds.), *Readings in Art Education*. Waltham, Mass.: Blaisdell, 1966.

Gallup, George H. "The Fourth Annual Gallup Poll of Public Attitudes Toward Education," *Phi Delta Kappa*, 1972, 54:33-46.

Gronlund, N. E. *Stating Behavioral Objectives for Classroom Instruction*. New York: Macmillan, 1970.

Krathwohl, D. R. (ed.). *Taxonomy of Educational Objectives, Handbook II: Affective Domain*. New York: David McKay, 1964.

Lange, C. A., and B. K. Rose. "Community Involvement in Educational Accountability," *Phi Delta Kappa*, 1972, 54: 81-82.

Mager, R. F. *Preparing Instructional Objectives*. San Francisco: Fearon Publishers, 1962.

———. *Developing Attitude Toward Learning*. Palo Alto, Calif.: Fearon Publishers, 1968.

———. *Goal Analysis*. Belmont, Calif.: Fearon Publishers, 1972.

Popham, W. J., and E. L. Baker. *Planning an Instructional Sequence*. Englewood Cliffs, N.J.: Prentice-Hall, 1970.

———. "The Instructional Objectives Exchange: New Support for Criterion-Referenced Instruction," *Phi Delta Kappa*, 1970, 52:174-175.

Swan, J. "The Challenge of Environmental Education," *Phi Delta Kappa*, 1969, 51:26-28.

Terry, M. *Teaching for Survival*. New York: Ballantine, 1971.

Torrance, E. P. *Gifted Children in the Classroom*. New York: Macmillan, 1965.

———. *Guiding Creative Talent*. Englewood Cliffs, N.J.: Prentice-Hall, 1962.

Whitehead, A. N. *The Aims of Education*. New York: Macmillan, 1929.

Five

Enroute Objectives

Objectives: After completing your study of this chapter,
you will be able to (1) define a lesson, unit, course, and
program, (2) define and give examples of enroute, terminal, and general objectives, (3) describe the function of
enroute objectives in the "Cycle of the Instructional Process," (4) identify the role of objectives in developing
curriculum, (5) specify sources of academic objectives,
(6) describe the contributions of programed instruction,
published instructional programs, and teacher-constructed
programs, (7) specify the functions of logical and psychological order, (8) write a lesson's enroute objectives
that are functionally related to terminal objectives, (9)
specify enroute objectives for study skills and relate
these to academic objectives, (10) specify enroute social
objectives, (11) describe the contributions of enroute objectives to improving instruction, and (12) complete the
exercises in Chapter Five of the Classroom Instruction
Workbook.

This chapter, "Enroute Objectives," and the next
three chapters, "Elicitors," "Reinforcers," and
"Evaluation," describe components of the dynamic
process of instruction—that is, the actual interventions that bring about progressive changes in student
behavior. When you present your students with a workbook
exercise, you have determined that the skills acquired
through completing the workbook assignment will move the
students a step closer to the objectives of the course.
You have selected this assignment because the questions in
the workbook are elicitors that have high probability of
bringing forth the desired responses from your students.
Scoring the students' answers plus social approval have
high probability of providing reinforcement. You will use
the scores to evaluate the students' progress and identify
the level of achievement for the entering behavior of the
next assignment.

The process of instruction follows the "Cycle of the
Instructional Process," as described in Chapter One, including the interrelated functions of objectives, elicitors, reinforcers, and observed behavioral responses. The
next four chapters describe this ongoing process. Each
component—enroute objective, elicitor, reinforcer, and
evaluation—is dealt with in relation to the others, and
not as a mutually exclusive topic.

Each lesson, unit, course, or program has a terminal
point and therefore should have a terminal objective. Attaining any of these terminal objectives requires achieving a sequence of tasks described by enroute objectives.
The student's achievement of the lesson's terminal objective means that he has arrived at the end of the lesson,
or the terminal that connects him to the next lesson.

The word *program* is used to identify all the courses
offered in a particular subject through all the school's
grades or the whole school system. For example, the mathematics program offered by a public school system consists
of all the mathematics courses from kindergarten through
secondary school.

A *course* is usually a specific one-year offering, but may not run for the entire school year. One-semester and short courses are offered in many secondary schools. In most school systems, teachers are given curriculum guides or outlines of courses of study that indicate what is to be taught in each subject for each school year. These curriculum guides vary greatly in their specificity. The content of the curriculum is usually presented in units.

A *unit* is defined as a single topic having "oneness" as its main attribute. The content of a subject has many logical cores, such as topics, principles, and themes, around which learning experiences may be organized. Usually a unit is presented as a number of lessons, study and research sessions, field trips, and activity periods. The time required to accomplish a unit may vary from a few days to several weeks or even months.

A *lesson* deals with one component of the unit or main topic. A lesson may be completed in one period or may be accomplished over several periods. A second-grade social studies curriculum guide included a unit entitled "Knowing Our Community Helpers." The teacher presented this unit by devoting one period each day to the fireman, the mailman, the policeman, the street cleaner, the garbage collector, the delivery man, and so forth. Each of these lessons had as its terminal objective the pupils' understanding of the function of one of these community helpers. The enroute objectives for a lesson on the fireman included (1) identifying the fireman in a picture of a number of community helpers, (2) describing one's own experiences with and observation of firemen at work, (3) telling stories about firemen seen in movies and on television news broadcasts, (4) explaining how firemen fight fire, rescue people and animals, and save lives, (5) describing fire prevention, and (6) explaining how the fireman makes our community a better place in which to live.

A fifth-grade mathematics curriculum guide included a unit on decimal fractions. The teacher selected as the terminal objective for one lesson, "Multiply decimal fractions by 10." This was presented in one period in which the pupils performed the operation a number of times. The class spent about ten minutes of each of the next three mathematics periods solving problems requiring multiplication of decimal fractions by 10. During the following period the class completed a short test exercise. This lesson extended over a five-day period, although it did not occupy the total time devoted to mathematics for those five days.

A fourth-grade social studies curriculum included a unit on transportation and suggested that the unit should result in an understanding of the different types of transportation and should employ reading, spelling, science, health, music, and mathematics. The teacher identified the following terminal and enroute objectives for the lessons of this unit. The enroute objectives described behaviors of the students that, when achieved, would indicate attainment of the lesson's objectives.

Lesson I. Develop interest in the study of transportation:

1. Pupils discuss their travel experience

2. Examine pictures of different types of vehicles

3. View film "The Helicopter"

4. Listen to teacher read a story about a local train station

Lesson II. Understand some past and present contributions of the railroad:

1. Read "The Men Who Run the Trains"

2. Visit train station

3. Tell imaginative stories about trips we could take

4. Sing railroad songs

5. Set up a display of toy trains brought from home

6. Explain the past and present contribution of the railroad

Lesson III. Know the functions and modes of transportation by water:

1. View pictures of rafts, barges, rowboats, canoes, kayaks, sailboats, tramp steamers, freighters, ocean liners, hydrofoils, hovercrafts, and submarines, and discuss the function of each

2. List the jobs performed by people who operate these vessels—captains, harbor pilots, engineers, wireless operators, helmsmen, stewards, deckhands, and ticket agents

3. Trace shipping routes on maps and globes

4. Sing the song "My Boat"

Lesson IV. Know the types of land transportation:

1. Describe experiences riding various types of land vehicles, such as bicycle, wagon, horse, train, bus, and
automobile

2. Read "Gears and Gasoline"

3. Calculate the cost of a trip by public transportation
and by private automobile

4. Trace early land routes

Lesson V. Understand the social changes created by
air travel:

1. Describe experiences with air travel, including time
and distances

2. Trace air routes on maps and globe

3. Describe the jobs performed by pilots, stewardesses,
air traffic controllers, and travel agents

4. Explain the changes in people's lives resulting from
air travel

Lesson VI. Understand the health services provided
on public conveyances:

1. Practice safety measures through role playing (drama-
tization)

2. View pictures in travel brochures and describe the
safety features

3. Describe the methods of providing cleanliness

4. Discuss the care of the ill

5. Create murals by group project method

Lesson VII. Know about a variety of transportation
fuels and their application to different vehicles:

1. Read about James Watt and the invention of the steam
engine

2. Identify fuels used to produce steam

3. Describe the function of gasoline in the internal combustion engine

4. Identify uses of diesel fuel

5. Explain the function of rocket fuel

6. Discuss sources of energy and power, including solar energy, nuclear energy, and electricity

Enroute objectives may be thought of as the way stations on a journey. The final destination is a terminal objective, but the traveller may decide on a number of other terminals or connecting points that are important stops along the way. He can specify these beforehand, when planning the trip. These terminals or connecting points on his trip are analogous to the unit's or lesson's terminal objectives. A curriculum guide describes the important objectives to be achieved but usually leaves the specifics of how to accomplish these objectives to the teacher. The teacher is in the position of the traveller, who has a map showing the final destination and the places that must be visited on the way. How he achieves these objectives is his responsibility.

Achieving the way stations on the trip, or the enroute objectives toward a lesson or unit terminal, may occur either more rapidly than anticipated or may be delayed. For example, the teacher may encounter obstacles that must be overcome. Enroute objectives may have to be modified. Opportunities for enrichment, events of special interest, and happenings that inspire creativity may occur along the way. These should not be passed by. The immediate enroute objective should not exclude responding to these opportunities for learning. Enroute objectives are part of the dynamic process of teaching. The terminal objectives can be preplanned and remain relatively constant, but enroute objectives should be responsive to the immediate situation, as described in the "Cycle of the Instructional Process," in Chapter One.

Curriculum

After you have assessed your students' entering behaviors and have written a terminal objective for an instructional sequence, the next procedure is to identify the steps required to achieve those terminal objectives. These steps are the basis of the curriculum by which students enter the instructional sequence and achieve the desired terminal objectives. Enroute objectives describe student behaviors that indicate movement toward a terminal objective.

There is no absolute means of determining the ideal sequence of instruction in every subject or for each social development. Corey (1967) states that, as research into sequencing and curriculum development becomes more specific, it also becomes increasingly clear that there is not just one "best" and "most efficient" arrangement of instruction. Frequently the sequence of instruction or learning tasks has evolved from experience. Curriculum planning is often a common-sense approach that arranges learning tasks in a logical sequence related to the ages and stages of development of the children in the class. This approach is based on the principle of arranging learning tasks chronologically, from simple to complex, easy to difficult, familiar to unfamiliar, and specific to general. After a principle or generalization has been acquired, it is applied deductively from general to specific.

Bent (1969) provides four criteria to consider in establishing a curriculum: (1) the function and purposes of the school in society, (2) a knowledge of how pupils learn and mature, (3) the needs of the pupils, and (4) the structure of knowledge. Curriculum consists of learning experiences that have been selected to achieve general and specific educational objectives. Instruction takes place through time and therefore consists of a sequence of activities. Through arranging the sequence developmentally, the prerequisites for each new learning task are achieved progressively so that learning efficiency is maximized. This sequential concept is particularly relevant to achieving essential-level objectives but is less relevant to creativity and developmental objectives. Such essentials as fundamental skills in basic school subjects can be acquired most efficiently through a developmentally sequenced curriculum. Creativity can be encouraged and may occur at any or all stages of the child's education.

Basic reading and writing skills acquired systematically may be employed creatively by some children as they are being acquired. Others may require more mastery before creativity occurs, and some may achieve little beyond the essential level. Similarly, in art instruction, techniques can be acquired sequentially so that the student is equipped with the means of greater artistic expression. Instruction that provides the student with the means of expression and encourages individuality facilitates creativity. Under ideal conditions, all normal children will achieve the essential objectives, but creativity will differ greatly. Gifted children will learn some things rapidly and apparently out of normal sequence. Children's individual differences in ability, interest, and creativity will vary the points at which creativity and developmental objectives are achieved. For the reasons given above, developmental sequencing of enroute objectives is used with essential-level objectives. The creativity and developmental objectives that encourage development of individuality cannot be structured sequentially. Creativity and developmental objectives should constantly allow for individual differences.

Corey (1967) presents five competencies (mainly for achieving essential-level objectives) required for planning curriculum: (1) familiarity with the content and behaviors that describe the terminal objectives, (2) ability to determine the entering behavior of the class of students, (3) competence to analyze and state terminal objectives, (4) knowledge of the characteristics and influences of instructional environments, and (5) competence in procuring and interpreting feedback information. In the Competencies for Teaching system, these five competencies are achieved through (1) your background and knowledge of the subject matter you are going to teach, (2) your ability to determine the entering behavior of an individual and a class, (3) your ability to identify and write appropriate terminal objectives, (4) your knowledge of the effectiveness of elicitors and reinforcers, which are the stimuli of the instructional environment, and (5) your use of feedback from observed students' responses in adjusting the objectives, elicitors, and reinforcers, as described in the "Cycle of the Instructional Process," in Chapter One. The Competencies for Teaching system gives you the *means* for selecting or constructing a curriculum based on a sequence of enroute objectives, but the curriculum *content* must come from your academic preparation for teaching and from your study of curriculum.

Academic Objectives

The terms *curriculum* or *curricula* are used extensively to discuss enroute objectives. A curriculum is the subject matter as well as the objectives and instructional plans. This may include a set of materials developed by the teacher, by a group of specialists in a subject, or by a commercial publisher. Curriculum materials may even be developed by a major national project, such as the American Association for the Advancement of Science.

Enroute objectives are descriptions of behaviors identified as indications of progress toward terminal objectives. A curriculum refers to a larger area of educational responsibility than do objectives, but enroute objectives are an important component of a curriculum. A present trend is for teachers to hold common objectives, but to have considerable individual freedom of choice in how they attain those objectives.

Both the design of the curriculum and its execution are powerful influences in the lives of students. The curriculum guides the educational process that influences the child's intellectual, social, and cultural development and determines how he will respond in the future.

Curriculum is organized in accordance with principles and concepts of how to teach. Any sensible organization of subject matter considers the prerequisites for the steps along which students will progress, from the early components to the later components of the subject material (Green, 1967). These principles will be discussed as they apply to (1) programed instruction, (2) commercially produced developmental programs, and (3) teacher-constructed programs.

PROGRAMED INSTRUCTION

The basic characteristics of programed instruction ensure that: (1) the subject content is presented in small steps, (2) each step or frame requires the student to make a response, (3) the student is given immediate feedback about the correctness of his response, (4) the frames are sequenced developmentally to lead to the program's objectives, (5) the development, revision, and validation of the program are based on student responses, and (6) the execution of the program is a learner-centered, self-paced activity.

Programed instruction begins with entering behavior and proceeds by means of small-step enroute objectives toward the program's terminal objectives. An entering behavior required for most programs is the ability to read the instructions contained in the frames, but programs that start at the prereading level have been developed. Each frame has as its enroute objective either strengthening a response through repetition or introducing a new response, constituting a step toward the program's terminal objective. These steps are usually smaller than those employed by a teacher.

The advantages of programed instructions are the care and explicitness with which objectives have been described, the careful analysis leading to sequencing of the frames, and the rigorous attention paid to empirical evidence for improving the program. These characteristics make programed instruction particularly suitable for achieving some essential-level objectives. The convergent nature of programed instruction and its concern with precise behavioral objectives has directed program developers toward subjects in which objectives are relatively easy to identify and in which the emphasis has been at the knowledge and application levels of the cognitive domain. Using programed instruction to achieve other than knowledge, procedures, and relationships has been questioned (Deterline, 1967). When suitable programs are available, they are frequently the best choice for achieving essential-level objectives. These programs minimize differences in attainment at the essential level, thereby giving the teacher greater opportunity for maximizing individual differences in the students' development of higher-level skills, interests, applications, and permitting the teacher to enrich learning through deeper involvement with subject matter.

Although teaching machines are used in many schools, the most practical application of programed instruction to date is the programed textbook. These textbooks come in two main types—linear and branching. The frames of a linear program are sequential from the beginning to the end. In a branching program, the student's inadequate responses may direct him to additional frames that form a remedial loop. This allows the more competent student to avoid having to complete frames that his responses indicate he does not need.

Programed instruction is an important breakthrough in the science of teaching. Hoover (1971) describes five contributions of programed instruction: (1) it embodies many basic concepts of learning, (2) it is based on specific behavioral objectives, (3) it is more effective than conventional instruction for certain cognitive skills, (4) it supplements regular classroom instruction, and (5) it facilitates individualization of instruction.

Developing a large-scale program requires a great amount of time; developing a short programed unit of instruction, however, is a valuable exercise for a teacher. The experience of writing a program and being involved in an experimental approach to developing a unit of instruction can have positive transfer to teaching other units. The essential steps in programing instruction are not difficult to master, and much that you have learned in the Competencies for Teaching system, such as the procedure for identifying entering behavior and terminal objectives, is directly applicable to the process. Frames are developed as a logical sequence of step-by-step activities aimed at reaching the terminal objective. The frames are tested with a representative sample of students, and then revised until a high rate of successful response for each frame is obtained. A number of useful treatments of programing are available: Espich and Williams, 1967; Hoover, 1972.

PUBLISHED INSTRUCTIONAL PROGRAMS

Textbook publishers have made available some well-structured, well-produced instructional materials. Their strength lies in the intelligent selection of objectives, the careful development of curricula, and extensive research and field testing. The programs often provide clearly stated course objectives as well as objectives for the units and lessons. Using these materials permits the classroom teacher to devote his energies more fully to teaching rather than to preparing materials.

The following describes a few commercially produced instructional programs: The *Sullivan Series* (Sullivan Associates Programmed Reading, Webster Division, McGraw-Hill Book Company) provides a series of programed books that achieves the essential-level objectives of reading. This is accompanied by a series of readers that achieves developmental objectives. These materials are available in kits which include materials for assessing entering reading, teaching the program, and evaluating results.

The *SRA Reading Laboratory* (Science Research Associates, Inc.) is designed for individualized instruction of a class or a group. The materials are intended for reading improvement rather than for teaching beginning reading. The kit contains reading selections and comprehension, word-study, and vocabulary-building exercises. The level of these selections ranges from grade three through grade twelve. The materials are arranged so that the process is student operated—that is, the student corrects his own exercises and charts his progress toward the program's objectives of improved comprehension, vocabulary, and reading rate.

The *SRA Organizing and Reporting Skills* (R. A. Naslund and R. E. Servey, Science Research Associates, Inc.) is a kit designed to improve students' ability in composition, from fourth through sixth grade. The topics include: (1) the form of reports, (2) sticking to the point, (3) order in the paragraph, (4) quality in the paragraph, (5) taking notes, and (6) making an outline.

The instructional materials in these and similarly constructed programs are based on an analysis of the subject matter and the learning process; the exercises or activities are therefore presented to achieve a developmentally ordered series of objectives.

TEACHER-CONSTRUCTED CURRICULA

Because every area of knowledge has its own peculiarities and structure, the teacher should identify enroute objectives only after having achieved mastery of the subject to be taught. Developing an efficient sequence of enroute objectives for an entire course is a complex task. Curriculum developers must look outside of the course being planned and think through the entire program, from kindergarten through twelfth grade, and beyond. They must consider how the course integrates and correlates with other subjects, and how it relates to child development, the instructional process, and general educational objectives. To select the units and major activities necessary to provide suitable experiences, secure balance, and prevent overlaps and omissions in subject content, curriculum planners must first analyze the entire course of study. For these reasons, it is not recommended that inexperienced teachers attempt to construct a curriculum for a course, until they have had sufficient experience in planning and implementing lessons and units.

The trend today is for curriculum directors and state and national committees of curriculum specialists to prepare exhaustive sets of objectives. Being able to select from prepared lists those objectives which he or she identifies as appropriate simplifies the teacher's job. The teacher who selects rather than generates objectives has more time to devote to planning and instructing. A complete understanding of curriculum is essential to selecting appropriate objectives and making rational decisions in the classroom.

The principles of curriculum planning are useful guidelines for planning even short instructional sequences. Starting with a terminal objective for a lesson or unit, the teacher must break down the objective into component enroute objectives and order these enroute objectives into an instructional sequence. In some cases, this is simply a matter of listing the behaviors describing the terminal objective in the order of an instructional sequence. Chapter Four gave examples of terminal objectives, followed by specific behaviors describing the objectives. Attaining these behaviors was evidence that the objectives had been achieved. If these behavioral descriptions were arranged in an instructional sequence, they would constitute a set of enroute objectives. In cases requiring more extensive developmental steps, however, these behavioral descriptions would be an inadequate set of enroute objectives.

The decision about what should be taught first may be arrived at in several different ways. The overall direction of sequencing must be determined before beginning instruction (although some aspects of preplanning may be tentative and could be altered as instruction proceeds).

The sequence of instruction follows two main directions—the logical order and the psychological order. The *logical order* is based on such ideas as "first things first," "start at the beginning," or "crawl before you walk, and walk before you run." The logical order is appropriate for learning certain developmental tasks. As the child learns to walk, talk, or read, he tends to follow a logical, developmental progression that could not be reversed; that is, he could not learn to run, then walk, and finally to crawl. Learning some subject matter lends itself to the logical order, particularly those subjects that follow a pattern in which skills are developmentally cumulative. In courses of reading, handwriting, physical education, and industrial education, most of the learning follows a logical order; that is, the prerequisite skill must be achieved before moving to the next, since a prerequisite skill is a component of the next skill. In subjects in which learned skills are truly cumulative, much confusion, duplication of effort, and frustration can result from not following the logical order.

The *psychological order* is based on the child's needs and psychological processes of learning. For example, the logical order in which to teach history would be chronological, starting from earliest times and following a sequence leading to the present. The child would have to begin by learning about ancient history, which is very remote from his experience, and conceptualize time periods of thousands of years. As the course would progress, time periods would become shorter and the historical events closer to his experience. A psychological order might reverse the chronological progression—that is, the child learns about his own community and current events and then the historical events that contributed to making his present society. As his study progresses, he moves back in time, exploring the origins of civilization. The psychological order is based on principles of child development —it tends to be ordered by the child's immediate needs and to move toward the more abstract, higher levels of conceptualization.

Logical Order for Enroute Objectives

The organization of subject matter frequently dictates the sequence of instruction. Learning certain basic mathematical processes is prerequisite to learning other, more complex, mathematical processes. Advanced scientific principles are derived from the synthesis, or combination, of simpler concepts. Logical order is the basis of most professional training. The medical, dental, or engineering student begins with the least complex tasks and systematically adds skills until he becomes capable of more complex tasks.

The Competencies for Teaching system employs a developmental, logical order, starting with the acquisition of the component skills required for teaching first an individual, then a class, and finally applying these skills to solving complex problems. In the first phase of the system, Individual Instruction, the major components— referral, observation, diagnostic teaching, terminal objectives, enroute objectives, elicitors, reinforcers, concomitant development, and evaluation—are each a terminal objective that is achieved through a sequence of enroute objectives. For example, Chapter Four of the first phase, "Observation," lists six enroute objectives: (1) interview a teacher or parent, (2) observe a child and identify deficits and interfering behaviors, (3) delineate critical behaviors, (4) observe and obtain base rates, (5) identify effective elicitors, and (6) identify high-probability reinforcers. Successive components of Individual Instruction incorporate the skills attained during the observation phase, as the student completes the textbook, workbook, and record activities corresponding to the chapter.

The logical order applies when the prerequisite skill is a component of successive performances. A child cannot read a story unless he knows the words in the vocabulary. He cannot write a word unless he can form the individual letters. He cannot solve simultaneous equations until he can solve simple equations. The logical order for sequencing enroute objectives is based on a hierarchy, proceeding from the simplest to the most complex (Gagné, 1967).

Psychological Order for Enroute Objectives

Achieving creativity and developmental objectives does not necessarily follow the logical order. At any age and at any time, a child may produce a creative response or become motivated and develop rapidly in his area of special interest. He may become so interested in a project that he independently seeks out the information he needs to complete it, and in the process, acquires knowledge out of logical sequence. Learning that satisfies his immediate interests and needs can have far-reaching effects on other learning by contributing to a positive attitude toward learning in general.

Discovery plays an important part in the learning process. When the learner feels that he has discovered his own solution, he experiences the satisfaction of independent accomplishment. At that moment it does not matter whether his creative effort or discovery has been made by others many times before, so long as it is original with him. Opportunities for learning through discovery can be scheduled in a logical sequence, but the student's own discoveries cannot be scheduled. Only the opportunities and encouragement for discovery can be scheduled. The student's discoveries will occur in a psychological order when the individual is ready and motivated. Providing opportunities for creativity and discovery improves the probability of creative responses, occurring in the future, but such individualistic responses will occur only as the learner is able to generate them.

From kindergarten through high school, the students' interests and perceived needs are the basis of the psychological order of objectives. If education seems irrelevant to students, the problem has developed because the students' perceived needs were omitted as a source of educational objectives. In many low-income, urban schools serving children from minority groups, instruction is ineffective because it is remote from the things that concern the students and seems too abstract or academic. Successful programs have been implemented by teachers who have allowed the children's areas of concern to determine the objectives. Through interviews, discussions, and questionnaires, the teacher identified what the children felt they should be doing and what they wanted to learn. By using this as a starting point, the teacher and students developed a psychologically ordered curriculum that maintained the students' interest.

Every highly successful curriculum follows the psychological order, but every psychological order is not highly successful. The logical order is the only efficient sequence for learning cumulative, complex behaviors, but the logical order will be effective only if the learner is developmentally ready for the learning tasks in the sequence. In other words, when the child is developmentally and experientially ready for a logical sequence, the logical sequence also meets the criteria of a psychological order.

The sequence of enroute objectives may be either forward or backward. Logical order is an example of forward sequencing. In teaching a child to read, you may communicate the objective by reading fluently and well to him, but the child must achieve the objective through successive stages of proficiency. It is not possible to teach the child to read by starting with difficult material.

Many sequences are learned more efficiently when the last step in the sequence is learned first. This backward sequencing is particularly appropriate in learning procedures in which the terminal behavior is not dependent on the enroute behaviors, as in memorizing a poem, a piece of music, and so on.

Suppose that the objective is for the student to learn to recite a poem. He should first read the poem from beginning to end several times. Then he should memorize the last stanza; then the last two, always reciting them through to the end; then the last three, and so forth until the entire piece is committed to memory. The result of this procedure is faster learning than if the first stanza were memorized first, and the final performance will be much smoother. The familiar experience of getting "stuck in the middle" is the result of interrupting the piece at that point and returning to the beginning, when memorizing the poem. It does no harm to start in the middle, but it creates problems to stop in the middle.

If a student who is learning to play a piece of music plays to a certain point and then starts again from the beginning, he is learning to get "stuck" at that point. Backward sequencing in learning the measures of the musical piece makes it possible to play the piece through to the end every time, even during the earliest stages of learning. In this manner, the student always knows what is ahead, whereas in conventional sequencing the student knows only what is behind. Through backward sequencing, the student finally plays the piece through from beginning to end, always knowing what is ahead.

In teaching a young child to dress himself, you would begin by letting him complete the last step in putting on each garment and gradually allow him to do more and more, until he can perform the entire task from beginning to end.

In a course in drafting, a lesson objective is for the student to understand and apply the fundamentals of orthographic projection—that is, drawing plans and an elevation projected onto horizontal and vertical planes. The teacher employed the following backward sequencing of enroute objectives.

Enroute Objective 1. Given a pictorial representation and plan of a rectangular block, the students will draw the front elevation.

Enroute Objective 2. Given a pictorial representation, plan, and front elevation of a rectangular block, the students will draw an end elevation.

Enroute Objective 3. Given a pictorial representation, front, and end elevation, the students will draw the plan.

Enroute Objective 4. Given a pictorial representation of a rectangular block, the students will draw the plan, front elevation, and end elevation.

In this lesson, the students completed final stages of the drawing three times so that all three views had been drawn before the task was undertaken from beginning to end. This application of backward sequencing is accomplished by presenting the learner with an incomplete product—a drawing, sentence, assembly, or solution to a problem. During successive steps he provides more and more of the solution until he produces all steps of the complete procedure.

It is important to note that the student never carries out any step backwards. He is learning everything in a forward direction. When the final desired step, or the solution, can be learned first, as in reciting the last stanza of a poem or completing the last step in a procedure, the most efficient way to learn is to move back through the procedure, step by step, until the connection between the terminal objective and the entering behavior is complete.

Lesson Enroute Objectives

Two types of curriculum will be used to illustrate the specification, or writing, of enroute objectives. The first is a commercially published mathematics program and the second is a curriculum guide for reading developed by a school district. The descriptions of these programs will provide only sufficient information for you to identify the relationship of the general and terminal objective to the enroute objectives.

PUBLISHED MATHEMATICS PROGRAMS

Commercially published programs of study in various subjects include textbooks for the students, teacher's textbooks and manuals, diagnostic and achievement tests, workbooks, charts, records, and graphs for evaluation, as well as a variety of other teaching aids. An example of a commercially published program is the *Modern School Mathematics: Structure and Use* (Duncan et al., 1967, Houghton Mifflin Company).

Modern School Mathematics: Structure and Use is an elementary program consisting of student textbooks, workbooks, a teacher's textbook, teacher's manual, and diagnostic tests. These components provide for: (1) assessment of entering behavior, (2) plans for dealing with individual differences, (3) terminal objectives at the various instructional levels, (4) developmental curriculum, and (5) evaluation instruments and procedures. The general features that apply to all elementary grades will be discussed first, followed by a specific example from the sixth-grade course to demonstrate how to specify enroute objectives for a lesson.

Entering Behavior and Individual Differences

Entering behavior is assessed through diagnostic testing. The continuity of testing in the program emphasizes making special provisions for students of differing ability. Suggested activities for the more able students, after they have attained the essential-level objectives, are based on:

1. Extending the process to more difficult examples (for example, three-place addition could follow two-place addition)

2. Discovering different, more sophisticated ways of performing operations

3. Describing by means of broader generalizations

4. Developing shortcut methods and individualized procedures

5. Applying the mathematical ideas (for example, devise and build an apparatus to demonstrate mathematical principles to the class)

6. Developing material for the number table or bulletin board

7. Producing a variety of projects (for example, draw graphs to represent the number of students in each class or the height of plants grown in the classroom, keeping a diary of the activities engaged in during different times of the day)

8. Helping slower students

9. Working with puzzles, novelties, and quizzes, such as magic squares and sets of number pairs

10. Drawing geometric shapes and observing and recording these shapes as they occur in everyday experiences

11. Setting up a store in the classroom

12. Organizing a mathematics club and discovering interesting materials for the club

13. Conducting group discussion of a question, such as the relative merits of different ways of performing a number operation

Suggested activities for helping less able students to attain essential-level objectives are based on:

1. Providing alternate experiences with concrete materials to explain the process, rather than discussing it in the abstract (for example, if a place-value chart has not helped students understand a process, let them try again using sticks or colored rods)

2. Introducing each process in its simplest form but not requiring the less able to work with anything but the simplest form

3. Encouraging the pupils to write down every step (for example, in addition problems, allowing students to write down the partial sums)

4. Encouraging pupils to make diagrams or use representational materials

5. Helping these students build up sets of arithmetic cards for various number operations and concepts

6. Giving frequent short periods of drill, gradually working up to the more difficult examples

Terminal Objectives

The general objectives for the total program are: (1) understanding mathematical concepts and (2) acquiring mathematical skills. The general description of the program to achieve these objectives is as follows (Duncan, et al., 1967):

The material to be learned is structured so that it follows a logical sequence of presentation. This points the way to the most useful generalizations and provides the groundwork for discovery. *Discovery is the essence of learning.* A student who is personally involved in his work and encouraged to find answers for himself not only acquires a firm grasp of concepts and skills but also develops an attitude of self-reliance which is indispensable in learning and using mathematics. The pattern of reinforcement used throughout the program secures the retention and refinement of basic understanding and skills. The whole program is designed to be a source of enjoyment, because students learn more effectively and use their knowledge more readily when they enjoy their work.

Curriculum

This elementary mathematics program emphasizes teaching procedures as well as content and uses up-to-date information on how children learn, in order to ensure retention and understanding of the mathematical concepts. The teacher's edition of the textbook suggests manipulation, demonstration, and discovery activities to be used before the students engage in the exercises in their textbooks. Using colored rods and illustrations of sets helps the students link the concrete with the abstract. The lessons present the concepts, developed through this concrete-to-abstract approach, in progressively increasing abstract contexts. As well as helping the students to understand the abstract concept, such diversified learning opportunities enable them to develop generalizations effectively.

The mathematical features of the program are based on procedures to make fundamental mathematical concepts and skills meaningful and therefore more readily learned. Consistently using the language and ideas of sets emphasizes mathematical structure.

A Sixth-Grade Lesson

Each lesson described in the teacher's edition of the text presents the objectives, including key mathematical ideas to be presented, describes how the concepts are developed, and suggests procedures and activities.

In the sixth-grade course, a unit on number theory includes lessons on factorization. A terminal objective for one of these lessons requires the student to "develop the concept of a greatest common factor and to use prime factorization to determine the greatest common factor."

The four enroute objectives leading to this terminal objective are as follows:

Enroute Objective 1. Name the prime factors of a number using repeated division.
Problems used to attain this objective.

1. $24 \div 2 = 12$
   $12 \div 2 = 6$
   $6 \div 2 = 3$

   Prime factors are: $2 \times 2 \times 2 \times 3$

2. 30   3. 48   4. 54

Enroute Objective 2. Name the common factors of a pair of numbers.
Problems used to attain this objective.

5. 24   1, 2, 3, 4, 6, 8, 12, 24
   30   1, 2, 3, 5, 6, 10, 15, 30

   Common factors of 24 and 30 are: 1, 2, 3, 6

6. 40   7. 36   8. 14
   60   27   42

Enroute Objective 3. Name the greatest common factor for pairs of numbers.
Problem used to attain this objective.

9. 24 common factors = 1, 2, 3, 6
   30 greatest common factor = 6

Enroute Objective 4. Name the greatest common factor using prime factorization for pairs of numbers.
Problems used to attain this objective.

10. $30 = 2 \times 3 \times 5$
     $18 = 2 \times 3 \times 3$
     GCF $= 2 \times 3 = 6$

In this example a well-constructed, commercially produced elementary mathematics program was selected to illustrate the relationship between general objectives, terminal objectives, and enroute objectives. Examples of the type of problem used to attain the enroute objectives were included to show the link between enroute objectives and elicitors.

DISTRICT READING PROGRAM

The Wiseburn School District in Hawthorne, California, has developed curriculum guides for a number of subjects. The following briefly describes program, course, unit, lesson, and enroute objectives in the Wiseburn School District Elementary Reading Program. This discussion starts with the total program's general objectives and moves in stages to a lesson's specific enroute objectives.

General Program Objectives

The overall objectives for the district reading program, for kindergarten through sixth grade, provide the general direction for the courses in the program. The four objectives are: (1) to acquire reading skill for word attack, (2) to acquire reading skill for comprehension, (3) to gain information, experience pleasure, appreciate beauty, and develop imagination, (4) to develop skills in reading at various rates appropriate to each child's purpose and to the material.

Stated behaviorally, the terminal objective for the reading program is that by the end of the sixth grade, the pupils will achieve a minimum score of eighty percent on District Subject Mastery Tests measuring three areas of comprehension skills: literal, interpretive, and critical.

Third-Grade Course Objectives

In the third-grade section of the curriculum guide, one of the objectives is that the students acquire reading comprehension. The terminal objective for the third-grade reading course defines a minimum score of eighty percent as the essential level to be achieved by pupils at the end of the third grade, on the District Subject Mastery Tests, which measure three areas of comprehension skills: literal, interpretive, and critical.

Unit Objectives

The curriculum guide describes three units in the interpretive and comprehension areas of third-grade

reading as: (1) recognizing main ideas, (2) drawing conclusions, making inferences, identifying emotional attitudes, and (3) classifying and identifying relationships.
     The second unit, which consists of drawing conclu-
sions, making inferences, and identifying emotional attitudes, has been broken down and presented as three terminal objectives: (1) supply logical outcomes from stories
when the ending is missing, (2) make why, what, when, and
where inferences from titles, and (3) interpret attitudes
and feelings of the main characters in stories.

Lesson Objectives

     For purposes of illustration, the third objective—
interpret attitudes and feelings of the main characters in
stories—has been selected as the objective for a lesson.
Two enroute objectives employed in attaining this terminal
objective are: (1) given a paragraph and a list of emo-
tions, the student will identify the emotion depicted, and
(2) given a short story, the student will locate and list
the words that identify the main character's feelings.
     This example extracted from a school district's cur-
riculum guide presented a brief description of the relationship between general program objectives, course objectives, unit objectives, lesson objectives, and enroute
objectives.
     A valuable exercise for the student teacher is to ex-
amine well-prepared programs and go through this deductive
process, from the general objectives to the specific enroute objectives. Of course, your teaching will be in
the other direction, starting with enroute objectives and
leading toward the general objectives. The ability to
identify appropriate enroute objectives, which describe
behaviors facilitating the development of higher mental
processes—conceptualization, and creativity—is essential
to fully competent teaching. To the casual observer, the
teacher's ability to change student behavior positively is
the obvious indication of a good teacher; but only if the
students' behavior is meaningful in relation to achieving
general educational objectives is the teacher a maximally
effective educator.

Enroute Study Skills

While acquiring skills and subject content, the pupil also
acquires the skills of learning. If the pupil acquires
the ability to learn independently, to solve problems, and
to evaluate his own accomplishments, the probability is
increased that he will learn continuously throughout his
life. Continuous learning has long been an objective of
education. There is general agreement that the proper
business of the school is to teach students to think.
Yet this goal has frequently failed to become a tangible

reality because thinking has been treated as a global process that encompasses anything that goes on inside the brain, from fantasizing to constructing a concept of reality.

The theory that reflective thinking or rational thought could not occur until a sufficient body of factual information had been accumulated was a traditional idea in education, which inhibited students from acquiring thinking skills. This tradition was based on the idea that the acquired knowledge would be useful later, when the student is thinking. Another assumption that interfered with the development of productive thought was that independent thought was an automatic by-product of studying and of acquiring the products of the disciplined thoughts of others.

Memorizing a mathematical formula or the steps in a mathematical process, for example, requires only rote memory. Providing the first-grade child with a set of counting rods that are a model of the number system, so that he can make his own mathematical discoveries, elicits responses that are at a higher level in the cognitive domain. The difference is not in the academic content but in the teaching and learning processes. In the first case, the student is learning about mathematics and in the second he is behaving as a mathematician. By behaving as writers, researchers, historians, and mathematicians, students are more likely to become involved in thought processes than if they are being asked only to memorize facts about these subjects. Learning history and doing historical research are qualitatively different activities (Bruner, et al., 1956; Bruner, 1960; Bruner, 1966).

Learning to think is not distinct from achieving the enroute objectives in various subjects. Developing higher-level thought processes depends more on *how* things are taught than *what* is taught. If the pupil studying geometry in a mathematics course has concomitant experiences in other subjects, which require geometric solutions, then understanding, transfer, and retention are enhanced. The student applying his geometric skills in studying the structure of the Egyptian pyramids, in learning about ancient navigation techniques in social studies, and in drafting and sheet metal layout in industrial education, has a much improved opportunity to learn problem solving by employing his knowledge of geometry, than if mathematics study were restricted to the mathematics period. The same applies to all subjects. Curriculum design based on correlation and integration results in increased application and proficiency in problem solving, and fosters creativity and generalization.

Thinking is a general term describing internal or inferred processes. The evidence that thought exists is based on subjective experience and observing behavior of others' speech, writing, and actions, indicating their application of rational processes, scientific method, knowledge, or creativity.

Certain study skills can be identified, including attending, independent study, problem solving, and self-evaluation. Attending to a task or to instruction refers to looking at and listening to the appropriate object or event. This includes shifting attention appropriately. The student must be able to attend to the teacher during the presentation of an explanation or demonstration and then shift to his own study or the task at hand. The ability to control attention is fundamental to effective study.

Developing independent study skills, or learning how to learn, will help the student adapt to an age of rapid and radical change. Hoover (1972) states that a goal for secondary school should be that, by the time a student graduates, he should be fully qualified to direct his own learning. Achieving this objective requires that students learn to use libraries, resource centers, and other sources of information efficiently. Learning to use reference materials is an important part of independent study and can be taught as an integral part of instruction to achieve a subject area objective. The ability to use reference materials can then be employed by the student in completing his independent research projects.

In an educational program, problem solving consists primarily of applying what has been learned. Problem solving is a method of instruction for engaging students in critical, inferential, differential, analytical, and deductive thinking. This method is based on the assumption that the student should be involved in processing his own information. The student selects his own problem and becomes motivated to gather information about himself and the world around him. As he organizes that information, he uncovers principles, theories, generalizations, as well as developing his own explanations. When he applies his generalizations and theories to predict or control his behavior or environment, he validates his ideas and produces new data. In this type of problem solving, the inductive-deductive process is a continuous cycle. Attempts have been made to evaluate the inductive and deductive approaches separately. In the inductive method, the student makes his own generalizations from specific data and experiences. This method appears to result in greater retention (Bent, 1969). The deductive method starts with the theory or generalization and then looks for supporting evidence. In practice, solving real problems usually involves both processes. The student attempting to solve a problem usually has a hunch or a vague generalization early in his investigation. This influences which data he collects. The data clarify his explanations, theories, and abstractions, which in turn influence his treatment of the data, thereby producing new data.

Guiding students through the steps of scientific method may contribute to reflective thinking and rational thought processes, but scientific method should not be taught as though it were the one and only way to solve problems. Its sequential steps—identifying a problem, gathering data, delineating, defining, establishing criteria, formulating hypothetical solutions, ordering the solutions, testing, and evaluating—have a rational basis, but in practice several of these activities may be occurring simultaneously.

Self-evaluation or internalized reinforcement is required for self-maintenance of directed learning. The student who rates his own performances and products, and derives satisfaction from successfully attaining his own objectives, has acquired one of the most important characteristics of independent study.

These behavioral characteristics, which contribute to study skills, cannot be learned apart from learning the content of a subject. The student cannot learn to think without thinking about something, and he cannot learn to learn without learning something. Acquiring study skills is not a separate area of study but a concomitant development achieved through the way students are taught and the way they learn.

Enroute Social Objectives

It is essential for the child to acquire the social behaviors that make it possible for him to learn in a group and also for his behavior not to interfere seriously with the learning of others. Beyond these essential-level social objectives, the developmental and creativity objectives include positive social contributions. It is desirable for students to acquire skills in human relations and social problem solving, and for some eventually to contribute positively to solving major social problems.

Essential-level social behaviors can be taught, using the same curriculum concepts as are used for academic subjects (Sheppard, Shank, and Wilson, 1972). The social curriculum consists of steps or enroute objectives that direct the child from his present functioning to the desired terminal behavior. The child who lacks the essential social behaviors for classroom participation may have to learn to (1) sit at his desk, (2) attend to and complete a task, (3) engage in parallel activities, (4) take turns, and (5) cooperate in a joint project. Similarly, the social objectives for a class can be based on a logical developmental sequence.

Social objectives based on the students' needs beyond the classroom must include behaviors that enable them to pursue worthwhile social goals. For example, students might engage in a great deal of valuable discussion of higher humanistic goals, but without developing specific behaviors necessary to perform humanistically, their learning may remain at a verbal level.

Some schools are emphasizing study of the future, or survival training, to help students learn to cope with changes they will probably have to live with tomorrow. For example, in one classroom an attempt was made to help the students conceptualize the relevance of population, and to assist them in making rational and responsible decisions about population. One enroute objective called for the class to explore the problems of living and working in less space. An effective activity employed in achieving this objective included roping off half the classroom and then exploring the problems created by doubling up at desks and functioning under crowded conditions.

Some educators suggest a social objective of evolving from a competitive society to a cooperative society (Kincaid, 1972). Cooperation requires a different set of skills, attitudes, and values than those required for competition. Achieving this objective would require identifying, adopting, and putting into practice a significantly different curriculum for social development than has been employed in the past. What is taught and how it is taught are inseparable if these new social objectives are to be achieved.

Improving Instruction

The enroute objective is an essential component in improving the teacher's or student teacher's performance. The important feedback that influences the teacher's behavior is derived from observing students' responses. If the teacher has only a vague or general idea of the intended response, the feedback can be misleading. It is therefore particularly important that the beginning teacher identify specifically the intended behaviors which the pupils are to produce. The teacher's observation of the students' behavior will then indicate when the teacher is becoming effective.

This feedback is the basis of a method for educating teachers, called *microteaching* (Allen and Ryan, 1969; Borg, 1970). Microteaching is accomplished by requiring the student teacher to conduct a short (about five-minute) lesson with a small group of students. The lesson is then evaluated by the teacher with the help of a supervisor. The same lesson is then immediately repeated with a different group of students to determine whether teaching techniques have improved. Microteaching provides a systematic means of studying the teaching-learning process and discovering the most effective techniques and skills needed by the teacher.

A process similar to microteaching may be achieved by employing enroute objectives and evaluating the teaching performance in relation to achieving the objective. In Phase One, Individual Instruction, the teaching records provided systematic feedback based on observation of behavioral responses in relation to enroute objectives.

The feedback can be enhanced by tape-recording each instructional sequence and then replaying the tape immediately after the lesson. Evaluating achievement of the enroute objectives in relation to the teacher's performance provides valuable feedback for continually improving instruction.

Assignment

After studying this chapter, complete the exercises in Chapter Five of the Classroom Instruction Workbook.

References

Allen, K., and W. Ryan. *Microteaching*. Reading, Mass.: Addison-Wesley, 1969.

Bent, Rudyard K., and Adolph Unruh. *Secondary School Curriculum*. Lexington, Mass.: D. C. Heath, 1969.

Borg, Walter R. *The Mini Course: A Microteaching Approach to Teacher Education*. Beverly Hills, Calif.: Macmillan, 1970.

Bruner, J. S. *The Process of Education*. Cambridge, Mass.: Harvard University Press, 1960.

————. *Toward a Theory of Instruction*. Cambridge, Mass.: Harvard University Press, 1966.

————, Jacqueline J. Goodnow, and G. A. Austin. *A Study of Thinking*. New York: John Wiley, 1956.

Corey, M. "The Nature of Instruction," in P. C. Lange (ed.), *Programmed Instruction: The Sixty-Sixth Yearbook of the National Society for the Study of Education, Part II*. Chicago: The University of Chicago Press, 1967.

Deterline, A. A. "Practical Problems in Program Production," in P. C. Lange (ed.), *Programmed Instruction: The Sixty-Sixth Yearbook of the National Society for the Study of Education, Part II*. Chicago: The University of Chicago Press, 1967.

Duncan, E. R., L. R. Capps, M. P. Dolciani, W. G. Grant, and M. Zweng. *Modern School Mathematics: Structure and Use*. Boston: Houghton Mifflin, 1967.

Espich, J. E., and B. Williams. *Developing Programmed Instructional Materials*. Palo Alto, Calif.: Fearon, 1967.

Foshay, Arthur W. "Curriculum Design for the Humane School," *Theory into Practice*, 1971, 10:204-207.

Frost, J. L. and G. T. Rowland. *Curricula for the Seventies*. Boston: Houghton Mifflin, 1969.

Gagné, R. W. "Curriculum Research and the Promotion of Learning," in *AERA Monograph Series on Curriculum Evaluation*. Chicago: Rand McNally, 1967.

Gooler, D., and D. Grotelueschen. "Curriculum Development Accountability," *Education Leadership*, 1971, 29: 165-169.

Green, Edward J. "The Process of Instructional Programming," in P. C. Lange (ed.), *Programmed Instruction: The Sixty-Sixth Yearbook of the National Society for the Study of Education, Part II*. Chicago: The University of Chicago Press, 1967.

Hoover, K. H. *Learning and Teaching in the Secondary School*. Boston: Allyn and Bacon, 1972.

Kincaid, G. L. "Curriculum for the 70's: Cooperation Is the Name of the Game," *English Journal*, 1972, 61:723-727.

Sheppard, W. C., B. Shank, and D. Wilson. *How to Be a Good Teacher: Training Social Behavior in Young Children*. Champaign, Ill.: Research Press, 1972.

Six

Elicitors

Objectives: After completing your study of this chapter,
you will be able to (1) describe the functional relationship between elicitors and enroute objectives, (2) define
instructional media—"hardware" and "software," (3) discuss the function of books, manipulative materials, and
equipment, (4) describe effective teacher behaviors for
eliciting pupil attention, (5) describe teacher behavior
for eliciting pupil task behavior, (6) describe other
eliciting events, such as field trips, visitors, direct
experience, independent study, simulation, and class discussion, (7) implement the procedure for developing questioning skills, and (8) complete the exercises in Chapter
Six of the Classroom Instruction Workbook.

Each enroute objective is achieved by manipulating
eliciting and reinforcing events to influence pupils' behavior in a positive direction, toward
either essential-level objectives or creativity
and developmental objectives. Pupils may achieve some
enroute objective with very little assistance from the
teacher, requiring only that the teacher communicate the
objective to the pupils and they will find their own ways
to achieve it. The elicitor in this case is communicating
the objective. Familiar examples of the objective as an
elicitor are projects or term papers, in which the student
is informed specifically or generally about the nature of
the end product. Valuable as this technique is, it cannot
be relied on for achieving many essential-level skills.

Elicitors should be organized in a developmental sequence so as to bring forth the essential-level behaviors
described by the enroute objectives. Elicitors may be
simple or complex. A simple elicitor may be (1) a command
or a question to which the pupil responds, (2) a self-
instructional worksheet or other self-instructional material, or (3) simply communicating the objective. A complex elicitor may combine such elements as the teacher's
explanation or demonstration, instructional materials,
students' assignment sheets, and group interaction.

Eliciting stimuli do not always bring forth the exact
behaviors that are anticipated (except for simple reflexes, such as contraction of the pupil of the eye on exposure to bright light, or salivation when food is placed
in the mouth). When selecting elicitors to bring forth
those behaviors described in the enroute objectives, the
teacher is working in an area of probability. The more
relevant the elicitor to the objective, the higher the
probability that the appropriate behavior will occur.
Frequently the same objective can be achieved by using
a number of different elicitors. In many cases there is
more than one "best" elicitor.

Effective teaching is a dynamic process that must be responsive to the pupil's needs. If the pupil does not answer a question, the teacher may reconstruct the question, add more cues, or ask another question to explore the pupil's prerequisite knowledge or understanding. For the teacher to be able to adjust elicitors successfully, it is essential that he or she have knowledge of the components of elicitors.

The following discussion explores the components that constitute elicitors by describing (1) instructional media, (2) teacher behavior, and (3) other eliciting events.

Instructional Media

Instructional media consist of materials and equipment. A piece of printed material may be presented in a number of different ways, each using different equipment. For example, the material may appear in a book. It may be reproduced on a chart. It may be transferred to a slide and projected on a screen. In each case the content is the same but the equipment is different. The material along with the equipment for presenting it constitute the media. The material and the book are one medium. The material and the chart are another medium. The projector and the projected image are another medium.

The pupil's response is influenced not only by the material but also by means of presentation. A still picture may be printed in a textbook. It may appear in a filmstrip. It may be projected from an overhead transparency or pinned on a bulletin board. The still picture is the material. The projector with which it is shown or the bulletin board on which it is displayed is the equipment. The material and the equipment together constitute the medium.

Two terms commonly used to discuss media are *hardware* and *software*. Hardware consists of the concrete elements of the media, such as the motion picture projector and the film, the paper and the binding of the book, the tape and the tape recorder. The software is the content, ideas, knowledge, information, and concepts represented on the film, printed in the book, or recorded on the tape. The motion picture, the book, and the tape are the means of transmitting the software.

There are many types of media employed in complex combinations to form the elicitor. The following brief examination of some of the categories of media reveals the wealth of possibilities in selecting effective elicitors.

Real Things. These are the actual events, people, animals, plants, objects, and demonstrations to which pupils respond.

Verbal Presentations. Words are the most common symbols of communication. They occur in speech, books, printed notices, projected media, and on signs, chalk-boards, and bulletin boards.

Graphics. Drawings and other symbolic representa-tions occur on charts, posters, graphs, maps, diagrams, animated cartoons, and in many other media.

Photographs. Still pictures record the real object or event in the same size, larger, or smaller than the object or event represented.

Motion Pictures and Television. These media simu-late events that otherwise could not occur in the class-room. By "recreating" reality in the classroom, they can transport the class to simulated or real events anywhere in time or space.

Audio Recordings. Recording tapes, phonograph rec-ords, and film sound tracks permit voices and sounds to be stored and reproduced at will.

Programs. Programed instruction presents sequences of information to elicit predetermined responses.

Simulation. Simulators, which produce close approxi-mations of actual events or processes, are a highly effec-tive way of eliciting complex skills or behaviors. Simu-lators used in training drivers and pilots simulate, or imitate, the essentials of the real environment. Simula-tors have been developed in medical training for teaching certain aspects of anesthesiology and surgery. Examples of simulation are computer games, games of economic, so-cial, and geographic conditions, and the workbooks in the Competencies for Teaching system.

BOOKS, MANIPULATIVE MATERIALS, AND EQUIPMENT

To help the teacher identify the elements that will constitute effective elicitors, the discussion of instruc-tional media is divided into three parts: (1) books, (2) manipulative materials, and (3) equipment.

Books

Books for instructional purposes fall generally into four main categories: textbooks, workbooks, readers, and programed books, although one book may contain elements from all categories.

Textbooks. Textbooks are specifically prepared for instructional purposes. Each chapter usually deals with a particular subject, and the content within the sections of each chapter are arranged with headings that indicate the structural organization of the subject matter. A textbook also makes the content readily available by including an index. The text is arranged so that the student can move about in the material, skip what is already known, turn back when necessary, and review selectively (Pressey, 1963).

Textbooks use a number of means to help the student reach the desired objectives in the subject matter. A textbook's organization develops the subject matter from simple to complex, easy to difficult, and concrete to abstract. The student's understanding of the subject matter is facilitated through descriptions, definitions, and illustrations. Students can become further involved in the subject by using the quizzes or questions provided and through the individual or group projects suggested (Smith and Smith, 1966).

Workbooks. Workbooks contain instructions, outlines for studying content, and spaces for student responses—questions to be answered, items to be checked, or blanks to fill in. Maps, diagrams, and other illustrations may also be included. A workbook may stand by itself or be directly related to a textbook. A textbook presents the basic information and the workbook gives the student opportunities for applying the acquired knowledge. A workbook related to a textbook supplements the text and provides self-instructional exercises to develop skills. Well-constructed workbooks can provide an outlet for written expression, develop transfer and generalization, offer variety, accommodate individual differences, and ensure order and continuity of thought (Dale, 1969).

Readers. Readers consist of short literary pieces arranged developmentally. Most use some form of controlled vocabulary so that the pupil is never confronted with too many new words in one exercise. Supplementary readers enrich learning by providing opportunities to select content in the pupil's areas of interest, and at his vocabulary level.

Programed Books. Programed instruction is presented in a sequence of frames, each of which elicits a response from the learner. The program then reinforces each correct response by providing knowledge of results. Programed books usually require the learner to respond to each frame with a written response—a word, symbol, or phrase. There are two kinds of programed books: linear and branching.

Linear programs consist of material presented in a fixed sequence of frames. The student reads the information in a frame, writes his answer to a question, checks his answer against the correct response, and repeats this process again and again until he reaches the end of the program.

Branching programs consist of material divided into small units so that the responses determine the student's movement through the program. Errors lead to presentation of further information, including explanations of why the answer was incorrect. Then the program requests another response or requires the student to review previously presented material. Branching programs recognize individual differences by allowing more able students to move quickly through the program and slower students to move through the program at their own pace (Espich and Williams, 1967).

Most programs are designed to teach basic knowledge or skills; however, some programs have been developed to teach creative problem-solving techniques (Dale, 1969).

Manipulative Materials

Although most instructional materials require some psychomotor activity, such as handwriting or drawing, manipulative materials demand primarily psychomotor activity. The objectives of using many manipulative materials are to develop neuromuscular coordination and refine perception. Pegboards, formboards, and Montessori materials develop coordination and perception of size, shape, and position in space. Concepts are sometimes taught with manipulative materials. For instance, blocks, counting sticks, abacus, and arithmetic rods may be used to teach number concepts. Providing the young child with a concrete model of the number system permits mathematical experiments to be performed through manipulating the materials. By using raised plastic or beaded letters, the child can trace the shape of the letters with his finger while pronouncing or saying the letter. This elicits a multisensory response involving visual, auditory, tactile, and kinesthetic stimuli.

Manipulating real objects can develop skills in handling objects from the child's natural environment. Environmental samples—stones, insects, seeds, and leaves—can be used to supply substance to the ideas being taught and give the pupil experiences in preparing, classifying, organizing, and displaying real things. Household, scientific, and mechanical equipment provide opportunities to observe, handle, manipulate, operate, disassemble, and assemble objects from real life.

Manipulative games and puzzles offer a rich source of activity contributing to motor and perceptual development. They also require cognitive skills. The equipment used in physical education, industrial education, commercial education, and home economics elicits manipulation and contributes to the child's psychomotor and cognitive development.

Equipment

Instructional media increasingly make use of equipment. Not many years ago, the teacher's instructional equipment consisted of a chalkboard, a globe, and some charts. Today the teacher may employ television, motion pictures, recordings, language labs, overhead projectors, teaching machines, and other audiovisual devices. The future will see additions to this list.

Television. Television is an electronic means of transmitting moving or still visual images with accompanying sound over a cable or through space. One of its major educational contributions is its potential for communicating a wide variety of content. Television can bring models of excellence and the world of distant reality into the classroom. The immediacy and reality of television make the content appealing and understandable to pupils of varying ages and educational levels (Dale, 1969).

The effective use of educational television depends primarily on the classroom teacher. There are many high-quality educational television programs, but unless the pupils know the objective of their viewing and engage in relevant follow-up activities, the program will be of limited educational value. Television establishes a common base of experience for all the pupils who see a given program. It brings to the classroom people, places, and events that otherwise could not be seen. It allows programs to be recorded and shown at appropriate times. Sources of educational programs are educational television channels, tape-rental libraries, cable television, and some special commercial programs.

Closed-circuit television can be used to give the class a closer view of a demonstration or to transmit a demonstration or lesson to rooms throughout the school (Gerlach and Ely, 1971).

Videotaping is useful for recording intricate experiments or demonstrations that are difficult to reproduce. Using videotape eliminates the need to prepare difficult demonstrations repeatedly for successive classes. Taping guest lectures, art demonstrations, musical or sports events, and other activities that are available on a one-time basis is a successful application of videotape. Videotaping student and class projects or performances, such as making a documentary of class activities to show on parents' day, is another valuable use of television which provides opportunities for every child to participate.

Motion Pictures. A motion picture film is a series of still pictures taken in rapid succession so that when projected it gives the viewer an illusion of motion. Motion pictures can show color, close-ups, microphotography, time-lapse, montages, X-rays, telescopic photography, slow motion, stop-action, and animation. They can show things that are difficult or impossible to present by other media. A wide variety of material is available on 16 mm and 8 mm films made for instructional purposes. These include lectures, field trips, dramatic productions of literary works, historical events, and scientific demonstrations that are too difficult, dangerous, expensive, or time-consuming for the teacher to replicate. Research indicates that more learning takes place when teachers prepare pupils for a film viewing and then follow the showing with appropriate activities. Research reveals also that students should attend passively during the film presentation, since activities such as taking notes interfere with attention to the film (Lumsdaine, 1963).

The 8 mm cartridge film is simple to load and project since no threading is required. It is inexpensive and can be shown to an individual or to a small group. It consists of an endless loop and is ideal for showing a single concept or technique.

Films are appropriate for introducing new information or concepts and for reviewing those already taught. Films used innovatively can elicit unique responses, foster creativity, and motivate discovery activities. The following lists a few innovative uses:

1. Show a short film on any topic with the sound turned off, and then ask the class to figure out from visual cues what happened and what the people said

2. Show parts of a film in reverse and ask pupils what happened

3. Show only part of a film and discuss possible endings

4. Show short films with the sound turned off; then, with the sound on but no picture, ask students who said what

A motion picture camera or a still camera in the hands of a student can be a valuable instructional device. Frequently, student-made films are qualitatively better than a traditional term paper, and making a film or slide presentation appears to sharpen observation and increase motivation.

Filmstrips. A filmstrip is a series of 35 mm still pictures, called frames, that are projected sequentially. The filmstrip may be accompanied by a phonograph record or audio tape that provides sound effects and narration. Because each frame is shown separately, the class can take as much time as needed to study or discuss each picture.

Filmstrips elicit attention and active participation from pupils (Gerlach and Ely, 1971). Students can operate the projector, read the captions, and ask questions about the frames. Two methods of using filmstrips effectively to review material are: (1) partially advancing the frame so that the caption is not visible and then requesting the students to say what the accompanying narration should be, and (2) having the class write a point-by-point summary after having viewed the filmstrip.

Slide presentations are easily and inexpensively produced. A teacher or pupil can assemble an effective slide presentation, arranging the sequence of slides to meet specific objectives.

Tapes and Tape Recorders. Audio recordings can be used for teaching listening skills. A wide variety of records is available for nearly all subjects at all levels. The tape recorder can record messages and replay them in addition to playing prerecorded tapes. The cassette recorder has increased the portability, ease of operation, and versatility of using the tape recorder for educational purposes. Tape recorders and language laboratories have been used effectively for speech correction and foreign language instruction. The teacher can prepare spelling dictation and tests on tapes so that he or she is free to help individuals and supervise pupils' activities. The tape recorder is a teaching device that can be used by students and teachers to (1) store data, (2) provide a means of self-evaluation for the teacher, (3) improve speech, (4) review material for individual students without consuming the teacher's time, (5) narrate visual materials, and (6) develop inflection and expression in reading.

Charts, Diagrams, and Maps. Charts are used to illustrate such phenomena as (1) the relationships among individuals in an organization, (2) the ingredients in a product, (3) the steps in a process, or (4) the sequence of events in a historical period. Diagrams are explanatory drawings used to describe the structure of such things as an electric motor, a house, the nervous system, the plot of a novel, or the organization of a process. Maps are a representation of the surface of the earth, or some part of it, showing size and position according to scale.

Models. Models are mock-ups or simulations that imitate a real thing that is too large, too small, or too inaccessible for instructional purposes. For example, the actual human eye or the earth cannot be examined and taken apart for instructional purposes. Models provide the simulation of reality required for teaching students about the solar system, how to brush your teeth properly, the shape and terrain of the earth, traffic safety, and so on.

Kits. Kits are assembled materials for specific instructional purposes. For example, the SRA Reading Laboratories are kits that help individualize group instruction. They contain charts for guiding students, booklets for reading, tests, cards for related activities, progress charts for students to keep track of their own progress, and a teacher's manual.

The Peabody Language Development Kits are a series of language development programs that stress reception, expression, and conceptualization of oral language. Motivation is built into the materials in the following ways: presenting activities that allow for free movement; including attractive pictures and puppets; pacing activities to keep interest high; encouraging children to engage in the same activities simultaneously; and using elements found to be of high interest value to most of the children for whom the kit was devised. The kit materials, stored in a compact metal carrying case, include: (1) a manual that contains 180 daily lessons, information on research and development, and lists of materials, (2) a set of full-color 7" × 9" stimulus cards arranged in thirteen different categories, used to build vocabulary and stimulate associated thinking, (3) a set of large "Story" and "I wonder" cards to stimulate imagination and continuity in story telling, (4) a set of 350 interlocking colored plastic chips used as reinforcers, (5) two soft hand puppets name "Peabo" (Peabody) and "Telsie" (Tell and See) to be used by the instructor and the children to motivate and draw out the total group, especially the withdrawn and distractible, and (6) a tape recording containing six favorite fairy tales as told by a male speech model, and songs and music for introducing and concluding "Language Time."

Effectively using instructional media can heighten motivation, provide variety, accommodate individual differences, encourage active participation, and widen the range of student experience (Dale, 1969).

Teacher Behavior

Anyone offering his services as a teacher should be an expert in subject matter. He or she should also be enthusiastic about education and have a desire to instill the love of learning in children. Teaching is a skilled profession and the successful teacher must enjoy performing the skills of the profession. He must *like* to teach. He should be interested in his pupils, his subject matter, and in teaching. These attributes, along with the skills required to organize student tasks logically, provide clear explanations, ask well-phrased, thought-provoking questions, use the chalkboard and other instructional media effectively, accommodate individual differences, manage classroom routines, establish positive relationships with pupils, and behave ethically are all essential to complete success in teaching.

It is also considered desirable for the teacher to be well groomed and appropriately dressed, be poised and able to handle situations with confidence, speak with a clear, pleasing voice, use correct language, and relate well to parents, other teachers, and supervisors.

Desirable as all these general characteristics may be, their presence will not ensure that such a person's teaching will be unqualifiedly successful. Ideally these desirable characteristics should be encouraged and developed along with the specific competencies of effective teaching.

The teacher must be able to analyze pupils' entering behavior, identify educationally relevant objectives, and select appropriate instructional media, as well as elicit attention to the appropriate stimuli and involve the pupils in the activities of learning.

It is essential that the teacher be able to elicit pupils' attention and progressive changes in pupils' behavior. These will be discussed separately as (1) teacher behaviors as cues to elicit attention, and (2) teacher behaviors as cues to elicit task behaviors.

ATTENTION CUES

The pupils' attention to appropriate stimuli is essential to efficient learning. Through the teaching-learning process, pupils should learn to differentiate between relevant and irrelevant stimuli. In developing the pupil's repertoire of study-related behaviors, some of the first objectives are that the student attend to a teacher, attend to a task, and attend to each as differentiated stimuli.

Children who do not learn to respond to stimuli differentially experience serious learning difficulties. The child who responds equally to the sound of the truck passing in the street, the rustle of papers on the desk beside him, and the noise in the hall will usually have both learning and behavior problems. Such a child tends to exhibit a random, rather than a discriminative, response pattern.

In the teaching-learning process, attention is primarily concerned with the pupil's looking and listening. Of course, attention involves feelings and senses other than sight and hearing, but usually when a teacher wants a pupil's attention, he wants the pupil to look and listen. A child may face the teacher, have his eyes open, and appear to be attentive, although he may be attending to his own inner thoughts or to inappropriate stimuli, such as the teacher's eye glasses. Attention is an internal phenomenon that is essentially unobservable and unmeasurable by the teacher or outside observer. It is an inference based on the observation that the pupil is looking in the direction of the appropriate stimuli, has eye contact with the teacher, or appears to be attentive. When a child appears to be looking at a book, watching the teacher, or observing the television screen, it can be inferred that he is attending (Haring, 1968). This inference is supported by the fact that children who appear to be attending show by their responses that they were attending to instructions given by the teacher.

A teacher points to questions on the board and tells the class to begin work. The pupils write their names, the title of the assignment, and the date on their papers and then begin writing answers to the questions. It is now evident that the pupils have been attending to the teacher's instruction, his pointing finger, and the words on the board.

Although the pupils' later responses to learning tasks are the only completely accurate or objective measures of attending, for practical purposes looking in the direction of appropriate stimuli and the appearance of attending will be called "attention." The purpose of attention is to increase the pupil's rate of appropriate responses.

A teacher is a stimulus—a complex stimulus consisting of many characteristics and capable of a wide range of behavior. A teacher talks, smiles, frowns, presents instructional media, demonstrates equipment, points to assignments on the board, asks questions, tells pupils what to do, wears particular kinds of clothes and hair styles, and responds differently to pupils' performances. The teacher's function is to elicit attention so that the pupils, at appropriate times, listen to what the teacher says, watch what the teacher does, and follow instructions.

The teacher may elicit attention for a variety of purposes. The discussion that follows describes two reasons for eliciting attention. The first reason is to attain creativity- and developmental-level objectives. This is pupil attention for the purpose of facilitating interest, motivation, and modeling behavior. The second is attention required for pupil attainment of essential-level responses.

Interest, Motivation, and Modeling

Achieving essential-level objectives should result in the pupils' experiencing the joy of accomplishing set tasks, but education should be more than achieving essential-level objectives. It should include experiences to which each pupil responds in his own unique way. These experiences contribute to attaining creativity and developmental objectives. When a teacher reads an exciting supplementary story to the class, all that is required of the pupils is that they listen or pay attention. Reading the story is not followed by a test or assignment. If the story is read well, the pupils will probably enjoy hearing it. This may motivate them to read, and it may increase their fondness for the teacher and their enjoyment of school. These outcomes are desirable side effects rather than essential-level objectives. Similarly, a dramatic rendition of a poem, telling a funny anecdote, playing amusing games, riddles, and guessing contests can make the classroom a more enjoyable place and the teacher a more enjoyable person.

Teacher behavior contributes immensely to the attractiveness of the classroom experience. An attractive classroom decorated with pleasing colors, comfortable furniture, adequate lighting and ventilation, interesting art objects, animals, and plants stimulates pupils to enjoy the classroom environment. Similarly, sympathetic teacher behavior creates the classroom's social environment.

Teaching is enjoyable when pupils like you and like what you are doing. When you present amusing stories, surprises, humor, and satisfying experiences, your pupils will tend to model your behavior. If you display enthusiasm for your subject matter and make teaching a happy routine, your pupils' enthusiasm and their enjoyment of learning will increase. Teaching is a performing art. It has often been compared to acting. To be effective, both acting and teaching must be convincing. The teacher and the actor must command attention and keep the performance interesting. However, here the similarity ends. The purpose of teaching is education and the purpose of acting is usually limited to entertainment. The actor may play the role of a villain or a fool—both unsuitable roles for the teacher.

The teacher should begin by playing the role of an enthusiastic instructor who is concerned for the educational welfare of every child. By playing that role he or she will become that teacher. It is probable that if you respond to your pupils with this attitude, you will treat them with professional fairness. It is simple to be interested in the bright, attractive, well-behaved child. As a professional, though, you have an ethical responsibility to teach every child, including the hostile, unwilling, unfortunate, undesirable, or personally unattractive. Your situation could be likened to that of the physician. He must provide his best professional services to the patient even when he feels that the patient has been foolish and neglectful of his health. Through learning to play this role, you will become a truly professional teacher.

If your attitude is that teaching is interesting and exciting, the pupils will be more likely to respond in similar ways. If you use amusing examples and humorous commentary, the pupils will find that learning is fun. If you pair subject matter with positive comments and events, you will elicit from your pupils positive reactions to subject matter. New content should be paired with methods, experiences, and content that elicited positive responses in the past. If the new instructional presentation contains elements that the pupils already respond to positively, the probability is good that they will enjoy the new content or activity.

Interest, motivation, and modeling behavior are side effects of good teaching. Activities that do not require specific responses other than that the pupil listen, watch, or pay attention, make valuable contributions to achieving such nonspecific objectives as fostering individuality and positive attitudes toward learning. The presentation of events, objects, stories, and humor can make classroom participation more interesting to pupils. The enthusiastic teacher stimulates modeling behavior; and by pairing learning with positive experiences, learning becomes a positive experience.

Attention for Essential-Level Responses

Attention cues are essential for any instruction directed by a teacher. The teacher must have the students' attention before presenting an explanation or a demonstration. The prerequisite for any instruction intended to achieve an essential-level objective is the pupils' attention to that instruction. The purpose of the attention cue is to elicit attention to the teacher. Once attention is secured, instruction can begin. Attention should be maintained throughout the instructional procedure.

Let us discuss the characteristics of effective instructional materials to illustrate the principles of teacher behavior for eliciting attention. Instructional materials that elicit attention effectively are stimuli of high impact value and those that limit distraction. Large, clear, and brightly colored materials elicit attention because of their vividness and their strong effects on the senses. Instructional materials of low stimulus value (small, pale, confusing) and cluttered with irrelevant detail are more likely to result in inattention or even distraction.

The first factor for the teacher to consider is how to heighten the stimulus value of the attention cue and the second is how to reduce distracting stimuli. The stimulus value can be heightened by such behaviors as a slightly raised voice (when cueing attention) and by deliberate, controlled, and emphatic gestures. Slight pauses before attention cues to ensure that all pupils are attending before proceeding, and avoiding irrelevant movements and words, are ways of reducing distracting stimuli.

Examples of irrelevant movements are fidgeting with a pointer, chalk, ruler, or other piece of equipment used in a lesson or demonstration. Examples of irrelevant or distracting words are excessive warnings about all the "don'ts" and all of the things that could go wrong. These can become so distracting that pupils pay more attention to the wrong things than to the right things to do.

The following description outlines a general procedure that can be used for cueing attention, which will result in the pupils' eventually learning to respond to minimal cues. It is not intended to be followed ritualistically. After pupils learn to respond to your attention cues, they will attend when you use only one cue or part of the procedure. In the beginning it is best to stand in front of the class when cueing attention.

1. Tell the class what will happen when they attend. So that attention is rewarded, it is good practice to start with interesting material. "Everybody! Pay attention and I will show you an interesting experiment." "Look here! I will show you a funny picture." After attention has been immediately reinforced a number of times, the reward can be gradually delayed. "Class! Watch and I will show you how to construct an equilateral triangle," or "Everybody! Listen and I will explain how to solve this problem."

2. Pause and observe that all eyes are on you. If they are not, repeat "Everybody!"

3. Repeat the key cue word, "Look!" "Listen!" "Watch!" or "Pay attention!"

4. Immediately show the picture, or give the demonstration or explanation.

5. If the instruction requires attention to an object, picture, or chalkboard illustration, use hand signals to cue attention. This should be done with very deliberate gestures. Hold your hand out in plain sight and observe by looking from side to side that you have everyone's attention. Then point directly to where the pupils are to attend. Pause briefly in that position before proceeding.

6. Praise attention. "Everyone is watching—very good." Or later when the class is experienced at attending, "Good!"

7. If a pupil, Joe, is not attending, praise another child who is attending, "Bill is watching—good." If this fails, call the inattentive pupil by name, "Joe, look at me." Always use the name at the beginning of the command. Do not repeat this for Joe if he remains inattentive on future occasions, since being called by name and singled out for special treatment may be reinforcing to him. Instead say, "Joe, look at Bill. He is paying attention. Bill, that is very good." Repeat the class attention cue, "Everybody! . . ." and so on.

With practice the steps in this procedure can be per-formed very quickly. A long or drawn-out set of attention cues is self-defeating. The goal is to be able to cue attention quickly and direct it to the relevant material, demonstration, or explanation. Cues should have suffi-cient stimulus value to elicit attention but should not be distracting. Shouting, slamming a book on the desk, or other startling stimuli are attention-getting but usually attract attention to themselves rather than to the in-struction that follows. Eliciting fear will result in avoidance behavior. This will inhibit the appropriate shifting of attention essential to effective learning.

When the class has learned to attend to instruction, the reinforcement for completed tasks supports the whole chain—attention to teacher, attention to instruction, and task completion. High attention rates can be main-tained by occasional or intermittent reinforcement after attention has been elicited.

TASK CUES

Cues to elicit task behavior range from simple to complex. A teacher may tell the class, "Turn to exercise #15 in your arithmetic workbook, read the directions, and then answer the questions." In another situation, the teacher motivates pupils by showing practical applications of a mathematical procedure, explains and demonstrates the step-by-step procedure for solving the mathematical prob-lem, asks questions during the demonstration, requests pu-pils to tell him how to solve the problem while he follows their instructions, and then assigns the class some prob-lems to solve using the demonstrated procedure. The task cue in the first example was a simple command, and in the second example was a complex instructional routine con-sisting of (1) activities to relate the new content to past learning, (2) examples to motivate the pupils' inter-est, (3) demonstrations of the task behavior, (4) ques-tions, (5) discussions, (6) explanations, and (7) finally the assignment, informing the class what to do and when to do it.

Task cues have two parts—instructional routines and assignments. Instructional routines consist of showing, demonstrating, and telling pupils how to do something. Assignments tell them what to do and when to do it. An assignment may be a verbal command given at the conclusion of an instructional sequence: "Now, sketch this still-life model." Other types of assignments given at the conclu-sion of instructional routines are textbook and workbook exercises, research assignments, projects, assignment sheets, tests, and homework. Assignments are also given during some instructional routines. Demonstrations are frequently divided into segments. The teacher demonstrates a segment of a total procedure and then assigns pupils to do that segment. This is followed by a demonstration of the next segment, and so forth.

Instructional Routines

The teacher's presentation of a lesson, or an instructional sequence to elicit the accomplishment of a learning task, also consists of two parts—attention cues and task cues. The task cue can be simply an assignment, but if the teacher wishes to introduce new content in the form of information or skills, some kind of instructional routine must be used to present the new content. The usual sequence of the lesson is first attention cues, then instructional routine, and finally assignment. The instructional routine must be started only when the attention of all pupils has been obtained. The instructional routine employed depends on the subject matter and the objective of the lesson.

Inquiry and Expository Method. There are two general approaches to instructional routines—inquiry and the expository method. The inquiry method relies on the pupil's own discoveries. Although the teacher may guide the pupil's activity and ask questions to focus his attention on relevant phenomena, the objective is for the pupil to discover his own meanings. This approach has also been called "learning by doing" and is based on the inductive process. In the inductive process, the learner discovers the relationships among things and extracts the common elements. When a pupil studies objects, processes, or events and discovers common elements, unifying principles, generalizations, or rules, he is involved in the inductive process. The inquiry or inductive method requires the learner to discover principles and make discoveries for himself. Induction proceeds from the specific to the general or from known data to generalizations.

The expository method requires that the teacher communicate the generalization, rule, or procedure, and that the pupils apply the generalization, rule, or procedure in solving problems or completing assignments. The expository method is based on the deductive process. Deductive teaching proceeds from rules or generalizations to examples and subsequently to conclusions or to the application of the generalization. In deduction, the pupil arrives at particular facts by applying previously established laws, conclusions, propositions, or generalizations.

In practice, few lessons are purely expository or purely inquiry. For example, in mathematics instruction if the teacher guides the pupils in discovering certain mathematical solutions and principles, the pupils will probably have greater understanding, improved recall, and increased motivation. In teaching handwriting and spelling, the teacher demonstrates the correct formation of letters and words and the pupils imitate what the teacher has demonstrated. Both kinds of instruction are valuable, particularly when they are applied appropriately. Inquiry leading to discovery is an important process that gives the pupil unique learning experiences which contribute to a different kind of involvement in the learning process than that of the expository method. On the other hand, it would be wasting the pupil's time for him to have to rediscover all of the past achievements of mankind through the inductive process. Although it is important for the pupil to learn that he can make his own discoveries, it is important also that he learn to use the discoveries of others.

Demonstrations. The teacher presents a demonstration as an instructional routine to show how things are done. It may be to clarify a generalization by showing how a general principle operates in a particular situation. For example, the teacher may present a demonstration to illustrate a scientific principle. The other purpose of a demonstration is to elicit modeling behavior. The teacher demonstrates how to write, read, hit a ball, or construct a project so that the pupils can model the demonstrated behavior.

Demonstrations are highly expository because their purpose is to elicit active modeling of teacher behavior. Models, mock-ups, and actual equipment are used effectively in successful demonstrations. The teacher combines showing materials along with procedures, explanations, cautions, reasons for actions, while pointing out the important features of each step. Demonstrations are mandatory in safety education, industrial arts, home economics, music, physical education, and science.

Reasoning. The higher mental processes are developed and the higher levels of the cognitive domain are attained primarily through instructional routines based on rational thought and the processes of problem solving. Reasoning power is most active when the pupil is faced with a problem or a new situation. The teacher should be acutely aware of the need for creating new and challenging situations for the class. One important way of challenging pupils is by giving them practice in inductive and deductive reasoning.

The pupil should be taught to consider all the possibilities that his classmates, his teacher, and he can think of, or generate. Briefly, the inductive process can be summarized in the following steps:

1. A problem is presented and defined

2. Various hypotheses or possible explanations are proposed

3. Procedures are devised for testing each hypothesis in turn, and factors not being tested are controlled

4. Data are collected systematically

5. The data are searched for common elements or relationships

6. Conclusions are made based on the evidence obtained

7. The result is applied to similar problems or situations

Throughout the inductive process, the pupil should be encouraged to be critical of his and others' ideas whenever these are based on unsubstantiated evidence.

In deductive reasoning, the pupil must first consider and understand what the problem is. Second, he must select the appropriate principle to apply. Third, he must verify the results to see if his reasoning was correct. In applying instructional routines for deductive reasoning, the teacher should: (1) propose challenging problems, (2) guide pupils in analyzing the meaning of problems, (3) question pupils so that they choose appropriate principles, rules, and courses of action, (4) reinforce application of correct procedures to solve problems, and (5) assist pupils needing help in verifying their answers.

Teaching Creativity and Individual Development. An activity is creative if it originates with the pupil. Most new learning contributes to individual development because the pupil gives his own interpretation and relates it to his own unique experience. In this discussion of instructional routines for creative endeavor, however, the objective is to achieve overt creative responses. When a pupil writes a composition that is original; draws, paints, or otherwise creates a unique design; builds a model or project of his own; invents an original dance step; composes a tune; or arranges a display, he is making an overt creative response. Creativity may be spontaneous, as when a pupil produces an original thought or design, or it may result from training, as when a pupil writes a poem that shows careful regard for what he has learned about form and grouping ideas.

Although genuine creativity is a unique talent that cannot be taught directly, it can be encouraged. During instructional routines, in which the teacher is explaining and demonstrating techniques for constructing a project, several completed models can be shown illustrating a wide variety of possibilities. These models should be removed at the end of the presentation to prevent direct copying. Discussing the possible uses of learned techniques and encouraging experimentation will facilitate the pupil's creative development in achieving essential-level objectives in subjects such as composition, music, and art. It also encourages the occurrence of creative activities during free or contingent reinforcement time.

The teacher can elicit many creative responses by initiating leading experiences. The teacher may relate the beginning of a story and ask the pupils to describe an ending. As each pupil offers his own ending, other pupils are encouraged to try to produce unusual or creative endings. When the teacher generates purposeful activity by presenting leading initial experiences, the pupils become involved and are stimulated by one another.

Not all types of creativity can be produced in a group situation. Some people require long periods of germination, quiet contemplation, research, and experimentation, but an atmosphere can be established in the classroom to support creative expression. The value of generating a purposeful activity by introducing a beginning experience for the class is that the pupils become interested in the experience and then each has a chance to communicate his ideas and feelings. Every child's contribution should be accepted without ridicule.

The presentation of the initial leading experience can encompass a wide range of activities. The teacher may show the class a picture and ask the pupils to tell stories about the people in the picture. The pupils can be asked the following: "Can you describe what the characters in the picture are doing now?" "What were they doing before this scene?" "What will they do next?" "If you were there in the picture, what are the sounds you might hear?" "What would you smell?' "How would you feel?" "What would you be doing?" Some pupils will respond by applying what they have learned directly, involving little or no originality. Although this is not a creative response, it might prove to be a valuable developmental activity for those pupils. Applying learning to a range of problems or in a variety of situations contributes to transfer, generalization, and understanding. Other pupils will produce original responses involving unique observations, synthesis of ideas, or original thought. Both developmental and creative responses are valuable and should be encouraged.

Questions. The act of questioning is nearly as old as language itself and has long been an important teaching technique. Questioning is both a technique for obtaining feedback from pupils during instruction and a method of instruction. It is a component of most instructional procedures. Because of the importance of questioning in eliciting attention as well as in developing higher-order responses, and because of the complexity of developing effective questioning skills, this topic will be dealt with more fully later in this chapter.

Structuring Instructional Routines

A teacher's presentation of a lesson consists of a sequence of task cues which elicit responses that facilitate the pupils' accomplishment of an assignment. The sequence of task cues may include presenting instructional media, explanations, demonstrations, and questions. The sequence is organized so that the task cues form a structure leading to the behaviors required for accomplishing the assignment. The teacher's presentation of this sequence is the instructional routine.

The most effective instructional routines are those that elicit a high level of pupil involvement and interaction. Questioning is the most versatile method of eliciting involvement during an instructional routine. At the conclusion of the first step of a demonstration, the teacher asks, "What do you think the next step will be?" After the next step, the teacher asks, "Why did I do that?" Later the teacher asks, "How will this turn out?" The teacher should also elicit questions from the pupils by asking, "Have you any questions?" "What kind of questions would you like to ask?" By asking questions, the teacher can involve the pupils in thinking about the content of the lesson and, at the same time, obtain feedback from the students indicating the effectiveness of instruction.

An effective instructional routine consists of dynamic interactions between teacher and pupils, in which the pupils are prepared for task activity. Because the process is dynamic, only the basic structure of the instructional routine can be effectively preplanned. The lesson plan should list the lesson's terminal and enroute objectives and the instructional materials required. The lesson should also contain key questions. The teacher should be prepared and confident that he is able to present clear explanations and skillful demonstrations. Preplanning gives the teacher a guide so that the lesson progresses logically and none of the key points is missed. At the same time, this type of lesson planning does not limit the flexibility required for dynamic interaction with the class. Lesson planning will be described more fully in Chapter Nine, "Classroom Management."

Assignments

A lesson assignment is a learning task to be performed by the pupil in response to instruction. At the conclusion of the instructional routine, or in some cases, throughout the routine, the class is assigned a learning task. To be valid and relevant the assignment must require the pupil to demonstrate the behaviors described by the lesson objectives. Written assignments can be constructed so that tasks representing essential-level objectives are readily differentiated from those representing higher-level developmental or creativity objectives. For example, if the assignment is a written test, the first set of questions could require essential-level responses, the next set could be more difficult, requiring a higher-level developmental response, and the last question could be open-ended to accommodate creative responses. All pupils are expected to achieve the essential-level tasks. Those who do not should receive individual remedial instruction. The developmental and creativity-level tasks will be achieved with varying degrees of success, thus recognizing individual differences.

Assignments constructed on this model, with essential-level tasks at the beginning, can be used effectively in contingency management. If the teacher notes that a pupil consistently has difficulty completing assigned tasks and is therefore unable to earn sufficient reinforcement time, the teacher can cross out part of the pupil's assignment and inform him that he is eligible for a reinforcement activity upon completion of the top part of the assignment.

Assignments should be specific enough to achieve something measurable. An assignment such as, "Read the next two chapters," is usually of less value than, "Read the next chapter and list three main points." Textbooks, workbooks, assignment sheets, and other printed or mimeographed assignments are useful because of their specificity. They are also helpful for the pupil who has been absent and wishes to catch up.

In making assignments, it is good practice to repeat the objectives. In the case of assignment sheets, the objective can be stated on the sheet as the introduction to the assignment. For example, a teacher of a business class wrote on the top of an exercise sheet, "The object of this assignment is that you develop the ability to alphabetize a random group of surnames quickly." When the assignment consists of individual projects, investigations, or experiments, the pupils should be encouraged to write their own objectives. For instance, one pupil wrote, "My purpose in building and testing an experimental domestic solar water heater is to determine its capability, under local climatic conditions, to provide a continuous supply of hot water."

When the assigned task has been communicated to the pupils, each must know *why*, *how*, and *when* he is to do it. Assignments may sometimes be started immediately upon conclusion of the instructional routine and will be completed in times varying from a few minutes to a full period. Some assignments may extend over several periods and require library or other research facilities.

The decision to assign homework is influenced by the policies of the school and community. Home conditions vary to such a degree that assigning extensive homework could possibly create serious conditions of inequality among the students. Because of variations in parents' educational backgrounds and differences in social atmosphere, physical facilities, and privacy, the home can be either an ideal or a hostile environment for study. For these reasons, homework should not be used for introducing new material. Homework can be used effectively for additional practice in developing skills, when it has been established that the pupils have already acquired the skill at a functional level. Reviewing notes is also an appropriate homework activity. A number of supplementary activities can be assigned: making maps and scrapbooks, writing letters to pen pals, or collecting materials that are readily available in the community.

Eliciting Events

There is a wide variety of eliciting events other than instructional media and teacher behavior, which contribute to the educational process. These events include field trips, visitors coming to the classroom, pupils' direct experiences, simulation, class discussions, group projects, and independent study. Although the teacher may initiate these events, the teacher is not necessarily the primary source of elicitation during the activity.

Field Trips. Field trips offer a dimension of reality that the classroom cannot supply. Pupils frequently passively observe rather than actively live the event they are learning about. The value of the field trip as an eliciting event is related to the kinds of questions and discussions that it produces and how it correlates with and enriches the classroom experience. The educational outcomes of the field trip depend in large measure on the preparation and follow-up provided by the teacher. Preparation should include the information required to make the trip meaningful. Two important aspects of preparation are explaining to the class the objectives of the trip and asking the pupils questions to help focus attention on the important aspects of the trip. These same questions can be used in follow-up discussions in the classroom. The field trip establishes a common base of experience for discussion and for individual or group projects.

Visitors. Inviting experts or authorities to visit
the classroom—for example, a traffic officer who discusses and demonstrates traffic safety—provides a real
experience that frequently has greater eliciting power
than would the same message presented by the classroom
teacher. Persons from the community, such as nurses, doc-
tors, truck drivers, newspaper reporters, telephone line-
men, and so on can present valuable information and be
motivating influences at all levels of education. Representatives of various professions not only tell about the
world of work but also help to show pupils the value of
education for professional success.

Direct Experiences. Direct experiences with real
things, in which the pupil learns from his active participation, comprise eliciting events in which the pupil
learns for and about himself. The teacher may initiate
the event and provide the material, but the pupil is allowed to manipulate or experiment at will.

Independent Study. Independent study is rapidly increasing in importance. Students must learn how to learn
in order to adapt to an age of rapid and radical changes.
Once a student has been guided in locating information and
assembling it for a particular purpose, he can then be expected to undertake reference tasks with little assistance
from the teacher. Projects and assignments requiring library research and other independent study techniques are
particularly valuable to the superior and college-bound
student, who will be expected to continue to use this approach in college and during his work life as well. Independent study at the secondary level can accommodate individual differences. The bright or gifted student who is
impatient with restrictive routine tasks will frequently
accept a challenging independent reference or research
project. The less able student can be helped to identify
an objective that requires locating limited specific information.

Simulation. Simulation has been an effective means
of teaching complex skills. Pilot training using the Link
Trainer and administrator training using "in-basket, out-
basket" role playing are examples of simulation used in
professional training. By using simulation in the classroom, it is possible to create social or physical environments that are less threatening than the real world and
that provide opportunities for exploring and practicing
appropriate responses. Improving pupils' interpersonal
relationships can be achieved through role playing and
exchanging roles to develop empathy and understanding of
others. Some of the problems in applying for a job, giving testimony as a witness, or dealing with an angry member of your committee can be explored and resolved in a

simplified simulation that eliminates unimportant elements and stresses the significant ones. Both the participants and the observers may learn constructive solutions to problems. The classroom can become a "grocery store" where pupils practice making change, a "courtroom" for replicating a trial, or the "council chamber" of a city hall, in which the pupils play the roles of elected officials.

Recently a number of simulation games have been developed for teaching-learning purposes. Most of these simulation games resemble table games with sets of rules, boards, markers, and cards, but the purpose is quite different. The simulation game involves the pupil in active decision making, using rules that apply to real-life situations. A consumer game, for instance, involves the players with the economic problems of installment buying. Consumers compete to achieve maximum points for making specific purchases while minimizing their credit charges. Credit agents would compete to make the most advantageous lending transactions. A democracy game simulates the legislative process, and an ecology game develops strategies for defending pure water and clean air against polluters.

Class Discussion. Class discussions develop an interchange of ideas among pupils. The preferred seating arrangement for a class discussion is a circle in which each participant can see who is speaking and who wishes to speak (although other seating arrangements are possible). Ideally, class discussions should involve all pupils in conversations that approach problems analytically and from different points of view. Group discussion may arrive at a solution, a meeting of minds, or a compromise embodying the ideas expressed by the participants. Productive discussion improves communication skills, helps arrive at solutions democratically, and fosters logical approaches to problem solving. For most pupils, class discussion is a stimulating experience that helps develop skill in decision making as well as helping to ensure closer correspondence between pupils' interests and class activities. Class discussions can take several forms, including town meetings, panel discussions, debates, interviews, forum-lectures, parliamentary procedures, buzz sessions, and brainstorming sessions.

The content or subject matter of the discussion may emerge from the pupils' interests and experiences or may be introduced by the teacher. Topics of interest to the group might include immediate concerns, such as planning a class party, homework, appointing a classroom committee, student government, group projects, social conduct in the classroom or the school, family, self, community, leisure, jobs, feelings, and personal problems. Pupils are frequently interested in larger issues, such as censorship, ecology, juvenile delinquency, the drug problem, crime, overpopulation, and other social issues. If the pupils introduce the topic for discussion, the teacher should usually offer advice or information only when called upon to do so. The teacher should assume the role of moderator, consultant, and mature participant.

The teacher can provide guidance to assist the class in learning about the processes of discussion. Informal discussion can be used for a variety of purposes, some of which may go no further than giving everyone an opportunity to speak and voice an opinion. If the purpose of the discussion is to solve a problem or come to a conclusion, the teacher may offer guidance, when needed, in applying the rational process.

Discussion can be based on the inductive or deductive process. The inductive method, in which pupils make their own generalizations from specific instances, and the deductive method, in which pupils start with a generalization and seek supporting evidence, are two different approaches to a discussion. Acquiring understanding of the processes involved helps the pupils develop the means to advance their own inquiry and discovery. The pupils' acquisition of the rational process is more important than the content of the discussion because the process will contribute to continuous learning. Reasoning is applicable to studying any subject, through communicating, discovering relationships, applying facts or principles, solving problems, analyzing, gathering and organizing data, estimating, drawing conclusions, and verifying.

In employing critical thinking as a problem-solving method, the teacher initially leads the group in formulating problems and employing subject matter. The teacher guides the discussion through the steps of identification, delimitation, definition of the problem, formulation of hypotheses, gathering data, analyses of data, and drawing conclusions. This method applies knowledge of various subjects to real problems or lifelike situations. It helps maintain a balance between cognitive, affective, and psychomotor objectives, since solutions to real problems frequently involve knowledge from many different areas as well as mental skills, feelings, and actions.

Discussion centered around problem solving is a means of eliciting involvement in critical, inferential, differential, analytical, and deductive thinking. It is a means of correlating subject matter because subject boundaries are transcended in the process of finding solutions.

Class discussion elicits individual and group responses that would not occur in other circumstances. Free and open discussion frequently leads to constructive action on the part of the pupils. Class projects, such as making a videotape of the class to show on parents' day, forming a social committee to handle certain classroom activities, organizing the class to prevent litter in the classroom, solving classroom behavior problems, and other worthwhile activities have resulted from class discussion. As for discussions leading to action, it is the teacher's responsibility to clarify any relevant limitations imposed by school rules and society's laws.

Each of these eliciting events involves some degree of teacher participation, but most of the responses in the activity are elicited: (1) by the people and things encountered on the field trip, (2) through seeing and listening to the classroom visitors, (3) by interacting in the simulation activity, and (4) by interacting with other pupils during class discussion.

Developing Questioning Skills

The question-answer exchange is a traditional teaching technique that has endured the test of time. Socrates directed questions to his pupils to make them think, organize and reorganize their experiences, answer questions, and derive conclusions. He countered questions with questions, each more penetrating than the last, each eliciting a new question.

It is man's nature to question and be curious. Most children are inquisitive and like to ask questions— indeed, they should be encouraged to do so. The teacher can encourage questions both by answering a child's questions and by asking questions that help focus the child's questions. A child should be asked questions of increasing difficulty, each based on the answers that preceded it, so that the final answer to the child's original question becomes obvious to him. Another helpful method of answering a child's questions is to turn the problem over to the class for discussion and analysis (Grossier, 1964). Although children's questions are an important part of the teaching-learning process, the balance of this discussion will deal with the teacher's questions as elicitors.

COGNITIVE LEVELS

The teacher's questions can be used to elicit responses for all levels of the *Taxonomy of Educational Objectives, Handbook I: Cognitive Domain* (Bloom, 1956). The teacher can ask questions to elicit (1) knowledge, (2) comprehension, (3) applications, (4) analysis, (5) synthesis, and (6) evaluation (Borg, Kelly, and Langer, 1970).

Knowledge

Questions that elicit recall of facts, symbols, observations, definitions, dates, and so on are at the knowledge level. Some examples are questions that ask "Who?" "What?" "Where?" "When?" and requests for definitions, such as "*What* is the meaning of the word 'plateau'?"

Comprehension

Questions that elicit descriptions, main ideas, and comparisons are at the comprehension level. Examples are questions such as, "*What* happened in the experiment?" "*What* is the central idea of this paragraph?" "*How* are these two countries alike?" "*How* are they different?"

Application

Questions that elicit application of techniques, principles, formulas, and rules for solving problems are at the application level. Examples are questions such as, "If Joe has 36 cents, *how* many 6-cent pencils can he buy?" "*What* use can we make in the school cafeteria of what we have just learned about controlling bacteria?" "From the information on this chart, *how* does the amount of rainfall affect the kinds of agricultural products a region can produce?"

Analysis

Questions that elicit identifying causes or motives, inferences, and locating evidence to support generalizations are at the analysis level. Examples are questions such as, "*How* does Carl Sandburg, in the poem 'Chicago,' express his feelings of joy?" "If we have a very cold winter without much snow, *what* effect will this have on agricultural crops?" "*What* evidence can you find to support the principle that air expands when heated?"

Synthesis

Questions that elicit problem solving, making predictions, and original communications are at the synthesis level. Examples are questions such as, "*How* can we construct a table to show the same quantities in common fractions, decimal fractions, and percentages?" "*How* can we solve this dilemma?" "*What* will happen now that man has landed on the moon?" "*What* would be a good title for this picture?" "*How* can we improve our procedure?" "On what basis (*how*) should a man with heart disease choose an apartment?" "*What* do you predict would happen if this lake were to dry up?"

Evaluation

Questions that elicit opinions about issues or judgments about the validity of ideas, the merit of solutions to a problem, and the quality of performances and products are at the evaluation level. Examples are questions such as, "From our study of the English people, *what* have they produced that has benefited mankind?" "Do you agree with George?" "Do you think that this is the best way to proceed?" "*What* is your judgment?" "*Which* song do you prefer?" "Would it be better to try another procedure?" "Under *what* conditions would the statement 'seeing is believing' be in error?"

PRESENTATION

A teacher may ask questions first to ascertain that pupils have the information and understanding required for new learning or for more interpretive questions later on, and second to elicit higher-order processes, such as judgment, application, interpretation, analysis, comparisons, evaluations, relationships, and creative endeavor. When you have identified the purpose or cognitive level, you are ready to begin questioning your pupils. It is good practice to preplan a few key questions, which will be the objectives for your questioning. Key questions will keep the process directed toward a goal. Questioning is a dynamic enterprise in which the pupils' responses become the elicitors for further questions and responses from the teacher and the class. Some of the factors in successful questioning are: (1) attention, (2) voice, (3) pause, (4) approval, (5) participation, and (6) distribution.

Attention

Questions are effective attention cues. As a lead-in to key questions, you might present a series of stimulating, entertaining, humorous, or current-interest questions. For example, a teacher had written two preplanned questions: "*How* was the concept of balance built into the American Constitution?" and "*How* does balance contribute to strength?" The attention questions leading to these key questions were, in part, as follows:

Teacher	"What are the chances of our football team's winning the next game?" (pause) "John?"
John	"They look pretty good."
Teacher	"In what way do they look good?"
John	"Well, we're pretty good in most positions and we have a well-balanced team."
Teacher	"You feel that balance contributes to strength?"
John	"Yes."
Teacher	"Do you feel that balance contributes to strength in government, also?"

In eliciting attention, it is usually more effective to ask a question of the whole class or group before calling on an individual to respond. This alerts all pupils to the possibility that they might be called upon.

Questions that relate to pupil interests are effective attention cues. "*What* sports do you like to play?" "*What* sports do you like to watch but do not play?" Use questions that motivate the class. "Would you like to make a collection of seeds and display them for the entire school?" Provocative questions that challenge beliefs and superstitions are also effective. "*What* influence could a black cat's crossing your path have on tomorrow's game?" Attention questions should be clear, brief, thought provoking, and limited in scope.

Questions leading to key questions frequently ask for facts. This focuses attention on the data that must be used when answering the more interpretive questions asked later on. The teacher must know what facts and understanding the pupils possess before presenting questions requiring them to apply rational thought and to form conclusions.

Voice. As a teacher, your voice is one of your major means of communication. The tone, volume, and clarity of your voice should be pleasant to listen to and not require pupils to strain to hear you. To evaluate your voice and avoid developing problems in voice production, tape-record your voice under comfortable conditions when you are relaxed. Save this recording for comparison with a recording made during questioning and other teaching activities. Listen to the tapes of your questioning procedures and evaluate your voice. Learn to avoid excessive loudness, shrillness, harshness, too rapid speech, or unclear enunciation. Questions should be asked in a pleasant or friendly manner and express anticipation of an answer.

Pause. The pause is the time between your presenting the question and calling for an answer. You should ask a question, pause briefly, and then call on a pupil to respond. "*What* are some current causes of inflation?" (pause) "Kathy?" A short pause is used for knowledge-level and recall questions. "*What* is nine times eight?" (short pause) "Irene?" Higher-level questions require that pupils have time to formulate adequate responses.

Encourage longer and more thoughtful pupil responses by pausing for three to five seconds after asking a question, then call upon a pupil. "What might be the immediate effect of the new military budget on public welfare service?" (three- to five-second pause) "Susan?" Your students will not automatically give longer and more thoughtful responses when you first begin using longer pauses; therefore, you must clarify what you want your students to do. "Please think over your answers carefully." "When I call on you, I want a complete answer." Then pause for three to five seconds before calling on a student. If you pause and then accept a low-level answer, pausing will not mean anything special to the student since any kind of answer will appear to be acceptable. Pausing becomes meaningful to the student only if your reaction to the response indicates that pausing is your signal for a more complete and thoughtful answer (Borg, Kelly, and Langer, 1970).

Approval. The elicitor-behavior-reinforcer process applies to questioning as it does to other instructional procedures. All acceptable responses should be reinforced with a smile, nod, gesture, or word of praise. Incorrect responses should be shaped through questions leading to acceptable answers, and then reinforced.

Participation. All pupils in the class should be encouraged to participate. This can be achieved by presenting questions ranging in level of difficulty to accommodate pupils' individual differences. *What* (or *who*) and *where* questions can be directed to the less able pupils and *how* and *why* questions can be directed to the more capable pupils.

Teacher	"*Where* did Dick and Jane go?" (pause) "Bill?"
Bill	"To the farm."
Teacher	"*Who* went with them?" (pause) "Mary?"
Mary	"Mother and father."
Teacher	"*How* did they get there?" (pause) "Ted?"
Ted	"They drove in the family car along a country road."
Teacher	"*Why* do some people live on farms?" (pause) "Kate?"

With this manner of questioning, the primary teacher was able to involve pupils ranging in ability from Mary's to Ted's. Although Mary should not be denied the opportunity to contribute or answer the questions asked of Ted, the questioning sequence above permits all pupils to participate.

Distribution. Questions should be presented first to the entire class or group and subsequently to individuals. Calling on pupils should be distributed to achieve the widest possible participation. Questions should be directed both to volunteers and to nonvolunteers, so that all pupils are encouraged to respond.

QUESTIONING TECHNIQUES

The following procedure for developing your questioning technique is based on the model of cybernetic feedback, described in Chapter One. The form used for questions in your Classroom Instruction Record provides the structure for carrying out this procedure.

Written Questions

Prepare four written questions. After you have gained experience, you may use any appropriate number. Using four questions is suggested here to learn the techniques of effective questioning because experience has shown that this method leads to successfully developing skill in questioning. Usually the first question will require an answer at the knowledge or comprehension level. The other questions can elicit higher-order responses and require pupils to analyze statements and ideas critically. "In *what* situations would the statement 'One picture is worth ten thousand words' be in error?" Pupils can be led to creative responses with: "*What* techniques could we use to make similar pictures?" Such higher-order questions should be challenging and require the pupils to compare, evaluate, draw inferences, and appraise results.

Factual questions require either recall or finding answers in texts or reference books. Higher-order questions require problem solving and reasoning from the pupils. Given a higher-order question, the pupil may have to compare, analyze, interpret, organize, and evaluate to produce a correct answer. Opinion questions require pupils to supply as many facts as they can to support their opinions. These questions may sometimes be controversial and not have definite answers. "*Why* would you like to live in China?" should provoke a controversial discussion and elicit facts to support the proposition. The purpose of this kind of question is not to settle an issue or impose the teacher's opinion on the class, but to have pupils think about issues.

During preparation, the teacher should answer the questions, thinking of all possible answers, and then reword questions that are ambiguous or grammatically incorrect. The questions should then be written on the form in the Classroom Instruction Record.

The Process

Initially, the student teacher in classroom instruction should work with small groups of from two to six pupils. This is easily arranged if the pupils are working at tables. If they are seated in rows of desks, it may be desirable to have a small group meet with you in a reading corner or activity area. Turn on your tape recorder before you begin your questioning. This will give you feedback for assessing your performance after you have conducted the questioning session.

After eliciting attention, ask your first question, keeping in mind the suggestions made earlier regarding presentation. Depending on your pupils' response, you may use one of the following processes:

Correct. If you receive a correct response immediately from a pupil, provide reinforcement and move on to the next question.

Redirect. In redirection, you direct the same question to several other pupils after the first has responded with an appropriate answer. The question is not repeated or rephrased, even though more than one pupil responds with the correct answer. The pattern during redirection is question-answer-answer-answer. Reinforce those who provided acceptable answers after all have made their responses.

Rephrase. If the response is unsatisfactory, you may reword the same question to clarify its meaning.

Prompt. Prompting employs a series of cues or hints used to help a pupil who has given a weak, incomplete, or incorrect answer. You should try to help the pupil develop an appropriate answer by asking easier questions to lead him to the answer. Prompting questions directs the student's thought from one aspect to another of the same topic, forming a connected series.

Pupil Clarification. This type of clarification is used when you want the pupil to amplify a partially acceptable answer. In some instances, the pupil may give a response that is either poorly organized, lacking detail, or incomplete. In pupil clarification, the teacher does not add information—he requests the pupil to do so.

Replay for Feedback

After you have presented the sequence of four questions, replay the tape and tally the number of times you employed the above processes for the first question. Then assess the question according to the pupils' responses and make recommendations regarding future use of the question. On completing the assessment of the first question, repeat the process for questions two, three, and four.

Assessment

Assess each question according to the following classifications: (1) adequate, (2) easier, (3) harder, (4) specific, (5) open-ended, or (6) clearer.

Adequate. If the question elicited the responses that you intended and did not require excessive rephrasing, prompting, or pupil clarification, it should be considered adequate. In this case, you would use the question in its present form in future presentations.

Easier. If it required excessive prompting to obtain the answer, the question was probably too difficult. In this case, the assessment would be that the question should have been made easier.

Harder. If the responses indicated that the question was not adequately challenging, then your assessment will indicate that the question should have been made harder.

Specific. If it required excessive pupil clarification, or the question elicited too many different or conflicting answers, then the question should have been more specific.

Open-Ended. If the purpose of the question was to elicit an explanation but was answered with one word, a phrase, or a "yes" or "no," it should have been more open-ended. For example, a teacher wanted to elicit a discussion of the social contribution made by the abolition of slavery but asked a rhetorical question: "Lincoln was right in freeing the slaves, wasn't he?" A more open-ended question would have been, "What are some of the changes in society that followed the abolition of slavery?"

Clearer. If rephrasing the question was required, the question should have been made clearer.

Recommendations

If your assessment of the question indicates that it needs improvement, rephrase the question as you would present it the next time. If you identify inadequacies in the process you used to elicit responses, make recommendations regarding your next presentation of the question.

Evaluation of Presentation

After you have listened to your tape and completed your assessment of each question, evaluate your presentation according to the descriptions provided earlier: (1) attention, (2) voice, (3) pause, (4) approval, (5) participation, and (6) distribution.

SUCCESSIVE QUESTIONING SEQUENCES

After you have presented your first sequence of questions to the first group of pupils, and after you have completed your assessment of each question and evaluated your presentation, you should present the improved sequence to other groups. Each assessment, evaluation, and recommendation will improve your questions and presentation. The forms in the Classroom Instruction Record provide for six presentations. These may be used for six presentations of the same four-question sequence, or they may be used for two or three different four-question sequences, with only one or two repetitions of each sequence.

Assignment

Complete the exercises in Chapter Six of the Classroom Instruction Workbook.

References

Becker, W. C., S. Engelmann, and D. R. Thomas. *Teaching a Course in Applied Psychology*. Chicago: Science Research Associates, 1971.

Bloom, B. S. (ed.). *Taxonomy of Educational Objectives, Handbook I: Cognitive Domain*. New York: David McKay, 1956.

Borg, W. R., M. L. Kelly, and P. Langer. *Effective Questioning: Elementary Level*. Beverly Hills, Calif.: Macmillan Educational Services, 1970.

Dale, E. *Audiovisual Methods in Teaching*. New York: Holt, Rinehart and Winston, 1969.

Espich, J. E., and B. Williams. *Developing Programmed Instructional Materials: A Handbook for Program Writers*. Palo Alto, Calif.: Fearon, 1967.

Gerlach, V. S., and D. P. Ely. *Teaching and Media: A Systematic Approach*. Englewood Cliffs, N.J.: Prentice-Hall, 1971.

Grossier, P. *How to Use the Fine Art of Questioning*. New York: Teachers Practical Press, 1964.

Haring, N. G. *Attending and Responding*. Belmont, Calif.: Fearon, 1968.

Lumsdaine, A. A. "Instruments and Media of Instruction," in N. L. Gage (ed.), *Handbook of Research on Teaching*. Chicago: Rand McNally, 1963.

Pressey, S. L. "Teaching Machine and Learning Theory Crisis," *Journal of Applied Psychology*, 1963, 47:1-6.

Smith, K. U., and M. F. Smith. *Cybernetic Principles of Learning and Educational Design*. New York: Holt, Rinehart and Winston, 1966.

Seven

Reinforcers

Objectives: After completing your study of this chapter, you will be able to (1) define and illustrate positive reinforcement, negative reinforcement, and extinction, (2) apply the principles of reinforcement to classroom instruction, (3) identify the role of teacher behavior in reinforcing pupil responses, (4) describe "Grandma's Law," the "Premack principle," and contingency management in the classroom, (5) define token reinforcement and describe the implementation of token economies in the classroom, (6) identify levels of reinforcement and methods of facilitating development of higher-level reinforcers such as knowledge of results and self-evaluation, and (7) complete the exercises in Chapter Seven of the Classroom Instruction Workbook.

Chapter Five discussed enroute objectives and Chapter Six described elicitors to bring forth the behaviors required to achieve these objectives. This chapter will present the means of strengthening desirable behaviors as they occur and eliminating undesirable behaviors.

Most behavior is affected by its consequences. If the consequences that follow a behavior result in the behavior's recurring, the consequences are said to be *reinforcing*. A reinforcer is defined solely by its effect on behavior. Reinforcing consequences result in the behavior's being maintained or increased. Aversive or punishing consequences result in the behavior's being decreased. Neutral consequences result in the behavior's tending to decrease through a process called *extinction*.

There are two basic types of reinforcement, positive and negative. *Positive* reinforcement occurs when rewarding consequences follow a behavior. *Negative* reinforcement occurs when the consequence of a behavior is the removal of an unpleasant stimulus. The effect of either positive or negative reinforcement is to increase or maintain a behavior. Negative reinforcement is responsible for much incidental learning in everyday situations. Individuals learn to escape aversive, or unpleasant, stimuli by such behaviors as (1) closing the window to shut out the draft, (2) picking up a baby to stop his or her crying, (3) moving out of the heat of the noonday sun, (4) taking off shoes that are pinching the feet, and (5) making excuses to get out of uncomfortable situations. In the classroom, negative reinforcement takes place when a pupil who is experiencing discomfort, embarrassment, or failure leaves the classroom for a drink of water. If this behavior terminates or reduces the unpleasant stimuli, the pupil will continue to leave the room. Staying home or dropping out may be even more effective behavior for terminating the aversive stimuli (Sulzer and Mayer, 1972).

The Competencies for Teaching system employs mainly positive reinforcements in the instructional process. However, all teachers should be aware of the operation of negative reinforcement, even if it will not be used consciously as an instructional technique. Positive reinforcement appears to be more easily managed in classroom instruction. The teacher specifies observable behavior, identifies highly reinforcing events, and arranges the environment so that rewarding consequences immediately and consistently follow appropriate behavior. The teacher provides rewarding consequences for desirable behavior and ignores, or extinguishes, inappropriate behavior.

Reinforcing consequences employed in an instructional procedure should have the following characteristics: (1) be clearly linked to the behaviors described in the enroute objectives, (2) immediately follow the appropriate behavior, (3) be administered consistently during the students' acquisition of new responses, (4) be frequent and appear early in a learning sequence, (5) be applied at each step in a learning sequence, and (6) be applied on a variable schedule after the behavior has been acquired.

The following discussion illustrates practical applications of reinforcement principles in classroom instruction. Although the teacher may employ a combination of methods, for purposes of explanation they will be described separately as teacher behavior, contingency management, and token economies.

Teacher Behavior

The most readily available and important reinforcer for a teacher to use is social reinforcement. Teacher attention and approval are powerful influences on pupils' behavior. The teacher's social reinforcers include praise, facial expressions, physical contact, and other gestures and words of approval.

PRAISE

Verbal expressions of approval are effective reinforcers for nearly all pupils. In praising the class, address the class by saying, "Everyone (brief pause) was really paying attention," or "Class (brief pause), you worked very well." In praising an individual pupil, use his or her name at the beginning of the statement: "Jane (brief pause), that's exactly right." If the behavior was not an assigned task, it is desirable to describe the behavior: "John (brief pause), you're doing a good job of cleaning the tables" (Sheppard, Shank, and Wilson, 1972).

Any word, phrase, or description that communicates approval will be effective. If a pupil offers an appropriate answer, appropriate praise may be simply, "Good!" On the other hand, one pupil, who had been habitually slow to start work, performed better on a particular day. The teacher went to him and said, "Steve, you got to work quickly. That's very good." Some praising statements that are potential reinforcers are:

"Yes."	"I like that."
"Right."	"Good for you."
"Great."	"That's better."
"Good."	"You really pay attention."
"Excellent."	"Show the class."
"Clever."	"That is interesting."
"Exactly."	"Let us all give Jimmy a round of applause."
"Very good."	"That was very kind of you."
"Thank you."	"Good idea."

Generally, the most effective praise is a rewarding statement that describes the pupil's performance. Use short statements signifying approval or correctness: "Good"; "That's right"; "You have five correct answers"; "That was thoughtful of you." It is less effective to praise or flatter the child: "My, but you are clever"; "You are a smart little girl." The reasons for praising performance rather than the child are complex. In many cases, praising the child is effective, but the insecure child may feel that he or she is acceptable only when correct. Parents and relatives may use similar terms of endearment in a noncontingent way—that is, independent of the child's present behavior—so that this type of praise is less effective as reinforcement. The child who has been criticized excessively may be reluctant to accept that he is smart just because the teacher tells him so. His confidence would be enhanced realistically by objective evidence that he was right and that his performance was praiseworthy. Telling your pupils that you think they are competent, intelligent, good, and kind can improve the general attitude of the class. Although this is good practice, it is advisable to reserve such praise for the purpose of *eliciting* feelings of confidence rather than for reinforcing behavior.

EXPRESSIONS

Facial expressions and physical gestures are signals that can enhance the reinforcing value of praise or be effective by themselves. These expressions include nods, winks, smiles, laughs, attending and looking interested, hand claps, and pointing.

PHYSICAL CONTACT

Nearness to the teacher can be reinforcing, particularly after the pupils have experienced the teacher as a source of other social reinforcements. A touch on the cheek, hugs, pats, handshakes, and other appropriate physical contacts can be reinforcing. Walking with pupils and joining them in group activity can be rewards for appropriate behavior.

SOCIAL REINFORCERS

Most social reinforcers are conditioned, or learned. Early in the infant's life he is responsive to being held or having physical contact with his parents, but the other social reinforcements are acquired through experience. Research on the effectiveness of social reinforcement in classroom instruction consistently indicates its potential for facilitating learning.

Hall, Lund, and Jackson (1968) studied the effects of the teacher's attention as social reinforcement on the study behavior of first- and third-grade pupils. The study behavior that was reinforced was attention directed toward the appropriate object, person, or task. Teacher attention consisted of moving to the pupil's desk, making a comment, or giving a pat on the shoulder. When a pupil was engaged in desirable study behavior, the teacher would attend to that pupil but would ignore the pupil's other behaviors. The technique effectively gave the teacher more classroom control and increased the students' academic achievement because of the increased time spent in study. This research indicated the contingent use of teacher attention to be a quick and effective means of establishing desirable classroom behavior.

Thomas, Becker, and Armstrong (1968) studied the effects of teacher behavior on pupils' classroom behavior. They found that teachers can effectively influence students' behaviors by using their own behaviors as social reinforcement. Two types of teacher behavior were studied: disapproving behavior and approving behavior. When the teachers increased their disapproving behaviors, such as scolding, grabbing, pushing, yelling, and belittling, the pupils increased their movement, interaction with other pupils, the noise level. The teachers' critical comments appeared to increase some of the pupils' misbehaviors on which the criticisms were contingent. The more often a teacher told first-grade pupils to "sit down," the more often they stood up. Praising sitting increased sitting behavior. When teachers increased their approving behaviors, such as praise, physical contact, and smiles, the pupils increased the frequency of their appropriate task behaviors. The result was that academic achievement increased beyond grade level.

Hart, Reynolds, Baer, Brawley, and Harris (1968) compared frequent noncontingent reinforcement with contingent reinforcement in developing the cooperative play of a preschool child. The results of the study showed that noncontingent reinforcement had little effect in developing cooperative play. Only when the teacher paid attention to the child engaged in cooperative play (that is, the reinforcement was *contingent*, or dependent, on the occurrence of the appropriate behavior) were the desired behaviors effectively increased and maintained.

Madsen, Becker, and Thomas (1968) studied three means of controlling student behavior in elementary classrooms: (1) rules, (2) praise of appropriate behaviors, and (3) ignoring inappropriate behaviors. The results were as follows. First, rules alone had little effect on inappropriate behavior. Second, ignoring inappropriate behavior produced inconsistent results. Third, a combination of ignoring inappropriate behavior and praising appropriate behavior was highly effective in reducing the incidence of inappropriate behavior. And fourth, praise is a means of developing effective classroom management.

The evidence from these studies supports the proposition that teacher behavior is an important and powerful reinforcer of pupil behavior. Praise and other expressions of approval contingent on appropriate academic or social behavior, and ignoring, or extinguishing, inappropriate behavior appear to be the most effective combination of teacher behaviors to facilitate effective classroom learning.

To be maximally effective, praise should be appropriate to the pupil's developmental level. With young children, praise may be effectively expressed by nods, smiles, pats, winks, and words, such as "yes," "good," "very good," "I like the way you do that," and so forth. With elementary pupils, nods, smiles, and other gestures of approval are effective. Words that describe desirable performance and reinforce self-evaluation are appropriate for secondary pupils. "See how you are improving." "You are becoming an expert in this." "Do you see what an effective job you have done?" "That is an interesting observation." "Will you discuss this with the class?" Reinforcement that involves self-evaluation helps the pupil learn to internalize the reinforcement process. To maintain maximum effectiveness, the teacher should use a variety of behaviors to express approval.

Contingency Management

Events are said to be *contingent* when the occurrence of one is dependent on the occurrence of the other. When a behavior is followed by a consequence, the consequence is said to be contingent on the behavior. A contingency is the relationship between a given response and its environmental consequence (Sulzer and Mayer, 1972). Contingency management in classroom instruction refers to arranging consequences so that appropriate learning and social behaviors are followed by satisfying activities.

Lloyd Homme (1969) summed up the concept of contingency management, or contingency contracting, in "Grandma's Law," which states, "First clean up your plate, then you may have your dessert." Stated generally the rule would be, do what you *have* to do, then you can do what you *want* to do. Preferred activities as reinforcers are important to the teacher because they are a practical way to motivate pupils. The teacher need only observe what behaviors pupils engage in frequently when they are free to choose an activity. By making these activities contingent on the completion of essential-level tasks, the pupils become motivated to achieve since essential behaviors are reinforced. "Grandma's Law" is significant because of its effect beyond the immediate contract. "Johnny, eat your spinach and then you can have your pie," not only (1) motivated Johnny to eat his spinach, and (2) reinforced him for eating his spinach, but (3) resulted in Johnny's developing a taste for spinach, even to the point of its possibly becoming one of his preferred foods.

"Grandma's Law" is known also as the "Premack principle" (Premack, 1963 and 1965). David Premack stated, "For any pair of responses, the more probable one will reinforce the less probable one." The practical application of the Premack principle is the basis of contingency management; that is, the higher-frequency behavior is made contingent on a lower-frequency behavior in order to increase the rate of occurrence of the lower-frequency behavior.

In an experimental program for emotionally disturbed children, Haring and Phillips (1962) employed a constructive approach for motivating pupils who refused to do assigned tasks. They employed consequences rather than punitive measures. A pupil was not permitted to move to other activities or to play until essential obligations had been met. Access to activities that pupils enjoyed were the consequences of task completion. The methods employed by Haring and Phillips, of which consequences were a part, produced significant gains over other methods studied in both academic achievement and behavioral improvement. They concluded that using consequences proved more effective and was less apt to increase tension than did employing verbal threats and punishment.

In an experimental project at the University of Washington, Haring and Kunzelmann (1966) designed classrooms that had "high strength areas," which were accessible contingent on achievement in a "low strength area." The high strength area contained materials for high-probability behaviors, including equipment for racing slot cars, painting, reading, crafts, and other activities that pupil behavior had indicated were most probable when a wide choice of activities was available. In the low strength area, the pupils earned points as they studied. These points were exchanged for time in the high strength area. The results indicated that this contingency management resulted in increased study behavior and motivation.

Homme (1969) developed a system of contingency management based on the concept that the likelihood that behavior will recur depends on its consequences. He viewed the teacher as a "contingency manager" and suggested that the essential characteristic of an excellent contingency manager was a willingness to reinforce successive approximations toward the terminal objectives. In practice, the contingency manager specified a certain amount of low-probability behavior that was required before the pupil engaged in a high-probability behavior.

The Premack principle (higher-probability responses reinforcing lower-probability responses) can be employed in self-management. Pupils who experience effective teacher-managed contingencies can gradually be taught to assume responsibility for managing their own contingencies. Self-management can begin with the pupil's identifying his or her attainment of an essential-level objective and then deciding on the nature of the reinforcing activitity. Later the pupil can determine his own requirements for achieving essential-level tasks. At this stage, the pupil is able to determine both the dimensions of his learning tasks and the nature of his reinforcing activities. At present, there is a lack of research indicating to what extent self-management of contingencies can be taught to pupils at different levels of development.

"In the regular classroom, the procedures of reinforcement should be natural and relevant to teaching-learning routines, both in timing and in selecting reinforcers. The most appropriate time for reinforcement is at the completion of a learning task or assignment. The most natural and available reinforcers are pleasurable activities related to academic subjects, and games, art projects, crafts, and music.

The most efficient use of contingency management requires organizing or structuring the classroom so that activities the pupils prefer are used as rewards for desired behaviors. Arranging different areas of the classroom to support various types of activities can facilitate contingency management.

TASK AREA

An area containing student desks or work tables creates the setting for group instruction in academic subjects. In this area, the pupils carry out textbook or workbook tasks and written assignments. Student desks that can be grouped to form tables permit flexibility and variations in grouping. The task area should be organized so that instructional materials are near at hand and readily available to teacher and pupils.

REINFORCEMENT AREA

The contingency-managed classroom must offer the pupil enjoyable activities. These activities may be accommodated in an area separated from the task area by a partition or other divider. Haring and Kunzelmann (1966) employed a glass partition that prevented interaction between pupils in the task and reinforcement areas, while permitting the teacher to supervise both groups. The more common practice is to set up a designated reinforcement area in part of the classroom. This area can be separated from the task area by low shelves or bookcases to physically divide those pupils working on assignments from those engaged in reinforcing activities.

The equipment and materials in the reinforcement area should be suitable to the pupils' ages and interests. The following are a few of the materials found to be effective with various age groups.

THREE TO SIX YEARS

Picture Dominos

Golden Book Records

Lego plastic construction blocks

Stepping stones

Magnetic boards with numbers, letters, and symbols

Crayons, construction paper, paste, paints, and clay

SIX TO NINE YEARS

Tinker Toys

Dominos

Puzzles

Twist boards

Picture-card games

Paints

NINE TO TWELVE YEARS

Comic books

Arts and crafts materials

Pets in cages

Science fiction stories

Checkers

Parquetry Design Blocks

Tumble Words

TWELVE TO FIFTEEN YEARS

Scrabble

Recordings of popular music

Maps or globes

Cassette tape recorders

Typewriters

Board games

Looms

Arts and crafts materials

FIFTEEN TO EIGHTEEN YEARS

Science materials

Tape recorders

Magazines

Television

Model kits—cars, rockets, etc.

Scrabble

Chess sets

Movie projector and films

Slide projector and slides

Cameras and film

Many activities, such as listening to music, reading, handicrafts, viewing slides and motion pictures, painting, and playing games are engaged in by pupils of all ages and developmental levels. Some reinforcing activities, such as talking, writing letters, dancing, studying with a friend, or reading a library book, do not require special materials in the reinforcement area. Sometimes pupils will bring materials from home—records, magazines, or pets. It is good practice to add new materials and to remove those that are not used. By changing or rotating the materials to suit the pupils' current interests, the reinforcement area will maintain its effectiveness.

The most important reinforcers are those directly related to educational objectives. Activities that apply and enrich essential-level learning should receive high priority. When a pupil has learned to use the library card catalog, for example, he should be given activities in which properly using the catalog is rewarding. When a pupil has learned the concepts of longitude and latitude, he should be given many opportunities to apply this knowledge in locating cities, rivers, and other geographical information. These and similar reinforcing activities broaden the child's application of his learning and increase the probability that he will continue to use what he has learned.

MANAGEMENT OF SEPARATE AREA CLASSROOMS

Classrooms having separate task and reinforcement areas can be organized in several different ways. An effective and straightforward approach is simply to require that all pupils begin assigned tasks at the same time. The teacher signals the class to assemble in the task areas by ringing a bell or flicking the room lights. When the class is assembled, a lesson is presented or a task assigned. The assignments may be the same for all pupils or may be individualized. When each pupil finishes the assignment, first the teacher checks it and then the pupil proceeds to the reinforcement area, where he engages in an activity of his choice. When the last pupil to enter the reinforcement area has had a minimum of three minutes' reinforcement time, the teacher signals the class to assemble in the task area for the next lesson or assignment. This provides for individual differences in the time required to complete a task and permits individualization of reinforcement. Contingency management ensures that every child has a number of reinforcing experiences.

On the first day of initiating this type of contingency management, pupils should be oriented to the task area and be given a very short assignment. When all have completed the task, the class is then taken to the reinforcement area and shown the variety of activities available. After a few minutes of exploration, the class is signalled to return to the task area, where a second short task is assigned. This time, as each pupil completes the task, he or she is sent to the reinforcement area. If a teacher's aide is available, orientation to the reinforcement area can be individualized. Initially, the teacher sends each pupil to the aide in the reinforcement area as he or she completes the assignment. As soon as the system is operating effectively, the difficulty and length of the tasks are increased and the reinforcement time extended. Approximately ten to fifteen minutes' reinforcement time per hour appears to be most effective.

MANAGEMENT OF CLASSROOMS HAVING ACTIVITY CENTERS

Activity centers, or designated specialized areas, can be employed as reinforcement areas. The management procedure is the same as described above, except that the pupils may be in a number of different areas for their reinforcement activities. When an activity area is full, games or materials may be brought to the pupils' desks in the task area.

MANAGEMENT OF COMBINED AREA CLASSROOMS

In secondary school classrooms, which are usually devoted to teaching only one subject, contingency management can be employed in a single area. Pupils are assigned the essential-level task of the course. As the assignment is completed, each pupil may select an activity or learning task to perform at his desk. For example, a mathematics teacher provided each pupil with a "reward" pass. One side of the pass was yellow and had the word *TASK* printed on it; the other side was blue and had the word *REWARD* printed on it. The pass was placed on the upper left-hand corner of the pupil's desk. When a pupil was engaged in an assigned task, the yellow side was turned up. When the assignment had been completed, the pupil turned the pass over and began another activity, such as reading, writing a letter, or doing another mathematics assignment. The pass alerted the teacher to those pupils who had completed assignments. The teacher visited each pupil who displayed a blue pass and then evaluated the assignment with the pupil. Classrooms employing this system of contingency management have also provided popular reading materials, games, and other items that pupils could use as reinforcement activities.

Flexibility

Contingency-managed classrooms can be organized and operated in many different ways. Pupils can be provided with task lists that prescribe assignments, such as chapters to study, workbook exercises, tests, and so on. Each pupil can then be put on an individual schedule and permitted to move from task to reinforcement after completing each assignment. Individualization such as this can be accomplished through a system called *contingency contracting* (Homme, 1969; Sulzer and Mayer, 1972).

Through innovation and experimentation, the teacher can find many ways to implement the principles of contingency management. The week before Christmas vacation, a teacher reinforced each pupil's performance on a variable schedule by rewarding the pupil with a Christmas tree ornament. The pupil was allowed to place his ornament on the class Christmas tree when and where he pleased. At other times of the year, the teacher used decorating the bulletin board, adding to a collage mural, and decorating the classroom for a party in a similar way. Such activities as carrying messages, making inventories of materials, helping the teacher, and any other activity regarded as a privilege can be employed contingently to strengthen desirable behaviors.

Token Economies

A token is an object that can be exchanged at a later time for another object or activity. If the object or activity obtained with the token is reinforcing, through conditioning, the token acquires reinforcing value. Tokens such as money, poker chips, or check marks initially have little reinforcing value, but through experience in exchanging them for valued objects or activities, they become powerful reinforcers. Check marks, stars, points, chips, or similar items that can be easily dispensed and later exchanged for more valuable back-up reinforcers acquire conditioned reinforcing properties. A *back-up reinforcer* is an object or event that has already demonstrated its reinforcing effect.

The advantages of token reinforcers are that (1) they can be dispensed immediately following the desired behavior, (2) they can be counted and recorded, and (3) the time of exchange for back-up reinforcers can be arranged so as not to interfere with assigned tasks.

TOKENS DISPENSED IMMEDIATELY

Tokens that have become conditioned reinforcers can
be dispensed unobtrusively for appropriate social or academic behavior without interrupting that behavior. This
allows for greater precision of reinforcement than reinforcement given only on completion of an assignment. Tokens paired with praise and later exchanged for back-up
reinforcers acquire powerful reinforcing properties. They
become conditioned social reinforcers that can be exchanged for pleasurable activities or materials.

The most practical system of dispensing tokens is the
work-record card. This is a form usually containing a
grid of 100 or 200 squares. The teacher moves about the
room, praising the pupils' performance, and placing checks
in the squares on each pupil's card. A schedule of points
can be established, such as two points for starting work
promptly, three points for demonstrating good work habits,
and five points for correct answers. The teacher tells
the pupil how he has earned the points as the checks are
being given: "Jane, you started work on time, so here are
two checks. You worked well, except when you were drawing
pictures on the cover of your notebook, so here is one
check for being a good student. You have all correct except this answer, so here are four checks for your work."
Bonus points can be awarded for outstanding production or
citizenship: "Here are two bonus checks for helping Marcia
when she spilled the paint."

Other systems have used plastic discs, bonus stamps,
washers, and play money as tokens. The bonus stamps are
saved in a book until the required number of pages are
filled and exchanged for a desired object or activity.
Another system used washers or poker chips with a hole
drilled in the center. These were dispensed by dropping
them onto a peg mounted in a wooden base placed on the
pupil's desk or table. Play money was used with young
children so that they could make purchases of back-up reinforcers at a classroom store.

Tokens (checks on a work-record card, gold stars,
bonus stamps, play money, marbles stored in a jar, plastic
chips strung on a ring, poker chips, or holes punched in
a card) should be dispensed to the pupil as soon as
earned. The amount of work required to earn tokens can be
gradually extended. The value of the token economy is in
the exchange system that allows the pupil to be immediately rewarded and save his tokens for back-up reinforcers.
In other words, tokens acquire the same properties as currency. Every economic system uses some type of currency
as the means of exchange, because of its versatility.
Money can be used to obtain almost any product or service
and can be either spent for immediate gratification or
saved for more valuable purchases. Even pupils who have
a history of unsatisfactory school progress have been

willing to work for such back-up reinforcers as tickets to sports events, movie or theater tickets, and recordings of popular music. The following are a few suggested back-up reinforcers:

FOODS

Apples	Peanuts	Cookies
Raisins	Breakfast cereal	Popcorn (candied)
Oranges	Candy bars	Fruit juice

MATERIALS

Colored pencils	Model kits	Puzzles
Crayons	Picture books	Marbles
Toys	Dolls	Clay
Balloons	Games	Records
Balls	Coloring books	Paints

PRIVILEGES

Showing outstanding work to the principal

Playing games in class

Doing art to illustrate studies

Spending extra time with the teacher

Choosing an activity for self or class

Extra free time

Setting up equipment

Choosing music or a song to sing

Raising the school flag

Taking the class pet home for a holiday or weekend

Being in a skit or play

Taking first turn

Carrying messages

Selecting own seating

Supervising an activity

Using the typewriter

Listening to recordings

TICKETS

Transportation

School events

Trading stamps

Sports events

Movies

Theater

USING TOKENS WITH EMOTIONALLY DISTURBED OR CULTURALLY DISADVANTAGED STUDENTS

Although social approval and activity reinforcers are effective for nearly all children, they are not always maximally effective for some children. These children are generally included in the populations called emotionally disturbed or culturally disadvantaged. This does not imply that all disturbed or disadvantaged children do not respond well to social and activity reinforcers, but that concrete and more enduring reinforcers tend to be more effective with many of these children. Insecure children appear to find stacks of plastic chips or checks on work-record cards reassuring because they can be counted and recorded.

Urban schools, in which disadvantaged pupils frequently experience low academic achievement, should employ reinforcement systems to motivate culturally deprived children. Motivation results from using proper and adequate reinforcers. There is a difference between the reinforcement histories of middle-income and indigent children (Green and Stachnik, 1968). Middle-class parents begin shaping their children's behavior early in life, motivating them to learn and exert effort in school by rewarding behavior they regard as acceptable. By the time their children enroll in school, they have had a sustained history of reinforcement for achievement. Many low-income parents desire and envy educational achievement but lack the skills required to implant such a value system in their children.

Green and Stachnik (1969) suggest that an alternative to low academic achievement—declining success as disadvantaged pupils move through school, high dropout rates, eventual unemployment—is to pay students for acquiring academic skills. Although the suggestion that pupils be paid for academic achievement may appear unconventional, on closer examination it could provide the basis of a truly compensatory education. If the middle-class child receives a variety of effective reinforcers, in effect being "paid" for achievement with approval, gifts, and money, why not pay the low-income or indigent child at school? In higher education, achievement is paid for with direct financial rewards called scholarships. An effective but less radical way of translating this concept into a viable classroom program is to implement token economies with back-up reinforcers that are powerful incentives for disadvantaged pupils. Tokens should always be contingent on performance and should follow the desired behavior as quickly as possible. For pupils who have a history of underachievement, initially the tokens can be dispensed for an approximation of the desired performance. As the program progresses, through a shaping process, the criteria for reinforcement would gradually be raised.

The token can be effective reinforcement for the disturbed child because it provides a dependable reinforcer for those who have difficulty maintaining appropriate social and emotional responses. The child retains the token until he wishes to exchange it. This gives him a feeling of security. If the teacher pairs the token with praise, the child can learn to respond more appropriately to social approval. The token can be an effective reinforcer for the disadvantaged or disturbed child because it does not require the verbal or social developmental level of the middle-class child.

EXCHANGE FOR BACK-UP REINFORCERS

In establishing the exchange system, ask your pupils what things they would like as back-up reinforcers, or rewards. With the pupils' help, select reinforcing activities, prizes, or foods that are practical, available, and appropriate to their developmental levels. Post a list giving the point value of each reinforcer. For example, five marbles cost one completed work-record card; a model car kit costs ten completed cards. Young children will work for privileges such as taking care of class pets and presenting at "Show and Tell," whereas secondary pupils will work for privileges such as being team captain, attending an assembly program, watching television, building a project, teaching younger children, and studying with a friend. The selection of back-up reinforcers must be based on observing your pupils and their involvement in the exchange system. This is particularly important with secondary pupils.

Initially, the exchange procedure might be held at the end of each day and later, delayed to the end of the week. Of course, certain privileges must be purchased when available. The pupil who wants to run an errand must turn in the required points at that time. During the exchange procedure, the pupil can spend his completed work-record card or other tokens, or he may save them for a larger reward.

Tokens can be used to increase socialization by rewarding the group for an individual's performance. For example, a teacher wished to improve the behavior of a class reputed to have an excessive rate of misbehavior. She wished also to increase cooperation among the pupils. She began by rewarding the class for each ten minutes in which no disruption occurred, by dropping a marble in a jar in full view of the pupils. She also rewarded individual performance by dropping a marble in the jar. Disruptive behavior decreased and individual achievement increased. Cooperation grew and the class members helped individuals who previously had exhibited misbehavior and learning problems. Each time the jar was filled with marbles, the class was given a treat, such as a party, a movie, or a field trip.

By pairing the presentation of tokens and back-up reinforcers with praise, the need for future tokens is reduced and the teacher's praise becomes more reinforcing. Tokens are often used in conjunction with contingency management because they give the teacher a means of bringing many different kinds of behavior under the influence of reinforcement. After tokens take on the properties of currency and become generalized reinforcers, they can be given at any time and cause minimal disruption of the learning activity. Maintaining learned behaviors by using tokens does not depend on long-term continuation of the tokens. Research indicates that behaviors acquired through the use of token economies are readily transferred (Bushnell, 1968).

A token economy is particularly effective for establishing new behaviors because tokens can be dispensed immediately to shape desired behavior. Through pairing with social reinforcement the tokens can be phased out. A practical approach to employing token economy in the classroom is presented in Neisworth, Deno, and Jenkins (1969).

Reinforcement Development

Chapter Nine of *Individual Instruction* (Peter, 1975) presented a model of reinforcement at seven developmental levels: (1) primary, (2) social-verbal, (3) material, (4) manipulation, (5) token, (6) knowledge of results, and (7) self-evaluation. This model is valuable to the teacher because it can be used to identify the pupil's level of reinforcement development and to provide experiences that will facilitate achievement of higher levels of development. A significant goal of education is to ensure that the child becomes motivated, self-monitoring, and self-reinforcing. When this goal is achieved, the pupil is eager to learn and experiences the joy of accomplishment without needing an externally administered reinforcement system. This chapter will not repeat the explanation of the developmental model of reinforcement and how to ensure that the pupil becomes self-motivated and that learning becomes self-rewarding. (For a complete discussion, refer to L. Peter, *Individual Instruction*, 1975.) The following discussion assumes that you understand the model.

PRIMARY REINFORCERS

During the first few months of life, the baby's main satisfactions are derived from the gratification of his biological needs. Throughout life, the reinforcers that maintain or perpetuate life are referred to as primary reinforcers. Food, water, sex, shelter, and warmth are examples of primary reinforcers. Some primary reinforcers can be extremely powerful, especially when an individual has been deprived of the reinforcer for a long time.

Risley (1968) used food to reinforce language and modeling behavior in culturally disadvantaged preschool children. The study indicated that dispensing pieces of fruit or other snacks contingent on appropriate use of language, including talking at appropriate times, resulted in significant increases in these behaviors.

Although food as reinforcement is effective and its use is justified in working with culturally deprived preschool children as well as in some other special cases, it is neither practical nor desirable to use primary reinforcers consistently. Food may be used effectively as a back-up reinforcer or occasionally paired with higher-order reinforcers to strengthen their influence. Conditioned reinforcers can be dispensed more easily than primary reinforcers and in most cases do not produce satiation. A *conditioned* reinforcer is an object or event that, through frequent pairings with primary or strongly conditioned reinforcers, assumes reinforcing properties. For example, while mother is feeding baby she talks to him, smiles at him, and pats him. Through time, smiles, praise, and attention become conditioned reinforcers.

SOCIAL-VERBAL REINFORCERS

Most children come to school having had sufficient consistent affection and attention rewarding their appropriate behavior so that praise and other expressions of acceptance are conditioned reinforcers. By using praise and attention, the teacher can reinforce appropriate behavior, and by pairing these social reinforcers with tokens, they can condition such higher-order reinforcers as self-evaluation.

Once reinforcers begin to serve as reinforcers for a wide range of behaviors, they are called *generalized* reinforcers. Well-developed generalized reinforcers are only minimally dependent on fluctuating conditions such as deprivation or satiation. Praise, smiles, money, or tokens are normally reinforcing irrespective of the amount of praise, smiles, money, or tokens the individual has received in the immediate past. If all pupils in the class can be reinforced by praise, approval, tokens, and good grades, the teacher can be more effective and teaching becomes easier. The teacher need not be concerned about providing too much praise or about how long a period has passed since the last time the pupil was praised.

Wasik (1969) studied behavior modification techniques with second-grade culturally deprived children who displayed inappropriate classroom behaviors. The study reported that culturally deprived children are already at an academic disadvantage when they begin school, and that when these children demonstrate aggressive, antisocial, or resistive behaviors, they become even further handicapped. In this study, teachers used three treatment variables: (1) social reinforcement—praise, attention, and teacher proximity, (2) withholding of social reinforcement, and (3) time-out, or removing the child from social reinforcement. The results indicated that social reinforcement effectively helped to establish and maintain appropriate classroom behaviors and to diminish disruptive behaviors.

If a pupil fails to respond according to expectations when provided with tokens, praise, or grades, it may be that these are not powerful enough generalized reinforcers. The solution is to strengthen the generalized reinforcer by pairing it with a highly effective reinforcer. This might be a material, manipulative activity, or primary reinforcer.

MATERIAL REINFORCERS

Material reinforcers are generally used as back-up reinforcers, but some teachers have used materials directly. Individual beads for stringing, pop beads, and marbles have been dispensed as immediate reinforcers. Material reinforcers used occasionally in this way can provide novelty and produce increased motivation.

MANIPULATION REINFORCERS

Any satisfying manipulative activity can provide reinforcing consequences. In contingency-managed classrooms, activity centers offer opportunities for manipulation as reinforcement.

TOKEN REINFORCERS

The token is the most versatile and valuable generalized reinforcer the teacher can use. In a class of preschool children, Bushell, Wrobel, and Michaelis (1968) studied the effects of a token economy on study behaviors, including attention to task and cooperation among the pupils. The teachers paired colored washers with praise to reinforce pupils as they worked. At a certain time each day, if the students had earned enough washers they could buy a ticket to a special event, such as a short movie, a trip to a park, an art project, a story session, or a special gym period. These special events occurred outside of the regular classroom. The pupils increased all of their study behaviors when earning tokens.

Kuypers, Becker, and O'Leary (1968) studied the effects on third- and fourth-grade pupils of a token system not employing other procedures such as time-out, shaping, and differential social reinforcement. Their findings support the proposition that a token economy is not a magical procedure that will operate effectively without consideration of other influences. They found that shaping procedures should be used, and, initially at least, tokens should be paired with social reinforcement.

KNOWLEDGE OF RESULTS AS A REINFORCER

When knowledge of results becomes a powerful generalized reinforcer, the pupil becomes motivated to achieve and complete tasks. Programed instruction offers the most precise use of knowledge of results as a reinforcer for instruction.

SELF-EVALUATION AS A REINFORCER

Self-evaluation is the highest order of reinforcement and is often referred to as *internal reinforcement* or *intrinsic motivation*. Pupils should be reinforced for evaluating their own social and academic behavior. As discussed earlier, learning depends on cybernetic feedback to strengthen and direct the learning process. This is more apparent in learning a psychomotor task than in learning a cognitive task. For example, a pupil is learning to toss a basketball through a basket. He takes a position in front of the basket, holds the ball, sights the target, flexes his muscles, and releases the ball. If the ball goes through the hoop, the feedback through his senses reinforces all the behaviors that produced the satisfactory outcome. If the ball failed to go through the hoop, the feedback indicates to the pupil that he should apply more power or make other modifications on his next throw. If he does not evaluate the feedback and modify his behavior, his practice will be of little value in learning how to score baskets.

Employing feedback in academic learning is more complex because, in many cases of initial learning, the pupil is unable to identify the correct response. He must depend to some degree on the teacher's informing him of the correctness of his responses. As soon as possible, the teacher should structure situations that facilitate self-evaluation. Sharing objectives with the class is the first step in developing self-evaluation. The next is involving the pupil in establishing and learning to meet his own criteria of acceptable performance.

Rating scales can be used as external criteria to help the pupil evaluate his work. The teacher provides samples of successfully finished products. The pupil learns to evaluate his success by comparing his work with the samples of other pupils' work. This method is particularly useful for evaluating the relative quality of work such as writing, drawing, and arts and crafts. Whatever methods you use to develop self-evaluation skills in your pupils, it is essential that you initially provide extrinsic reinforcement for the pupil's own evaluation. When self-evaluation becomes a powerful generalized reinforcer, the pupil is freed from reliance on external reinforcement. His own self-evaluation becomes the feedback that reinforces his own behavior. Developing intrinsically motivated, self-monitoring pupils, who are reinforced by self-evaluation, is an ultimate purpose of education.

Assignment

Complete the exercises in Chapter Seven of the Classroom Instruction Workbook.

References

Becker, W., S. Engelmann, and D. Thomas. *Teaching: A Course in Applied Psychology*. Chicago: Science Research Associates, 1971.

Bushell, D., P. Wrobel, and M. Michaelis. "Applying 'Group' Contingencies to the Classroom Study Behavior of Pre-School Children," *Journal of Applied Behavior Analysis*, 1968, 1:55-61.

Green, R., and T. Stachnik. "Money, Motivation, and Academic Achievement," *Phi Delta Kappa*, 1968, 69:228-230.

Hall, R., D. Lund, and D. Jackson. "Effects of Teacher Attention on Study Behavior," *Journal of Applied Behavior Analysis*, Spring 1968, 1:1-12.

Haring, N., and E. Phillips. *Educating Emotionally Disturbed Children*. New York: McGraw-Hill, 1962.

————, and H. Kunzelmann. "The Finer Focus of Therapeutic Behavioral Management," *Educational Therapy*, 1966, 1.

Hart, B., N. Reynolds, D. Baer, E. Brawley, and F. Harris. "Effect of Contingent and Non-Contingent Social Reinforcement on the Cooperative Play of a Preschool Child," *Journal of Applied Behavior Analysis*, 1968, 1:73-76.

Homme, L. *How to Use Contingency Contracting in the Classroom*. Champaign, Ill.: Research Press, 1969.

Kuypers, D., W. Becker, and K. O'Leary. "How to Make a Token System Fail," *Exceptional Children*, 1968, 35:101-109.

Madsen, C., W. Becker, D. Thomas. "Rules, Praise, and Ignoring: Elements of Elementary Classroom Control," *Journal of Applied Behavior Analysis*, 1968, 1:139-150.

Meacham, M., and A. Wiesen. *Changing Classroom Behavior: A Manual for Precision Teaching*. Scranton, Pa.: International Textbook, 1969.

McAllister, L., J. Stachowiak, D. Baer, and L. Conderman. "The Application of Operant Conditioning Techniques in a Secondary School Classroom," *Journal of Applied Behavior Analysis*, 1969, 2:277-285.

Neisworth, J., S. Deno, and J. Jenkins. *Student Motivation and Classroom Management*. Newark, N.J.: Behavior Technics, 1969.

Premack, D. "Rate Differential Reinforcement in Monkey Manipulation," *Journal of the Experimental Analysis of Behavior*, 1963, 6:81-89.

————. "Reinforcement Theory," in D. Levine (ed.), *Nebraska Symposium on Motivation*. Lincoln, Neb.: University of Nebraska Press, 1965.

Risley, T. "Learning and Lollipops," *Psychology Today*, 1968, 1:(8)28-031; 62-65.

Sheppard, W. C., S. B. Shank, and D. Wilson. *How to Be a Good Teacher: Training Social Behavior in Young Children*. Champaign, Ill.: Research Press, 1972.

Sulzer, B., and G. R. Mayer. *Behavior Modification Procedures for School Personnel*. Hinsdale, Ill.: The Dryden Press, 1972.

Thomas, D., W. Becker, and M. Armstrong. "Production and Elimination of Disruptive Classroom Behavior by Systematically Varying Teacher's Behavior," *Journal of Applied Behavior Analysis*, 1968, 1:35-45.

Wasik, B., D. Senn, R. Welch, and B. Cooper. "Behavior Modification with Culturally Deprived School Children: Two Case Studies," *Journal of Applied Behavior Analysis*, 1969, 2:181-194.

Eight

Evaluation

Objectives: After completing your study of this chapter, you will be able to (1) define tests, measurement, and evaluation, (2) describe the process of evaluation, (3) construct teacher-made paper-and-pencil tests using true-false, matching, multiple-choice, completion, short-answer, and essay questions, (4) administer teacher-made tests, (5) mark tests and evaluate results, (6) construct and administer performance tests, (7) design systems for pupil self-evaluation, and (8) complete the exercises in Chapter Eight of the Classroom Instruction Workbook.

Many of the decisions, strategies, and interventions in the process of instruction are based on feedback regarding pupil performance. Much information comes from directly observing your pupils' behavior. The teacher must continually evaluate feedback and make decisions about how to plan future instructional strategies. Evaluation is a continuous process that underlies all effective teaching and learning. Dynamic, productive evaluation provides cybernetic feedback that should be used to modify elicitors, reinforcers, and enroute objectives to sustain progressive changes in pupil behavior. In addition to this continuous, longitudinal approach, evaluation can be based on specific samples of behavior obtained at appropriate times during an instructional program. Specific samples of behavior are called *tests*.

Chapter Three described standardized tests. This chapter will discuss teacher-made tests. The teacher is frequently required to produce measuring instruments—that is, checklists, rating scales, and paper-and-pencil tests—when standardized tests are not suitable for the specific needs of a particular program. The teacher-made test should elicit a sample of pupil behavior that can be used to evaluate the pupils' attainment of an educational objective. This informs the pupil about his progress and indicates to the teacher the effectiveness of instruction. Testing is a sampling technique used to measure student performance.

Measurement and Evaluation

Evaluation is the process of finding the value of, or appraising the worth of, something. As used in education, evaluation is a systematic process of determining the extent to which educational objectives have been achieved. Systematic evaluation always assumes that objectives have already been identified. Without being able to refer to established criteria, or objectives, it is impossible to judge the degree of progress.

The evaluation procedure consists of first obtaining an appropriate sample of pupil performance, and then comparing the sample with the objective. An appropriate sample of pupil performance can be obtained from directly observing pupil behavior, assessing a product of pupil behavior, or from testing. The sample of pupil performance is the data used in making an evaluation.

Evaluation may involve qualitative or quantitative appraisal. Qualitative descriptions of pupil performance in art, music, composition, and social behavior are frequently evaluated subjectively. Qualitative methods of appraisal do not depend on measurement. Quantitative evaluations involve measurements such as counting occurrences of a behavior and obtaining base rates, marking an assignment and assigning a numerical score, or administering a test and obtaining a score. Measurement provides the data used for evaluation.

A test is a measuring device for obtaining data used for evaluation. Tests can be constructed to sample a variety of performances. For example, tests may be classified by the nature of the responses they elicit. *Achievement* tests measure knowledge of subject matter or content already studied in class. *Diagnostic* tests sample essential-level skills to help the teacher determine subsequent instruction. *Speed* tests measure reading rates or the frequency of correct arithmetical responses within a given time period. The questions or items in a speed test are all of the same level of difficulty, and the score represents the total number of correctly completed items. *Power* tests measure the degree of mastery of basic skills through a series of increasingly difficult questions. The total number of completed items represents the pupil's power to solve difficult problems. *Performance* tests sample how a task is executed, such as how the pupil operates a machine, throws a ball, or follows safety procedures.

To be valid, testing must sample and measure the performance described in the lesson, unit, or course objectives. The Competencies for Teaching system does not require you to develop objectives for testing because you use the same objectives for testing as you do for instruction. You are required, however, to identify test items that constitute a representative sample of the performance described in the instructional objectives. The *Taxonomy of Educational Objectives* (Bloom, 1958; Krathwohl, 1964) can be useful in determining whether test items sample the appropriate levels of performance.

The sections that follow will describe two general classifications of teacher-made tests: paper-and-pencil tests which require pupils to write or select answers, and performance tests which involve observing and recording pupils' behavior.

Paper-and-Pencil Tests

The most frequently used method of measuring pupil achievement is the paper-and-pencil test. The main requirement of a valid test is that it be constructed to elicit and measure behaviors described in the instructional objectives.

Gronlund (1971) suggests four factors that influence the final value of a paper-and-pencil test: (1) the type and quality of questions used, (2) the construction and content of the total test, (3) the procedures followed in administering the test, and (4) the use made of the test scores. These factors are described below.

TYPES OF QUESTIONS

There are two general categories of test items, objective and essay. An *objective* question is one in which the answer can be marked right or wrong objectively, since there is a limited number of correct responses. The responses consist of short answers, completions or filling in blanks, identifying true or false statements, matching related words or statements, and selecting correct responses from multiple choices. A key or template can be used to score many of these tests. Different scorers would mark an objective test in essentially the same way and arrive at similar scores.

The *essay* question tests ability to write effectively and to organize facts from a fund of knowledge. The essay question can elicit descriptions of interrelationships between topics in a given field and explanations of cause-and-effect relationships. Essay questions can deal also with controversial issues in which there is no "correct" answer. Such responses as explanations of basic understanding and comprehension of a topic cannot be scored objectively. Scoring an essay is subjective, and the validity of the score depends on the expertise of the scorer and his or her ability to evaluate the response to the essay according to the objectives of the course. Even among highly qualified scorers, essays are often evaluated differently.

The type of test question should be selected on the basis of the kind of response that would best represent the teacher's objective. If, for example, the objective is for the pupil to recall specific facts or to apply formulas or procedures, objective questions would be most appropriate. But if the objective requires that the pupil explain his understanding of a topic, an essay question would be more effective.

Not all items on a paper-and-pencil test are stated in the interrogative form, although they may be generally referred to as "questions." Many are stated as declarative sentences to which the students are instructed to respond.

True-False Questions

The true-false question should be used to test an absolute fact about which there is no disagreement. The advantage of this type of question is the speed with which the students' knowledge of a great many facts can be tested and scored. A variety of forms is used, but the question usually consists of a statement to which the pupil responds by either writing the word *true* or *false* or circling the letter "T" or "F."

A whale is a mammal.	(T) F
Turtles and lizards are mammals.	T (F)

True-false questions are most frequently used to measure attainment of lower-level objectives, but they can be used to identify the correct statement of a fact, the definition of a term, and the students' understanding of a relationship or procedure.

Fact:

Mark Twain was the pseudonym of Samuel Clemens.	(T) F

Terminology:

Ohm is the unit used to measure flow of electricity.	T (F)

Relationship:

Ounce is to pound as inch is to foot.	(T) F

Procedure:

The position of secretary of state is filled by presidential appointment with Senate confirmation.	(T) F

The true-false question can be used for assessing reading comprehension.

Below are ten statements based on the above paragraph. If the statement is true, circle "T"; if false, circle "F."

A disadvantage of using true-false questions is the students' tendency to guess at the answer. There is a fifty-percent chance that the correct answer can be obtained by guessing. As a consequence, the validity of the students' level of achievement of the objective as measured by the test is questionable.

A modification of the usual true-false question can increase its validity in determining whether the pupil knows the answer or is guessing. The test can be modified by underlining the important word, phrase, number, or symbol in the true-false question. A line is provided next to the response column. The pupil is directed to circle "T" or "F." If the statement is false, the pupil is directed to write a replacement for the underlined part of the sentence in order to make it true.

<u>Ernest Hemingway</u> wrote *The Old Man and the Sea*. _____ Ⓣ F

The mathematical symbol ≥ represents "less than." _____ T Ⓕ

Particles of positive electricity are called <u>electrons</u>. *protons* T Ⓕ

<u>Water</u> can be in liquid, solid, or gaseous form. _____ Ⓣ F

In designing true-false tests, the responses should be aligned in columns to prevent confusion for the pupil and to contribute to ease of marking for the teacher. The statements should be brief and clear, avoiding double negatives and other unnecessary complexities.

Matching Questions

Matching questions can be used to measure knowledge of factual information and understanding of relationships. Usually a matching question consists of two columns of items that have some common relationship. The pupil is directed to select the item in the second column that matches the item in the first column and write its letter in the blank.

Identify the part of speech.

B 1. it   A. noun

E 2. or   B. pronoun

D 3. big   C. preposition

A 4. car   D. adjective

G 5. run   E. conjunction

                      F. adverb

                      G. verb

There are many kinds of relationships that can provide items for matching questions.

Persons—achievements

Objects—names

Plants—classifications

Foreign words—English translations

Authors—books

Causes—effects

Quotations—authors and/or books

Symbols—concepts

Rules—examples

Dates—events

Terms—definitions

A matching question can sample a large amount of content in a short period of time.

Match the name of the element with its symbol.

_B_	1.	Fe	A.	Gold
_G_	2.	Ag	B.	Iron
_I_	3.	Sn	C.	Lead
_C_	4.	Pb	D.	Mercury
_A_	5.	Au	E.	Nitrogen
_H_	6.	Na	F.	Potassium
_F_	7.	K	G.	Silver
_D_	8.	Hg	H.	Sodium
			I.	Tin
			J.	Uranium

The matching question is suitable only when there are sufficient related items in a given instructional sequence. The items to be matched should be homogeneous, that is, the content of the question should deal with one area of study. The directions should indicate whether the response may be used only once or more than once. The columns should be kept brief—about eight to ten matches are sufficient. The columns normally contain unequal numbers of items. It is also advisable to list the items in some logical order—alphabetical, numerical, or chronological. The response blank is normally placed before the left-hand column. This avoids confusion and expedites marking.

Match each fraction in the first column with its name from the second column. The names in the second column may be used one or more times.

_____	1.	4/4	_____	5.	7 1/3	A.	common
_____	2.	7/8	_____	6.	1/4	B.	whole
_____	3.	9/7	_____	7.	6/1	C.	improper
_____	4.	2/2	_____	8.	1 1/2	D.	mixed

Multiple-Choice Questions

The multiple-choice question is widely used because of its versatility, objectivity, and ease of scoring. It can be used to test all subjects. The multiple-choice question has two parts. The *stem* consists of a question or an incomplete statement. This is followed by from three to five *alternatives*, consisting of words, numbers, or symbols that are possible answers to the question or completions of the statement. The pupil is directed to read the stem and the alternatives and then to select the correct or best alternative.

The multiple-choice may be presented as a question:

D 1. What kind of weather is most likely when nimbostratus clouds are present?

A. sunny and warm

B. windy or foggy

C. cool and hazy

D. rainy or snowy

or it may be presented as a statement requiring completion:

B 2. In the northern hemisphere, the longest day in the year comes in the month of

A. March

B. June

C. September

D. December

Multiple-choice questions are useful for testing achievement at all cognitive levels. The limitations of multiple-choice questions are in measuring problem-solving processes and in assessing organization, composition, and presentation skills.

Objectives in all subject areas include attaining basic knowledge of facts, terminology, principles, and procedures. These are usually considered to be essential levels on which pupils build higher levels of learning.

Multiple-choice questions are particularly suitable for measuring the following essential levels of cognitive learning.

Facts:

_C_ 1. Winston Churchill is best known as

    A. an inventor

    B. an artist

    C. a statesman

    D. an explorer

Terminology:

_A_ 2. Hue refers to

    A. color

    B. lightness

    C. oils

    D. perspective

Principle:

_C_ 3. The United States Constitution establishes judicial review as

    A. an alienable right

    B. a requirement on all federal cases

    C. a check-and-balance system

    D. a guarantee for lawyers

Procedure:

_B_ 4. In the scientific process, which step comes first?

    A. collect data

    B. identify the problem

    C. define the problem

    D. formulate a hypothesis

Bloom (1956) presents examples of multiple-choice questions for all cognitive levels, including application, analysis, evaluation, and cause-and-effect relationships. You should study these examples before attempting to write higher-level multiple-choice questions. Questions can be presented in a number of ways to sample various levels of learning.

Simple Form. The simplest form tests recognition of facts.

_A_ 1. A right triangle always contains

A. one 90° angle

B. two equal sides

C. two 45° angles

D. a 30° angle

Reverse Form. This type is too difficult for elementary grades and should be used at the secondary level only.

_C_ 2. All of the following were post-Impressionist painters except

A. Cézanne   C. Rembrandt

B. Van Gogh   D. Gauguin

Multiple-Response Form. One or more of the alternatives may be correct. Because of its difficulty, it should be used only with advanced pupils.

_A, B, D_ 3. Which of the following terms applies to graphs?

A. axis   C. rank

B. coordinates   D. ordinate

Order Form. This is used to test chronological order or procedural steps.

_____ 4. The event that occurred first was the

    A. purchase of Florida

    B. purchase of Louisiana

    C. acquisition of California

    D. purchase of Alaska

Cluster Form. This is the most difficult type.

_____ 5. What is the chronological order of the following events?

    A. the purchase of Florida

    B. the purchase of Louisiana

    C. the acquisition of California

    D. the purchase of Alaska

The correct combination is

    A. ABCD   B. ACDB

    C. BACD   D. DABC

Three considerations will help you construct and write multiple-choice questions. First, the stem of each question must be stated as clearly and concisely as possible. Too many words may result in confusion and test only those pupils who have a high level of reading comprehension. The stem should contain as much of .the question as possible. In the following example, question 2 is an improvement over question 1.

_____ 1. In the problem $4X + 5 = 13$,

    A. X = 1   C. X = 3

    B. X = 2   D. X = 4

_____ 2.   In the problem 4X + 5 = 13, X equals

A. 1   C. 3

B. 2   D. 4

Second, in constructing multiple-choice questions, all the alternatives should be plausible, but there should be only one correct or best alternative. Alternatives should all be on the same topic, of similar length, and of consistent grammatical construction. The alternatives, "all of the above" and "none of the above" should not be used too frequently on any one test.

Third, unnecessary clues to the correct answer should be avoided. Subjects of the stems should agree with verbs in the alternatives. If an *a* or *an* divides the stem from the alternatives, it is best to place these articles with the alternatives. The length of the alternatives should not provide a clue to the answer. For example, in poorly constructed tests, the correct alternative may be longer than the incorrect alternatives.

Completion Questions

The completion question requires the pupil to supply the answer by writing a word, phrase, number, or symbol in a blank, either to answer a question or to complete a statement.

Completion Question:

What is the name of the U.S. president whose domestic reform program was called the New Deal?

_____

Completion Statement:

The name of the U.S. president whose domestic reform program was called the New Deal was

_____

The completion question can be used for any subject at any grade level. A main advantage of completion questions is that they require the pupil to produce the answer by recalling a fact or a process.

1.   The name of the capital city
      of the state of California
      is   _____

2. Identify each of the following fractions as either common, whole, or improper.

    1/4   _____

    5/4   _____

    4/4   _____

    3/4   _____

Completion questions can elicit simple problem-solving behaviors.

3. $1/4 \div 232 =$ _____

4. If 96 pupils are to be equally divided into 4 classes, each class would contain

   _____ pupils.

Completion questions can be used to measure pupils' ability to interpret data from drawings, diagrams, charts, and graphs.

5. How many degrees are there in angle B

   in the following triangle?   _____

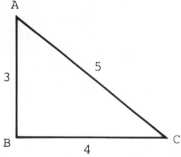

6. What was the approximate number of people unemployed in the United States in 1972?

   _____

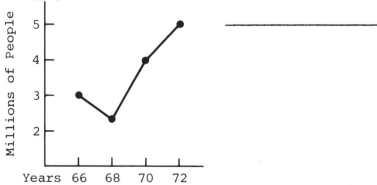

Constructing completion questions is relatively simple. However, there are three points to consider to ensure that they effectively measure appropriate performance. It is usually best to place the blank for the response at the end of the statement or question. This allows the reader to comprehend the meaning before having to make a response. For example, question 2 is preferable to question 1.

1. _____ is the author of *A Separate Peace*.

2. The author of *A Separate Peace* is _____ .

Placing all the response blanks in a single column on the right side of the test paper will expedite marking. Each blank should be of equal length to preclude giving an unnecessary clue to the answer.

The question should be stated explicitly enough so that the desired answer is specified. For example, question 2 is preferable to question 1.

1. NaCl is _____

2. The common name for NaCl is _____

The first question could be answered correctly with any of a number of responses: sodium chloride, a chemical compound, or a base. The second question specifies the desired response, so that if the pupil knows the answer he will write "salt." Avoid ambiguous questions that may be open to more than one interpretation. In the question, specify the type of response—name, number, or symbol. If the response should be a number, indicate the units in which it should be stated. For example, question 2 is preferable to question 1.

1. A triangle contains _____

2. The number of degrees in a triangle is _____

Short-Answer Questions

The short-answer or short-essay question requires a phrase or sentence response. Each question should be worded so that only one correct answer can be given. For example, recall of a definition requires a short answer.

1. Define the term *sphere*.

2. Define the term *cube*.

Short-answer questions can elicit more complex responses also. For example, a test paper contains diagrams of three dry cells connected (a) in series, (b) in parallel arrangement. This is followed by three short-answer questions.

1. How are the cells connected in diagram (a)?

2. How are the cells connected in diagram (b)?

3. What is the total voltage of the three dry cells in diagram (a)?

Essay Questions

Although responses to essay questions are scored subjectively and marking is time-consuming for the teacher, they do test areas of performance that objective questions cannot. Essay questions can test:

1. Basic understanding of a topic as a whole

2. Interrelationships (including cause and effect) of topics in a given area

3. Understanding of controversial issues

4. Ability to organize facts and approach problems by presenting evidence from background knowledge

5. Ability to write effectively and keep to the topic, using correct grammar, spelling, paragraphs, and structure

Essay questions should generally be reserved for objectives that cannot be measured effectively in any other way. This includes objectives using verbs such as the following: *explain, express, describe, formulate, integrate, organize, outline, present, produce, state, evaluate,* and *create.* An essay question can draw parameters to give the pupil structure and boundaries within which to organize and present his answer. For example, the following statements limit answers but still allow pupils to select and organize supporting information.

1. "From the material you studied in this unit, select two. . . ."

2. "What, in your opinion, are the three. . . ."

3. "Choose two examples from those studied in this unit and describe the relationship between. . . ."

4. "Using the alpha principle, how would you apply it in solving. . . ."

Essay questions may be open-ended and provide opportunities for creativity. An essay response can be a poem, a description, an explanation, a report, a criticism, or an evaluation. Complex essay questions can combine characteristics of both structured and open-ended questions. For example:

Of all the contemporary problems facing the human race, select the one you consider most critical and outline a plan of attack on the problem. Then briefly evaluate what effect your plan would have.

TEST CONSTRUCTION

Each teacher-made test is constructed for a specific purpose. It may be constructed for a single lesson and consist of a few questions related to the lesson topic. It may be a weekly quiz to assess progress in a subject. It may be a unit test designed to measure achievement of essential-level objectives before beginning the next unit. Or it may be a midterm or final examination. Obviously, each kind of test should be constructed to satisfy the particular instructional objectives, but there are a few general rules that provide some guidance:

1. Limit the types of questions on any one test. Pupils should not have to read many different directions and should not have to change procedures and kinds of thought processes too often.

2. Write questions to elicit behaviors described in the objectives.

3. Group questions by type, such as true-false, multiple-choice, and so on. Within each group, questions should be arranged in order of difficulty.

4. Make sure directions are clear and concise, and include general directions for the test as a whole and specific directions for each different type of question. When testing young children or those who are inexperienced with a particular type of question, it is good practice to illustrate a new type of question with a sample of a completed question. On comprehensive tests, the points or value allotted to each question should be indicated and the approximate time that should be devoted to each section of the test should be stated.

5. For objective questions, place all choices of answers or answer blanks in a standard position for ease of responding and marking.

The Comprehensive Test

The purpose of the comprehensive test is to measure achievement of the course's or unit's objectives. A comprehensive test usually contains a variety of questions because it is designed to measure the complex achievements of relatively longer instructional sequences than do lesson tests or weekly quizzes. A test consisting of two or three kinds of questions, including essay questions, allows the teacher to measure a broad range of behaviors and to assess some performances in depth. For example, the following is a selection of questions from a comprehensive biology test in a general science course.

Plants—Seeds, Roots, Stems, and Leaves

True-False Questions

1. Heliotropism is the tendency of young
   plants to grow toward the light.   (T)   F

2. Germination needs light to begin.   T   (F)

3. A bean seed has a single seed coat.   T   (F)

4. The thorns on a rose bush are modi-
   fied leaves.   (T)   F

5. Water evaporation from leaves is regulated by guard cells.   (T)   F

6. The water lily does not contain breathing pores.   T   (F)

7. More chlorophyll is produced by leaves of plants growing in the dark than by those growing in the light.   T   (F)

Completion Questions

1. The epidermis of a tree protects its inner bark and prevents   *evaporation*

2. The name of the process by which water enters roots is called   *osmosis*

3. The breathing pores of a leaf are called   *stomata*

4. Another word for decayed leaves is   *humus*

Multiple-Choice Questions

1. A tomato can best be classified as a   *D*

    A. root   B. seed

    C. stem   D. fruit

2. The tree from which cork is made is an   *A*

    A. oak   B. alder

    C. ash   D. elm

3. Which of the following is an example of a taproot?   *B*

    A. onion   B. dandelion

    C. bean   D. corn

4. Water is best retained in soil that contains   *D*

    A. seeds   B. gravel

    C. limestone   D. humus

Essay Questions

1. Describe the life cycle of the bean.

2. In what ways are angiosperms useful to man?

3. Explain the differences between monocotyledon and dicotyledon with respect to their (a) appearance, (b) seeds, (c) stems, and (d) leaves.

TEST ADMINISTRATION

The physical and psychological environment in which the test is given should ensure that each pupil is given a fair and equal chance to demonstrate his achievement of the objectives being measured. The physical environment should provide adequate work space, quiet, and sufficient light and ventilation. The psychological environment should not arouse excessive anxiety during testing. The teacher should assure the pupils that time limits are adequate to allow them to complete the test and that the test's results will be used to help them improve their learning. The teacher should avoid (1) giving too many instructions before the test, (2) giving hints to pupils who ask questions, and (3) interrupting students during the test.

MARKING AND EVALUATION

Marking objective questions is a comparatively simple task. One type of scoring key can be made by writing the correct answers on a blank copy of the test. Or, a more convenient key to use is a strip key—a narrow slip of paper with a column of correct answers, made by cutting the answer column from a master copy of the test. Scoring then becomes only a matter of comparing the answers on the key or master copy with the answers on each pupil's paper.

A scoring stencil is efficient for marking true-false and multiple-choice questions. This is made by cutting holes in a copy of the test where the correct answers should appear. The stencil is placed over the pupil's paper and the correct answers are checked and counted. When scoring is done by template (scoring stencil), each paper should also be scanned to see that only one answer was entered for each question.

It is good practice to mark each correct answer with a check or other correct mark to indicate and reinforce correct responses. The word *check* means a test of accuracy and a "check mark" is a symbol to show approval or verification of something (Webster, 1968). The check mark is widely used to indicate correctness or completion in checking off tasks or items in business, industry, and other human endeavors; however, for some strange reason some educators use check marks to indicate wrong answers. This practice is indefensible: first, using checks to indicate errors confuses the meaning of a commonly used symbol, and second, it conditions aversive stimuli for a symbol that should be paired with positive reinforcement. If you are working in a school that uses check marks to indicate incorrect responses, it is advisable for you to use a "C" for correct. The "X" is a universal symbol for wrong or incorrect, so it can be used when you wish to indicate error, but it is usually necessary to mark only correct responses. In scoring multiple-choice tests, it is good practice to draw a vertical line through the proper answer in an item missed by the pupil to let him know what the correct response should have been.

On an objective test, each correct response should be counted as one point. This avoids complications in scoring. The pupil's score on an objective test, or for the objective items on a comprehension test, should be simply the number of items answered correctly.

An aide might be assigned the task of scoring an objective test by using a key. Carefully constructing objective test items contributes to both ease and efficiency of marking. The time spent on preparing the questions and the format of the test is compensated for by the time saved in administration and scoring.

Scoring essay questions is a time-consuming but useful chore. It is essential that the essay be read and evaluated carefully to see how well it meets the criteria established by the question. Questions intended to elicit creative writing and expressions of feelings are scored subjectively, and the quality of the evaluation depends to a considerable degree on the teacher's ability to make literary judgments.

Essay questions can be constructed so that scoring is less subjective. Preparing an outline of expected answers and wording the question to restrict the answers to those expected helps the teacher establish criteria and a point system for scoring. When marking essay questions, read and evaluate the same question on all papers, preferably without knowing whose paper you are marking. This helps lessen the subjectivity.

In the Competencies for Teaching system, testing evaluates both teaching and learning. A goal of teaching is to help pupils attain the instructional objectives. Testing periodically evaluates the effectiveness of instruction. When a test reveals a weakness in most pupils, subsequent class instruction should be designed to remedy the deficit. On the basis of your evaluation of test results, the class may be divided into groups for remedial instruction, or individual follow-up procedures may be undertaken. In some classrooms, pupils who have few or no errors on the test are assigned as coaching teams to help those needing assistance in a specific area.

If the test is constructed to measure essential-level objectives, it is important that remedial instruction be provided for those who fail to attain the minimum prerequisite requirements for subsequent instruction. The quiz is an effective device for determining whether essential-level objectives are being achieved. In addition, comprehensive tests can be constructed so that the questions at the beginning of each group of items measure essential-level skills and knowledge. The latter items can test power, creativity, and developmental levels. In this way, both essential- and higher-level learning are tested. Such a format permits the teacher to distinguish the students' level of attainment of both types of objectives during evaluation.

Test results should be reviewed with the class to give the pupils an opportunity to identify their mistakes and learn the correct answers. Unless there are rules to the contrary (as sometimes apply to final examinations), after the test papers have been graded, they should be returned and the pupils should be encouraged to examine them in detail. In the case described earlier of multiple-choice questions marked with a template, the pupils should reread the questions and observe what their responses should have been. After the pupils have reviewed their tests and had an opportunity to ask questions or request clarification, the papers may be collected again. This is obviously an important step if the teacher intends to use the same test again with another class. The test scores and the pupils' review of the test provide feedback that can help direct subsequent learning as well as subsequent teaching.

Performance Tests

Performance tests are most appropriately used to measure psychomotor performance in cases where assessing skills is essential. For example, in the road-test portion of a driver's examination, the applicant must demonstrate his control of the vehicle and his ability to drive safely. In this performance test, it is important that the driver not only be able to reach an objective (drive where told), but also that he exercise caution, obey traffic laws, and operate the vehicle with requisite skill. Performance tests must use real or simulated situations and sample the actual behaviors required.

In schools, performance tests are used in such areas as physical education, industrial arts, home economics, art, music, and driver education. Performance tests are essential in certain aspects of safety education. For example, in learning to use a power lathe, the pupil must demonstrate that he can operate the machine without injuring himself. In physical education, to avoid serious injury, it is important that the pupil demonstrate prerequisite skills before attempting advanced physical activity. Well-designed programs in any subject requiring safety precautions use performance testing and a system of checking to ensure that essential prerequisites have been acquired before allowing students to undertake advanced activities.

Because direct observation is the means of obtaining data and because much performance testing requires the teacher to observe one pupil's performance at a time, its use should be restricted to essential applications only. While supervising class activities, the teacher is observing performance regularly as part of the ongoing instructional process. In marking papers and paper-and-pencil tests, the teacher is observing the products of performance. But the performance test is a specific procedure that is best employed (1) to assess performance of essential psychomotor or safety skills, and (2) to judge performances of speech, singing, playing musical instruments, acting, and so on.

Performance is measured according to checklists or rating scales. The checklist is most appropriate for essential-level and safety skills. The teacher observes that the pupil performs each of the required component skills to an acceptable standard and checks them off. As in the driver's test, only after the pupil has demonstrated that he can perform all of the necessary essential-level skills is he allowed to progress to the advanced activity. The checklist indicates only the presence or absence of each required skill. It does not indicate the range of quality in the performance.

Performing arts are judged according to the quality of various components of the performance. Rating scales provide a structure to facilitate adjudication by (1) specifying the particular aspects of the performance to be assessed, (2) helping maintain similar criteria for all pupils, and (3) scoring the specific observations that are used in the overall evaluation (Gronlund, 1971).

A number of formats are used for rating scales. The three main types are numerical, verbal, and graphic. A numerical scale uses the lowest number to indicate poor performance and the highest number to represent superior or outstanding performance. For example, the following rating scale was used in a speech class. The teacher circled the number evaluating the performance of each component skill:

A.	Enunciation clear	1	2	3	4	5
B.	Correct use of grammar	1	2	3	4	5
C.	Subject well organized	1	2	3	4	5
D.	Effective use of words	1	2	3	4	5
E.	Pleasing voice	1	2	3	4	5

Verbal rating scales are constructed so that words describing the component skills are checked or circled. Examples of words used in evaluation are: *poor, fair, good,* or *never, seldom, frequently, always.*

Graphic rating scales may use the basic graphic methods employed in statistics. One of the simplest and most effective is the bar graph, in which the height of each bar indicates the level of performance of a particular skill.

Self-Evaluation

The development of self-evaluation can be encouraged by having pupils participate in marking and evaluating some of their own tests. They can be given keys and templates or rating scales with which to evaluate their own performances. Examples of high-quality products or performances can be used for means of comparison with their own products and performances. For instance, the pupil can compare his handwriting with a model paper and then employ a rating scale to assess the characteristics of his own handwriting. In the same way he can evaluate his shop project, painting, sewing, or sculpture against a sample. In oral reading, singing, and speaking, he can compare a tape recording of his performance with a sample recording of a high-quality performance.

Pupils who are accustomed to having someone else evaluate their performance will frequently find it difficult to evaluate their own. Because self-evaluation is such an important aspect of effective learning, it should be taught systematically. Initially, pupils should be given rating scales for simple tasks and be reinforced for their evaluations. This procedure can be gradually extended until several aspects of a performance are evaluated. Rating scales for self-evaluation can contribute significantly to developing the student's intrinsic motivation and internalized reinforcement.

Assignment

Complete the exercises in Chapter Eight of the Classroom Instruction Workbook.

References

Bloom, B. S. (ed.). *Taxonomy of Educational Objectives, Handbook I: Cognitive Domain*. New York: David McKay, 1956.

————, J. Hastings, and G. Madaus. *Handbook on Formative and Summative Evaluation of Student Learning*. New York: McGraw-Hill, 1971.

Educational Testing Service. *Making the Classroom Test: A Guide for Teachers*. Princeton, N.J.: Educational Testing Service, 1959.

Gronlund, N. *Measurement and Evaluation in Teaching*. New York: Macmillan, 1971.

Krathwohl, D. (ed.). *Taxonomy of Educational Objectives, Handbook II: Affective Domain*. New York: David McKay, 1964.

Webster, N. *Webster's New Twentieth-Century Dictionary*. New York: World Publishing, 1968.

Nine

Classroom Management

Objectives: After completing your study of this chapter, you will be able to (1) identify the purposes of classroom management, (2) arrange the physical facilities of the classroom, (3) schedule group learning activities, (4) plan lessons, (5) individualize instruction, (6) describe the role of reports and records in management, (7) implement effective discipline, (8) conduct a classroom program, and (9) complete the exercises in Chapter Nine of the Classroom Instruction Workbook.

The Competencies for Teaching system is designed to help the teacher acquire (1) teaching skills, (2) a conceptual model of the instructional process, and (3) relevant concepts of educational psychology, all of which are essential to effectively teaching any subject, at any educational level, in any classroom. Effective classroom management applies the learning principles and processes that you are acquiring through the Competencies for Teaching system. Although an elementary classroom accommodating a wide range of activities and subjects will have a different physical arrangement and organization from a secondary classroom in which a single subject is taught, the management of each should be based on the same conceptual model of the instructional process.

Well-arranged facilities and efficient routines for handling equipment and materials increase cooperation among pupils. The teacher whose classroom is well ordered and whose instruction is well organized will tend to have pupils who have orderly study habits. For some pupils, the classroom is the only environment in which they have an opportunity to learn about organization.

The primary purpose of a well-organized instructional environment is efficiency. This includes efficient instruction and use of teacher's and pupils' time as well as efficient use of instructional media. The efficient use of the physical classroom should facilitate achievement of essential-level objectives while promoting an atmosphere that fosters imaginative and creative activities.

Management in the classroom includes: (1) arranging the physical facilities, (2) scheduling group learning activities, (3) individualizing instruction, (4) employing additional personnel, (5) using reports and records, (6) carrying out discipline, and (7) conducting the classroom program.

Arranging the Physical Facilities

Furniture and equipment in the classroom should be arranged to provide a variety of activity areas or learning centers. Students' desks or worktables are arranged for group instruction so that they create a task area where the majority of essential-level objectives are assigned and where many are achieved. The balance of the space should be designated as subject or activity areas.

Organizing the elementary classroom into specialized activity areas makes it possible to centralize the materials, equipment, and pupils who are involved in a particular activity. The location in the classroom of the specialized areas should be based on three major considerations: their relationship to the room's fixed features, the functional relationships among the areas, and the classroom's primary pathways.

The classroom's fixed features—its doors, windows, lighting, closets, and sinks—should obviously be considered when organizing the specialized centers. "Messy" activities such as clay modeling and those requiring water (paints) should be located near the sink and not impede access to the sink from other areas. Closets and shelves should be employed to make materials readily accessible to the space designated for their use. All specialized activity centers should be organized around the fixed features required when engaging in these activities.

The functional relationships among the areas influence their location. Quiet areas should be grouped away from areas that generate noise. For example, the reading area should be comfortably quiet and uninterrupted by through-traffic. "Messy" areas that require special cleaning facilities should be grouped together.

The primary pathways for entering and leaving as well as for moving from area to area within the classroom must facilitate the pupils' orderly movement. If primary pathways or traffic routes are not planned efficiently, pupil traffic may create considerable disorder. For instance, children in certain activity areas need to dispose of waste materials. Placing small waste receptacles in these areas can reduce unnecessary traffic. These small waste receptacles can be emptied daily into the classroom wastebasket. The traffic pathways should resemble those of a well-organized business office. Such an arrangement would ensure that pupils will be appropriately dispersed throughout the activity areas, making maximum use of the facilities, under conditions of minimal congestion and little hindrance from cross-traffic.

Most specialized areas should accommodate four or more pupils. Limiting the number of occupants in an area permits (if it does not ensure) quiet interaction. Some areas should be expandable and contractible according to interests and needs.

Special areas are defined by furnishings and dividers that separate that area from the rest of the classroom.

Using different colors for each area can create a visual definition as well. Color-coding equipment can also be used to ensure that materials are returned to the correct area. This is helpful when materials from a specialized area are brought to the task area for instruction or an activity of the total group. The organization and display of the materials in an area should receive special attention. The attractiveness of the materials and their aesthetic arrangement elicit the pupils' attention and curiosity. It is important to strike a balance between an abundance of attractive materials that may stimulate a child's interest and a distracting clutter that could discourage him. The pupil should be able to locate and replace easily the materials he needs. Every item should have a specifically designated space, and everyone should learn to put things back into their assigned places.

The reading or library area should contain a reading table with chairs and attractively displayed books, magazines, dictionaries, encyclopedias, newspapers, articles, and reading-list suggestions. A pupil who has extra time may go to the library corner between assignments to read. This causes less disturbance than when a child gets a book, takes it to his desk, reads it while other pupils are completing their assignments, takes the book back to the shelf, and then returns to his seat. Of course, if the library corner is fully occupied, the above procedure may be unavoidable. Bookshelves can form the dividers for the area, which should be carpeted, comfortable, and quiet.

The science areas should contain collections of minerals, seeds, bulbs, plants, wood, insects, shells, live animals and fish in appropriate containers, cages, and aquariums. There should be ample working surfaces to permit pupils to examine objects and experiment with equipment. For primary children this area can also be a manipulative game area.

The arts and crafts area may include paints, brushes, chalk, crayons, scissors, paper, drawing boards, easels, clay, sand, tools, and other materials for creative activities. It should also contain smocks to protect clothing, plastic buckets and boxes for storing clay and other materials, as well as shelves on which finished products may be displayed.

The music area should contain such instruments as the following: piano, radio, record player, tape recorder, and rhythm-band instruments. Appropriate to the age of the pupils, it should also have other musical instruments, song books, sheet music, and similar musical materials.

The social studies area can be provided with a globe, maps, charts, models, pictures of historical and geographic interest, and a sand table for building model cities, mountain ranges, and so forth.

The mathematics area should contain concrete materials for mathematical experimentation, including abacus,

Cuisenaire rods, measurement devices, picture cards, flashcards, geometrical forms, mathematical diagrams, and pictures illustrating mathematical applications.

Booths or carrels can provide private spaces for study, rest, or reading. Any area set aside for a special activity should have all the equipment and materials necessary for that activity neatly stored, labeled, and displayed.

A classroom that has well-arranged facilities lends itself naturally to contingency management. The activity centers serve as reinforcers for pupils who have successfully completed their essential-level tasks. Many of the essential-level objectives will be achieved at the students' desks in the general task area, but some will be achieved in the specialized centers. The key to effective contingency management is immediately following the successful achievement of an essential-level task by permitting the student to engage in an activity that he or she enjoys. When a student achieves self-satisfaction in a particular subject, he may continue to explore that subject area during his reinforcement time. The pupil who does not achieve this degree of satisfaction in a subject will select a different and more rewarding activity. This reinforcement may in time result in accelerated achievement in the academic or troublesome subject, which may eventually produce its own intrinsic reinforcement. The gifted student will frequently achieve essential-level objectives in much less time than the average pupil and thereby spend more time in enrichment activities, achieving creativity and developmental objectives.

The teacher may encourage pupils to bring reinforcing materials from home. These should be placed in appropriate areas. An efficient contingency-managed classroom can readily achieve both individualization of instruction and attainment of essential-level objectives. The classroom whose facilities are organized into a variety of centers for simultaneous activities provides an ideal physical setting for contingency management.

The physical facilities of the secondary classroom can be arranged along the same principles as those described for the elementary classroom; however, the arrangement will be based on the specialized purpose of the classroom. The physical organization of classrooms in the science, physical education, social studies, industrial education, and home economics departments is based on their specialized needs.

Scheduling Group Learning Activities

Confronted with the problem of scheduling group learning activities to accomplish prescribed curricula in various school subjects, the teacher should begin with writing daily schedules. In secondary schools and some elementary schools, the daily schedules are dictated by the school's timetable. This general schedule controls the number of periods per week and the amount of time allotted to each subject. When timetables are not provided, many schools indicate the approximate allotment of time for each subject or activity. Even when the teacher is permitted flexibility in scheduling, there are usually fixed times when school begins, for recess, lunch, dismissal, as well as for school assemblies, the use of the gymnasium, and other special facilities.

Some classrooms are operated on fixed schedules. The following is an example of a fifth-grade daily timetable:

9:00- 9:15	Opening exercises and attendance
9:15-10:05	Reading—workbook, discussion, directed study
10:05-10:30	Fine arts—music, art, crafts
10:30-10:45	Recess—organized games
10:45-11:05	English—composition, grammar
11:05-11:30	Physical education—health, hygiene, safety
11:30-12:00	Group projects
12:00- 1:30	Lunch
1:30- 2:20	Mathematics—arithmetic, problem solving
2:20- 3:00	Science and social studies
3:00- 3:15	Spelling and writing

This fixed schedule was managed in a Competencies for Teaching classroom. Lessons were taught and task assignments were designed so that almost all children achieved essential-level objectives each period, well within the allotted time. This provided time for reinforcement activities during each period of the day except for opening exercises, physical education, and group projects.

A flexible schedule in which a week's activities are designed to provide the correct balance between subject areas is preferable because more time may be required to achieve an essential-level objective than a fixed schedule specifies. It is more efficient to ensure that the class members have achieved an objective and that they have had time for a reinforcing activity than it is to stop and begin another activity because of a fixed schedule.

Team teaching, specialist teachers who instruct children from several classrooms in one subject, and vertical grouping (that is, grouping children according to their performance level in a particular subject) may limit the flexibility available to the classroom teacher. Each classroom teacher must adjust to the school's fixed schedule for assigned library periods, specialists' schedules, and time limits imposed by the school's timetable.

PLANNING LESSONS

It is important for each school day to be a succession of varied and stimulating activities designed to develop pupils to their maximum capacities during the time available. A *lesson plan* is simply an outline prepared in advance of teaching, so that time and materials will be used efficiently. The Competencies for Teaching system encourages the teacher to prepare lesson plans. These consist of brief statements of the minimum essentials that must be determined for a lesson to be taught effectively. Excessive detail should be avoided because pupils do not conform to elaborate, formal, written specifications and do not give the exact responses or answers that such a plan requires. There is a tendency for the teacher who prepares elaborately detailed plans to become tied to the plans and to ignore meaningful incidental experiences not anticipated during planning.

Various types of lessons require different kinds of lesson plans. The present discussion deals primarily with lessons for achieving essential-level objectives in basic school subjects. Enrichment lessons, such as field trips, review-and-drill, or practice lessons do not require lesson plans in the formal sense. The teacher should identify the purpose or objective of exploratory learning activities, but the desired outcomes are in each pupil's individual creativity and personal development. Class discussions following a field trip and group discussion about projects are most effective when they center on the pupils' interests. The teacher may preplan the stimulus events to start such lessons and may contribute questions during the discussions, but the objective is to involve the pupils in working toward their own unique solutions. In other words, planning for achievement of creativity and developmental objectives through informed, incidental, and enrichment activities requires the teacher's careful consideration, but the preplanning should be limited primarily to identifying stimulus events to initiate these learning activities.

On the other hand, achieving the essential-level objectives delineated by a curriculum almost demands preplanning the lessons. Preplanning is required because the direction in which the lesson is to move is predetermined by the curriculum. Essential-level objectives are convergent and predictable, whereas creativity and developmental objectives are divergent and unpredictable.

Before writing an essential-level lesson plan, the teacher should study the course and unit objectives and select the topic for the lesson. Then the lesson and enroute objectives are identified and written, as described in Chapter Five, "Enroute Objectives." Next the teacher describes how to introduce the lesson so that attention, interest, and motivation are elicited. Finally the elicitors to bring about the behaviors described in the enroute objectives are listed, including the instructional materials, the methods of presentation, some of the key questions to ask the pupils, and the assignment or test to be performed by the pupils. To prepare the elicitor list efficiently, the teacher must be familiar with the physical assets of the school and the availability of audiovisual equipment and instructional materials. The lesson plan should also specify the reinforcement that will be provided for correct responses.

Once this preplanning is completed, the teacher has a clear guide for effective action. She or he knows the materials that must be obtained or prepared before instruction begins. She has a clear statement of objectives describing pupil behavior, so that feedback from observing pupils' performance, including students' answers to questions, keeps her informed about the students' progress. She has an introduction or opening for the lesson with which (1) to relate the lesson to previous learning, (2) to interest the class by asking about their experiences or by telling an interesting story, showing a sample product resulting from the successful completion of the lesson, displaying a visual aid or other novel stimulus material, and (3) to share the lesson's objective with the class. The teacher has a list of things to do, materials to present, show, or demonstrate, key questions to ask, and an assignment or test for the students to perform at the end of the sequence. She has also identified some of the reinforcers she will employ. Her lesson plan is an outline of essentials that will make the teaching efficient by keeping the lesson moving in the right direction and avoiding wasted time and unnecessary repetition or duplication of effort.

The following example of a third-grade arithmetic lesson illustrates the procedure of lesson planning. The topic of the final unit of the course is "Roman Numerals." The purposes of the unit are to teach the everyday uses of Roman numerals, how to read Roman numerals, and how to write Roman numerals. The teacher's plan for the first lesson in this unit included the following.

Arithmetic—Grade III

Topic: Roman Numerals   Lesson: 1

<u>Objectives</u>—Know Roman numerals I to XII

1. Identify uses of Roman numerals.

2. Recall the letters in Roman numerals I to XII.

3. Arrange volumes of *The Book of Knowledge* in order by numbers using the order on the clock face.

4. Write Arabic and Roman numerals from 1 to 12 and I to XII.

<u>Introduction</u>

1. Show pictures and tell story "Grandfather's Clock."

2. Ask questions about where pupils have seen Roman numerals.

3. Show pictures of classroom sign, "Grade III," monument with date in Roman numerals, school timetable with grades in Roman numerals, and Queen Elizabeth II and Pope Paul VI.

4. Visit the Official Opening plaque in the front hall of the school.

<u>Elicitors</u>

Instructional Materials:

Clock face with Roman numerals
The Book of Knowledge
Picture of monument
Grade III sign
Books with chapters in Roman numerals
School timetable
Pictures of Queen Elizabeth II and Pope Paul VI

Method of Presentation: Explain equivalence of Arabic and Roman numerals. Demonstrate writing Roman numerals I to XII.

Questions:

    Where have you seen Roman numerals?

    Which letters are in I to XII? (*I, V, X*)

    How many grades are on this timetable?

    What time does the clock show?

Assignment—Mimeographed assignment sheet (see sample)

Reinforcement—Praise, check marks, taking correct or corrected assignments home to parents.

Roman Numerals

Date: _____   Name: _____

1. Fill in the blanks on the clock with Roman numerals.

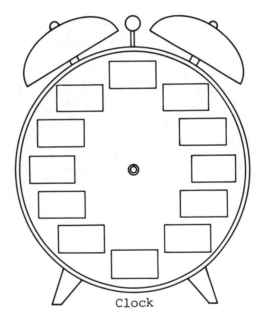

Clock

2. Draw the clock hands on the clock for 3 o'clock.

3. Opposite each number write Roman numerals.

2. _____	6. _____	10. _____	1. _____
5. _____	8. _____	12. _____	7. _____
4. _____	9. _____	3. _____	11. _____

4. Opposite each Roman numeral write our (Arabic) number.

    V. _____   IX. _____   IV. _____

    II. _____   VII. _____   XI. _____

This sample lesson plan was completed during one mathematics period; however, a more complex lesson might take more than one period. For example, a field trip or an experiment might be included. Students might be introduced to the lesson and then be required to do some library research or home study to complete the assignment. In either case, the format of the lesson plan would remain the same.

Now return and study the lesson plan and imagine that you are teaching this introductory lesson on Roman numerals to an advanced third-grade class. The lesson objective, "Know Roman numerals I to XII," describes what the pupils will know at the termination of the lesson. The four enroute objectives are guideposts toward that objective and describe pupil behaviors indicating achievement of the lesson's objectives. In the introduction you involve the pupils and relate the lesson to their experience with Roman numerals both in school and outside of school. The elicitor you have selected brings forth behaviors that involve the pupils in learning about Roman numerals I to XII and transferring and generalizing their knowledge. You asked many questions that elicited pupils' recalling Roman numerals in various situations. The lesson plan listed only a few key questions that you considered important to remember. The pupils' assignment was completed in pencil. As each pupil indicated completion, you checked and praised correct answers. The students erased and corrected incorrect answers. The assignments were taken home to share with parents. You probably observed that this type of outline lesson plan provided adequate guidance to keep the lesson moving in the right direction. An outline lesson plan requires a minimal amount of your time for preparation while providing the essential structure needed for efficient teaching. By filing this plan, the next time you teach this lesson you will have a ready reference for the materials and preparation needed for the lesson.

After the lesson was completed, you evaluated the results and made some notes regarding how to improve the next presentation. The student teacher or any teacher wishing to improve instructional skills is advised to (1) write an outline lesson plan, (2) tape-record the teaching of the lesson, (3) listen later to the tape and evaluate each part of the lesson plan and its effects, and (4) revise the plan for the next presentation.

Each teacher should have his own lesson plans to suit his style and situation. The above example is not presented as an ideal lesson plan but only as an illustration of the value of this type of outline plan. Published lesson plans and those available in schools and media centers can be helpful, but in most cases the teacher should adapt them to fit the particular situation.

Individualizing Instruction

During the individual instruction phase of this system, you acquired the skills of a tutor, that is, teaching in a one-to-one situation. Tutoring, or individual instruction, differs from *individualized instruction* in that the latter term usually implies individualizing instruction within a class. Individualizing instruction is an effort to meet the educational needs of each child as a separate human being. Recently there has been a growing emphasis on individualization, or treating each child as a unique entity within the classroom. Individualizing instruction is based first on the idea that no two children learn in precisely the same way or at the same pace, and second, on the observation that progress for any given child is uneven.

Individual instruction, or tutoring, as employed in the first phase of the Competencies for Teaching system, has two main functions. The first is to provide extensive and intensive individual instruction for a child. The second is to offer the student teacher the means of acquiring skills that can be used either in the tutorial situation or in individualizing instruction in the classroom. Integrating methods from individual instruction into the classroom helps adapt group instruction to try to meet each child's particular needs.

The methods of group instruction described in this textbook accommodate individual differences in practical ways that are not too demanding of teacher time. For example, contingency management allows children different amounts of time to complete essential-level tasks and permits individualization of reinforcement. Token economies allow children flexibility in timing and selecting reinforcement. Programed instruction is self-paced. Individually initiated projects and self-evaluation contribute to personalizing education. Competencies for Teaching classrooms provide for these and other means of individualizing instruction within the framework of group instruction.

GROUPING

One important traditional means of accommodating individual differences is *grouping*. Achievement patterns vary widely from subject to subject and from student to student. Primary classrooms have usually consisted of three reading groups—one for the top, one for the average, and one for the slow readers. Some schools are formally organized for grouping so that each pupil attends the class for each of his basic subjects at his level of achievement. For example, this method would permit a pupil to attend reading with a third-grade reading group and mathematics with a fifth-grade mathematics group. A full description of the various grouping plans is beyond the scope of this chapter. Some books that provide useful information on grouping are listed in the references at the end of this chapter: Benton (1962), Goodland and Anderson (1959), and Matthews and Chalmers (1959).

PROGRAMS FOR ACCOMMODATING INDIVIDUAL DIFFERENCES

There has been a number of experimental designs for individualizing instruction. All have essentially the same goal—to offer alternatives to traditional lockstep education. Some of the more notable programs are (1) individualized instruction, (2) self-selected education, (3) continuous progress education, and (4) the open classroom.

Individualized Instruction

Although individualized instruction is part of most classroom instruction, there have been attempts recently to develop personalized educational programs for each pupil. An objective of individualized instruction is to make education a pleasant experience and to help pupils develop independent behavior.

In most individualized instruction programs, the classroom teacher has the assistance of at least one teacher aide and, in some cases, volunteers. Because there is no formal group instruction, the aides or volunteers are available to help each child, as needed, with whatever subject or unit of instruction the child is working on. Whenever possible, instruction is built into the materials available to the pupil. The teacher, teacher aides, and volunteers answer questions or provide other help when pupils reach an impasse. The teacher aides and volunteers also correct assignments, mark tests, and assist in keeping records. Individualized instruction programs tend to make considerable use of programed instruction, teaching machines, child-operated audiovisual equipment, and computer terminals for computer-assisted instruction.

Individualized instruction may range from highly permissive, allowing each pupil to engage in activities of his own choice, or it may be highly structured, in which the teacher examines each pupil's progress and prescribes each day's instruction. In a structured program each pupil is given assigned tasks. When he feels that he has mastered a unit of study he asks to be tested. In this structure, the teacher is responsible for selecting assignments. The objectives of individualized instruction seek to: (1) develop the pupil's confidence in his own ability, (2) teach the child to be responsible for his own achievement, and (3) help the pupil realize that achievement is dependent on his participation and initiative.

Many programs of individualized instruction are currently in operation; however, the following have received widespread attention: Individually Prescribed Instruction (IPI), University of Pittsburgh; Individually Guided Education (IGE), University of Wisconsin; and Program for Learning in Accordance with Needs (PLAN), Westinghouse Learning Corporation.

Self-Selected Education

Personalizing education through "self-selection" has been part of the progressive movement in education for many years. Self-selected education emphasizes self-initiated learning activities, self-determined progress, self-selected materials, self-scheduling, and self-evaluation. The pupil plans his own education while the teacher is available as a consultant, counselor, and monitor.

Self-selected education is based on the theory that the pupil knows best *what* he needs to learn at a particular time, *how* he can best learn it, and *when* he has learned it. For many pupils this seems to hold true. For these students, self-selected education develops positive attitudes toward learning. A serious limitation occurs, however, when the child withdraws from an area of greatest need. Within the program, the pupil may either return to his area of need or he may continue to withdraw. Most parents and teachers will not accept that a child of normal ability does not need to learn to read, for example, even though the child may not wish to read. In other words, most teachers and parents are not willing to grant children total freedom of choice regarding what they are to learn and how they are to learn it.

Continuous Progress Education

In continuous progress education, each pupil advances from level to level in a subject at his own rate. Instead of being grouped into grades, pupils are brought together to be taught a subject according to their readiness to learn certain skills. Each pupil moves forward after mastering a particular skill, with no time limits imposed. In continuous progress education, grades are unnecessary, making possible nongraded schools. The pupil engages in continuous progress in each academic area rather than being placed in a grade. Grades in subjects also become irrelevant. Some continuous progress programs grant only one score—a pass mark. As soon as the pupil earns a pass mark, he or she progresses to the next course. A modified version of this system grants a pass mark for mastering the essential-level objectives, and an honors mark for outstanding achievement of creativity- and developmental-level objectives.

Although some continuous progress education can be employed in an individual classroom, its full implementation requires that the whole school employ the system. Computer scheduling can make it possible for an entire school system to plan continuous progress education. To be effective, continuous progress scheduling requires precise and relevant terminal and enroute objectives. Even though continuous progress scheduling is applicable to all levels of education and is consistent with the best available knowledge about human learning, individual differences, growth, and development, it presents problems that are to date unresolved. For example, how do we identify the point at which one graduates from elementary, secondary, or higher education? Does graduation consist of a certain number of courses or units completed? Does it consist of an average amount achieved in all courses? How will graduation from continuous progress programs relate to traditional standards of professional training and certification? At present there are no generally accepted answers to these questions.

The Open Classroom

"Open education" incorporates many aspects of the other methods of individualization described earlier. The "open classroom" is not so much a specifically definable method as it is the provision of a generally supportive environment in which teachers guide and manage learning in a partnership with their pupils. Cooperatively planning educational activities and sharing objectives are essential components of open education. The emphasis is on both individual and cooperative learning, in which the pupil works to achieve both personal and group objectives.

The "open education" movement has been implemented most successfully in the British infant schools. The British infant school has no exact counterpart in American education. British children begin their formal education at five years of age and remain in the infant school through their seventh year. At eight years of age, they move on without an examination to the junior school, where they remain through the age of eleven. The British refer to infant and junior schools together as "primary" schools.

The basis of the open classroom in the British infant school is called the "integrated day," in which the child exercises a great degree of choice about what he does and when he does it (Taylor, 1972). It is called the integrated day because it is a form of organization in which the activities "form a whole," in contrast to the traditional classroom, in which there is a series of separate subject periods. Although children exercise a high degree of choice, the teacher integrates the daily program to ensure that learning takes place. The central direction may be less obvious than in the traditional classroom, but the structure of the successfully integrated program must be even more methodical and carefully planned than is necessary when there is a more clearly defined structure. Taylor emphasizes the importance of this integrated structure in the British infant school and outlines a systematic sequence of stages for making a transition from a traditional classroom to an open classroom.

There has been a long-standing need to open up the classroom and further individualize and humanize education, but there are liabilities in the wholesale and sudden adoption of a program developed for a different educational system from a different society. Therefore, although some valuable lessons can be learned from the British experience with open classrooms, it is not recommended that the total British model be imported and implemented.

To begin with, English school children generally bring from their homes and communities a cult of respect and obedience for adult authority much less common in American children. In addition, the teacher in the English school occupies a different status in the community from that of the teacher in the American school, and as a consequence, he or she is granted more autonomy by parents and educational authorities than is the American teacher. Expectations of public education in the two countries are quite different, directly related to educational requirements for employment in each country. (American employers frequently require a higher level of academic education and insist more often on a college diploma as a prerequisite of employment than do English employers.) For these reasons, it seems more practical for teachers in America to develop classrooms consistent with American needs. Hertzberg and Stone (1971) describe a particularly "American approach" to the open classroom.

DEVELOPING INDIVIDUALIZATION

The Competencies for Teaching classroom permits individualizing education while ensuring achievement of essential-level objectives. This is accomplished through contingency management based on developmentally sequenced enroute objectives—an effective means of achieving essential levels based on sound learning principles. Personalizing education to achieve individual, creative, and developmental objectives is attained by providing a more open situation that allows pupils to choose and manage their individual learning activities. This would include the choice of continuing with a learning task that has become engrossing. So far, the description of the Competencies for Teaching classroom has shown how special activity centers and reinforcement areas can provide for differences in interest and rates of learning. A classroom managed along these lines is a good place for the teacher to begin individualizing instruction. Through the use of contingency management, the teacher is able to exercise control of the learning process. Once the teacher is confident that the classroom management is effective, he or she may wish to attempt more individualization by exploring some of the approaches described above. Take care, however, to implement only one innovation at a time so that its outcome may be precisely identified and evaluated.

Effectively managing the classroom makes a significant contribution to attaining all educational objectives. The most important of these objectives is that the child *learn*. All of the arguments, no matter how convincing, and all of the new theories of instruction, no matter how popular, are worthless unless they result in the pupils' learning more effectively and to greater purpose.

To achieve a balance between essential-level activities and individualization it may be helpful to look at the extremes. Some educators have become so devoted to the idea of permissiveness and openness that they condemn straightforward teaching and believe that it is enough to supply pupils with instructional materials and leave it to the pupils to find their own way. These educators imply that to direct the pupils' learning is somehow a violation of individuality and freedom. Some of these educators appear to make a virtue of having noisy or unorganized classrooms. In *The Open Classroom*, Kohl (1969) goes so far as to suggest that if another teacher is upset by the noise coming from your classroom, "Perhaps you can find that teacher's weakness and complain about it, instead of being defensive about the noise in one's own room." Hostility toward the traditional educational establishment may be justified, but antagonizing professional colleagues is counterproductive and presents maladaptive models of behavior for pupils. In direct contrast, the extreme of traditional authoritarian education is typified by a teacher's lecturing in front of rows of silent, bored children deprived of their rights as individuals by a prisonlike school system. The liabilities of a lockstep educational system have become increasingly evident.

The pupil's own investigations and discoveries create a large measure of his excitement and satisfaction in learning. Sharing his findings with his classmates and his teacher adds to his enjoyment of learning through discovery. These independent activities are tremendously worthwhile, but so is learning that some things are important enough that the class members should attend at one time to what the teacher has to say. Learning that attaining certain essential-level objectives is valuable for everyone and experiencing efficient group methods of achieving them are important aspects of socialization. Learning to conform only to externally imposed demands limits individual potential. Learning to conform only to individual needs limits social development. The pupil who is learning to meet both his own and the group's needs is developing convergent and divergent behaviors essential to the dynamic process of adjustment.

Personnel

The Competencies for Teaching system is concerned with developing essential teaching skills that can be used in a variety of instructional situations. Basically, classroom instruction consists of the teacher's interaction with the class. Instruction in many classrooms, however, involves additional personnel.

THE TEACHER AIDE

A teacher aide employed by the school system can relieve the teacher of a great many nonteaching duties and facilitate the teacher's professional task of teaching. Studies have shown that a large portion of the teacher's day is given over to duties that require little or no professional teaching competence. These duties were traditionally perceived as teaching functions. One study showed that teachers spent an average of twenty-six percent of their teaching time on such nonteaching routine chores as completing attendance sheets and other records, collecting class funds for a variety of projects, cleaning chalkboards, helping children with their clothing, monitoring lunchrooms, supervising playgrounds, and so forth (Morse, 1960).

Physicians, lawyers, engineers, and architects use the services of secretaries, clerks, draftsmen, and technicians to relieve them of paperwork, routine tasks, and nonprofessional duties. Unfortunately, the highly skilled, truly professional teacher has been required to spend many precious hours in nonprofessional activities, when the evidence is quite clear that the learning process would be facilitated if the competent teacher actually had time to teach.

Employing a part-time or full-time teacher aide provides greater opportunity for the teacher to use his professional skills. Some of the duties that a teacher aide could assume include: (1) maintaining the classroom, (2) supervising playground and lunchroom activities, (3) assisting the teacher, (4) assisting pupils, and (5) performing clerical tasks.

Maintaining the classroom refers to such duties as: preparing the classroom each morning—checking lighting, ventilation, bookshelves, and supplies; assisting pupils in keeping desks, storage of supplies, reading tables and chairs, books, plants, cages, and aquarium in order; preparing instructional materials—filmstrips, projectors, screen, record player, word cards, and so forth, and returning them when no longer needed; assisting in assembling bulletin board displays and keeping them current; and keeping chalkboards clean and ready for use.

Supervising playground and lunchroom activities includes: supervising pupils moving from the classroom to the playground or lunchroom, assembling materials for games, helping to supervise playground activities, and assisting in supervision during lunchtime.

Assisting the teacher includes: reading stories for pupils during story time; making charts, word cards, displays, or other teaching materials; helping individuals or groups of pupils follow instructions; operating audiovisual equipment; preparing materials in advance of instruction—cutting paper, mixing paints, and so on; and supervising the class when the teacher is called from the classroom.

Assisting the pupils includes: helping children with coats and overshoes, accompanying children to administrative offices or the school's medical or dental clinic; working with children during recreational activities, helping children in need of special practice after skills have been taught by the teacher, and observing children for problems including indications of illness.

Performing clerical tasks includes: taking attendance and making attendance reports, typing and duplicating teacher-prepared materials, collecting and recording special accounts for photographs or Junior Red Cross, and assisting in other secretarial tasks.

These lists indicate only a few of the possible duties that a teacher aide could perform. The qualifications determined by each school system's board of education, the amount of time available, the legal specifications of the teacher aide's role, and the teacher's ability to organize and delegate responsibility determine the functions that the teacher aide can assume. Only experience will permit further delineation and clarification of the teacher aide's potential (Esbensen, 1966). The background and required special training of teacher aides varies so greatly that sweeping generalizations about their functions are unwarranted at this time.

VOLUNTEERS

Volunteers, particularly in nursery school, kindergarten, and the primary grades, are being used increasingly in many schools. The volunteers are usually mothers of children in the school, but a number of volunteers are being recruited from other groups as well.

TEAM TEACHING

Team teaching results in a variable personnel structure for the classroom. For example, one team consisted of a teacher who acted as the team leader, three other teachers, a teacher aide, and seventy-eight first-grade pupils. Under the direction of the leader, the teachers and teacher aide planned the program for the total group. The program included group instruction in lettering for all seventy-eight pupils simultaneously. An overhead projector magnified on a large screen the teacher's demonstration of how to form letters. Each child could see the demonstration more clearly than if it had been conducted in a regular-sized class with the teacher using the chalkboard. Also, three teachers and an aide supervised and assisted individuals having difficulty carrying out the instructions. Later the large group was rearranged into smaller groups, each having one teacher. This type of team teaching requires sharing objectives and the responsibility for achieving them among the teachers and aides. Efficiently operated, a team can use more effectively each teacher's special strengths and talents.

Records and Reports

The requirements for record-keeping vary from school to school. Some school principals expect the teacher to keep extensive anecdotal records (describing students' behavior and performance) and submit previews of each day's lessons. Some schools provide the teacher with a daybook in which to keep these records. In most schools, teachers are responsible for such records as attendance, grades, classroom requisitions, and certain anecdotal summaries. The teacher must become familiar with the forms used in his or her school, since the requirements vary widely from one district to another.

Making reports of students' progress, as in all other aspects of teaching, ought to be an integral part of the instructional process. Reporting practices influence the pupils' and parents' feelings and behavior. The progress report can be either a powerful reinforcement or a punishment influencing the pupil's motivation. The traditional methods of reporting contradict sound learning principles. The old system of comparing a student's achievement through ranking or assigning letter grades according to a curve provides a very inaccurate picture of the student's progress.

A number of attempts have been made to resolve the problems of traditional grading and reporting. "Pass-fail" is growing in popularity because it reduces competition for grades. Another attempt, written evaluations, summarizes the student's strengths and weaknesses but risks being excessively subjective. "Contract grading" occurs when the student and teacher agree in a written "contract" on the content to be covered and the criteria to be used in grading. "Performance curriculum" communicates to the student a sequence of behavioral objectives so that he knows how many of these he must achieve to be awarded a particular grade.

Ungraded schools and other systems that individualize instruction can establish different criteria to measure performance to evaluate an individual's achievement. Such criteria avoid the problem of evaluating an individual's performance in relation to that of others. When students know the objectives they have to attain, they can pace themselves. Learning is more effective when the essential level of each objective, criterion, or performance standard must be achieved before others are attempted. Reporting that communicates the objectives attained by the student provides an accurate description of the progress. The Progress Report used in *Individual Instruction* employs this method of reporting. Some form of criteria-referenced measurement appears to be essential for the process of individualized instruction to be complete and effective.

At present, however, there is little agreement among educators about grading and how to report progress. The teacher is usually required to use the method adopted by the particular school or school system.

Discipline

As used in education, the word *discipline* has several meanings. It is used to refer to a branch of knowledge or study. It is used also to describe the results of study or training. The individual who develops self-control, orderliness, and efficiency is said to have discipline or a disciplined mind. In a different sense, it is used to mean punishment inflicted in an attempt to correct behavior. It is used also as a general term for the teacher's control of pupil behavior. The following brief discussion will deal with discipline for the sake of correcting and controlling behavior.

The methods described throughout the Competencies for Teaching system are designed to develop the pupil's self-discipline. Achieving self-evaluation as a reinforcement leads the pupil to self-monitoring and self-correcting behavior, which is the goal of self-discipline. The Competencies for Teaching method supplies interventions for dealing with behavior disturbances while offering the teacher effective means for strengthening desirable behavior and eliminating undesirable behavior. These teaching methods for effective classroom management will result in minimizing problems in behavior and discipline.

Serious, chronic behavior disorders require a long-term, consistent instructional program based on sound learning principles. Some children who have behavior problems benefit greatly from individual instruction, in which they acquire the essential behaviors for successful classroom participation. The next phase of the Competencies for Teaching system, *Therapeutic Instruction*, will present further information about remediating behavior disorders. The present discussion focuses on temporary behavioral upsets that may occur in normal children in even the best-managed classrooms.

Everyone suffers some degree of loss of behavior control from time to time. This can occur in the normally well-adjusted individual because of extreme provocation, stress, or temporary physical illness. When the individual intent on achieving a worthwhile goal is continually interrupted by another person, he may be provoked into a violent verbal or physical outburst. A highly competent, mature individual may become aware of his heightened anxiety and take corrective action by becoming assertive and heading off the offender before his or her frustration reaches the breaking point, or by stopping the activity until he or she regains control. Although many adults have not learned to cope with frustrating circumstances constructively, the teacher should not be discouraged from trying to help children cope more effectively with frustration. The classroom should be managed so that frustration-provoking conditions are minimized. It is, of course, impossible to eliminate these conditions entirely. Interactions among children will sometimes lead to altercations and disruptive behavior. Or, frustration and personal difficulties can result in the child's temporary loss of behavior control.

For the normal individual, stress occurs when one is confronted by a situation with which he feels he cannot cope. When one is confronted with a problem, anxiety rises. If the individual has a repertoire of behaviors that are appropriate for the situation, anxiety is reduced and feelings of satisfaction ensue. In the classroom, the child may sustain anxiety about a learning problem to the point of temporarily losing emotional or behavioral control. Temporary physical illness—a cold, a headache, or a stomach ache—can result in reduced tolerance for annoyances, causing the child to be more easily upset.

In a well-managed classroom, one child's temporary upset does not always create serious problems for the rest of the class. Whenever the pupil can regain control and find his own solution, he should be encouraged to do so.

When a child loses his temper and appears unable to bring it under control quickly, the teacher should firmly command the child to stop the behavior and then allow him time to regain his composure. If this fails, the child should be given time-out. If, during the episode of misbehavior, property is damaged or materials upset, the child should be required to replace the materials or correct the damage. Any discussion of the problem should take place after the child has regained his composure. Attempts at rational discussion while the child is upset are unproductive and even harmful. Under highly charged emotional conditions, individuals can acquire irrational ideas and prejudices to justify the misbehavior.

The teacher can provide the most effective remediation in these situations by first, applying a sound educational solution, and second, having a preplanned intervention procedure. A sound educational solution is based on the teacher's viewing the child's misbehavior as an opportunity for the child to learn behavioral control. This is in contrast to some counterproductive measures, such as responding to the upset by giving the child reinforcing attention consisting of either reprimands or sympathy, treating the incident as a serious, not-to-be-forgotten offense causing the child to feel excessive guilt, or becoming upset and establishing a maladaptive model of how to cope with problems. By applying the model of the instructional process, the teacher can achieve a sound educational solution.

When the teacher observes that a child's behavior is out of control or is excessively disruptive, the terminal objective for the teacher's intervention should be to bring the behavior under control in such a manner that the child learns self-control. The first eliciting cue must obtain the child's attention and the second elicitor must stop the behavior. Usually, calling the child by name will get his attention, but sometimes it is necessary to go to the child and touch him or take him by the hand. The next step is to command him to stop. If this fails, he should be told to leave the area and sit in a chair set apart from the areas occupied by the other pupils. A chair at the side of the room and near the teacher's desk has been found effective because it adds the teacher's proximity as an aid to control. The next eliciting cue is to tell the child that after a specified time he may return to classroom activities. For example, he may be told that five minutes after he has settled down quietly in the chair he can return to normal activities. An additional cue in the form of a prediction is frequently helpful in controlling behavior and in building the child's confidence that he can solve his problem. For example, the teacher can tell the child, "In a few minutes you will settle down, and then, after your time-out, you will return to your work, pick up your books, and all will be well again." During this time-out, the child should not receive any reinforcement. If reinforcement is given during this period, it may be too close in time to the maladaptive behavior. The child should not be reinforced for a behavioral sequence that begins with his dropping out of an appropriate activity, misbehaving, then behaving properly during time-out. Reinforcement should be reinstated only after he is back in the classroom activity and has earned the reinforcement.

Later, the teacher may help conceptualize behavioral control by counseling the child; that is, the teacher helps the child see that by stopping his behavior himself, he would have been able to avoid the difficulties he created. This facilitates internalization of control so that next time the child may stop his own misbehavior. Of course, stopping behavior is not the ultimate goal of self-discipline; it is only the first step. Every child should receive the help he needs to arrive at constructive alternatives. If a pupil is frustrated in solving problems, he should stop and seek help or try a different approach. If he is being bothered by another pupil, he should learn how to be assertive in requesting cessation of the annoying behavior. If conflict arises between pupils, they should be encouraged to analyze the difficulty or seek arbitration. These solutions require social maturity that can be acquired only over time.

By applying sound educational solutions to the temporary behavior disorders of normal children, the teacher contributes to the development of self-directed behavior. Self-control that leads to manufacturing constructive alternatives is consistent with good mental health. By learning adaptive behaviors, the pupil avoids excessive anxiety under normal circumstances. Through acquiring constructive alternatives, problem solving, and other adaptive behaviors, the pupil derives satisfaction while avoiding excessive repression.

Some of the traditional approaches to discipline were based on the idea that the child should repress his feelings and be unresponsive to frustration, boredom, interference, or other provocation. Moderate repression is a normal adjustment mechanism but excessive repression is maladaptive. Through generalization of the procedure described above, the teacher can manage behavior disturbances so that the pupil internalizes adaptive behavior control.

By preplanning intervention procedures, the teacher can discipline effectively when necessary and avoid confusion, indecision, and anxiety. The teacher's confidence and competence in handling behavior problems reassures the child and helps him learn self-management. The preplanned general procedure described below helps the teacher act with confidence and competence.

GENERAL PROCEDURE FOR DISCIPLINE

1. <u>Warning</u>. When a pupil misbehaves, call him by name, warn him to stop the behavior, and then redirect him back to the task at hand. If the misbehavior stops, allow him a short time to settle down. After he has returned to his learning task and is engaged in appropriate activity, reinforcement should be reinstated. If you feel that the child requires a stronger warning, go to him, elicit his attention, command him to cease the misbehavior, and tell him that he is to be back to work in one minute. The time limit is up to the teacher's judgment, based on the degree of disturbance, but for a normal child it should not be a long period of time. If the child does not appear to be seriously upset, a limit of ten to thirty seconds is usually effective.

2. <u>Classroom Time-Out</u>. If, after the above procedure, the pupil is not responding appropriately, he should be given time-out. This means that he has time-out from positive reinforcement. In the classroom, this is best accomplished by having the pupil sit apart from other class members for a few minutes, during which time he is not allowed anything with which to work or play. Sitting quietly by while classmates are actively engaged in activities for perhaps fifteen minutes usually results in the pupil's returning to classroom activities and behaving appropriately. It is essential that the pupil not get reinforcement from classmates during time-out. Inform the class that to help this pupil "we must all leave him alone while he is sitting in this chair." It is important also that the pupil not escape from completing essential-level tasks because of time-out. If he was engaged in an essential-level task, he must return and complete it even though his classmates may be engaged in a more enjoyable activity.

3. <u>Isolation Time-Out</u>. If the misbehavior interferes with others or is severe, the child may be isolated for time-out. He or she may be taken or sent into the hall or a suitable room for isolation. The child should be told that he can return either when he feels ready to go back to work or that he can return in a specified time. In most cases, five to twenty minutes is an effective time-out. Long periods of time-out should be avoided.

Time-out is effective only when it occurs in the context of much positive reinforcement for behaviors that are incompatible with misbehavior. If the classroom is not positively reinforcing, taking the pupil out of the room is not time-out from reinforcement. In fact, placing him in the hall may allow him an escape from an uncomfortable situation and thus reinforce misconduct. Negative reinforcement occurs when the behavior (misconduct) removes the aversive stimuli (removes the child from the classroom to isolation). In this situation, isolation reinforces misconduct.

4. <u>Refer the Pupil</u>. Rarely will the misbehavior persist after a number of repetitions of the above procedure. If the classroom is giving the child ample reinforcement for appropriate behavior, and reinforcement is withheld for inappropriate behavior, behavior control and improvement will result. If improvement is occurring, the teacher should persist with the procedures just described. Most other methods may produce undesirable side effects.

When the misbehavior persists, is dangerous to the child or others, or when it causes excessive interference with classroom activities, the teacher should send or escort the child to the principal's office. The child may spend time-out at the office or be sent home for a specified time. In most schools, the decision to send the child home must have administrative approval.

A well-managed Competencies for Teaching classroom will have few behavior problems. When problems do occur, they should be accepted as opportunities to teach adaptive self-control. Almost every case will respond to warnings, direct interventions in the classroom, or time-out. Only in extreme cases of severe or dangerous behavior should it be necessary to refer the problems to the principal. In these cases, though, the teacher has a responsibility to inform the school administration about the problem. It may be decided that the parents should be consulted or that special diagnostic services should become involved. Even if the services of the school administration, school psychologist, counselor, school health services, visiting teacher, or social worker do become necessary, the classroom teacher should persist with the reinforcement of appropriate behavior and the nonreinforcement of misbehavior.

The preceding general description obviously cannot provide the specific that must be determined by each situation. Experience and feedback will help the teacher acquire progressively more effective strategies for dealing with behavior problems.

PUNISHMENT

Punishment is a natural part of learning. When we make certain kinds of mistakes, discomfort or pain follows. Carelessness with sharp or hot objects causes physical injury which in turn results in our learning greater care in handling these objects or in avoiding them in the future. This kind of natural punishment occurs in many kinds of learning. The individual who suffers embarrassment in a social situation tries either to improve his social behavior or to avoid social encounters in the future. The student who injures himself in a sports activity tries either to improve his performance or to avoid the activity in the future.

There is no question about the effectiveness of punishment and the fact that it is a natural part of the learning process. The question that the educator must answer is whether imposed punishment is effective in achieving educational objectives. Punishment consists of aversive stimuli that follow behaviors and weaken the probability of the behavior's occurring in the future. Punishment operates in a manner similar to reinforcement but has the opposite effect on behavior. Punishment weakens the behavior it follows, whereas reinforcement strengthens the behavior it follows. Punishment is more effective when it is immediate, as is reinforcement. Schedules of punishment operate in the same way as do schedules of reinforcement, only they achieve the opposite effect.

Although punishment is effective, it should usually be avoided as a means of dealing with misbehavior. Just as reinforcers can be conditioned, so can punishments. Pairing the teacher's presence with positive reinforcers results in the teacher's presence, by itself, becoming a more powerful reinforcer. Pairing the teacher's presence with the infliction of pain results in the teacher's presence, by itself, becoming unpleasant. The child punished by a teacher may try to avoid not only the punishment but also the source of the punishment. The teacher who punishes a child conditions negative attitudes toward that teacher. This attitude may generalize and spread to other teachers. Also, place conditioning may occur—that is, the child develops avoidance of school and school work as well as avoidance of the teacher.

Imposed punishment, such as the infliction of pain or embarrassment, produces side effects that are inconsistent with educational objectives. Instead of the child's developing a positive attitude toward teacher, school, and learning, punishment teaches him to avoid and escape from the source of punishment. To avoid the punishment that follows misconduct, a child learns to be sneaky and to blame others. To avoid the punishment that follows making mistakes, the child learns to cheat. If attending school becomes associated with failure, frustration, embarrassment, and punitive or inadequate teaching, the child may learn to avoid school by being truant or by developing psychosomatic illness. Because imposed punishment can have such undesirable side effects, it is an inappropriate means of dealing with most behavior problems.

There are occasional circumstances in which punishment may be required. When the problem behavior is so intense that either the child or other persons may be in danger of injury, punishment may be appropriate. Self-destructive behaviors, such as running in front of cars, violent aggression against other persons, and dangerous activities with knives or fire could produce irreparable damage. Imposed punishment immediately following dangerous acts will usually put a stop to the behavior. Again, punishment is effective only when it occurs in a context of much positive reinforcement for behaviors that are incompatible with the punished behavior. Punishment does not correct behavior. It does not teach appropriate behavior. It only inhibits the behavior that was punished. For the punishment to produce lasting benefit, the child must be in a milieu in which his appropriate behaviors are receiving ample reinforcement.

Time-out from positive reinforcement is more effective than pain or imposed embarrassment because reinforcement is withdrawn in such a way that pupils know the steps required for earning back the reinforcers, for example, settling down for the required time-out and then returning to the classroom activity. In one case, a teacher separated two boys who were fighting during recess. They were sent to spend the balance of recess in the principal's waiting room. They learned that to enjoy the recess activities they must engage in nonviolent behavior. Withdrawal of privileges (or positive reinforcement) for a time-out period, followed by the opportunity to regain the privileges, presents the pupil with an educational situation in which he can learn to improve his behavior and self-discipline.

Unfortunately, much of the literature on the subject of discipline is not based on sound learning principles and is therefore unreliable as a source of effective techniques. A few sources that you may find valuable are: Green (1963); Haring and Phillips (1962); Meacham and Wiessen (1969); Phillips, Wiener, and Haring (1960); and Larson and Karpar (1963).

Conducting the Classroom Program

Effective management of the physical facilities and learning activities in the classroom can produce an environment of joyous accomplishment for teacher and pupils. Inadequate management can produce undesirable outcomes. The Competencies for Teaching classroom, based on essential-level tasks and creativity and developmental objectives provides continuous meaningful activity. Carefully preparing and arranging the physical facilities, daily schedules, and lesson plans are essentials of good classroom management. The methods you acquire throughout the Competencies for Teaching system will facilitate the effective operation of your classroom. Your experience will help you refine your skills so that your gratification from teaching increases. So long as you attend to feedback and continue to improve, teaching and classroom management will be a challenge and a source of satisfaction.

The following are a few general ideas about conducting classroom instruction which are beneficial to the overall success of the program. In the beginning, met with a new class, it is important for you to have prepared a number of interesting assignments so that pupils establish immediately that this classroom is a place of meaningful activity and achievement. Your students' promptness is encouraged by making the day's opening exercises interesting and by the teacher's own examples of promptness. Show enthusiasm for teaching and interest in your pupils and they will respond with more enthusiasm for learning. Develop the ability to be spontaneous and to adapt to situations as they arise. Learn the names of your pupils as soon as possible. Use a seating plan until you can identify your students by name. Contribute to improved learning by developing daily schedules that provide each pupil with a happy ending for each school day.

Competent teaching is our profession's most effective public relations, so essential to maintaining high-quality education. Institutions and government departments compete vigorously for larger shares of the tax dollar. Unless teachers maintain good public relations, voters and politicians will develop negative attitudes toward schools, cut funds, resist salary increases, and force educators to make do with inadequate buildings and equipment. How can teachers compete for public attention against the tremendous financial power of the mass media of advertising and entertainment—also bidding for the same attention?

Overwhelming evidence has shown that children acquire knowledge and develop their capacities best when they understand the reasons for doing school work. Free people are entitled to understand the reasons for the work they are asked to do. The teacher who helps pupils to understand the reasons for school work will produce large dividends in improved learning for the child, in parental approval, and in public support for education.

The basic purpose of public education is to help all pupils develop whatever capacities they possess. The teacher who recognizes that individual pupils possess a wide variety of capabilities and who expresses recognition for even limited accomplishment stimulates further progress and increased parental cooperation. Already it has become urgent for pupils to learn more and to continue learning throughout their lives, and it will be disastrous for education if schools use competitive evaluation, marking, and reporting procedures that impede learning.

Relationships between teachers and pupils have a far-reaching influence on public understanding. Every day, pupils convey their impressions about school directly to their parents. The teacher who corrects a child's behavior or work early in the day so that the child can redeem himself in his own eyes, in the eyes of his classmates, and in the eyes of the teacher, is contributing to both high-quality teaching and public relations. The teacher who is strong enough at the end of the school day and at the end of the school week to communicate his desire to meet the class on the next school morning is performing a constructive educational act. The teacher who reviews the achievements and the successful experiences of individual pupils and of the class at the close of the school day is establishing a positive attitude toward future learning while, at the same time, enhancing the probability that the child will present positive messages about his school experiences to his parents. The child's happy attitude in turn produces parental reinforcement of positive school performance.

Assignment

After completing your study of this chapter, do the exercises in Chapter Nine of the Classroom Instruction Workbook.

References

Burton, W. H. *The Guidance of Learning Activities*. New York: Appleton-Century-Crofts, 1962.

Esbensen, T. "Should Teacher Aides Be More Than Clerks?" *Phi Delta Kappa*, 1966, 47:237.

Goodlad, J. S., and R. H. Anderson. *The Nongraded Elementary School*. New York: Harcourt Brace and World, 1959.

Green, A. S. *The Elementary School Classroom Discipline Manual*. Minneapolis, Minn.: T. S. Denison, 1963.

Haring, N. G., and E. L. Phillips. *Educating Emotionally Disturbed Children*. New York: McGraw-Hill, 1962.

Hertzberg, A., and E. F. Stone. *Schools Are for Children: An American Approach to the Open Classroom*. New York: Schocken Books, 1971.

Kohl, H. R. *The Open Classroom*. New York: The New York Review, 1969.

Larson, G., and R. Karpar. *Effective Secondary School Discipline*. Englewood Cliffs, N.J.: Prentice-Hall, 1963.

Matthews, W. D. E., and M. W. Chalmers. *School and Classroom Management*. Toronto, Canada: J. M. Dent and Sons, 1959.

Meacham, M. L., and A. E. Wiessen. *Changing Classroom Behavior*. Scranton, Pa.: Instructional Textbooks, 1969.

Morse, A. D. *Schools for Tomorrow Today*. Garden City, N.Y.: Doubleday, 1960.

Phillips, E. L., D. N. Wiener, and N. G. Haring. *Discipline, Achievement and Mental Health.* Englewood Cliffs, N.J.: Prentice-Hall, 1960.

Taylor, J. *Organizing the Open Classroom.* New York: Schocken Books, 1972.

Ten

Classroom and Community

Objectives: After completing your study of this chapter,
you will be able to (1) relate certain social changes to
changes taking place in public education, (2) acknowledge
the need for continuous professional growth by applying
relevant psychological theory and learning principles,
(3) describe such programs as early childhood education,
nongraded elementary schools, secondary schools without
walls, work-study programs, community education, and instructional technology, and (4) complete the exercises in
Chapter Ten of the Classroom Instruction Workbook.

Public education has recently seen some bold and
some feeble attempts at meeting the challenges of
an increasingly diverse school population, com-
pounded by justly unyielding demands for quality.
Some of these attempts indicated that escalating past efforts would not suffice. For example, "Evaluating the
More Effective Schools," a study of compensatory education
(Fox, 1968), indicated that increasing administrative and
special services, along with establishing a comprehensive
program to provide sufficient teaching staff, did not significantly improve teaching nor did it affect children's
functioning and achievement levels. Typically, compensatory educational efforts involved piecemeal supplements to
existing programs or intensive efforts in a single area of
a program.

Some educators are trying out promising new programs
to bring about fundamental improvement in the schools.
There appears to be general agreement that if schools are
to be significantly better, they will have to be substan-
tially different from those of the past. The role of the
public school, educational content, and method of instruction, are all undergoing searching reappraisal.

The need for change in public education has come
about primarily because of dramatic social change. In
recent years, schools have had to respond to demands from
the community, the courts, and the state legislatures.
The demands for education for all children, high-quality
education, equal educational opportunities for minority
children, early childhood education, educational relevance, and accountability are examples of recent issues
that have produced a series of changes in the public
schools. There have been major community, demographic,
and sociological changes that must be accommodated by the
schools of the future. Life style, even in rural areas,
has become more urbanized as towns and villages disappear
to be replaced by the big city and its urban sprawl. The
cities are of such magnitude that most citizens do not

participate actively in community affairs or government. The resultant sense of loss of community is heightened by the ever-increasing mobility of the family. The individual feels that much of his life is controlled by bureaucracies and is regulated by rules and red tape. These factors, along with poverty, racial strife, crime, and the drug culture have challenged public education's capacity to maintain its position as a relevant social institution.

The responses of public education to these social changes have created a variety of programs—early childhood education, compensatory education, work-study, schools without walls, and community education. Each of these programs, and those that may emerge in the future, will influence the concept of what constitutes a classroom.

Transfer and Generalization of Teacher Training

The Competencies for Teaching system attempts to develop teaching skills that are adaptable to a wide variety of teaching situations, so that the teacher will continue to be effective as the process of social change takes place. The Competencies for Teaching system integrates the practice of teaching with relevant educational and psychological theories, thereby ensuring instructional practices based on sound learning principles.

The distinction between an engineer and a mechanic is based on the engineer's knowledge of the sciences basic to his profession, whereas the mechanic may make repairs using established procedures without understanding the technical principles underlying the structure or operation of the machine. A profession usually differs from a trade by its greater emphasis on understanding the underlying scientific principles, which permits greater flexibility in applying and refining one's professional skills. The civil, mechanical, electrical, or structural engineer engaged in building bridges, tunnels, generator plants, transmission lines, and highways must base construction, operation, and supervision on scientific principles derived from mathematics, physics, electricity, and chemistry. The practice of engineering consists of a repertoire of skills and knowledge supported by scientific understanding. Similarly, the practice of medicine consists of skills and knowledge supported by scientific understanding of anatomy, physiology, and chemistry. An engineer, physician, or teacher who has studied the general principles basic to the practice of his profession is best able to meet new situations and adapt his practice to accommodate change.

The professional teacher meets new situations intelligently and creatively and is able to employ new materials and processes effectively. Teaching, like the other professions discussed earlier, is not based on one theory or one discipline. Everything involved in the practice of teaching forms the basis of the profession. Competencies for Teaching provides a conceptual model of the process and a system for acquiring skills to implement the process.

It is important to distinguish a system from a theory. For example, when applying the Competencies for Teaching *system*, you will evaluate pupils' entering behavior. In doing this, you may use direct observation or tests based on measurement *theory*. In identifying terminal objectives, you may bring to bear information derived from philosophy, sociology, subject content, curriculum, and child development. In establishing enroute objectives, you will use your background in child development and curriculum. In selecting elicitors, you will put into practice your knowledge of classical, or *respondent*, conditioning (in which selected stimuli elicit responses) and instructional media in addition to employing your skills in eliciting attention and task behavior. In reinforcing responses, you will use your knowledge and understanding of learning principles based on *operant* conditioning (in which reinforcing emitted behaviors increase the probability of the responses' occurring in the future). In measuring outcomes, you will employ evaluation techniques based on mathematical and statistical theory. The formal system of Competencies for Teaching does not limit the appropriate applications of theory and knowledge from other disciplines any more than the practice of medicine and engineering limits the application of theory and knowledge relevant to those professions.

The Competencies for Teaching system does not assume that teaching is based solely on one theory or discipline. Note that in the discussion above, child development, philosophy, sociology, curriculum, learning principles, and test and measurement theory were all combined in making professional decisions. Educational psychology is valuable to teaching because it describes how a child developmentally acquires progressive changes in behavior.

In the past, educators have placed great trust in psychology, particularly learning theory, which describes the conditions under which children learn. McDonald (1964) surveyed theories of learning and instruction and concluded that no single psychological theory included all the characteristics needed by the educational practitioner. He commented that psychologists do not create theories to be acceptable to nonpsychologists, and that there appears to be no good reason for education to be committed to any single psychological theory short of a comprehensive "science of man."

Educational practitioners should be eclectic, that is, select the "best" approaches from all available doctrines, so that learning principles are applied appropriately in the instructional process. The Competencies for Teaching system is designed to help the teacher make pragmatic decisions about the techniques that will work in teaching pupils social and academic skills. It is a system that helps teachers become more rational in selecting instructional stimuli and more sophisticated in selecting educational interventions. The system is successful if it teaches essential skills and provides an adequate background of knowledge and theory so that the teacher becomes a self-initiating agent of change, who makes the classroom the most effective educational environment possible.

Changes in Programs and Classrooms

To this point, the Competencies for Teaching system has emphasized the teacher and the teacher's influence in the classroom. This chapter will deal briefly with some of the changes resulting from influences outside of the classroom and the interrelationship of community and classroom.

EARLY CHILDHOOD EDUCATION

A contemporary sociological and educational development is the widespread reawakening of interest in the very young child. Great educators of the past—Pestalozzi, Froebel, and Montessori—emphasized the importance of the child's experiences before the age of six. Although kindergarten for five-year-old children has had considerable support over the years, until recently most prekindergarten programs were supported privately. National concern for the problems of the rural poor and the inner-city child focused attention on providing compensatory education for these culturally different children during the four-year span beginning at two years of age and extending through age five. The civil rights movement and policies adopted at the federal level resulted in funding prekindergarten educational programs. A variety of nursery school and day-care center programs emerged. Project Head Start, part of the war on poverty, was the most notable example of the newly awakened interest in early childhood education.

The bulk of evidence reported by the government-sponsored Westinghouse study (Cicirelli, 1969) supports the conclusion that Project Head Start was unsuccessful in increasing the intellectual abilities of disadvantaged or culturally different children. Although these findings indicated that Head Start had done little to prevent scholastic failure during attendance in elementary school, the growth of early childhood programs has continued. This can be justified educationally because all preschool programs are not identical and research is beginning to discover the effectiveness of certain curriculum models. Successful early childhood education, which compensates for cultural differences and gives children common forms

of experience as prerequisites to effective transactions
and interactions in the school's academic and social environment, could significantly change the role of the primary classroom. If enriched environments were provided
for all children during this critical stage of language
and social development—the prekindergarten years—the
primary grade teacher could spend less time on readiness
and compensatory activities.

NONGRADED ELEMENTARY SCHOOLS

The nongraded plan is a program for ensuring each
child's continuous progress (as described more fully in
Chapter Nine). Instruction is individualized so that
learning moves along sequential steps that are not restricted by grade levels. Pupils' progress is evaluated
according to the objectives achieved. The pupils receive
no failing marks. They either receive a pass mark or that
part of the record is left blank. Progress reports specify only those objectives that have been achieved. The
nongraded elementary school is based on school-wide individualized instruction and flexible grouping.

SECONDARY SCHOOLS WITHOUT WALLS

The concept of "schools without walls" is based on
using community resources instead of the conventional
classroom. High school students may attend art classes
in museums, economics seminars in banks, auto mechanics
classes in service stations, and social studies classes
at city hall. The most notable example of schools without
walls is the Parkway Program in Philadelphia (Greenberg
and Roush, 1970). John Bremmer, the director of the program, catalogued ninety community institutions that cooperate in providing learning facilities. The Parkway Program operates within the general requirements for a high
school diploma in the state of Pennsylvania. In addition
to the academic curriculum, the students are encouraged to
investigate special problems in an area of their interest.
Although adopting programs using schools entirely
"without walls" will probably be limited to very few
school districts, schools are increasing their use of community resources as educational facilities. Using the
community as the classroom has the potential for revitali-
zing secondary education.

WORK-STUDY PROGRAMS

The possibility of combining school and work experiences to provide alienated high school students with exploratory employment has been offered to those seeking a

terminal high school program leading to employment. The program adapts the school curriculum to the pupils' academic level. Classroom instruction is designed to assist the pupils in their work experience. Each work-study program must evolve from local needs and be developed by local personnel using local educational and community employment resources (Burchill, 1962).

COMMUNITY EDUCATION

Community education is based on an expanded concept of the public school's function. It advocates greater community use of all school facilities, especially the community's use of school buildings that are empty in the evenings, on weekends, and during summer vacation. Community education attempts to involve the residents of a community in developing their own educational goals. This is a new involvement of the community in education and of education in the community. The residents who have been frustrated in their attempts at involvement and identification are given opportunities for meaningful participation in problem solving in a way that promotes a sense of personal identity and community membership. The community education concept is a means of bringing together people in large cities into smaller operational units, which fosters interaction among the people living in an area served by a school.

It is beyond the scope of this chapter to describe community education programs and how they operate. The teacher interested in the basic concepts, functions, and operations of community education is advised to read: *Education and Public Understanding* (McClosky, 1967), which describes the basic concepts and functions of public relations in improving support of public education; *The Community School: Basic Concepts, Functions, and Organization* (Totten and Manley, 1969), which explains the goals, programs, and role of the school in a total community education program; and *The Power of Community Education* (Totten, 1970), which describes the application of community education concepts, methods, and procedures to solving human and community problems.

INSTRUCTIONAL TECHNOLOGY

Technology is applied scientific development. Developments in electronic technology, such as television and computers, along with developments in systems analysis, programed instruction, and audiovisual equipment have made possible a new educational specialty—instructional technology. The classroom teacher can use instructional technology to achieve educational objectives more efficiently. Technology does not replace the teacher nor does it necessarily make instruction less humanistic. New technology, tools, or media used appropriately can give the teacher more time to help pupils analyze, criticize, evaluate, and synthesize their experiences.

One of the most challenging developments in instructional technology is computer-assisted instruction. The computer is a powerful tool for storing and manipulating coded information electronically, but by itself, it can tell us nothing about how learning occurs. Computer-assisted instruction can be only as effective as the learning principles and subject matter incorporated into developing the computer program.

A single computer can store many instructional programs and serve many terminals. This permits the simultaneous individual instruction of a number of pupils. Each program is paced to the individual's needs. It can assess individual progress and automatically initiate remedial work as required, all the while performing these functions with less error and more speed than could a human instructor.

In the usual computer installation, each terminal contains a typewriter keyboard and a screen similar to that of a television set. A frame is presented on the screen and the pupil is required to select or to type a response. The computer evaluates the response and decides where to go in the program for the next frame. Finally, the computer informs the pupil how well he did in the program. The computer stores individual records for reporting achievement and scheduling students' future courses.

Summary

These brief descriptions of the community's influences on the classroom are far from complete. Early childhood education, nongraded elementary schools, secondary schools without walls, work-study programs, community education, and instructional technology are only a few of the current efforts to enrich and modernize education. Some of these programs are already exerting widespread influence and others are still regarded as being in the experimental stage. The programs described in this chapter represent the kinds of changes that expand the traditional concept of the classroom from four walls that isolate the student from the outside world to one of an environment that will be a constructive influence on the child's early life, that will accommodate continuous, progressive learning for nongraded groups of students, that may be outside of school walls entirely, that may be part of a total community educational program, or to a classroom that may use computer-assisted instruction to permit each child to learn at his own rate and to receive immediate reinforcement for his accomplishments.

Whatever the present or future concept of the classroom, the teacher's effectiveness will depend on his or her mastery of the instructional process. The effective use of the classroom and appropriate implementation of technology can be achieved only by a teacher who can select appropriate educational objectives and plan the experiences necessary to reach these objectives. Advances in technology and restructuring the educational environment can assist the teacher but they cannot perform the essential task of the classroom teacher—to interact dynamically with children to promote learning and development.

Assignment

Complete the exercises in Chapter Ten of the Classroom Instruction Workbook.

References

Burchill, G. W. *Work-Study Programs for Alienated Youth: A Casebook*. Chicago: Science Research Associates, 1962.

Cicirelli, V. *The Impact of Head Start: An Evaluation of the Effects of Head Start on Children's Cognitive and Affective Development*. Springfield, Va.: U.S. Department of Commerce Clearinghouse, 1969.

Fox, D. J. "Evaluating the More Effective Schools," *Phi Delta Kappa*, 1968, 50:593-597.

Greenberg, J. D., and R. E. Roush. "A Visit to the 'School without Walls': Two Impressions," *Phi Delta Kappa*, 1970, 52:480-484.

McCloskey, G. *Education and Public Understanding*. New York: Harper & Brothers, 1967.

McDonald, F. J. "The Influence of Learning Theories in Education (1900-1950), *63rd Yearbook of National Society for the Study of Education*, 1964, 63 (Part 1):1-16.

Totten, W. F., and F. J. Manley. *The Community School: Basic Concepts, Function, and Organization*. Galien, Mich.: Allied Education Council, 1969.

————. *The Power of Community Education*. Midland, Mich.: Pendell Publishing, 1970.

Claffroom Inftruction Workbook

Laurence J. Peter

Forrest G. Wisely
Illinois State University at Normal

To teach is to learn.

Japanese Proverb

One

Introduction

Objectives: When you have completed this chapter, you will
be able to (1) demonstrate correct use of this workbook,
(2) explain the purposes of this workbook, (3) identify
the three types of frames used, (4) explain the reasons
for studying educational psychology, (5) define learning,
(6) define simulation and its function, and (7) describe
the use of the Classroom Instruction Record.

The procedure for using this workbook is the same
as that used in the first volume of this series,
Individual Instruction.

1. Move a card that covers the width of the page down
   to the heavy black line.

2. Read all the material you have uncovered.

3. Write your response in the space provided.

4. Move the card down to the next heavy black line.

5. Compare your response for content and meaning with
   the answer provided. Your answer does not have to
   follow word for word the one provided.

6. If your answer does not contain the same content
   and meaning as the one given, reread the frame
   and correct your response.

7. When you are satisfied that your response is correct,
   continue with the next frame.

If your answer does not agree in content and meaning with

the answer provided, you should _____ your re-

sponse.

correct

The format of this workbook is programed instruction, but
because it is part of a total system (including textbook
and record book), and because it is not intended to be

used separately from the other components, it does not meet all the generally accepted specifications for programed texts that are designed to be used independently.

The main difference in this workbook from traditional linear programs is that some frames stand alone and require responses based on information contained in the textbook. The format of this workbook is

_____ .

---

programed instruction

This Classroom Instruction Workbook is designed to be used along with the text, *Classroom Instruction*. Its purposes are (1) to further develop information presented in the textbook, (2) to present new content that is useful to the classroom teacher, and (3) to provide opportunities to respond to simulations of classroom situations that could occur during your practicum (student teaching) or future teaching.

One of the purposes of this workbook is to give you an opportunity to respond to _____ that may occur in the classroom.

---

situations

To achieve the three purposes of this workbook, three types of frames are used. They are (1) *continuation* frames that extend and expand some of the material presented in the textbook, (2) *educational psychology* frames that present new information about learning principles and other aspects of educational psychology which can be applied to classroom instruction, and (3) *simulation* frames that provide you with opportunities to develop effective responses for classroom application.

The three types of frames used in this workbook are (1)

_____ , (2) _____ , and (3)

_____ .

---

(1) continuation (2) educational psychology (3) simulation

Continuation Frames

Continuation frames may either extend or expand on the content of the corresponding chapter in the textbook. For example, an important concept presented in Chapter One of the textbook is the feedback-control process.

This feedback-control process is called _____ .

---

cybernetics

The following describes the three primary functions of a cybernetic system.

1. Movement toward an objective is initiated.
2. Comparison is made between the outcome of the actions and the desired objective.
3. The detected difference redirects succeeding behaviors.

A detected error in performance is the _____ that redirects succeeding performance.

---

feedback

Pupils in a physical education class are learning to play shuffleboard. A pupil's disk falls short of the target. On the next trial he pushes the disk harder and comes closer to the desired target. This improved performance

is the result of _____ from his detected error.

---

feedback

The cybernetic process in Competencies for Teaching is illustrated in the following diagram, "Cycle of the Instructional Process." The three feedback loops provide the teacher with information to continually improve and modify elements in the instructional process.

Objective

R
Reinforcer

E
Elicitor

feedback

feedback

feedback

feedback

Observed
Behavioral
Response

Feedback is derived from the _____

_____ .

---

observed behavioral response

The information that indicates to the teacher that the
elicitor, reinforcer, or objective should be modified or

changed is called _____ .

---

feedback

Feedback may result in the teacher's modifying any or all
of the following.

1. _____   2. _____   3. _____

---

(1) elicitor   (2) reinforcer   (3) objective

The means of achieving progressive changes in behavioral response toward an objective are (1) _____ and (2) _____ .

---

(1) elicitors   (2) reinforcers

You establish an objective and present a task to your pupils. They do not respond. This feedback indicates that you should modify the _____ .

---

elicitor

You reinforce an appropriate behavioral response. After repeated cycles of instruction, the behavior has not increased in strength. This feedback indicates you should change to an effective _____ .

---

reinforcer

If repeated attempts with a variety of elicitors and reinforcers fail to establish a behavioral response, you may decide that an error was made in identifying the appropriate _____ .

---

objective

You identify an objective and then observe that the behavior has already been established. This feedback indicates that you should move to another _____ .

---

objective

You communicate an objective to your students. They demonstrate that they can perform the task without further instruction. You should do two things: (1) _____ the behavior and move to the next (2) _____ .

---

(1) reinforce   (2) objective

Feedback indicates check marks are reinforcing but teacher praise is not. To establish praise as a reinforcer, teacher praise and check marks should be _____ .

paired

You observe one of your pupils while he is working on a science project. Upon completion he smiles and admires his work. This feedback indicates that this pupil's self-_____ is a reinforcer.

evaluation

Educational Psychology Frames

Educational psychology has developed a substantial body of knowledge applicable to teaching. Some of this information is presented in the textbook and some in the workbook. This psychological information establishes a basis for making many instruction decisions.

A body of knowledge that teachers can use in making instructional decisions is _____ .

educational psychology

All professions derive their content from a variety of disciplines. Just as physics and mathematics are the foundation of certain engineering professions, and anatomy and physiology are the basis for medical training, educational psychology establishes the foundation for teaching.

Education, like other professions, derives its content from many _____ .

disciplines

Topics to be included in this classroom instruction phase are: (1) learning principles, (2) reinforcement, (3) extinction, (4) behavior, (5) growth and development, (6) intelligence, (7) tests and measurement, and (8) statistics.

A knowledge of learning principles enriches classroom teaching by providing a basis for decisions that increase learning.

Learning principles are useful to the teacher if they
lead to _____ learning.

---

increased

Reinforcement is a variable that the teacher applies after
a behavior has occurred to increase the probability of
that behavior's recurring in the future.

For instruction to move forward effectively, teachers
should use _____ .

---

reinforcement

The extinction of an undesirable behavior by not reinforcing it is a useful technique because it allows instruction to move in constructive directions.

The nonreinforcement of an undesirable behavior is a
process called _____ .

---

extinction

Studying behavior, behaviorism, and behavioral analysis
gives teachers a means of obtaining objective evidence
about pupils' learning and educational progress.

To determine the success of instruction, teachers observe
pupils' _____ .

---

behavior

The study of growth and development is an important aspect
of educational psychology because it helps the teacher understand and respond to individual differences.

Through recognizing variations in individual development,
the teacher can _____ more appropriately to
each child's needs.

---

respond

The collection and statistical analysis of data about pupils help the teacher to (1) measure their students' levels of knowledge and performance, (2) predict future performance, and (3) evaluate outcomes of instruction.

Teachers evaluate outcomes of instruction through the

(1) _____ and (2) _____

_____ of data about their pupils.

---

(1) collection   (2) statistical analysis

Topics from educational psychology will be presented in sequence of frames as in the following example.

LEARNING

Changes in behavior result from (1) maturation, (2) temporary physiological changes, and (3) experience.

Change in behavior that results from experience is called

_____ .

---

learning

A group of pupils cannot multiply single-digit numerals. They are presented an instructional program. After completing the program the pupils are able to multiply single-digit numerals. From this observation we say the

pupils have _____ to multiply single-digit nu-erals.

---

learned

Learning takes place within the learner. It cannot be directly observed or measured. We can observe pupils' behavioral responses to given elicitors, but we cannot

observe the process of _____ .

---

learning

Since learning takes place within the learner, we infer
learning has taken place by observing his _____
_____ .

behavioral responses

A class is given some lessons on library research. On
their next social science assignment, the pupils find the
required information in the library. From their behavior
we have objective evidence that the pupils have _____
to use the reference works in the library.

learned

We infer that learning has taken place when we observe
progressive changes in a pupil's _____ .

behavior

Simulation Frames

The classroom teacher is required to possess a wide range
of complex competencies and skills. He or she must be
able to plan and implement instructional sequences, evaluate the effects of instruction, manage the classroom, and
deal effectively with problems as they develop.

The teacher does not normally have the luxury of post-
poning a response. In most instances the teacher must
respond effectively in the _____ .

present

The simulation frames are representative of many real
classroom situations. They enable you to analyze a situation and make a response while avoiding the normal risks
of the real situation. The immediate feedback (the correct response) provides a solution that has high probability of being effective if transferred to a real classroom situation.

Simulation frames are representative of _____
classroom situations.

real

Simulation allows you to analyze situations and make decisions while avoiding the risks inherent in the

_____ situation.

---

real

Pupils in other professions learn skills through simulation. Student architects build models, prospective lawyers conduct mock trials, and medical trainees work with plastic models of the human body and its organs.

Learning professional skills while avoiding the risks inherent in the real situation can be achieved through

_____ .

---

simulation

The following are examples of simulation frames. Treat each frame as an individual simulation game.

Tim helps other pupils who are having difficulty with their science workbooks. You decide that this form of cooperative social behavior is desirable and wish to maintain it. You should therefore _____ Tim's helping behavior.

---

reinforce

You observe improved achievement in mathematics after you begin giving extra points for completed assignments. Using this feedback, you could improve achievement in completing social science assignments by giving _____

_____ .

---

extra points

Frequently one of your pupils waves his hand and shouts out, "I know, I know!" when you ask the class a question. To extinguish this undesirable behavior, you should

_____ the pupil when he is exhibiting this type of behavior.

---

ignore

The pupils in your biology class usually enter the room in an orderly fashion, go to their assigned laboratory tables, and begin preparing for the day's assignment. Since your pupils respond to verbal praise, you should

reinforce their behavior by _____ them.

---

praising

A pupil sitting at the front of the room regularly "clowns around" and makes the class laugh. To decrease the opportunity for this pupil to make the class laugh, you should

move him away from the front of the room and _____ the behavior when it occurs.

---

ignore

One of your pupils throws tantrums. Each time he "acts out" you send him to the counselor but his tantrums do not decrease. It is possible that being sent to the counse-

lor's office is _____ .

---

reinforcing

Assignment

The classroom practicum (student teaching) provides opportunities for implementing the knowledge and skills presented in the Classroom Instruction Textbook and in this workbook. The Classroom Instruction Record is another aid in practicing what you have learned. The instructions and forms contained in the Classroom Instruction Record will help you record and evaluate your practicum experiences.

The main difference between the individual instruction practicum and the classroom instruction practicum is in your control of the structure and sequence of classroom activities. Unlike individual instruction, during which you studied a portion of the instructional process and then carried it out in the practicum, this phase must accommodate the needs emerging from your placement in a classroom. Some of the assignments in the Classroom Instruction Record may be carried out in an order different from their arrangement in the record book. Such variables as the time of year at which you begin your practicum, specific needs of your classroom, and special events influence the order in which you fulfill your practicum assignments. It is unnecessary to attempt to carry out the practicum assignments in direct relationship to the chapters in the textbook and workbook.

During the orientation period given by your practicum school, you should:

1. Study the general instructions and contents of the Classroom Instruction Record, and

2. Complete the forms, "Teaching Assignment" and "Practicum School."

Two

Competencies for Classroom Instruction

Objectives: When you have completed this chapter, you will
be able to (1) respond to different classroom teaching
situations, (2) solve various school problems, (3) identify feedback, elicitors, reinforcers, shaping, modeling,
extinction, and time-out in the learning process, and (4)
begin the assignments in the Classroom Instruction Record.

Classroom teaching is a process involving many fundamental
teaching skills. The successful teacher must have the
ability to elicit and reinforce progressive changes in the
academic and social behaviors of his or her pupils. The
most important outcome of this phase of the system is for

you to learn effective teaching _____ .

---

skills (behaviors)

This chapter presents simulations of problems teachers encounter, allowing you to learn interventions useful in
real teaching situations. Simulation exercises represent

_____ teaching situations.

---

real

Each simulation frame will elicit a response to the prob-

lem presented. You will be required to _____ to
each frame.

---

respond

The solutions presented, with which you can compare your
responses, provide feedback to reinforce your responses.

Your appropriate responses will be _____ by the
solutions presented.

---

reinforced

These simulation exercises, by eliciting and reinforcing your responses, will assist you in _____ teaching skills.

---

learning (acquiring)

Learning has been defined as changes in behavior resulting from experience.

It is the first year of school for your pupils. When asked a question, they do not raise their hands before answering. It can be said that these pupils have not

_____ the behavior of raising their hands before

answering a question.

---

learned

After demonstrating and explaining appropriate hand-raising behavior, the pupils raise their hands before answering a question. The demonstration and explanation

_____ the pupils' hand-raising behavior.

---

elicited

The most appropriate method of maintaining your pupils' hand-raising behavior would be to reinforce it for the next few periods by calling on only those pupils who

_____ .

---

raise their hands

Your pupils put their books and other materials away before leaving the classroom. To maintain this desirable

behavior you would _____ it.

---

reinforce

Henry frequently loses his temper when he is unable to do an assigned task. Occasionally he asks for help when he is having difficulty. To increase the number of times he asks for help when in difficulty, this behavior should be

_____ .

---

reinforced

Mabel is a talker. She also enjoys your attention. If you respond with, "Mabel, be quiet!" each time she talks

out of turn, you are probably _____ her talking-out-of-turn behavior.

---

reinforcing

Your physical education class is learning to play volley-ball. As the pupils learn each step, you tell them how well they are doing. This praise reinforces each new be-

havior and _____ the probability that it will be maintained.

---

increases

Your students plan a field trip quickly and efficiently. Praising them for this type of cooperative social behavior

will tend to _____ the probability of its oc-

curring in the future.

---

increase

When your students have completed their reading assign-ments, you allow them to play their favorite class game.

The (1) _____ is a reinforcer that will increase

the chances of the pupils' (2) _____ reading assignments in the future.

---

(1) game   (2) completing

John completed his arithmetic assignment and you gave him ten grade points. The reinforcer in this situation was receiving the _____.

grade points

You told a group of pupils, "Your science project is excellent!" The reinforcer in this situation was the

_____ .

praise (sentence)

Pairing is a procedure used to establish a new reinforcer. It is accomplished by presenting a neutral stimulus along with an established reinforcer a sufficient number of times for the new stimulus to become a reinforcer by itself.

Verbal praise is an effective reinforcer for your pupils. To establish points as a reinforcer, you should _____ giving points with verbal praise.

pair

Your students enjoy free-reading time. You would like to establish check marks as reinforcers. You could accomplish this by pairing giving check marks with granting

_____ .

free-reading time

Letter grades are not reinforcing to your primary children. By pairing teacher attention with grades, you will establish grades as an effective _____ .

reinforcer

You observe that praise is not reinforcing to one of your pupils. For praise to become a reinforcer, you should pair it with an _____ reinforcer.

---

established (effective)

The Premack principle states that any high-frequency behavior can be used to reinforce a low-frequency behavior.

Your objective is that a group of boys complete their language assignments. You observe that the boys spend much of their free time playing checkers. From this observation you decide to use (1) _____ as a reinforcer when the boys (2) _____ their language assignments.

---

(1) playing checkers   (2) complete

Lou spends much of his free time reading stories about horses. To strengthen his participation in class projects, you can use the high-frequency behavior of _____ _____ as a reinforcer.

---

reading stories about horses

Your high school class spends a large amount of time socializing. Free time to talk can be used to _____ academic and other social behaviors.

---

reinforce

You allow your students free time after they have completed their workbook exercises. You observe that fewer and fewer students complete their workbooks in class. You might therefore conclude that free time (is / is not) an effective reinforcer for these students.

---

is not

Contingency refers to the relationship between a behavior and its consequence.

Bill received a star for correctly spelling twenty words. Receiving the star was _____ on correctly spelling the twenty words.

---

contingent

Unless a behavior is in a child's repertoire it cannot be reinforced. *Shaping* is one way of introducing a new behavior into a child's repertoire. Shaping is accomplished by reinforcing closer and closer approximations of the desired behavior.

To improve a pupil's handwriting, you should _____ each small step toward good handwriting.

---

reinforce

You want Marvin to sit at his desk and not get up too many times. By reinforcing increasing lengths of time that Marvin sits at his desk, you can _____ the desired behavior.

---

shape

Another way a new behavior is learned is through *imitation* or *modeling*.

Michael watched Jim operate the controls of a gasoline-powered model airplane. Later, Michael successfully operated the airplane. We could assume that Michael _____ Jim's behavior.

---

imitated (modeled)

The individual whose behavior is observed in learning the behavior is called the model.

In the preceding frame about Michael and Jim, the model was _____ .

Jim

You wish to develop cooperative social behaviors in a kindergarten class. When you observed Jill and Jane sharing a toy, you remarked to the class, "Look how nicely Jill and Jane are sharing." In this instructional situation you used the two girls as _____ .

---

models

You read aloud a story in which the main characters helped their parents with the household chores. The characters in the story may become _____ for your pupils' future behavior.

---

models

Modeling plays an important role in young children's learning, including learning of speech, psychomotor activities, and social behaviors.

At home the most important models are the child's parents. In the classroom, the teacher is one important _____ .

---

model

You do not become upset and lose your temper when problems arise in your classroom. From observing you, your pupils learn to remain calm and deal with unexpected events.

This behavior was learned through _____ .

---

modeling

Both adaptive and maladaptive behaviors can be learned through modeling.

Gary pushes other pupils aside in the lunch line. Unless you respond quickly to deter this behavior, it is highly probable that some of the other pupils will _____ Gary's behavior.

---

model

As a teacher, you must not only establish desired behaviors but also decrease or eliminate undesirable ones. One method of doing this is by withholding reinforcement.

You do not respond when a pupil waves his arm and snaps his fingers to gain attention. By not attending to this behavior, it may be _____ .

---

eliminated (decreased or extinguished)

The term used to identify this process is *extinction*.

Extinction of undesirable behaviors is accomplished by _____ reinforcement.

---

withholding

Some inappropriate language can be _____ by not responding to it.

---

extinguished

There are two situations in which extinction should not be used. First, desirable, adaptive behaviors should not be extinguished, and second, dangerous or destructive behaviors usually should not be treated by extinction methods.

A number of pupils cleaned up their tables after lunch. A few pupils left their dirty dishes and papers on their tables. No attention was given to those pupils who cleaned up their tables. It is highly probable that this desirable behavior will be _____ .

---

extinguished

Extinction should not be used when the undesirable behavior is destructive or dangerous.

Ann often becomes frustrated over something she cannot do and begins throwing books and other school equipment. The use of extinction (is / is not) appropriate in this situation.

---

is not

Melvin tries to draw attention to himself by occasionally making strange noises. It is possible that if you and the class ignore his noises, they will be _____ .

---

extinguished (decreased)

When you first begin ignoring a disruptive behavior in an attempt to extinguish it, the behavior may become more intense temporarily. You must continue to ignore the new intensity because any response from you will probably

_____ this increased level of disruption.

---

reinforce

Another way to eliminate undesirable behaviors is to reinforce desirable behaviors that cannot be performed simultaneously with the undesirable behaviors—that is, they are incompatible.

When given an assignment, Debora works on it and eventually finishes it. She also takes time to talk to those sitting close to her. You observe that these two behaviors do not occur simultaneously. It is therefore important for you to _____ her for working on the assignment.

---

reinforce

Undesirable behaviors may be eliminated by reinforcing competing or incompatible behaviors.

Debora should be reinforced when she is working. Working on an assignment that has been given and talking to her neighbors at the same time are _____ behaviors.

---

competing (incompatible)

Tim pays attention for short periods of time but is easily distracted. To decrease the number of times Tim responds to a distraction, you should reinforce him for

_____ .

---

attending

To improve Tim's study habits, you should withhold reinforcement when he fails to attend to an assigned task and

praise him for _____ to the assigned
task.

---

attending

By reinforcing the acceptable competing behavior, you can
decrease the time required to extinguish undesirable behaviors.

Kevin has the bad habit of shouting when he wants to answer a question. Whenever he raises his hand and does not
shout out, you should call on him. This will reinforce

the desirable behavior and help _____ the undesirable behavior.

---

extinguish

Carol often turns in messy homework. You can increase the
number of times she turns in tidy homework by reinforcing

her each time she turns in _____ homework.

---

tidy

Time-out is a term used to describe a procedure in which a
pupil is deprived of reinforcement for a specified period
of time.

Because Mark persisted in interfering with his neighbors,
you made him sit in a chair at the back of the room where
he had no materials to work with and no reinforcement for

five minutes. Mark was given _____ for five
minutes.

---

time-out

Time-out involves moving a disruptive or uncooperative
pupil to a situation barren of both eliciting and reinforcing stimuli.

While the rest of the class continues with art projects, you make a misbehaving pupil sit in the hall for ten minutes. This is another example of the use of

_____ .

---

time-out

During time-out, the pupil should not receive any

_____ .

---

reinforcement

Allen threw a paper airplane, which caused the class to laugh. The pupils' laughter will probably (1) _____ Allen's behavior and tend to (2) _____ the chances of its recurring in the future.

---

(1) reinforce   (2) increase

You respond to Allen's airplane throwing by removing him from group activities for fifteen minutes. Your action will probably cause Allen's airplane-throwing behavior to

_____ .

---

decrease

From observing your response to Allen's undesirable behavior, the other pupils in the class will be _____ likely to model Allen's behavior.

---

less

Time-out is effective only when the situation from which the pupil is removed is positively reinforcing.

Arlene does not like mathematics and cannot do the assigned problems. She begins to talk and disrupt the
class. Would you increase Arlene's enjoyment of mathematics and her ability to do the assigned problems by

placing her in time-out? _____ .

No

The school counselor is liked by all the pupils. It is
fun to talk with her, and she always has something interesting to show them. Sending a pupil to the counselor's
office (would / would not) be an appropriate time-out
procedure for you to use.

---

would not

Dora enjoys the discussion period in English. However,
she will not remain quiet and allow other students to
present their ideas. The use of time-out (would /
would not) be appropriate with Dora.

---

would

Saul is a shy student. He does not participate in class
discussions or volunteer answers to your questions. The
use of time-out (would / would not) be effective for use
with Saul.

---

would not

Extinction and time-out can both be used to eliminate undesirable behaviors. The difference between the two is
that in using extinction, the reinforcement is removed
from the student, and in using time-out, the pupil is
removed from the reinforcement.

Bill tries to get your attention by tapping his pencil on
his desk. By not reinforcing this behavior with your attention, you are attempting to eliminate it through

_____ .

---

extinction

If, after several warnings, Bill continues to tap on his desk for long periods of time until he has disrupted the class, you may place him in _____ where he cannot attract your attention.

---

time-out

Assignment

Continue the exercises in the Classroom Instruction Record in conjunction with assignments made by your practicum teacher or supervisor.

Three
Entering Behavior

Objectives: When you have completed this chapter, you will
be able to (1) define entering behavior and list reasons
for determining it, (2) discuss ways of identifying entering behavior, (3) describe individual differences, (4)
discuss the importance of considering individual differences, and (5) identify the use and limitations of I.Q.

Entering behavior is the behavior pupils are capable of
producing before new instruction begins. Because most new
learning depends on previous learning, the first step in
teaching is to determine _____ .

entering behavior

Entering behavior may include the level of academic
achievement, social development, and the skills pupils
have prior to instruction.

Before beginning reading instruction, you survey your pupils' prerequisite knowledge and skills for reading. This
information provides a description of their _____

_____ .

entering behavior

One reason for establishing entering behavior is to provide you with information about where to begin instruction.

Three pupils in your class cannot identify all the letters
in the alphabet. Reading instruction for these three pupils should _____ with letter recognition.

begin

Your study of entering behavior may suggest that initially, pupils could be grouped for instruction.

The initial reading skill of four of your pupils is well beyond that of the rest of the class. This indicates that you could _____ these four together for reading instruction.

---

group

To increase the probability of placing pupils appropriately in instructional groups, you should first determine their _____ .

---

entering behavior

Entering behavior also provides a basis for selecting materials and methods for instruction.

The pupils in your biology class performed well in independent study projects in their previous science course. From this you decide to select (1) _____ and (2) _____ that provide opportunities for working independently.

---

(1) materials   (2) methods

One way of determining entering behavior is to use standardized tests. The score from a standardized test compares a pupil's performance with other pupils' performances of the same age or grade level.

Josh, a freshman, takes a standardized test. His score will be compared with the scores of other _____ .

---

freshmen

A test is standardized by administering it to a sample of individuals representing a particular group (population).

A standardized test to measure reading comprehension of third-grade pupils will have been administered to a sample population of _____ pupils.

---

third-grade

A battery of standardized achievement tests draws a profile of a pupil's strengths and weaknesses in various
areas.

A graphic representation of the scores from a battery of
standardized achievement tests indicates a pupil's

strengths and weaknesses and is called his _____ .

profile

A valid test accurately measures what it was designed to
measure.

An arithmetic aptitude test that accurately measures a

pupil's ability to learn arithmetic is a _____

test.

valid

You administer a valid reading comprehension test to your
pupils. Their performance on the test will indicate their

level of _____ .

reading comprehension

Test reliability refers to a test's ability to provide
consistent measurement.

John receives a high score on a test. If the test is reliable, John will receive a _____ score if he

takes the test again.

high

Entering behavior can also be determined through direct
observation.

Observation provides feedback to help you determine where

to _____ instruction.

begin

You can select objectives, elicitors, and reinforcers for an instructional sequence using the _____ obtained through direct observation.

---

feedback

Changes in the objectives, elicitors, or reinforcers during instruction can also result from the _____ gained through direct observation.

---

feedback

Individual Differences

Doris, a sixteen-year-old pupil, achieves a score of 112 on a standardized achievement test. Before you can assess her performance in comparative terms, you need to know

something about the _____ of the other sixteen-year-old pupils.

---

scores (performance, norms)

A *population* is a group of individuals having some common characteristic such as age or grade level.

Because Doris is a sixteen-year-old, she is a member of a _____ of all sixteen-year-olds.

---

population

A *norm* is a standard of performance considered typical for a given population.

If an average score is obtained for all sixteen-year-old pupils in a sample population, this average could be used as the _____ for the total population.

---

norm

The average score of the sixteen-year-old sample population was 100. This score represents the _____ for the sixteen-year-old population.

---

norm

You can now compare Doris's score of 112 with the norm score of 100. You can then state that Doris's performance was (above / below) the population's norm.

---

above

A table of average scores for this test obtained from five age groups is as follows:

Age Groups	Scores
14	65
15	85
16	100
17	115
18	125

The score expected for a typical seventeen-year-old pupil is _____ .

115

A fourteen-year-old pupil achieves a score of 100 on the test. His score would be equivalent to that expected of the typical pupil of age _____ .

---

sixteen years

A seventeen-year-old pupil who scored below the typical seventeen-year-old would have a score below _____ .

The time from an individual's birth to the present, expressed in months and years, is his chronological age (C.A.). Doris was sixteen years old yesterday, so sixteen years is her _____ age.

---

chronological

Intelligence is positively correlated with the ability to learn or to succeed in school.

Willis gets along well in school and receives high marks. It is highly probable that Willis would rank high in

_____ .

---

intelligence

The concept of intelligence was devised to help predict performance.

It requires an individual of average intelligence fifteen minutes to solve a particular problem. Carrie ranks above average in intelligence. You can predict that Carrie will probably solve the problem in (more / less) than fifteen minutes.

---

less

In 1905, Alfred Binet, a French psychologist, developed the first intelligence test to identify and separate those children who could from those who could not profit from school attendance.

Binet would accept the definition of intelligence as the

ability to succeed in _____ .

---

school

Almost all intelligence tests from Binet's time to today require pupils to respond to elicitors similar in many ways to those used in school. Success on the test indicates a high probability of _____ in school.

---

success

Some intelligence tests consist of a number of subtests to measure the various factors (variables) of intelligence. The subtest scores produce a profile.

An intelligence test not only measures an individual's ability to succeed in school, it may also provide a

_____ .

---

profile

It can also be said that an intelligence test measures an individual's aptitude for learning.

Betty achieves a high score on an intelligence test. It is highly probable that Betty also has a high aptitude for

_____ .

---

learning

An intelligence test may indicate general learning ability as well as specific strengths and weaknesses. Betty's test score may indicate her potential general success in school and aptitude for learning as well as her potential

_____ successes in various areas.

---

specific

There are two main types of intelligence tests—individual and group. Probably because of the factors of time and cost, the most frequently used intelligence tests are of the _____ type.

---

group

A teacher who has read the test manual can administer a group intelligence test to a class. Many of the group intelligence tests also have printed instructions and questions. This requires pupils to have some _____ skill.

---

reading

Pupils who have reading problems may therefore score
_____ on a group intelligence test.

---

low

A valid intelligence test is supposed to measure

_____ .

---

intelligence

So a pupil with a reading problem may receive a low score
on an intelligence test when he actually has high intellectual potential. In this case, the intelligence test

score would not be _____ .

---

valid

The concept of mental age (M.A.) was introduced by Binet.
It is used to indicate a child's level of intellectual
development.

Mary Ann's chronological age (C.A.) is eight years. She
has "average" intelligence, which would indicate her

mental age (M.A.) is also _____ years.

---

eight

Wayne is ten years old. His score on an intelligence test
was the norm for a typical twelve year old. Wayne's

chronological age (C.A.) is (1) _____ , and his

mental age (M.A.) is (2) _____ years.

---

(1) ten   (2) twelve

Thelma is thirteen years old. She achieved an intelligence test score equal to the norm for a typical twelve-
year-old. Her (1) _____ age is thirteen years,
and her (2) _____ age is twelve years.

---

(1) chronological   (2) mental

Wayne and Thelma have different (1) _____ ages, but their (2) _____ ages are the same.

---

(1) chronological   (2) mental

Regardless of chronological age, if a pupil's score on the Stanford-Binet equals the norm for the eleven-year-old population, his mental age is stated as _____ .

---

eleven years

Calvin's M.A. is nine years, and his C.A. is seven years. This would indicate that Calvin has "above normal" intelligence.

Joseph's M.A. is also nine years, but his C.A. is twelve years. Joseph probably has _____ intelligence.

---

below normal

The following table lists the M.A. and C.A. of three girls.

Name	M.A.	C.A.
Agnes	14	10
Bertha	10	10
Celeste	7	10

Comparing the M.A. and C.A., identify the girl whose intellectual development is:

"normal"   (1) _____

"above normal"   (2) _____

"below normal"   (3) _____

---

(1) Bertha   (2) Agnes   (3) Celeste

An intelligence test also yields an *intelligence quotient* (I.Q.). This is a ratio of M.A. to C.A. and is calculated by the formula:

$$I.Q. = \frac{M.A.}{C.A. \times 100}$$

From the table in the preceding frame, calculate the girls' I.Q.'s.

Agnes   (1) _____

Bertha   (2) _____

Celeste   (3) _____

---

(1) 140   (2) 100   (3) 70

Ten-year-old Bertha has normal intellectual development since she obtained an M.A. score equal to the average score of the ten-year-old sample population. Then an average I.Q. is _____ .

100

Complete the following table.

Name	M.A.	C.A.	I.Q.
George	12	10	(1) _____
Harvey	(2) _____	6	100
Irving	8	(3) _____	80

---

(1) 120   (2) 6   (3) 10

M.A. was defined as *level* of intellectual development. I.Q., a ratio of M.A. to C.A., represents the *rate* of intellectual development.

Since Bertha's M.A. is ten years at a C.A. of ten years, you can say that she has had an average _____ of intellectual development.

---

rate

Bertha's I.Q. of 100 indicates _____ rate of intellectual development.

---

average

You calculated Agnes's I.Q. at 140. Her I.Q. is above 100 and is considered to be an *accelerated* _____ of intellectual development.

---

rate

Celeste's I.Q., which is below 100, is considered to be a *slow* _____ of intellectual development.

---

rate

Therefore, what do we consider the rate of intellectual development of the following I.Q.'s to be?

above 100   (1) _____

100   (2) _____

below 100   (3) _____

---

(1) accelerated   (2) average   (3) slow

Although an I.Q. of 100 is considered to be average, the range of scores from 90 to 109 (Terman and Merrill, 1960) is considered as a *normal* rate of intellectual development.

Jean's M.A. of 9.5 years and C.A. of 10 years produces an I.Q. of 95. Jean's rate of intellectual development is considered to be in the _____ range.

---

normal

In the Terman and Merrill table, an I.Q. above 139 is classified as "gifted." Agnes's I.Q. of 140 places her in the class of _____ children.

---

gifted

Each classification in the table consists of a _____ of I.Q. scores.

---

range

Wechsler (1939) listed factors included in a description of intelligence. He included (1) the capacity to learn, (2) the knowledge acquired, (3) the ability to adjust or adapt, (4) the ability to think on an abstract level, and (5) the capacity to act toward a specific goal.

Wechsler's description of intelligence includes a number of _____ .

---

factors (variables)

The Wechsler Intelligence Scales for Children (WISC) determine I.Q. by comparing an individual's score with the scores of other individuals of the same chronological age. The Wechsler I.Q. is called a *deviation I.Q.*

A deviation I.Q. is found by comparing an individual's score with the scores of other individuals of the same

_____ .

---

chronological age

The 1960 revision of the Stanford-Binet Intelligence Scale (Terman and Merrill, 1960) substituted a deviation I.Q. for the older, ratio I.Q. The deviation I.Q. is generally used today. One of its several advantages is that it is a standard score that provides better correlation with different tests.

The type of I.Q. in general use today is a _____ I.Q.

---

deviation

An individual who correctly answers the same number of questions as the mean number correctly answered by the sample population of his same C.A. obtains a deviation I.Q. of 100.

Ted correctly answers 140 items on the Wechsler test. His mean number correct (in relation to the sample population's) is 140. Ted has a deviation I.Q. of _____ .

100

The number of correct answers above or below the sample population's mean will determine how many deviation I.Q. points a person will score above or below 100.

If the sample population's mean number correct is 125 and Robert correctly answers 145 questions correctly, you would assume his deviation I.Q. would be (above / below) 100.

---

above

The concepts of intelligence and I.Q. are useful for understanding differences in rates of learning.

Considering Bertha's I.Q. of 100 and Agnes's I.Q. of 140, you would expect Agnes to learn (faster / slower) than Bertha.

---

faster

Every psychological measurement has some degree of unreliability, so you can not be certain that a particular administration of an intelligence test yields an accurate score. However, the *standard error of measurement* allows you to know the range in which the real score might fall.

The standard error of measurement (does / does not) allow you to determine a completely accurate measurement.

---

does not

The error of measurement is approximately five points for I.Q.'s from 90 to 110 on the Stanford-Binet.

An I.Q. score achieved on the Stanford-Binet indicates that the real I.Q. is within _____ points of that score in either direction.

---

five

Mark's Stanford-Binet I.Q. is 107. There is a chance that on future I.Q. tests his score will range between (1) _____ and (2) _____ .

---

(1) 102   (2) 112

If two I.Q. scores are three points apart in this range, is it possible to say one is really higher than the other?

_____ .

No

Although the Stanford-Binet is quite a reliable intelligence test, it is important to remember that an I.Q. in the 90 to 110 range can vary approximately _____ points on subsequent tests.

---

five

It was stated earlier that correlation between I.Q. and academic achievement is high. Correlation refers to the degree of relationship between two factors (variables).

Since Agnes's I.Q. is higher than Bertha's, you could expect her academic achievement to be _____ .

---

higher

Bob's I.Q. of 104 is in the normal range. You could expect his academic achievement to be _____ .

---

normal (average)

I.Q. is useful for short-term predictions of learning achievement. You could make a short-term prediction after determining Celeste's I.Q. of 70 that she might have some _____ difficulties.

---

learning

Research indicates long-term prediction from I.Q. scores may not be valid. Honzik, Macfarlane, and Allen (1948) tested a group of children over a period of sixteen years. They found that a majority of children tend to have relatively stable I.Q.'s over a period of years, but a considerable number of children show consistent moves toward higher or lower I.Q.'s.

You can conclude from this that teachers should be cautious in making _____ predictions of future performance based on I.Q. alone.

---

long-term

A table of some of the findings of Honzik, Macfarlane, and Allen follows:

Change in I.Q. Points from 6 to 18 years	Percent of a Total Population of 222 (N = 222)
50 or more	0.5
30 or more	9.0
20 or more	37.0
15 or more	59.0
10 or more	85.0
9 or fewer	15.0

The table shows that I.Q. is not stable over a number of years and that it can _____ dramatically in some cases.

---

change

From the table you can see that for 59% of the population between six and eighteen years of age, I.Q. can change _____ points or more.

---

fifteen

I.Q. should be considered only one indicator of potential academic achievement.

In predicting a high-school pupil's success in college, you (should / should not) use only an intelligence test score.

---

should not

I.Q.'s tend to be invalid predictors of achievement for culturally different, socially deprived, or disturbed children.

A recent immigrant from Asia obtains a WISC score of 80. This score is probably not valid because his background

is _____ .

---

culturally different

Another limitation on the validity of I.Q. tests resulted from the assumption that mental development did not continue to increase after fifteen years of age. However, recent research indicates that mental development continues after _____ years of age.

---

fifteen

Still another limitation on the validity of the intelligence test score is its lack of ability to measure all the factors that can be used to describe intelligence, including creativity, motivation, or sense of humor.

An intelligence test cannot measure all the _____ of intelligence.

---

factors

A wide range of individual differences affect learning. For example, eyesight, hearing, and other physical health

factors may affect a pupil's _____ .

---

learning

A pupil's cultural and ethnic background, in particular his language development, influences _____ .

---

learning

Many influences in the social environment can affect a pupil's academic _____ either positively or negatively.

---

learning (achievement)

A child's excessive fears, anxieties, or emotional insta-bility can affect his academic and social _____ .

---

learning (achievements)

Individual differences in intelligence, culture, social environment, physical health, and emotional adjustment can affect a pupil's _____ .

---

learning

Assignment

Continue with the assignments in the Classroom Instruction Record in conjunction with assignments made by your prac-ticum teacher or supervisor.

References

Honzik, M. P., J. W. Macfarlane, and L. Allen. "The Sta-bility of Mental Test Performance between Two and Eighteen Years," *Journal of Experimental Education*, 1948, 17:309-324.

Terman, L. M., and M. A. Merrill. *Stanford-Binet Intelli-gence Scale*. Boston: Houghton Mifflin, 1960.

Wechsler, D. *Wechsler Intelligence Scale for Children*. New York: Psychological Corporation, 1949.

Four
Terminal Objectives

Objectives: When you have completed this chapter, you will
be able to (1) define terminal objective and state when it
is to be determined, (2) identify, define, and list the
advantages of the two types of terminal objectives, (3)
select the various types and levels of terminal objectives
appropriate for instructional sequences, and (4) evaluate
the use of the three levels of objectives.

Assessing such areas as level of academic achievement,
social development, and physical skills is the first
step in the process of instruction.

This initial assessment identifies pupils'

_____ .

---

entering behavior

Assessing entering behavior establishes a basis for determining the beginning level of instruction.

You are about to teach your pupils how to solve long division problems. By determining their entering behavior

in arithmetic skills, you will know where to _____
instruction in long division.

---

begin

Assessing entering behavior also provides a basis for advancing to the second step in the instructional process—
developing terminal objectives.

After determining entering behavior, your next step in the

process of instruction is to establish _____

_____ .

---

terminal objectives

A statement of the behaviors pupils are capable of producing *before* instruction begins is called _____

_____ .

---

entering behavior

A statement of the behaviors pupils will be capable of producing *after* instruction ends is the _____

_____ .

---

terminal objective

"The pupils in my French class have a vocabulary between 1000 and 1500 words." This is a statement of _____

_____ .

---

entering behavior

". . . . The pupils in my French course will write simple, grammatically correct sentences. . . ." This is a statement of _____ .

---

terminal objective

The two types of terminal objectives presented in Competencies for Teaching are *convergent* and *divergent*. Convergent objectives describe essential levels of learning for all pupils.

Pupils need basic reading skills to succeed in school. Therefore, most terminal objectives dealing with basic reading skills are _____ .

---

convergent

Convergent objectives also describe prerequisite learning for succeeding instructional sequences.

Terminal objectives for multiplication skills describe prerequisite skills in long division and are _____ objectives.

---

convergent

Divergent objectives describe performances that permit maximum individual development.

A number of pupils in your class complete assignments long before the rest of the class. To allow these pupils to develop to the maximum of their ability, you should establish _____ objectives for their instructional sequences.

---

divergent

The range of individual differences among pupils in a class is accommodated by divergent objectives.

Terminal objectives that allow for varying degrees of individual achievement are _____ objectives.

---

divergent

Some divergent objectives are developmental, that is, they encourage a pupil to strive to achieve his maximum ability.

Terminal objectives that encourage each pupil to develop his abilities to their maximum potential are _____ objectives.

---

divergent

A terminal objective, ". . . to solve problems using scientific method . . . ," can be achieved by pupils of varying abilities because the difficulty of the problems and the complexity of the solutions may vary. This terminal objective is a _____ objective.

---

divergent

Other divergent objectives encourage creative behavior, in which pupils do things that are new or unique to them.

Terminal objectives that do not have established criteria for outcomes allow pupils to be creative. These are _____ objectives.

---

divergent

In a beginning French course, a terminal objective, ". . . the pupils will have a minimum speaking vocabulary of 1000 words by the end of the semester . . . ," is a _____ objective.

---

convergent

The objective for the French course is convergent because it describes an (1) _____ level of learning that is (2) _____ for future learning.

---

(1) essential   (2) prerequisite

In the beginning French course, another terminal objective for the semester might be, ". . . the pupils will write letters to French-speaking pen pals. . . ." This objective would be classified as a _____ objective.

---

divergent

"Writing letters" is a divergent terminal objective that allows each pupil to _____ his own individual level in writing French.

---

develop

Because the pupils in your French course learn vocabulary at different rates, and because some pupils will develop the ability to write French prose more rapidly than

others, "writing letters" is a divergent objective that
will accommodate a range of _____ .

---

individual differences

The convergent and divergent objectives for an instructional sequence include (1) _____ levels of
learning for all pupils and accommodate a range of individual differences by encouraging each pupil to (2)
_____ to his maximum ability.

---

(1) essential   (2) develop

The following five frames present sets of objectives for
instructional sequences. Indicate which objectives are
convergent and which are divergent.

"At the conclusion of the unit on ecology, the pupils will
be able to:

Describe relationships between man and his environment.

(1) _____

Write a definition of ecology."   (2) _____

---

(1) divergent   (2) convergent

"By the end of the first semester of the physical education swimming class, pupils will be able to:

Float on their backs for one minute.   (1) _____

Demonstrate a variety of swimming strokes."

(2) _____

---

(1) convergent   (2) divergent

"At the end of the eighteenth-century literature course,
pupils will be able to:

Analyze an eighteenth-century English essay.

(1) _____

Name six major eighteenth-century literary works."

(2) _____

---

(1) divergent (2) convergent

"At the conclusion of the introductory industrial arts course, pupils will be able to:

Design and build a small table.   (1) _____

Identify the correct use of basic hand tools."

(2) _____

---

(1) divergent   (2) convergent

"At the conclusion of a unit on water colors in an introductory art course, pupils will be able to:

Make a color wheel.   (1) _____

Create a picture using water colors."   (2) _____

---

(1) convergent   (2) divergent

Most instructional sequences require a combination of both (1) _____ and (2) _____ terminal objectives.

---

(1) convergent   (2) divergent

Convergent and divergent objectives apply to learning outcomes on three levels: (1) essential, (2) developmental, and (3) creativity.

Convergent objectives applying to basic arithmetic operation skills describe _____ levels of learning.

---

essential

Essential-level objectives describe learning required of

_____ pupils.

Minimum expectations are described by essential-level objectives.

An essential-level objective describes the _____ learning you expect of all your pupils.

"After a unit on ceramics, pupils will be able to prepare a basic clay mixture for throwing pots. . . ."

This objective describes one of the (1) _____

learning outcomes expected and is at the (2) _____

level.

Essential-level objectives often describe learning outcomes that are prerequisite to future learning.

The skill, "to prepare a basic clay mixture," is a

_____ to throwing pots.

". . . Will be able to operate the potter's wheel . . ." is also an objective that describes an essential-level

skill that is _____ to throwing pots.

Essential-level objectives should describe a sufficient number of specific behaviors to indicate the minimum requirements clearly.

It is important to _____ essential-level objectives in sufficient detail to indicate the minimum requirements.

---

describe

Added to the objective, ". . . to prepare a basic clay mixture . . . ," might be these specific behaviors:

A. "To select the correct amount of materials"
B. "To add sufficient water"
C. "To mix thoroughly"

These specific behaviors clearly define the

(1) _____ learning of the (2) _____

level objective.

---

(1) minimum   (2) essential-

Divergent objectives describe learning outcomes on two levels: *developmental* and *creativity*.

Learning outcomes described by divergent objectives exist

on the (1) _____ and (2) _____ levels.

---

(1) developmental   (2) creativity

Developmental- and creativity-level objectives describe learning outcomes that provide opportunities for individual achievement.

Learning outcomes described by developmental- and

creativity-level objectives provide for _____

achievement.

---

individual

Developmental-level objectives provide for progress beyond the minimum level.

Pupils may achieve a (1) _____-level objective by (2) _____ beyond essential-level objectives.

---

(1) developmental   (2) progressing

A teacher provided additional and more difficult problems for pupils who had learned the basic operations of a slide rule.

These pupils were provided with an opportunity to achieve on the (1) _____ level because they were able to (2) _____ beyond the essential level.

---

(1) developmental   (2) progress

". . . To understand the process of growing plants" is a developmental-level objective that provides an opportunity for pupils to _____ beyond the essential level of simply listing a plant's stages of growth.

---

progress

In addition to providing for progress beyond the essential level, developmental-level objectives may also provide opportunities for in-depth study.

All the pupils were required to learn the names, locations, and dates of major events in the Civil War, but developmental-level objectives provided opportunities for them to study one or more of the events _____ .

---

in depth

In a science course, one of the objectives is: ". . . to identify cycles in nature. . . ." Three pupils made detailed charts of water and food cycles. Making the charts required the pupils to study these two cycles

(1) _____ and provided the opportunity for them to (2) _____ beyond the minimum requirements.

---

(1) in depth   (2) progress

Creativity-level objectives accommodate pupils' original responses.

Objectives that accommodate new or original responses are on the _____ level.

---

creativity

A pupil's responses at the creativity level are _____ for that pupil.

---

original (new)

A creativity-level objective, ". . . to write an essay . . . ," provides an opportunity for pupils to write something _____ .

---

original

An objective for a social studies unit is, ". . . to report on one aspect of local history." Two students, Frank and Kathleen, used tape-recorded interviews and film slides to report on the historical development of local housing. Since this type of response was original for these two pupils, it is on the _____ level.

---

creativity

There are two areas of creativity-level objectives: (1) problem solving and (2) individual expression.

Applying scientific method and producing solutions may achieve creativity-level objectives in the area of

_____ .

---

problem solving

The objective, ". . . to solve the problem of transporting people to and from their work more efficiently," is a (1) _____-level objective in the (2) _____ area.

Some problem solving is on the creativity level because there is not one specific solution to a problem.

The objective, ". . . to identify alternate solutions to a problem . . . ," provides an opportunity for pupils to be _____ .

---

creative

". . . To design a set of criteria to evaluate new products . . . ," is an objective on the (1) _____ level and does not restrict the possible (2) _____ to the problem of one "right" answer.

---

(1) creativity   (2) solutions

Another area of creativity-level objectives is

_____ .

---

individual expression

". . . To compose a song. . . ."
". . . To design a dress. . . ."
". . . To write a poem. . . ."

These objectives are on the creativity level because they give each pupil the opportunity to _____ himself individually.

---

express

Both developmental- and creativity-level objectives are open-ended because they permit a wide range of individuality in their responses.

The preceding transportation objective is open-ended because it allows for a _____ of possible solutions.

---

wide range

Which one of the following objectives is open-ended?

(1) ". . . State the law of conservation of mass."
(2) ". . . Describe advantages of using solar energy."

---

(2)

When pupils know the intended outcomes of an instructional sequence, they are more likely to concentrate their efforts toward achieving those outcomes. This can be aided by sharing the instructional objectives with your pupils.

Intended outcomes of instruction are more likely to be achieved when the objectives are _____ with your pupils.

---

shared

It is particularly important for essential-level objectives to be _____ with your pupils.

---

shared

Presenting your class with a course outline describing what they are expected to do is one means of _____ objectives.

---

sharing

Showing your pupils examples of pupils' best work from a previous instructional sequence is another way of

_____ instructional objectives.

---

sharing

Developmental- and creativity-level objectives can also be _____ without limiting the quality and quantity of an individual pupil's achievement.

---

shared

Showing a *variety* of pupils' creative products from past instructional sequences is another means of _____ objectives.

---

sharing

One way of sharing developmental- and creativity-level objectives is to _____ your pupils in the process of establishing their own objectives.

---

involve

The three methods of sharing instructional objectives with your pupils are:

To (1) _____ products that can be produced as a result of the instruction,

To (2) _____ lists of the instructional objectives, and

To (3) _____ pupils in establishing their own objectives.

---

(1) show   (2) provide   (3) involve

To review, the two types of objectives presented were

(1) _____ and (2) _____ .

---

(1) convergent   (2) divergent

The three levels of instructional objectives that have been presented are (1) _____ ,

(2) _____ , and (3) _____ .

---

(1) essential   (2) developmental   (3) creativity

Establishing objectives for an instructional sequence can be accomplished by one or a combination of the following methods:

1. Select them from prepared lists.
2. Write them yourself.
3. Develop them cooperatively with your pupils or with other teachers.

There are a variety of ways of establishing _____ for an instructional sequence.

---

objectives

There are three basic steps in establishing and writing an objective:

1. Describe the learning outcomes.
2. List the behaviors that demonstrate achievement.
3. State criteria for acceptable levels of performance.

The first step in establishing objectives is to

_____ the learning outcomes.

---

describe

"By the termination of the introductory course in Spanish, pupils will have a foundation for the use of the Spanish language."

This statement is one of the intended _____
of the course in Spanish.

---

learning outcomes

Statements of learning outcomes may be general and open to
many interpretations.

For example, "to know," "to understand," and "to apply"

are open to many _____ .

---

interpretations

The second step in establishing objectives is to

_____ the behaviors the pupils will exhibit when

demonstrating their achievement of the learning outcomes.

---

list

". . . To converse in Spanish. . . ."
". . . To write simple sentences in Spanish. . . ."
". . . To read sentences and short stories. . . ."

These statements are examples of intended specific

_____ .

---

behaviors

This second step requires using specific verbs to describe
pupils' behaviors.

Verbs such as "to read," "to speak," "to translate," and
"to write," describe pupils' _____ after instruction.

---

behaviors

On the creativity level, verbs such as "to design," "to construct," "to solve," and "to illustrate" are specific types of _____ but are sufficiently open-ended to allow for individual achievement.

---

behaviors

The third step in establishing objectives is to state the criteria to be used in evaluating the acceptable level of performance. This applies principally to essential-level objectives.

Stating the criteria for evaluating the acceptable level of performance applies principally to _____ - level objectives.

---

essential

The criteria of acceptable performance for the behavior, "to write simple sentences in Spanish," may be "to write ten sentences having two or fewer spelling errors and no more than three grammatical errors."

These statements are the _____ to be used in evaluating pupils' achievement of the objective.

---

criteria

The three steps in establishing objectives for an instructional sequence are:

Describe the desired (1) _____ .

List the specific (2) _____ that indicate achievement of the learning outcomes.

State the (3) _____ that will be used to evaluate the pupils' performance.

---

(1) learning outcomes   (2) behaviors   (3) criteria

Developmental-level objectives should be open-ended so as not to limit the pupil's individual development.

Fixed criteria for developmental-level objectives could
_____ pupil performance.

---

limit (restrict)

Creativity is a result of individual performance and expression. Fixed or predetermined criteria for evaluating
creativity could _____ pupil performance.

---

limit (restrict)

Statements of criteria for essential-level achievement
are required to evaluate the class performance of essential skills.

Stated criteria are not required nor are they desirable
for developmental or creativity objectives because they
could _____ individual pupil performance.

---

limit (restrict)

Assignment

Continue the exercises in the Classroom Instruction Record
in conjunction with assignments made by your practicum
teacher or supervisor.

Five

Enroute Objectives

Objectives: When you have completed this chapter, you will
be able to (1) describe the use of enroute objectives,
(2) describe developmental changes and predict the effects
of these changes as children develop, (3) use your knowledge of child development in writing instructional sequences, and (4) describe some of the work and findings of
Jean Piaget.

Enroute objectives describe component behaviors, or steps,
to be achieved in attaining a terminal objective.

Enroute objectives are components of, or _____
toward, a terminal objective.

---

steps

Enroute objectives provide guideposts on the way to a
terminal objective. They establish criteria for determining how well pupils are progressing.

Enroute objectives provide _____ for determining
how well pupils are achieving and where difficulties are
occurring.

---

criteria

The terminal objective for a lesson was, ". . . know Roman
numerals I to XII . . ."; the first enroute objective was,
". . . identify uses of Roman numerals. . . ."

Enroute objectives may describe steps toward a lesson's

_____ .

---

terminal objective

The second enroute objective for this lesson was, ". . .
recall the letters in Roman numerals I to XII. . . ."
This enroute objective indicates a required behavior and
helps the teacher select an appropriate elicitor to bring
forth the behavior.

The enroute objective helps the teacher select an appropriate _____ .

The third enroute objective was, ". . . arrange *The Book of Knowledge* in order by number. . . ."

This enroute objective identified instructional material that would be used to _____ the appropriate performance.

The fourth enroute objective was, ". . . write Arabic and Roman numerals from 1 to 12 and I to XII. . . ." The enroute objective describes a specific behavioral response.

The description of a specific behavioral response establishes _____ for evaluating achievement.

The lesson's terminal objective, "know Roman numerals," was described specifically by the enroute objectives.

Enroute objectives may be component behaviors describing the terminal objectives for a _____ .

Enroute objectives may describe component behaviors, or steps, required in achieving a unit's terminal objectives.

Enroute objectives may provide guideposts to indicate how well progress toward terminal objectives of a _____ is being achieved.

Enroute objectives may provide criteria for determining how well the terminal objectives of a course of study are being achieved.

Enroute objectives may describe the components of a

_____ of study.

---

course

Enroute objectives may be employed to describe the components or steps required to achieve the terminal objectives of a lesson, a unit, a course, or any program of instruction in which the terminal objective is achieved by acquiring component skills or steps.

Component skills or steps toward achieving terminal objectives are described by _____ .

---

enroute objectives

Understanding the structure of the subject matter being taught provides one basis for selecting a developmental sequence of enroute objectives.

Enroute objectives should be based on understanding the structure of the _____ being taught.

---

subject matter

Usually, enroute objectives consist of a developmental sequence. Understanding child development can contribute to the teacher's accuracy in selecting appropriate enroute objectives.

The teacher who understands _____ has a basis for accurately selecting appropriate enroute objectives.

---

child development

Child Development

Throughout life, an individual goes through many physical, mental, and social changes. Child development is the area of psychology that studies these changes.

Studies of the physical changes that take place at puberty are part of the study of _____ .

---

child development

The developing child is a constant challenge to the teacher. Knowledge of child development is important for the teacher in understanding how these changes affect learning.

Physical and mental changes in children affect their learning ability and can be better understood by studying _____ .

---

child development

Two of the major goals of child development are (1) to describe the changes in children as they grow and (2) to predict the effects of these changes.

One generalization from studies of child development is that a trend associated with all changes is toward increased complexity. As a child's psychomotor abilities develop, there will be a trend for psychomotor behavior to become more _____ .

---

complex

Generalizations such as "the trend toward complexity" are helpful to the teacher because they _____ changes in children as they grow and develop.

---

describe

The approximate time of occurrence and the usual effects of the physical and behavioral changes most children experience can be _____ from the findings of studies in child development.

---

predicted

Besides physical and mental development, each individual develops socially.

From complete dependence on others for satisfaction of needs to relative independence, individuals follow a similar sequence in their early _____ development.

---

social

Like other aspects of development, social development occurs in stages that are dependent on each other. (Social development was discussed in considerable detail in *Individual Instruction* and therefore will not be explored further in this chapter.)

Stages of social development are _____ on each other.

---

dependent

Child development studies seek to describe the internal and external forces that influence physical, mental, and social changes.

The changes in the growing and developing child are

_____ by both internal and external factors.

---

influenced

Internal factors that influence development are *hereditary*, and external factors are *environmental*.

A child growing up in a Spanish-speaking home develops the ability to speak the Spanish language. This development

results from _____ factors.

---

environmental

An infant's eyes turn brown. This change is the result of

a(n) _____ factor.

---

hereditary

Maturation is the process of development through which an individual acquires those characteristics associated with heredity.

Height, hair color, and other physical characteristics

develop through the process of _____ .

---

maturation

Some types of behavioral changes such as visual fixation and walking also develop through the process of

_____ .

---

maturation

Psychological studies have discovered that some changes take place with little influence from the environment in which the child is raised.

These changes take place through the process of (1) _____ and are associated with (2) _____ factors.

---

(1) maturation   (2) hereditary

Arnold Gesell studied the sequence of development common to normal children, which appeared to be determined by heredity.

If a change develops in a group of normal children experiencing a broad range of environmental differences, Gesell would say that the change was due to _____ factors.

---

hereditary

Gesell emphasized that knowledge about the maturational process would lead to the provision of better environmental situations for learnings.

Your knowledge of child development due to heredity may result in your ability to develop better _____ sequences.

---

instructional

Keeping the range of individual differences in mind, Gesell obtained norms for many areas of child development. Norms of this type help in achieving the goals of child

development by (1) _____ the changes that occur
and by (2) _____ when they normally occur.

---

(1) describing   (2) predicting

Norms can help you identify deficiencies in development or
explain changes that may seem unusual.

Gesell found that between the ages of two and three years,
normal children begin to use short sentences. A child entering kindergarten, who has the ability to use only
single words to express himself, would be considered

_____ in his development of language.

---

deficient

Another norm Gesell established was that after five years
of age, children have developed socially to the point that
they have enough independence from parents to adjust to
school.

After several days at school, a child who cries as soon as
his mother leaves him would be considered _____
in his social development.

---

deficient

Gesell's research indicates that children pass through a
number of specific maturational stages in the same sequence but at different rates.

The process of learning to walk is similar for most children but the stages may occur at different _____
for each child.

---

ages (rates)

It can accurately be said that children (do / do not)
mature at the same time.

---

do not

The concept of maturation, however, does not explain all of the changes in a child's development.

Child development is therefore concerned with more than

_____ .

---

maturation

External or environmental factors influence physical, mental, and social changes in children.

Besides being concerned with hereditary factors, child development is concerned with _____ factors that influence development.

---

environmental

The maturation process is concerned with the rate and amount of change an individual undergoes as a result of heredity. Environmental factors can either assist or retard these changes.

Heredity establishes that a child can grow to be tall. Disease or the lack of an appropriate diet are

_____ factors that can negatively affect the development of this characteristic.

---

environmental

The amount of time parents spend in verbal interaction with their children is a(n) _____ factor that influences the child's language development.

---

environmental

In most cases, the developmental changes in children cannot be attributed to a single factor. It is likely that both (1) _____ and (2) _____ factors interact to influence child development.

---

(1) hereditary   (2) environmental

Jean Piaget, a Swiss psychologist, employed a systematic approach to observation in studying the development of children's mental abilities.

Although it had been recognized before that children could manage increasingly complex intellectual problems as they matured, a systematic study of mental development was conducted by _____ .

Jean Piaget

Piaget's research involved the systematic _____ of children in their natural environments.

---

observation

One generalization Piaget made from his many years of observation was that there is a *continuous* and *progressive* change that characterizes mental development.

Throughout an individual's life, the ability to think and to understand is always _____ .

---

changing

Contrary to early psychological beliefs, Piaget found that an individual's mental development undergoes (no / more) changes after the age of fifteen years.

---

more

Central to Piaget's theory of the development of mental abilities is the child's interaction with the environment.

Besides maturation, mental development takes place through the child's interaction with the _____ .

---

environment

Piaget's studies establish that mental development is (1) _____ and (2) _____ throughout an individual's life. His studies indicate also that development is influenced through the process of (3)

_____ and through the child's (4) _____

with the environment.

---

(1) continuous (2) progressive
(3) maturation (4) interaction

According to Piaget's theory, mental development implies
an increasing ability to adapt to the environment.

As a child's mental abilities develop, he or she is in-

creasingly able to _____ to new or more complex

environments.

---

adapt

Piaget found that the mind is characterized by a tendency
toward adaptation. He describes two mental operations
that result in the ability to adapt: *assimilation* and
accommodation.

Assimilation and accommodation are the two basic mental
operations that result in the individual's ability to

_____ .

---

adapt

Assimilation is the mental operation of using previously
learned behaviors to respond to new environmental stimuli.

A pupil solves a new problem by using a previously

learned process. The pupil is said to have _____

previous learning.

---

assimilated

Responses to new stimuli that use previously learned be-

haviors are called _____ .

---

assimilation

Assimilation does not require learning any new

_____ .

---

behaviors

For assimilation to take place, however, there must be interaction with the _____ .

---

environment

Assimilation is one of the two complementary mental operations involved in interacting with the environment, which an individual uses in _____ .

---

adapting

The second operation is accommodation. Accommodation occurs when there is a change in behavior resulting from interaction with the environment.

Accommodation results in a _____ in behavior.

---

change

The process of mental development, through which new behaviors are learned, Piaget calls _____ .

---

accommodation

Whenever an individual is unable to assimilate new environmental stimuli, he _____ them by modifying the old behaviors or learning new ones.

---

accommodates

Like assimilation, accommodation takes place through an interaction with the _____ .

---

environment

The act of responding to new stimuli with an established behavior is (1) _____ , and the process of learning new behaviors is (2) _____ .

---

(1) assimilation   (2) accommodation

All the interactions an individual has with the environment involve both assimilation and accommodation. The reason for this may be that new behaviors are developed on the basis of previously learned behaviors. Most learning involves both (1) _____ and (2)

_____ .

---

(1) assimilation   (2) accommodation

The processes of adaptation and increasing mental ability occur in stages and involve qualitative changes in mental abilities.

Piaget believes all children pass through the same

_____ of mental development.

---

stages

The stages of mental development that normal children pass through occur within an approximate range of time.

Children normally learn to use short sentences to describe their experiences and express their desires within a range of _____ from twenty-four to thirty-six months.

---

time

"Stages" of development should not be understood to mean that each stage is distinct and has a definite beginning and an end.

Development is continuous and progressive but stages can be identified as occurring within an approximate range of

_____ .

Although the stages are not distinct and may not occur at the same time, Piaget believes they occur in the same

_____ for all people.

---

sequence

Piaget has identified four stages of development.

Piaget's work has resulted in his identifying four

_____ in child development.

---

stages

The four stages and their approximate age ranges are:

1. Sensorimotor   0 to 2 years
2. Pre-operational   2 to 7 years
3. Concrete operations   7 to 11 years
4. Formal operations   11 and up years

The first stage of development Piaget describes involves the child's sensing some stimulus in the environment and

reacting to it with a simple _____ response.

---

motor

A child sees a ball, picks it up, and throws it to his mother. This series of events would probably take place

for the first time during the _____ stage of a child's life.

---

sensorimotor

Around the age of two years, the child develops beyond the sensorimotor state and enters the _____ stage.

---

pre-operational

The pre-operational stage is the period in which the child develops mental abilities necessary for success in school.

Mental abilities necessary for positive school accomplishments are developed in the _____ stage.

---

pre-operational

During the pre-operational stage, the child learns to substitute language and mental images for the sensorimotor
responses he used in earlier life.

Instead of reaching out his hand toward some object out of
his reach, the child learns to ask for it during the

_____ stage.

---

pre-operational

Between the ages of seven and eleven years, a child is in
the stage of development Piaget calls the _____

_____ stage.

---

concrete operations

The concrete operations stage is characterized by the
child's learning to reason and to think logically.

A child is shown a quart of water poured into a number of
containers of different sizes and shapes. The ability to
understand that the amount of water remains the same develops in the _____ stage.

---

concrete operations

In this third stage of development, the child acquires the
ability to reason and to think logically, but these reactions are still involved with _____ situations.

---

concrete (real)

The fourth stage of mental development described by Piaget
is the _____ stage.

---

formal operations

The ability to use formal operations normally develops after _____ years of age.

The major development in the formal operations stage is that the child learns to think about hypothetical situations.

In the first three stages, the child reacts to concrete situations in his environment, but in the formal operations stage, he develops the ability to think about _____ situations.

Being able to think of what will happen if a certain thing is done develops during the _____ stage.

A child who understands that when a number is divided by another number larger than the first, the answer is smaller than one, is probably in the _____ stage of development.

Piaget's studies imply that instruction that jumps too far ahead of a child's mental development will probably be ineffective.

It is (probable / improbable) that a child eight years of age can successfully be taught abstract mathematical principles.

Another implication for teaching is that because children do reorganize their mental structures as a result of experience, teachers should provide experiences to challenge a child's mental abilities in order to bring about the next stage of development.

To help the child move from one stage of development to the next, the teacher should provide _____ at the next higher level of mental development.

---

experiences

In summary, Piaget and many other child psychologists believe that for maximum learning to take place, a child must have adequate (1) _____ of the mental operations and sufficient (2) _____ with the environment.

---

(1) maturation   (2) interaction

Although there are other theories of child development, Piaget's theory is possibly the most influential in the area of the development of _____ abilities.

---

mental

Assignment

Continue the exercises in the Classroom Instruction Record in conjunction with assignments made by your practicum teacher or supervisor.

References

Flavell, John H. *The Developmental Psychology of Jean Piaget*. Princeton, N.J.: D. Van Nostrand, 1963.

Gesell, Arnold, and I. Ilg. *Infant and Child in the Culture of Today*. New York: Harper & Row, 1943.

Inhelder, Barbel, and Jean Piaget. *The Early Growth of Logic in the Child*. New York: Norton, 1969.

Spencer, Mary Ann. *Understanding Piaget: An Introduction to Children's Cognitive Development*. New York: Harper & Row, 1971.

Six

Elicitors

Objectives: When you have completed this chapter, you will
be able to (1) define eliciting stimuli, (2) identify environmental events that are unconditioned and conditioned
stimuli, (3) understand classical conditioning and (4)
know the use of classical conditioning in the classroom.

An *elicitor* is defined as an environmental stimulus that
precedes and brings forth a behavior.

The school bell rings and your pupils take their seats.
The ringing bell is the _____ that elicits the
pupils' behavior.

---

stimulus

The behavior that is elicited by the stimulus is called a
response.

Taking their seats was the _____ the pupils made
to the stimulus of the ringing bell.

---

response

Another term for learning used by psychologists is *conditioning*.

When a psychologist says that an individual has been conditioned to perform some behavior, we might say that the
individual has _____ the behavior.

---

learned

Classical Conditioning

Events occur in the environment. For example, a beam of
light is directed toward your eye. The event in the environment, the light's shining in your eye, is a stimulus

that _____ a decrease in the size of the pupil
of your eye.

---

elicits

The decrease in the size of your pupil is a _____
to the elicitor.

---

response

The response is your behavior, contraction of your pupil,
brought forth by the _____ stimulus.

---

eliciting

A *reflex* is relationship between an unlearned response
occurring involuntarily in an individual and the stimulus
that elicits the response.

A stimulus-response association that is unlearned and involuntary in an individual is a(n) _____ .

---

reflex

The eyelid closes involuntarily when an object approaches
the eye. The movement of the object toward the eye is the
(1) _____ that elicits the (2) _____
of the eyelid's closing. This unlearned, involuntary
stimulus-response association is called a(n) _____ .

---

(1) stimulus   (2) response   (3) reflex

A reflex response is _____ by a stimulus.

---

elicited

A reflex occurs in a specific order. First the (1)
_____ is presented which elicits the (2)
_____ that follows.

---

(1) stimulus   (2) response

If a stimulus is too weak, it will fail to _____
a response.

---

elicit

If the light that strikes your eye is very weak it will
fail to _____ pupil contraction.

---

elicit

In order for your pupil to respond, the light stimulus
must have sufficient strength or intensity.

The point at which a stimulus will _____ a response is called the *threshold*.

---

elicit

The point at which the light will elicit pupil contraction
is called the _____ .

---

threshold

The term *threshold* refers to the weakest intensity or magnitude of a stimulus that is sufficient to elicit a response.

A teacher's softly spoken question that does not elicit
the pupils' response may be below their hearing

_____ .

---

threshold

If a response does not occur the stimulus may be

too _____ .

---

weak

The (1) _____ of a stimulus is the intensity

that is barely sufficient to (2) _____ a (3)

_____ .

---

(1) threshold   (2) elicit   (3) response

Around the turn of the century, Pavlov, a Russian physi-
ologist, discovered the *conditioned reflex*, the basis of
classical conditioning.

Classical conditioning is an area of learning concerned
with the acquisition of responses through the use of
formerly neutral stimuli.

The area of learning concerned with conditioning eliciting stimuli to formerly neutral stimuli is called

_____ .

---

classical conditioning

Classical conditioning occurs when two stimuli—one unconditioned (or reflexive) and the other neutral—are paired.

Classical conditioning procedures depend on _____
two stimuli.

---

pairing

If a stimulus that initially has no effect—that is, it is
neutral—is paired with an unconditioned stimulus—that
is, one that elicits an involuntary response—the pre-

viously neutral stimulus will become a _____
stimulus.

---

conditioned

"An unconditioned stimulus elicits a response." This
sentence is represented by the diagram:

$$US \longrightarrow R$$

US represents (1) _____

→ represents (2) _____

R represents (3) _____

---

(1) unconditioned stimulus   (2) elicits   (3) response

Through the process of classical conditioning, a neutral
stimulus becomes an elicitor, or conditioned stimulus
(CS).

A neutral stimulus (is / is not) an elicitor.

---

is not

The example below represents the pairing of an unconditioned stimulus with a neutral stimulus that has become
a conditioned stimulus:

US
CS

After a neutral stimulus has been conditioned it becomes

effective as an _____ .

---

elicitor

$$US \longrightarrow R$$
$$CS \dashrightarrow$$

In this diagram, the CS is directly under the US and indicates that the two stimuli were presented at about the

same _____ .

---

time

The broken line in the diagram indicates that the CS is acquiring the ability to _____ the response.

In summary, in the following diagram:

$$US \longrightarrow R$$
$$CS \dashrightarrow R$$

US represents (1) _____

⟶ represents (2) _____

CS represents (3) _____

⇢ represents (4) _____

R represents (5) _____

---

(1) unconditioned stimulus   (2) elicits   (3) conditioned stimulus   (4) is acquiring the ability to elicit the response   (5) response

Conditioning a neutral stimulus to establish a stimulus-response relationship may require a number of pairings of the US and the CS.

For conditioning to be successful, a _____ of pairings of the US and the CS may be required.

When the words *ice cream* are said to a baby, it is un-likely that he will respond. If he does not respond, the words are a _____ stimulus for him.

You place a small amount of ice cream in the baby's mouth, saliva flows, and he eats the ice cream. Ice cream can be called an _____ stimulus.

For the sounds of the words *ice cream* to elicit salivation, the words and the act of putting the ice cream into

the baby's mouth should be _____ .

---

paired

For the classroom teacher, the practical application of
classical conditioning is in the realm of emotional reactions. This has far-reaching implications because most
behavior is "emotional" to some degree.

Emotional reactions are associated with most

_____ .

---

behaviors

During the process of instruction, a teacher can condition
children to like or dislike, hate or love, fear or enjoy
the subject matter, the learning process, the teacher, or
the school.

During the instructional process, the teacher can condition pupils' _____ responses.

---

emotional

In teaching, it is frequently desirable to pair new
elicitors with established elicitors that are known to
bring forth favorable emotional responses.

Elicitors to which pupils respond positively or with satisfaction should be paired with _____ elicitors.

---

new

If the teacher involves pupils in an established activity
that elicits a favorable response and then introduces a
new elicitor, there is high probability that the new elicitor will, through conditioning, bring forth a positive

_____ .

---

emotional response

Assignment   Continue the exercises in the Classroom Instruction Record
in conjunction with assignments made by your practicum
teacher or supervisor.

References   Pavlov, J. P. *Conditioned Reflexes*. London: Oxford
University Press, 1946.

Seven

Reinforcers

Objectives: When you have completed this chapter, you will be able to (1) define reinforcement, (2) understand operant conditioning, (3) know the differences between and the uses of positive and negative reinforcers, and (4) identify and apply the different reinforcement schedules.

A reinforcer makes it more _____ that the pupil will respond in the same way again.

probable (likely)

The praise pupils receive after successfully completing an assignment will increase the _____ that future assignments will be completed.

probability

Operant conditioning or learning results from the association between a (1) _____ and its (2) _____ .

(1) behavior   (2) consequence (reinforcer)

The pupils' behavior of completing their assignments was _____ by praise, which will increase the behavior's occurrence in the future.

reinforced

When pupils complete assigned tasks so that they may select an activity in which they wish to engage, they are illustrating the fact that behaviors can be _____ by being reinforced.

_____

strengthened

When pupils are praised for specific behaviors, this reinforcement is presented immediately _____ the behavior occurs.

_____

after

When reinforcement is *presented* to pupils after their behavior, it is said that they are being positively

_____ .

_____

reinforced

Presentation of a stimulus that strengthens behavior is _____ reinforcement.

_____

positive

When a teacher employs positive reinforcement, the reinforcer is _____ to the pupil.

_____

presented

A pupil is given twenty points for successfully solving arithmetic problems. Presenting the pupil with the twenty points is an example of _____ .

_____

positive reinforcement

The purpose of positive reinforcement is to _____ the behavior it follows.

_____

strengthen

Another class of reinforcers strengthens behavior through
the termination of an unpleasant stimulus.

If presenting a reinforcer is called positive reinforcement, then terminating an unpleasant stimulus to

strengthen the behavior it follows is called _____
reinforcement.

---

negative

A pupil is negatively reinforced. This means his behavior
is strengthened by the _____ of a stimulus.

---

termination

If *presentation* is the key word in positive reinforcement,
then the key word in negative reinforcement is

_____ .

---

termination

When presentation of a stimulus reinforces the response it
follows, the stimulus is a (1) _____
_____ , and when termination of a stimulus reinforces the response it follows, the stimulus is a (2)

_____ .

---

(1) positive reinforcer   (2) negative reinforcer

You wish to escape from the discomfort of a loud noise.
You escape the discomfort by placing your hands over your
ears, thus reducing the effect of the noise.

The behavior of putting your hands over your ears was

strengthened by _____ reinforcement.

---

negative

Turning off a disturbing television program, closing the
window to terminate a cold draft, and turning away from an

unpleasant scene are all examples of escape behaviors that are subject to _____ reinforcement.

---

negative

In negative reinforcement, the stimulus is _____ by the behavioral response.

---

terminated

Peer group disapproval is aversive to most young people. Terminating other children's ridicule can be considered a _____ .

---

negative reinforcer

A boy is ridiculed for hesitating to break windows in a vacant building. When he breaks the windows he escapes being called a "sissy." Breaking the windows

_____ the group's ridicule.

---

terminated

The boy might have continued to decline to break the windows, or he might have made excuses, redirected the group's activity, or left the scene.

A diversity of responses might be reinforced by

_____ reinforcement.

---

negative

A child may escape the threats and anxiety created by an aggressive and threatening adult by adopting compliant behavior. The child may also respond by either counteraggression or attempts to escape from or avoid the adult.

These two behaviors are probably inconsistent with the adult's objectives. Counteraggression or escape from a

threatening adult is _____ if it results in reducing the threats.

---

reinforced

Negative reinforcement occurs naturally in many learning situations. The child fearful to attempt a jump in physical education class reduces his anxiety by making the jump.

Making the jump produces _____ from anxiety.

---

escape

The function of positive reinforcement is to _____ the behavior it follows.

---

strengthen (reinforce)

The function of negative reinforcement is to _____ the behavior it follows.

---

strengthen (reinforce)

Therefore, a behavior can be (1) _____ through the use of both (2) _____ and (3) _____ reinforcement.

---

(1) strengthened   (2) positive   (3) negative

Presenting a stimulus to strengthen behavior is (1) _____ , and terminating a stimulus to strengthen behavior is (2) _____ _____ .

---

(1) positive reinforcement   (2) negative reinforcement

According to the Premack principle, a (1) _____ _____ behavior can be used to reinforce a (2) _____ behavior.

---

(1) high-probability   (2) low-probability

"Eat your vegetables and then you may have some dessert,"
is an example of _____ Law.

Grandma's

Schedules of reinforcement indicate the times when reinforcement occurs and the amount of reinforcement provided
for a behavior. The kind of schedule used depends on
whether the behavior is being established or maintained.

The frequency and the amount of reinforcement are indicated by the _____ of reinforcement.

---

schedule

Reinforcing a behavior each time it occurs is called a
continuous schedule of reinforcement.

In contingency management, each time a pupil completes an
assigned task he is allowed to go to the reinforcement
area. In this case, task completion behavior is on a

_____ reinforcement schedule.

---

continuous

A continuous reinforcement schedule is used to establish
new behaviors.

New behaviors are best learned on a _____ reinforcement schedule.

---

continuous

To teach your pupils to put away their books before
leaving the room, you should use a _____ reinforcement schedule to establish this behavior.

---

continuous

The purpose of continuous reinforcement schedules is to
_____ new behaviors.

---

establish

B. F. Skinner's early experiments reinforced each occurrence of a behavior. Later he discovered that this
_____ reinforcement schedule was not always the
best for maintaining an established behavior.

---

continuous

Skinner found that established behaviors could be maintained with only *intermittent* reinforcement.

Reinforcing behavior other than for each occurrence is
called a(n) _____ reinforcement schedule.

---

intermittent

There are two types of intermittent reinforcement schedules: (1) *ratio* and (2) *interval*.

Besides a continuous reinforcement schedule, there are
two _____ reinforcement schedules.

---

intermittent

The two intermittent reinforcement schedules are (1)
_____ and (2) _____.

---

(1) ratio   (2) interval

A ratio reinforcement schedule reinforces according to the
number of _____ emitted.

---

behaviors

In ratio reinforcement schedules, reinforcement is based on the _____ of behaviors emitted.

---

number

A fixed-ratio schedule reinforces a behavior after the behavior has been emitted a fixed, or specified, number of times.

Reinforcement after a specified number of behaviors have been emitted is a _____-_____ reinforcement schedule.

---

fixed-ratio

A fixed-ratio reinforcement schedule is based on a _____ number of behaviors.

---

fixed (specified)

A variable-ratio reinforcement schedule reinforces a behavior after a variable, or inconstant, number of the behaviors has been emitted.

Reinforcing a behavior after a variable number has been emitted is a _____-_____ reinforcement schedule.

---

variable-ratio

You reinforce your pupils for cooperative play on the playground. Your reinforcement schedule will vary depending on your proximity to the child and a number of other factors. This is an example of a _____-_____ reinforcement schedule.

---

variable-ratio

A variable-ratio reinforcement schedule is based on a _____ number of behaviors emitted.

---

variable (inconstant)

You tell your kindergarten pupils that for every three correct responses to the alphabet flashcards, they will earn one point. This is an example of a _____-_____ reinforcement schedule.

---

fixed-ratio

An interval reinforcement schedule is based on the time between _____ .

---

reinforcements

Fixed-interval reinforcement schedules are based on a (1) _____ period of (2) _____ between re-inforcements.

---

(1) fixed   (2) time

Fixed-interval schedules reinforce after a fixed time has elapsed.

Reinforcing a behavior after a fixed period of time has elapsed is a _____-_____ reinforcement schedule.

---

fixed-interval

A teacher set a timer to ring every ten minutes. Pupils who are working when the bell rings are reinforced. This is an example of a _____-_____ reinforcement schedule.

---

fixed-interval

Variable-interval reinforcement schedules reinforce behavior after a variable period of time has elapsed since the last reinforcement.

Reinforcing a behavior after a variable period of time has elapsed is a _____ - _____ reinforcement schedule.

---

variable-interval

In the previous example, a teacher set the clock to ring at ten-minute intervals. A more effective method would be to set the time to ring after variable time periods so the pupils would not know when to expect it. This would be a _____ - _____ reinforcement schedule.

---

variable-interval

A variable-interval reinforcement schedule is based on _____ periods of time.

---

variable

The key point to remember about interval schedules is that they are based on the elapsed _____ between re-inforcements.

---

time

The difference between ratio and interval schedules is that ratio schedules are based on (1) _____ and interval schedules are based on (2) _____ .

---

(1) number   (2) time

But to maintain established behaviors, it is more effi-cient to change from continuous reinforcement to an _____ reinforcement schedule.

---

intermittent

A variable-ratio and a variable-interval reinforcement schedule are both effective in _____ an established behavior.

maintaining

In teaching, it is desirable to use a combination of reinforcement schedules, using a (1) _____ schedule to teach new behaviors and changing to a(n) (2) _____ schedule to maintain behaviors.

(1) continuous   (2) intermittent

Assignment

Continue the exercises in the Classroom Instruction Record in conjunction with assignments made by your practicum teacher and supervisor.

References

Holland, J. G., and B. F. Skinner. *The Analysis of Behavior*. New York: McGraw-Hill, 1961.

Skinner, B. F. *The Technology of Teaching*. New York: Appleton-Century-Crofts, 1968.

Eight

Evaluation

Objectives: When you have completed this chapter, you will
be able to (1) define evaluation, measurement, dependent
variable, independent variable, and other terminology used
in descriptive statistics, (2) organize, analyze, and describe data collected on pupil behavior, (3) understand
descriptive statistics used in standardized test manuals
and research reports, and (4) interpret the various types
of scores derived from testing.

After an instructional sequence is completed, it is time
to determine the students' level of achievement of the instructional objectives. This systematic process is called

_____ .

evaluation

Evaluating the achievement of instructional objectives

involves collecting _____ of behaviors described

in the objectives.

samples

Evaluation also involves comparing collected samples of

behaviors with the stated _____ for the instruc-

tional sequence.

objectives

Measurement

Collecting samples of behavior is called *measurement* and

provides the data used in _____ how well the

objectives have been achieved.

evaluating

In determining how well your pupils have learned to spell, you may give them a quiz. The quiz is a means of

_____ each pupil's spelling behavior.

---

measuring

The score on the quiz is called a *dependent variable*. Any change in pupil performance due to the influence of environmental factors is called a _____ variable.

---

dependent

The environmental factors that result in changes in dependent variables are called *independent variables*.

Instructional materials, methods of presentation, assignments, types of measurement instruments, and the consequences of performance are all _____ .

---

independent variables

You give each of your pupils ten cards with a word printed on each and instruct them to place the cards in alphabetical order.

The task of placing the cards in alphabetical order is the (1) _____ variable and the number of words correctly placed in alphabetical order is the (2) _____ variable.

---

(1) independent   (2) dependent

Half of a group of pupils studies biology using a self-instructional program in the learning lab. The other half of the group attends a regular lecture-lab class.

The method of instruction used in this study is the

_____ variable.

---

independent

An identical examination is given to the entire biology group to determine which method of instruction was more effective. The scores on the examination are the

_____ variables of the study.

---

dependent

Many types of independent variables for measuring pupil behavior have been discussed in the textbook: standardized achievement tests, teacher-made paper-and-pencil tests, and performance tests. The scores on any of these measuring instruments provide data for _____ the level of achievement of the instructional objectives.

---

evaluating

The purpose of this chapter is to show you how these scores can be treated to obtain maximum information for

_____ pupil achievement.

---

evaluating

Descriptive Statistics

Descriptive statistics is the basic method used to organize and analyze dependent variables.

The basic method used to organize and analyze a group of test scores is called _____ .

---

descriptive statistics

A number of symbols with which you should become familiar are used in descriptive statistics. They are:

$$x = \text{raw score}$$
$$f = \text{frequency}$$
$$\Sigma = \text{sum of}$$
$$M = \text{mean}$$
$$N = \text{total number of subjects in group}$$
$$s = \text{standard deviation}$$

Descriptive statistics uses _____ to represent various concepts.

The measurements a teacher makes of pupil behavior are normally a collection of numerical raw data. This is especially true of assignment grades, quiz or test scores, and points earned.

The information teachers collect concerning pupil behavior is called _____ .

---

raw data

Susan received a score of 23 for her science workbook. The 23 is her _____ .

---

raw score

The symbol normally used to indicate raw score is x.

Sam received a raw score of 49 on a sociology quiz. For Sam, x equalled _____ .

49

If each question on a quiz counted one point and Philip obtained an x equal to 19, this would indicate that

Philip's responses to _____ questions were correct.

19

The $x = 19$ Philip obtained on the quiz has little meaning by itself and is of no value in evaluating his performance without additional information. An $x = 19$ of a possible 100 points would probably indicate poor performance, whereas an $x = 19$ of a possible 20 points would indicate he performed very well.

Comparing the raw score with the total possible points is one method of _____ Philip's performance.

---

evaluating

The method normally used to compare an individual's score with the total possible points expresses the score as the percentage correct. This is done by dividing the raw score by the total possible points and multiplying by 100.

$$\frac{\text{raw score } (x)}{\text{total possible points}} \times 100 = \text{percentage score}$$

Jay's assignment was graded 40 of a possible 50 points.

His percentage score is _____%.

80

Evaluation should always be done in relation to the objectives set for the instructional sequence. However, comparing raw scores with total possible points or determining percentage scores indicates only individual achievement. It does not indicate the level at which the rest of the group performed the desired behavior.

Descriptive statistics helps compare an individual's performance with the rest of the _____ .

---

group

To make a collection of scores more meaningful, the first procedure to follow is to arrange them in numerical order. A numerically ordered collection of scores is called a *distribution*.

If a collection of scores were arranged in numerical order from the lowest score to the highest score, the arrangement would be a _____ .

---

distribution

The following scores were received by the self-instructional biology group. Arrange the scores in a distribution.

51, 51, 49, 53, 52, 51, 50, 51, 50, 52

49, 50, 50, 51, 51, 51, 51, 52, 52, 53

The number of times a particular score occurs in a distribution is referred to as that score's *frequency*.

The frequency of the score of 52 in the self-instructional biology group is _____ .

If 3 pupils obtained a score of 83 on an assignment, then the _____ of $x = 83$ would be 3.

---

frequency

Listing a group of scores in order with their corresponding frequencies is called a *frequency distribution*.

The following table of the preceding scores is called a

_____ .

Score	Frequency
x	f
49	/
50	//
51	////
52	//
53	/

---

frequency distribution

Another way of portraying a frequency distribution is by using a graph.

A visual representation of a frequency distribution can be accomplished by using a _____ .

---

graph

A *histogram*, or *bar graph*, is one type of graph used to illustrate a frequency distribution.

A bar graph that illustrates a frequency distribution is called a _____ .

---

histogram

The following graphic representation of the scores on a biology examination is called a _____ .

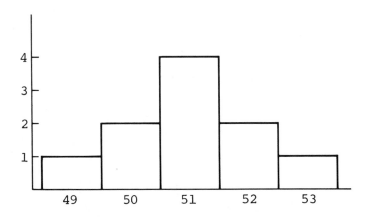

---

histogram (bar graph)

A *frequency polygon* is another type of graph used to illustrate a frequency distribution. Points and lines are used to indicate scores and their frequencies.

A graph illustrating a frequency distribution with points and lines is a _____ .

---

frequency polygon

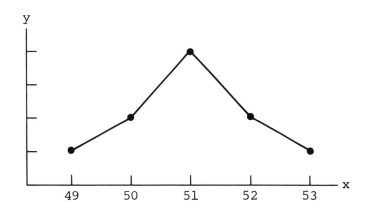

This graph of the biology scores is called a _____

_____ .

---

frequency polygon

The vertical side of a graph is called the y-axis, or the ordinate, and is commonly used to designate frequency (f).

Frequency increases as you move higher on the

_____ .

---

ordinate

By reading the number on the ordinate, determine the frequency of the following three scores indicated by the frequency polygon above.

A (1) _____

B (2) _____

D (3) _____

---

(1) 2   (2) 5   (3) 4

The horizontal side of a graph, the x-axis, or abscissa, is commonly used to designate the scores (x).

Normally the value of numerical raw scores increases as you move from left to right on the _____ .

---

abscissa

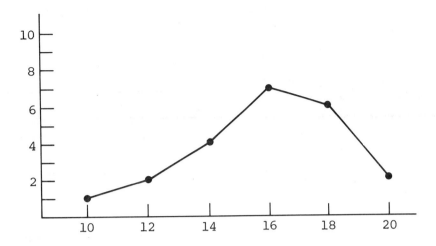

The score with a frequency of 4 on the histogram above

is _____ .

14

In review, a bar graph illustrating a frequency distribution is a (1) _____ , and a graph that uses
points and lines to illustrate a frequency distribution
is a (2) _____ .

---

(1) histogram   (2) frequency polygon

On both the histogram and the frequency polygon, the raw
score (x) is designated on the (1) _____ and
the frequency (f) is designated on the (2) _____
of the graph.

---

(1) abscissa   (2) ordinate

Measures of Central Tendency

In descriptive statistics, a score around which all the
scores in a group cluster is called a *measure of central
tendency*.

A score that describes the typical performance in a group
of scores is called a measure of _____ .

---

central tendency

Three measures of central tendency are (1) *mean*, (2) *median*, and (3) *mode*.

The mean, median, and mode are the average measures of a distribution's _____ .

---

central tendency (center)

The most useful measure of central tendency is the arithmetic *mean*, or average.

The number obtained by finding the sum (Σ) of a group of scores and dividing by the total number of scores is the arithmetic _____ .

---

mean (average)

The first step in determining the mean (M) is to find the _____ of all the scores.

---

sum

Using the frequency distribution of the biology examination scores, find the sum of all the scores (x).

x	f	$x \times f$
49	/	49
50	//	100
51	////	204
52	//	104
53	/	53
	$\Sigma x =$	_____

510

The next step is to determine the number of scores in the group.

$$N = \text{_____}$$

Complete the following formula for finding the mean of the group of scores.

$$\text{Mean} = \frac{\rule{5cm}{0.4pt}}{\text{total number of scores}}$$

---

sum of the scores

Write the formula in symbols for finding the mean.

$$(1) \ \rule{2cm}{0.4pt} = \frac{(2)}{(3)}$$

---

(1) M   (2) Σ x   (3) N

Complete the formula with the numerical values and find the mean of the self-instructional biology group.

$$M = \frac{(1) \ \rule{2cm}{0.4pt}}{(2) \ \rule{2cm}{0.4pt}} = (3) \ \rule{2cm}{0.4pt}$$

---

(1) 510   (2) 10   (3) 51

Determine the descriptive statistics for the following group of scores.

7, 8, 9, 10, 8, 9, 10, 11, 9

(1) x	(2) f	(3) $x \times f$
___	___	___
___	___	___
___	___	___
___	___	___
___	___	___

$N = (4) \rule{1.5cm}{0.4pt}$ $\Sigma x = (5) \rule{1.5cm}{0.4pt}$ $M = (6) \rule{1.5cm}{0.4pt}$

---

(1) x	*(2) f*	*(3) x X f*
7	*/*	*7*
8	*//*	*16*
9	*///*	*27*
10	*//*	*20*
11	*/*	*11*

N = (4) 9   Σ x (5) 81   M = (6) 9

The *median*, another measure of central tendency, is the middle score of a group of scores.

The midpoint of a distribution that divides the scores into two equal parts is the _____ .

---

median

What is the median value of the group of scores in the previous problem?

7, 8, 8, 9, 9, 9, 10, 10, 11

Median = _____

9

It is easy to determine the median of a group of scores with an odd N.   The median is the _____ score.

---

middle

When N is an even number, however, the score on each side of the middle must be considered in determining the median.   The median becomes the value halfway between these two scores.

What is the median of the following scores?

4, 6, 7, 10   Median = _____

6.5

What is the median of these six scores?

83, 85, 86, 90, 94, 97

Median = _____

The third measure of central tendency is the *mode*. The most popular score or the score that is achieved the most often is the _____ .

---

mode

What is the mode of this group of scores?

7, 8, 9, 10, 8, 9, 10, 11, 9

Mode = _____

9

If the score of 78 is received by more pupils in a class than any other score, then 78 is the _____ of the group.

---

mode

On a frequency polygon or histogram, the mode of a group of scores can be identified as the score at the highest point on the graph.

What is the mode of the group of scores as illustrated on the following histogram?

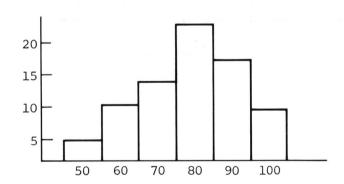

Mode = _____

It is possible to have more than one mode for a distribution. In this set of scores—55, 55, 60, 63, 63—both 55 and 63 are _____ of this distribution.

---

modes

When a distribution has two modes it is called *bimodal*. When a distribution has more than two modes it is said to be *multimodal*.

Identify the type of modality for each of the following distributions.

9, 9, 9, 10, 11, 11, 11, 12, 13   (1) _____

55, 59, 59, 61, 62, 62, 65, 69   (2) _____

76, 77, 78, 78, 79, 79, 80, 80   (3) _____

---

(1) bimodal   (2) bimodal   (3) multimodal

A distribution—2, 2, 5, 9, 11, 13, 13, 13, 13—has an N of 9 and a Σx of 81.

In this set of scores the mode is (1) _____, the median is (2) _____ , and the mean is (3) _____ .

---

(1) 13   (2) 11   (3) 9

The value of the mean, median, and mode in the previous distribution was (different / the same) for each case.

---

different

In a small group of scores, an extremely low or high score will affect the mean greatly.

5, 5, 6, 7, 12 $N = 5$ $x = 35$ $M = 7$

If the score of 12 had been 22—an extreme score for this distribution—the mean would have been _____ .

However, the median and mode are not affected by extreme scores. Regardless of the value of the last score in the previous distribution, the median would have been (1)

_____ and the mode would have been (2)

_____ .

---

(1) 6   (2) 5

Measures of Variability

In addition to frequency distribution, graphs, and measures of central tendency, a group of scores can be described by its *variability*.

Another descriptive statistic used to describe a group of scores is the group's _____ .

---

variability

Range is one measure of variability. The distance between the lowest and highest score is the _____ of a set of scores.

---

range

The range is found by subtracting the lowest score from the highest score. The range of this set of scores—24, 32, 35, 44—is _____ points.

20

A more useful measure of variability, which is based on all the scores within the distribution, is the *standard deviation (s)*.

Unlike the range, which is derived from the lowest and the highest score of a distribution, the standard deviation is based on _____ the scores in the distribution.

---

all

The standard deviation (s) is calculated to permit scores from various measurement scales to be compared.

The standard deviation allows scores on different scales to be _____ .

---

compared

The standard deviation is based on the differences of the scores from the mean of a distribution.

The differences are called "deviations from the mean" and are the basis for finding the _____ .

---

standard deviation

The standard deviation for a group of scores is determined in six steps.

<u>1. Calculate the group's mean.</u>

Obtain the (*M*) of the following group of scores.

x	f
10	/
8	/
7	/
6	/
4	/

Σx = (1) _____ N = (2) _____

M = (3) _____

---

(1) 35   (2) 5   (3) 7

2. Determine the deviations by subtracting the mean from
each score.

x - M = deviation

x	Deviations
10	(1) _____
8	(2) _____
7	(3) _____
6	(4) _____
4	(5) _____

(1) 3   (2) 1   (3) 0   (4) -1   (5) -3

3. Square the deviations.

x	Deviations	Deviations Squared
10	3	(1) _____
8	1	(2) _____
7	0	(3) _____
6	-1	(4) _____
4	-3	(5) _____

(1) 9   (2) 1   (3) 0   (4) 1   (5) 9

4. Determine the sum of the squared deviations.

x	Deviations	Deviations Squared
10	3	9
8	1	1
7	0	0
6	-1	1
4	-3	9
		_____

5. Divide the sum of the squared deviations by the total number of scores (N).

The answer is _____ .

4

The sum of the square deviations divided by the total number of scores is called the *variance*.

The variance of this group is _____ .

4

6. The final step is to find the square root of the variance.

The square root of the variance—that is, the standard deviation—for this group is _____ .

2

The specific definition of the standard deviation is, "the square root of the average of the squared deviations from the _____ ."

---

mean

When the scores of a measurement deviate a large amount, the standard deviation is large, and when the scores deviate very little, the standard deviation is _____ .

---

small

The amount of variability of a group of scores can be identified by the magnitude of the _____ .

---

standard deviation

The mean and standard deviation are the two statistics most used to compare scores and groups of scores.

To compare scores and groups of scores, the two most useful statistics are (1) _____ and (2)

_____ .

---

(1) mean   (2) standard deviation

The standard score used to compare performances on different scales is called the *z*-score and uses both the means and standard deviations of the distributions being compared.

The standard score is called a _____ .

---

z-score

The *z*-score is derived by using the following formula.

$$z = \frac{x - M}{s}$$

Jean receives a raw score of 44 on an arithmetic examination. If the distribution's mean is 40 and its standard deviation is 4, the *z*-score is _____ .

1

If Jean's raw score on a history examination is 21, and the distribution's mean is 19 and its standard deviation is 2, her *z*-score is _____ .

1

The value of a *z*-score indicates the number of standard deviations a score deviates from the mean.

Jean's *z*-score of 1 indicates that she exceeded the mean performance of the others who took the examination by

_____ standard deviation(s).

1

Jean's z-score on the history examination also indicates she exceeded the mean performance of the group by

_____ standard deviation(s).

1

In spite of the differences in numerical value of Jean's two scores, the z-scores indicate that her performances

on the two examinations were _____ in relation

to the relative performances of the others in the group.

comparable

Assignment

Continue the exercises in the Classroom Instruction Record in conjunction with assignments made by your practicum teacher and supervisor.

Nine

Classroom Management

Objectives: When you have completed this chapter, you will
be able to (1) describe the use of classroom management
and its advantages, (2) define a normal distribution curve,
and (3) understand the use of curves in interpreting raw
scores.

The objective of classroom management is to maximize all
of the variables leading to effective classroom learning.

Discussions about classroom management should be based on
_____ principles.

---

learning

Arranging physical facilities, scheduling group learning
activities, individualizing instruction, keeping records,
and maintaining discipline are all aspects of

_____ .

---

classroom management

Well-arranged facilities and efficient routines for handling equipment and materials increase _____
among pupils.

---

cooperation

Classroom management that supports adaptive behavior leads
to effective classroom learning. Getting along with others, self-reliance, and achieving educational success are
_____ behaviors.

---

adaptive

Maladaptive behavior is characterized by the child's inability to meet the demands of the environment satisfactorily.

The child who exhibits persistent difficulty in getting along with others or in achieving educational success has developed a pattern of _____ behavior.

---

maladaptive

As a child develops, he learns to depend more and more on himself to satisfy his needs.

A friendly, outgoing, self-reliant child is developing _____ behaviors.

---

adaptive

Adaptive social behavior is usually interpreted to mean "acceptable" social behavior.

In classrooms that encourage individual initiative and expression, creativity is an _____ behavior.

---

adaptive

A child who continually makes insulting remarks when others make mistakes is exhibiting maladaptive social behavior, since this is not _____ behavior in the classroom.

---

acceptable

Behavioral conformity should not determine acceptability of behavior. Creativity, originality, and leadership vary greatly among children and are acceptable behaviors that are not expressions of conformity.

Too much emphasis on conformity or typical behavior of the group could _____ creativity.

---

limit (restrict)

Contingency management refers to any procedure that arranges the environment so that some (1) _____ is made contingent on some desired (2) _____ .

---

(1) reinforcement   (2) behavior

Effective classroom management is based on _____ principles.

---

learning

More About Descriptive Statistics

Chapter Eight of this workbook stated that the two most useful statistics from a group of scores for interpreting individual scores were the (1) _____ and the (2) _____ .

---

(1) mean   (2) standard deviation

Another method of evaluating scores was the use of graphs. The two types of graphs used are the (1) _____ and the (2) _____ .

---

(1) histogram   (2) frequency polygon

THE NORMAL CURVE

The following distribution represents a particular measurement of a large group of pupils. This graph, which is a _____ , is symmetrical around the median score of the distribution.

A distribution that is symmetrical around the median is
called a *normal* distribution. The distribution represented by the preceding histogram could be described as a

_____ distribution.

---

normal

Drawing a smooth curve through the midpoints of each bar
of a histogram illustrating a normal distribution creates
a *normal distribution curve*.

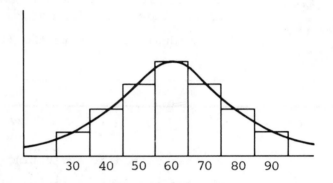

The curved line superimposed over the histogram is called

a _____ .

---

normal distribution curve

It is important to remember that normal distributions are
not associated with small N's (number of measurements) but

result from a _____ number of measurements.

---

large

The horizontal axis on a graph of a distribution indicates

the _____ obtained.

---

measurements (scores)

The vertical axis represents the _____ with which each measurement occurred.

---

frequency

The area under a curve represents all the cases in a sampling. Since a normal curve represents a very large or infinite number of possible measurements, the ends of a normal curve never touch the _____ axis.

---

horizontal

Standardized achievement and intelligence tests use very large samples. It is therefore probable that the distribution curve of these measurements would approximate a _____ curve.

---

normal

The normal curve is often called a "bell-shaped" curve because its shape represents a _____ .

---

bell

Specific characteristics must be present before a distribution curve can be called a normal curve.

First, a normal curve must be identical on its left and right sides. In other words, a normal curve is _____ around the mean.

---

symmetrical

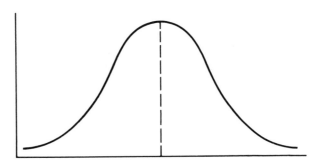

The center line in this diagram of a normal curve represents the average score, the middle score, and the score
achieved the most often.   Therefore, the mean, median, and
mode of a normal curve always have the _____
value.

---

same (identical)

Since the median is represented by the center line, there
is an _____ number of scores on each side of
this line.

---

equal

One of the mathematical properties of the normal curve are
the two points, one on each side of the central line,
where the curve changes from a convex curve to a concave
curve.   These two points are called *points of inflection*.

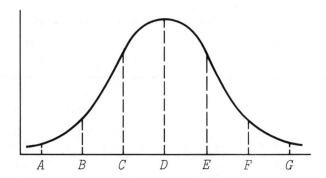

Points C and E on the preceding curve are called its

_____ .

---

points of inflection

On the following graph, three vertical lines have been
drawn.   The central-axis line has been designated zero.
The lines on each side of the central-axis line have been
drawn at the points of inflection.   The line on the left
has been designated as -1 and the line on the right has
been designated as _____ .

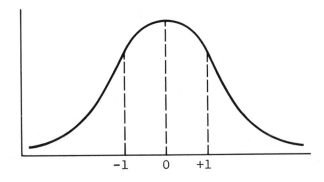

-1   0   +1

+1

In the graph above, the score represented by the line to the right of the central-axis line (drawn at the point of inflection) is said to be "one standard deviation above the mean." Therefore, the score represented by the -1 point-of-inflection line is said to be one standard deviation _____ the mean.

below

In a distribution of scores, the mean was 50 and the standard deviation was 5. What are the values of the scores indicated by the three lines, A, B, and C in the following illustration?

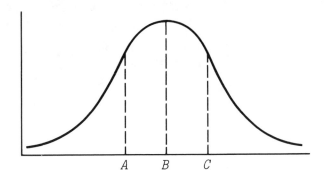

A   B   C

A = _____   B = _____   C = _____

A = *45*   B = *50*   C = *55*

The distance between the 0-line and the +1-line is the standard used to divide a normal curve into equal segments.

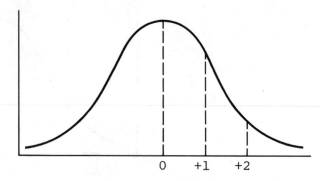

The +2 line represents two _____
from the mean.

We have stated that all the possible measurements of a
particular variable are represented by the area under the
curve, and that a normal curve is symmetrical around the
central-axis line. Therefore, the area under the curve to
the right of the central-axis line represents

_____% of the total number of measurements.

50

The area between the central-axis line and the +1 point-
of-inflection line is approximately 34% of the total area
under the curve of a normal distribution. It would there-

fore be true that _____% of the measurements of
the distribution would occur between the mean and one
standard deviation above the mean.

34

Using your knowledge of a normal distribution's symmetry,
can you state that the number of scores between the mean
and one standard deviation below the mean would represent

approximately _____% of the total scores?

34

This would mean that approximately (1) _____%,
or more than two-thirds, of the measurements of a normal

distribution occur between +1 and -1 (2) _____

_____ of the distribution's mean.

---

                                                    (1) 68   (2) standard deviation

The following normal curve indicates the approximate percentage of scores between +2 and -2 and +3 and -3 standard deviations of the mean of a normal distribution.

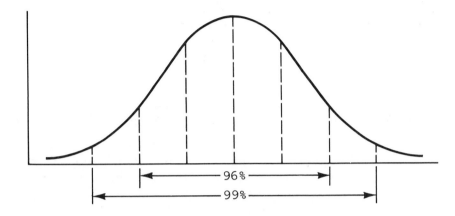

One interpretation from this graph is that close to 100% of all the measurements of a normal distribution are between (1) _____ and (2) _____ standard deviations of the distribution's mean.

---

                                                              (1) +3   (2) -3

From this illustration and the two numerical scores, answer the following questions.

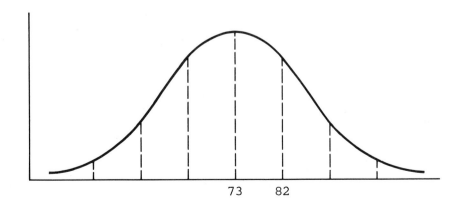

The mean of this sample population
is: (1) _____ .

The standard deviation is: (2) _____ .

The score that is -1 standard de-
viation below the mean is: (3) _____ .

The score that is +2 standard deviations above the mean is: (4) _____ .

The percentage of scores below 73
in the distribution is: (5) _____ .

The percentage of scores between
73 and 82 is: (6) _____ .

---

(1) 73   (2) 9   (3) 64   (4) 91   (5) 50%   (6) 34%

All sets of measurements do not have a normal distribution. The following distribution is described as bimodal.

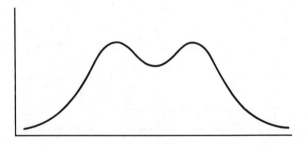

The two peaks of the curve represent the two _____
of the distribution.

---

modes

When the two peaks of a frequency curve are not equal in
height, the distribution is still considered to be

_____ .

---

bimodal

Another variety of curve that differs from the normal
curve is a *skewed* distribution.

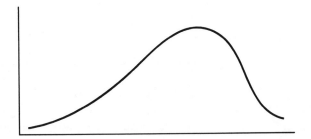

A skewed distribution (is / is not) symmetrical.

---

is not

A skewed curve represents a distribution that has more
scores occurring on one end than on the other. The end of
the curve having the fewer scores is called the "tail" of
the curve.

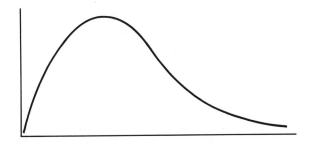

The tail on the right side of the curve represents a positively _____ distribution.

---

skewed

A negatively skewed distribution has the tail on the
_____ side of the curve.

---

left

In summary, a bell-shaped curve is called a (1)
_____ distribution; a curve having two peaks is
called a (2) _____ distribution; and a curve

that has one peak but is not symmetrical is called a (3) _____ distribution.

---

(1) normal   (2) bimodal   (3) skewed

Assignment

Continue the exercises in the Classroom Instruction Record in conjunction with the assignments made by your practicum teacher and supervisor.

Ten

Classroom and Community

Objectives: When you have completed this chapter, you will
be able to (1) describe some of the means and some of the
limitations of the public's understanding of education,
(2) identify some of the methods of communicating with the
public, and (3) know some of the community agencies involved in public education.

Education plays such an important part in individual and
societal well-being that citizens have long insisted on
participating in formulating educational policy.

Active public interest and public participation are

important influences in formulating _____ .

---

educational policy

Social changes have induced corresponding changes in public education. Early childhood education, work-study programs, and compensatory education are a few programs to
emerge as a result of public education's response to

_____ .

---

social changes

Informal communication between school and society takes
place during everyday child-parent discussions of activities occurring at school.

Many of the impressions the public has about the schools
come from child-parent _____ .

---

discussions

Understanding the reasons for schoolwork improves pupil
performance and also enables children to convey more specific information to their parents.

Sharing objectives with your pupils can influence the
_____ parents have about the schools.

---

impressions (understanding)

The amount of satisfaction and success pupils experience
will influence the _____ their parents have
about the worth of the schools.

---

impressions (understanding)

The parent-teacher conference is one means the teacher has
to _____ goals and achievements to parents and
thereby to the community.

---

communicate

Public education must compete with the propaganda skills
of the wealthy information and entertainment media for
public recognition and support.

Some of the best trained psychologists, communications
technicians, and public relations experts are employed in
creating television, newspaper, and magazine advertising
for new products and services. This results in powerful
competition for _____ to gain public recognition
and support.

---

education

Many worthy governmental as well as private services,
agencies, and organizations have intensified their public
communication efforts, creating more and more competition
with education for public attention.

Expansion of governmental and private information services
has created increased _____ with education for
public attention.

---

competition

Public education has not been in the forefront in recognizing and accepting the need for modernized methods of communicating with the public.

Educators have been primarily interested in the basic educational purposes of public schools and have had very limited budgets for public communication. Understanding and support of public education may be enhanced by

improved _____ .

---

communication (and budgets)

Communication is defined as, "an effort to establish commonness with another person or group by sharing information, ideas, or attitudes."

By exchanging information, ideas, or viewpoints, a

_____ understanding can be developed among people or groups.

---

common

Public education can develop common understanding and mutually agreeable working arrangements through improved

_____ .

---

communication

A continuing difficulty in developing common understanding has been the great variability and diversity of the information educators present to the public. The educational professions have not yet developed an adequate body of

scientifically verified information to create _____ understandings of public education.

---

common

Early childhood education, educational television, compensatory education, progressive education, discovery methods, phonics, controlled vocabulary, look-and-say, competency-based instruction, open classrooms, and a variety of special services, including psychology, counseling, and educational consultants, have each been promoted as a solution to educational problems. The public has had difficulty acquiring (1) _____ under-

standings of educational needs because of the (2)

_____ of educational information.

---

(1) common   (2) variability (diversity)

Most communication is on a person-to-person level. This direct form of communication is most effective. Although messages from advertising media are prolific, they are not as effective as personal conversations.

Face-to-face, two-way communication is an effective means

for teachers to develop _____ with members of the

public.

---

common understandings

The direct relationship between parents and teachers is the basis of the Parent-Teacher Association's strength. For decades, the PTA has supported educational improvement and has been the major agency for creating cooperative parent-teacher efforts.

Because of the stability and endurance of the PTA, it is

an important forum for developing _____ .

---

common understandings

Although the relative effectiveness of local PTA groups varies, a strong national organization provides dependable leadership and support for educational improvement.

Local units and state offices of the PTA are provided with

stable leadership by the _____ organization.

---

national

Although the PTA is a stable and effective means for developing common understanding, it has some very real limitations. For instance, the most active and numerous members are mothers of children in grades one to six.

The typical PTA member (is / is not) representative of the total community interested in education.

---

is not

Although the PTA has a large membership, it represents only a fraction of the parents who have children in school.

The PTA is further limited in its effectiveness because it does not represent _____ parents who have children in school.

---

all

Membership in the PTA does not include a representative portion of the middle-aged and older men and women who tend to exert much of the influence in the community power structure.

The PTA is likely to have inadequate contact with and support from many citizens of influence in the community

_____ .

---

power structure

PTA membership consists largely of relatively young parents who, as a group, have less vested interest in real property, and who tend to rely less on other types of investments for their income. The community power structure encompasses conflicting interests. Some participants are concerned with improving public education whereas others are concerned with limiting the taxes on real property.

The PTA is likely to represent those concerned with

_____ public education.

---

improving

Many citizens are members of civic, occupational, social, and cultural organizations whose combined influence on community action is considerable. Although education is not the major interest of these organizations, they have been known to sponsor study groups, scholarships, "career days," and other educational activities.

Some civic and professional organizations _____ educational activities.

---

sponsor

Some civic and professional organizations advocate budgets and educational programs that are in conflict with the needs of public education. To obtain the widest possible community support for education, it is important that these groups be involved in programs that will clarify educational values and objectives.

Members of groups that might otherwise oppose educational progress should be induced to participate in clarifying educational objectives in order to achieve the widest possible community _____ .

---

support

The actions and statements of the school board have a profound influence on public understanding and support for schools. Citizens elect school board members in order to establish local policies for public education.

The school board is the official agency connecting the citizens to the _____ .

---

schools

Influences on education come from individuals, communities, organizations, and governments. The PTA, the school board, and professional educational organizations all have

_____ on the organization and content of public education.

---

influence

The local, state, and federal governments also

_____ public education.

There are, in addition, groups of citizens organized for specific purposes. For example, local citizens' councils, study councils, advisory committees, and the National Citizens' Commission for the Public Schools stimulate public interest in public education.

School boards, PTA, citizens' councils, civic and professional organizations, and many other groups are participants in the relationship between classroom and

_____ .

---

community

Assignment

Check with your practicum teacher and supervisor to ensure that you have completed the practicum requirements.

Classroom Instruction Record

Laurence J. Peter

Arthur Margolese
University of Southern California

General Instructions

The Classroom Instruction Record is designed for use during student-teaching (practicum) in classroom instruction. It provides instructions and record forms to guide you through a developmental sequence for acquiring essential classroom teaching skills.

Independent Use. The teacher who is studying *Classroom Instruction* independently should follow the instructions and complete the forms, omitting those sections that apply to the practicum teacher. The independent student should act as his or her own supervisor in completing the assessment procedures.

Inservice Use. The inservice teacher uses all sections of the forms except those that apply to the practicum teacher.

Preservice Use. As a student teacher, you will use the total system of records. Your practicum in classroom instruction provides opportunities to observe, assist, and teach in the classroom of an experienced teacher, herein referred to as the *practicum teacher*. During your classroom practicum, you should seek opportunities to assist your practicum teacher with classroom routines, care and arrangement of supplies and equipment, extracurricular activities, and preparation, scoring, and interpretation of quizzes, tests, and evaluations.

Tape Recording. Tape recording should be made of your teaching. The recordings provide feedback for evaluating your presentations. The recordings are also useful for completing certain forms—Incidental Intervention, Questions, Single Task, and Lesson Plan. Although any portable tape recorder will suffice, it is preferable to use one that is lightweight, that can be attached to a belt or carried on a shoulder strap, is easy to operate, and is reliable. Specific desirable characteristics are that it use cassette tapes, be battery operated, have a built-in microphone, and have an automatic record-level control. The following cassette recorders are recommended: (1) Panasonic, Model 409, (2) Califone, Model AVIII, (3) Sony, Models TC40, TC45, TC55, or their equivalents.

Contents. This outlines the Classroom Instruction Record and briefly describes each form. The forms are arranged in a developmental sequence, but it may not be practical to complete all the forms in this order. For example, you may finish three of the Incidental Intervention forms early in the course and complete the balance later. Study the Contents and then examine each of the types of forms. Before using a form, you should study the parallel chapters of both the textbook and workbook in *Classroom Instruction* as indicated.

Completing the Forms. For each set of three forms, insert carbon paper behind the original and second copy of a form *before* making any entries. Use a pencil or ballpoint pen. When you have completed your entries on a form containing assessment columns, request an evaluation from either your practicum teacher or your teacher education supervisor.

Contents

ORIENTATION

These forms are to be completed early in your practicum (student teaching) assignment.

Circle Number as Completed

TEACHING ASSIGNMENT
This identifies the key personnel of your practicum assignment.

1 set

PRACTICUM SCHOOL
This is a directory of the personnel, procedures, and facilities of your practicum school.
Reference: Chapter One, *Classroom Instruction*.

1 set

TEACHING

The following forms record your instruction of pupils and provide you with feedback regarding your skill in various components of the instructional process. They also provide a means for your practicum teacher and supervisor to evaluate your success.

INCIDENTAL INTERVENTION
This is a record of informal or unplanned interactions with pupils who need assistance with academic or behavior problems.
Reference: Chapter Two, *Classroom Instruction*.

1 2 3 4 5 6

QUESTIONS
This form helps you develop questioning skills with small groups of pupils.
Reference: Chapter Six, "Developing Questioning Skills," *Classroom Instruction*.

1 2 3 4 5 6

SINGLE TASK
This form helps you learn to (a) develop an objective, (b) present a brief lesson, and (c) evaluate attainment of a single objective with a small group of pupils.
Reference: Chapters Three, Four, Five, Six, *Classroom Instruction*.

1 2 3 4 5 6

LESSON PLAN
This form is an outline to guide you in preparing, presenting, and evaluating a class lesson.
Reference: Chapters Three, Four, Five, Six, Seven, Eight, and specifically, "Planning Lessons," in Chapter Nine, *Classroom Instruction*.

1 2 3 4 5 6

ANCILLARY ACTIVITIES

CONCOMITANT EXPERIENCE
This form is a record of your supplementary experiences occurring during practicum.
Reference: Chapter Ten, *Classroom Instruction*.

1 set

Directions for Teaching Assignment

This form identifies the key personnel in your practicum assignment and introduces your practicum teacher to the classroom instruction phase of the Competencies for Teaching system. The relevant information should be entered on this form by inservice or preservice teachers. Those engaged in independent study may omit this form.

1. Student Teacher. Provide the required information.

2. Practicum Teacher. Enter the name of your practicum teacher, the school's phone number, and the name and address of the school. Discuss with your practicum teacher convenient times for meeting and planning your teaching assignments. Establish the procedure to follow in case of emergency or absence. Omit the file number on all forms. This file number is for office use by the college of education.

3. Supervisor. Enter the name of your teacher education supervisor and the office phone number. Fill in the address of your college.

4. To the Practicum Teacher. This section briefly describes the Competencies for Teaching system. If your practicum teacher is unfamiliar with the system, you should provide further information as required. Allow your practicum teacher to examine your Classroom Instruction Record so that he or she will be familiar with your assignment.

5. Signature. Sign and date the form. Distribute the copies as indicated at the top of each form.

Student Teaching

Follow your supervisor's recommendations regarding the procedure for reporting to your assigned practicum school. Plan to arrive at the classroom before the pupils enter so that you have an opportunity to become acquainted with your practicum teacher.

Acquaint yourself with the courses of study and other instructional guides. Examine the textbooks and study the accompanying teacher's manuals. Make or obtain a seating plan and begin learning the pupils' names. During the first week, make careful objective observations of the classroom proceedings and gradually assume responsibility for making incidental interventions.

Your classroom practicum will not provide you with opportunities to implement all of the techniques described in *Classroom Instruction*. You will benefit most by establishing a friendly working relationship with your practicum teacher and by learning methods of classroom management and instruction employed by your practicum teacher.

Competencies for Teaching—Classroom Instruction

Teaching Assignment

1. STUDENT TEACHER

Last Name	First	Initial	File Number

Current Address:	Street	City	State	Zip	Telephone
					( )

2. PRACTICUM TEACHER

Last Name	First	Initial	School Phone
			( )

Practicum School	Address: Street	City	State	Zip

3. SUPERVISOR

Last Name	First	Initial	Office Phone
			( )

College or University	Address: Street	City	State	Zip

4.

TO THE PRACTICUM TEACHER:

The *Competencies for Teaching* system provides a method for integrating theory and practice so that the student teacher acquires complex instructional skills in a developmental sequence. The forms in the Classroom Instruction Record provide the means of ensuring that certain essential classroom competencies are achieved. Your assistance in providing opportunities for the student teacher to accomplish these skills will help maximize the student teacher's success. By helping the student teacher assess his or her performance of the activities described on four forms—Incidental Intervention, Question, Single Task, and Lesson Plan—you will be providing feedback that can be used by the student teacher to improve instruction.

You may make your assessments on the basis of your direct observation of the student teacher's performance or by listening to a tape recording. Discuss your assessment with the student teacher and circle "S" for satisfactory or "N" for needs improvements.

The student teacher's practicum should not be limited to the items on the forms. He or she should be given opportunities to observe in your classroom and participate in your ongoing program, so that the student teacher gradually takes on more responsibility.

Your cooperation in implementing this system of accountability is appreciated by both the student teacher and teacher education supervisor.

5. Signature

STUDENT TEACHER	DATE

Competencies for Teaching—Classroom Instruction

Teaching Assignment

1. STUDENT TEACHER	Last Name	First		Initial	File Number
	Current Address: Street	City	State	Zip	Telephone ( )

2. PRACTICUM TEACHER	Last Name	First		Initial	School Phone ( )
	Practicum School	Address: Street	City	State	Zip

3. SUPERVISOR	Last Name	First		Initial	Office Phone ( )
	College or University	Address: Street	City	State	Zip

4. TO THE PRACTICUM TEACHER:

The *Competencies for Teaching* system provides a method for integrating theory and practice so that the student teacher acquires complex instructional skills in a developmental sequence. The forms in the Classroom Instruction Record provide the means of ensuring that certain essential classroom competencies are achieved. Your assistance in providing opportunities for the student teacher to accomplish these skills will help maximize the student teacher's success. By helping the student teacher assess his or her performance of the activities described on four forms—Incidental Intervention, Question, Single Task, and Lesson Plan—you will be providing feedback that can be used by the student teacher to improve instruction.

You may make your assessments on the basis of your direct observation of the student teacher's performance or by listening to a tape recording. Discuss your assessment with the student teacher and circle "S" for satisfactory or "N" for needs improvements.

The student teacher's practicum should not be limited to the items on the forms. He or she should be given opportunities to observe in your classroom and participate in your ongoing program, so that the student teacher gradually takes on more responsibility.

Your cooperation in implementing this system of accountability is appreciated by both the student teacher and teacher education supervisor.

5. Signature	STUDENT TEACHER	DATE

Competencies for Teaching—Classroom Instruction

Teaching Assignment

1. STUDENT TEACHER

Last Name	First	Initial	File Number

Current Address: Street	City	State	Zip	Telephone ( )

2. PRACTICUM TEACHER

Last Name	First	Initial	School Phone ( )

Practicum School	Address: Street	City	State	Zip

3. SUPERVISOR

Last Name	First	Initial	Office Phone ( )

College or University	Address: Street	City	State	Zip

4. TO THE PRACTICUM TEACHER:

The *Competencies for Teaching* system provides a method for integrating theory and practice so that the student teacher acquires complex instructional skills in a developmental sequence. The forms in the Classroom Instruction Record provide the means of ensuring that certain essential classroom competencies are achieved. Your assistance in providing opportunities for the student teacher to accomplish these skills will help maximize the student teacher's success. By helping the student teacher assess his or her performance of the activities described on four forms—Incidental Intervention, Question, Single Task, and Lesson Plan—you will be providing feedback that can be used by the student teacher to improve instruction.

You may make your assessments on the basis of your direct observation of the student teacher's performance or by listening to a tape recording. Discuss your assessment with the student teacher and circle "S" for satisfactory or "N" for needs improvements.

The student teacher's practicum should not be limited to the items on the forms. He or she should be given opportunities to observe in your classroom and participate in your ongoing program, so that the student teacher gradually takes on more responsibility.

Your cooperation in implementing this system of accountability is appreciated by both the student teacher and teacher education supervisor.

5. Signature STUDENT TEACHER | DATE

Directions for Practicum School

This form should be completed within a few days of your arrival at the practicum school. You may wish to consult your practicum teacher regarding where to locate the required information.

    1. Identifying Information. Enter the name of the school and the school district.

    2. Personnel. Enter the names of the personnel as indicated. You may wish to add the names and positions of others, such as department chairman, remedial teacher, counselor, or psychologist.

    3. Emergency Procedures. Describe the *Signal* used for *Fire drill* and the procedure to follow when the signal is sounded. Describe the *Signal* and *Procedure* for *other* emergencies, as they are dealt with in your school.
    Describe the procedure for referring a pupil to the school nurse or other medical services in cases of *Accident or Illness*.
    Describe the procedure for reporting a teacher's *Accident or Illness*.

    4. Facilities. Describe the *Location* of the facilities indicated and add others you may wish to locate.
    Check or list *Informational Materials* you have acquired.

    5. Signature. When you are satisfied that you have completed the form, sign in the appropriate space and distribute as indicated at the top of each form.

Competencies for Teaching—Classroom Instruction

Practicum School

1. School	District	File Number

2.	Principal	Secretary
PERSONNEL	Vice-Principal	Nurse
	Librarian	Custodian

3.			Signal	Procedure
EMERGENCY PROCEDURES	DRILLS	Fire		
		Other		
	ACCIDENT or ILLNESS	Pupil		
		Teacher		

4.	Audiovisual Materials	Location	INFORMATIONAL MATERIALS
FACILITIES	Cafeteria		☐ CLASS LIST
	Library		☐ DAILY SCHEDULE
	Nurse's Office		☐ TEACHER'S HANDBOOK
	Teachers' Room		☐ SCHOOL CALENDAR
			☐
			☐
			☐

5. Signature	STUDENT TEACHER	DATE

Competencies for Teaching—Classroom Instruction

Practicum School

1. School	District	File Number

2.	Principal		Secretary	
PERSONNEL	Vice-Principal		Nurse	
	Librarian		Custodian	

3.			Signal	Procedure
EMERGENCY PROCEDURES	**DRILLS**	Fire		
		Other		
	ACCIDENT or ILLNESS	Pupil		
		Teacher		

4.	Audiovisual Materials	Location	INFORMATIONAL MATERIALS
FACILITIES	Cafeteria		☐ CLASS LIST
	Library		☐ DAILY SCHEDULE
	Nurse's Office		☐ TEACHER'S HANDBOOK
	Teachers' Room		☐ SCHOOL CALENDAR
			☐
			☐
			☐

5. Signature	STUDENT TEACHER	DATE

Competencies for Teaching—Classroom Instruction

Practicum School

1. School	District	File Number

2. PERSONNEL	Principal	Secretary
	Vice-Principal	Nurse
	Librarian	Custodian

3. EMERGENCY PROCEDURES	DRILLS	Fire	Signal	Procedure
		Other		
	ACCIDENT or ILLNESS	Pupil		
		Teacher		

4. FACILITIES	Audiovisual Materials	Location	INFORMATIONAL MATERIALS
	Cafeteria		☐ CLASS LIST
	Library		☐ DAILY SCHEDULE
	Nurse's Office		☐ TEACHER'S HANDBOOK
	Teachers' Room		☐ SCHOOL CALENDAR
			☐
			☐
			☐

5. Signature	STUDENT TEACHER	DATE

Directions for Incidental Intervention

An incidental intervention is an unplanned event in which the student teacher helps a pupil or pupils solve an immediate behavior or learning problem.

When you observe pupils needing help, or when requested by your practicum teacher to provide help, intervene by employing the following procedure.

a. Turn on your tape recorder.

b. Intervene by asking questions, explaining solutions, demonstrating a correct procedure, suggesting references, resolving a dispute or fight, reinforcing appropriate behavior, and so forth.

c. Replay the tape and complete the Incidental Observation Record. If the intervention was not recorded, complete the form from memory.

1. <u>Identifying Information</u>. Each incidental intervention will be assigned a consecutive *Lesson Number* (1 to 6). The *Subject or Activity* identifies the nature of the program at the time of the intervention (for example, recess, reading, physical education, or lunch). *Number of Pupils* refers only to those involved in the intervention. If you taped the intervention, place a check in the box labeled *Tape Recorded*. Enter the approximate *Duration* (in minutes) of the intervention. *Note*: This type of indentifying information will be completed for each instructional form whether it is Incidental Intervention, Questions, Single Task, or Lesson Plan.

2. <u>Observation</u>. Describe what you observed before you intervened, such as, "Alice asked for help with an addition problem," or "Mike pushed his way through the lunch line."

3. <u>Intervention</u>. Describe what you did to help solve the problem. Listen to the replay of your tape and write a condensed report of your actions.

4. <u>Response</u>. From your memory of the event or from replaying your tape, describe briefly the response of the pupil or pupils to your intervention.

5. <u>Recommendations</u>. Evaluate the effectiveness of your intervention according to the pupils' response. Based on this evaluation, state your recommendations for future interventions. Indicate whether you consider your intervention to have been satisfactory, or describe the modifications you would make in similar situations in the future.

6. <u>Assessment</u>. When you have completed the form to your satisfaction, initial or sign your name in the space provided.

Obtain an evaluation of your intervention by either your practicum teacher or your teacher education supervisor.

a. At a convenient time for your practicum teacher, request an evaluation of your intervention. If the assessment is based on the practicum teacher's direct observation, check the box labeled *Direct*. If it is based on replay of a tape, check *Recorded*. Both may be checked when applicable. As each section is assessed, request that the practicum teacher circle either "S" for satisfactory or "N" for needs improvement. Your practicum teacher will then sign or initial the form in the space provided.

b. If the assessment is to be made by your teacher education supervisor, follow the same procedure as above. In either case, show the form to your supervisor, who will read the entries and will circle "H" for honors, "P" for pass, or "I" for incomplete. "I" indicates that the form requires more information before it is submitted. "F" indicates failure. Your supervisor will then initial or sign the form. You may make brief notes regarding suggestions for improvement in the space opposite each section. Enter the date and distribute the copies of the forms as indicated at the top of each form.

Competencies for Teaching—Classroom Instruction

Incidental Intervention

1. Student Teacher	Last Name	First	Initial	File Number	ASSESSMENT
Lesson Number	Subject or Activity	Number of Pupils	Tape Recorded □	Duration	PRACTICUM TEACHER □ Direct □ Recorded / SUPERVISOR □ Direct □ Recorded

2. OBSERVATION

S N | S N

3. INTERVENTION

S N | S N

4. RESPONSE

S N | S N

5. RECOMMENDATIONS

S N | S N

6. Signature	STUDENT TEACHER	PRACTICUM TEACHER	SUPERVISOR	DATE	H P I F

Competencies for Teaching—Classroom Instruction

Incidental Intervention

1. Student Teacher	Last Name	First	Initial	File Number	ASSESSMENT
Lesson Number	Subject or Activity	Number of Pupils	Tape Recorded ☐	Duration	PRACTICUM TEACHER ☐ Direct ☐ Recorded SUPERVISOR ☐ Direct ☐ Recorded

2. OBSERVATION

S N | S N

3. INTERVENTION

S N | S N

4. RESPONSE

S N | S N

5. RECOMMENDATIONS

S N | S N

6. Signature	STUDENT TEACHER	PRACTICUM TEACHER	SUPERVISOR	DATE	H P I F

Competencies for Teaching—Classroom Instruction

Incidental Intervention

1. Student Teacher	Last Name	First	Initial	File Number		ASSESSMENT
Lesson Number	Subject or Activity		Number of Pupils	Tape Recorded ☐	Duration	PRACTICUM TEACHER ☐ Direct ☐ Recorded SUPERVISOR ☐ Direct ☐ Recorded

2. OBSERVATION

S N S N

3. INTERVENTION

S N S N

4. RESPONSE

S N S N

5. RECOMMENDATIONS

S N S N

6. Signature	STUDENT TEACHER	PRACTICUM TEACHER	SUPERVISOR	DATE	H P I F

Directions for Incidental Intervention

An incidental intervention is an unplanned event in which the student teacher helps a pupil or pupils solve an immediate behavior or learning problem.

When you observe pupils needing help, or when requested by your practicum teacher to provide help, intervene by employing the following procedure.

a. Turn on your tape recorder.

b. Intervene by asking questions, explaining solutions, demonstrating a correct procedure, suggesting references, resolving a dispute or fight, reinforcing appropriate behavior, and so forth.

c. Replay the tape and complete the Incidental Observation Record. If the intervention was not recorded, complete the form from memory.

1. <u>Identifying Information</u>. Each incidental intervention will be assigned a consecutive *Lesson Number* (1 to 6). The *Subject or Activity* identifies the nature of the program at the time of the intervention (for example, recess, reading, physical education, or lunch). *Number of Pupils* refers only to those involved in the intervention. If you taped the intervention, place a check in the box labeled *Tape Recorded*. Enter the approximate *Duration* (in minutes) of the intervention. *Note*: This type of indentifying information will be completed for each instructional form whether it is Incidental Intervention, Questions, Single Task, or Lesson Plan.

2. <u>Observation</u>. Describe what you observed before you intervened, such as, "Alice asked for help with an addition problem," or "Mike pushed his way through the lunch line."

3. <u>Intervention</u>. Describe what you did to help solve the problem. Listen to the replay of your tape and write a condensed report of your actions.

4. <u>Response</u>. From your memory of the event or from replaying your tape, describe briefly the response of the pupil or pupils to your intervention.

5. <u>Recommendations</u>. Evaluate the effectiveness of your intervention according to the pupils' response. Based on this evaluation, state your recommendations for future interventions. Indicate whether you consider your intervention to have been satisfactory, or describe the modifications you would make in similar situations in the future.

6. <u>Assessment</u>. When you have completed the form to your satisfaction, initial or sign your name in the space provided.

Obtain an evaluation of your intervention by either your practicum teacher or your teacher education supervisor.

a. At a convenient time for your practicum teacher, request an evaluation of your intervention. If the assessment is based on the practicum teacher's direct observation, check the box labeled *Direct*. If it is based on replay of a tape, check *Recorded*. Both may be checked when applicable. As each section is assessed, request that the practicum teacher circle either "S" for satisfactory or "N" for needs improvement. Your practicum teacher will then sign or initial the form in the space provided.

b. If the assessment is to be made by your teacher education supervisor, follow the same procedure as above. In either case, show the form to your supervisor, who will read the entries and will circle "H" for honors, "P" for pass, or "I" for incomplete. "I" indicates that the form requires more information before it is submitted. "F" indicates failure. Your supervisor will then initial or sign the form. You may make brief notes regarding suggestions for improvement in the space opposite each section. Enter the date and distribute the copies of the forms as indicated at the top of each form.

Competencies for Teaching—Classroom Instruction

Incidental Intervention

1. Student Teacher	Last Name		First		Initial	File Number	ASSESSMENT
Lesson Number	Subject or Activity			Number of Pupils	Tape Recorded ☐	Duration	

ASSESSMENT

PRACTICUM TEACHER ☐ Direct ☐ Recorded   SUPERVISOR ☐ Direct ☐ Recorded

2. OBSERVATION

S N   S N

3. INTERVENTION

S N   S N

4. RESPONSE

S N   S N

5. RECOMMENDATIONS

S N   S N

6. Signature	STUDENT TEACHER	PRACTICUM TEACHER	SUPERVISOR	DATE	H P I F

Competencies for Teaching—Classroom Instruction

Incidental Intervention

1. Student Teacher	Last Name	First	Initial	File Number	ASSESSMENT
Lesson Number	Subject or Activity	Number of Pupils	Tape Recorded ☐	Duration	PRACTICUM TEACHER ☐ Direct ☐ Recorded / SUPERVISOR ☐ Direct ☐ Recorded

2. OBSERVATION

S N   S N

3. INTERVENTION

S N   S N

4. RESPONSE

S N   S N

5. RECOMMENDATIONS

S N   S N

6. Signature	STUDENT TEACHER	PRACTICUM TEACHER	SUPERVISOR	DATE	H P I F

Competencies for Teaching—Classroom Instruction

Incidental Intervention

1. Student Teacher	Last Name	First	Initial	File Number	ASSESSMENT
Lesson Number	Subject or Activity	Number of Pupils	Tape Recorded ☐	Duration	PRACTICUM TEACHER ☐ Direct ☐ Recorded SUPERVISOR ☐ Direct ☐ Recorded

2. OBSERVATION		S N S N
3. INTERVENTION		S N S N
4. RESPONSE		S N S N
5. RECOMMENDATIONS		S N S N

6. Signature	STUDENT TEACHER	PRACTICUM TEACHER	SUPERVISOR	DATE	H P I F

Directions for Incidental Intervention

An incidental intervention is an unplanned event in which the student teacher helps a pupil or pupils solve an immediate behavior or learning problem.

When you observe pupils needing help, or when requested by your practicum teacher to provide help, intervene by employing the following procedure.

a. Turn on your tape recorder.

b. Intervene by asking questions, explaining solutions, demonstrating a correct procedure, suggesting references, resolving a dispute or fight, reinforcing appropriate behavior, and so forth.

c. Replay the tape and complete the Incidental Observation Record. If the intervention was not recorded, complete the form from memory.

1. _Identifying Information_. Each incidental intervention will be assigned a consecutive _Lesson Number_ (1 to 6). The _Subject or Activity_ identifies the nature of the program at the time of the intervention (for example, recess, reading, physical education, or lunch). _Number of Pupils_ refers only to those involved in the intervention. If you taped the intervention, place a check in the box labeled _Tape Recorded_. Enter the approximate _Duration_ (in minutes) of the intervention. _Note_: This type of indentifying information will be completed for each instructional form whether it is Incidental Intervention, Questions, Single Task, or Lesson Plan.

2. _Observation_. Describe what you observed before you intervened, such as, "Alice asked for help with an addition problem," or "Mike pushed his way through the lunch line."

3. _Intervention_. Describe what you did to help solve the problem. Listen to the replay of your tape and write a condensed report of your actions.

4. _Response_. From your memory of the event or from replaying your tape, describe briefly the response of the pupil or pupils to your intervention.

5. _Recommendations_. Evaluate the effectiveness of your intervention according to the pupils' response. Based on this evaluation, state your recommendations for future interventions. Indicate whether you consider your intervention to have been satisfactory, or describe the modifications you would make in similar situations in the future.

6. <u>Assessment</u>. When you have completed the form to your satisfaction, initial or sign your name in the space provided.

Obtain an evaluation of your intervention by either your practicum teacher or your teacher education supervisor.

a. At a convenient time for your practicum teacher, request an evaluation of your intervention. If the assessment is based on the practicum teacher's direct observation, check the box labeled *Direct*. If it is based on replay of a tape, check *Recorded*. Both may be checked when applicable. As each section is assessed, request that the practicum teacher circle either "S" for satisfactory or "N" for needs improvement. Your practicum teacher will then sign or initial the form in the space provided.

b. If the assessment is to be made by your teacher education supervisor, follow the same procedure as above. In either case, show the form to your supervisor, who will read the entries and will circle "H" for honors, "P" for pass, or "I" for incomplete. "I" indicates that the form requires more information before it is submitted. "F" indicates failure. Your supervisor will then initial or sign the form. You may make brief notes regarding suggestions for improvement in the space opposite each section. Enter the date and distribute the copies of the forms as indicated at the top of each form.

Competencies for Teaching—Classroom Instruction

Incidental Intervention

1. Student Teacher	Last Name	First	Initial	File Number	ASSESSMENT
Lesson Number	Subject or Activity	Number of Pupils	Tape Recorded ☐	Duration	PRACTICUM TEACHER ☐ Direct ☐ Recorded SUPERVISOR ☐ Direct ☐ Recorded

2. OBSERVATION

S N   S N

3. INTERVENTION

S N   S N

4. RESPONSE

S N   S N

5. RECOMMENDATIONS

S N   S N

6. Signature	STUDENT TEACHER	PRACTICUM TEACHER	SUPERVISOR	DATE	H P I F

Competencies for Teaching—Classroom Instruction

Incidental Intervention

1. Student Teacher	Last Name	First	Initial	File Number	ASSESSMENT
Lesson Number	Subject or Activity		Number of Pupils	Tape Recorded ☐	Duration	PRACTICUM TEACHER Direct ☐ Recorded ☐ / SUPERVISOR Direct ☐ Recorded ☐

2. OBSERVATION

S N   S N

3. INTERVENTION

S N   S N

4. RESPONSE

S N   S N

5. RECOMMENDATIONS

S N   S N

6. Signature	STUDENT TEACHER	PRACTICUM TEACHER	SUPERVISOR	DATE	H P I F

Competencies for Teaching—Classroom Instruction

Incidental Intervention

1. Student Teacher	Last Name	First		Initial	File Number	ASSESSMENT
Lesson Number	Subject or Activity		Number of Pupils	Tape Recorded ☐	Duration	PRACTICUM TEACHER / Direct ☐ / Recorded ☐ — SUPERVISOR / Direct ☐ / Recorded ☐

2. OBSERVATION

S N | S N

3. INTERVENTION

S N | S N

4. RESPONSE

S N | S N

5. RECOMMENDATIONS

S N | S N

6. Signature	STUDENT TEACHER	PRACTICUM TEACHER	SUPERVISOR	DATE	H P I F

Directions for Incidental Intervention

An incidental intervention is an unplanned event in which the student teacher helps a pupil or pupils solve an immediate behavior or learning problem.

. When you observe pupils needing help, or when requested by your practicum teacher to provide help, intervene by employing the following procedure.

a. Turn on your tape recorder.

b. Intervene by asking questions, explaining solutions, demonstrating a correct procedure, suggesting references, resolving a dispute or fight, reinforcing appropriate behavior, and so forth.

c. Replay the tape and complete the Incidental Observation Record. If the intervention was not recorded, complete the form from memory.

1. _Identifying Information_. Each incidental intervention will be assigned a consecutive _Lesson Number_ (1 to 6). The _Subject or Activity_ identifies the nature of the program at the time of the intervention (for example, recess, reading, physical education, or lunch). _Number of Pupils_ refers only to those involved in the intervention. If you taped the intervention, place a check in the box labeled _Tape Recorded_. Enter the approximate _Duration_ (in minutes) of the intervention. _Note_: This type of indentifying information will be completed for each instructional form whether it is Incidental Intervention, Questions, Single Task, or Lesson Plan.

2. _Observation_. Describe what you observed before you intervened, such as, "Alice asked for help with an addition problem," or "Mike pushed his way through the lunch line."

3. _Intervention_. Describe what you did to help solve the problem. Listen to the replay of your tape and write a condensed report of your actions.

4. _Response_. From your memory of the event or from replaying your tape, describe briefly the response of the pupil or pupils to your intervention.

5. _Recommendations_. Evaluate the effectiveness of your intervention according to the pupils' response. Based on this evaluation, state your recommendations for future interventions. Indicate whether you consider your intervention to have been satisfactory, or describe the modifications you would make in similar situations in the future.

6. <u>Assessment</u>. When you have completed the form to your satisfaction, initial or sign your name in the space provided.

Obtain an evaluation of your intervention by either your practicum teacher or your teacher education supervisor.

a. At a convenient time for your practicum teacher, request an evaluation of your intervention. If the assessment is based on the practicum teacher's direct observation, check the box labeled *Direct*. If it is based on replay of a tape, check *Recorded*. Both may be checked when applicable. As each section is assessed, request that the practicum teacher circle either "S" for satisfactory or "N" for needs improvement. Your practicum teacher will then sign or initial the form in the space provided.

b. If the assessment is to be made by your teacher education supervisor, follow the same procedure as above. In either case, show the form to your supervisor, who will read the entries and will circle "H" for honors, "P" for pass, or "I" for incomplete. "I" indicates that the form requires more information before it is submitted. "F" indicates failure. Your supervisor will then initial or sign the form. You may make brief notes regarding suggestions for improvement in the space opposite each section. Enter the date and distribute the copies of the forms as indicated at the top of each form.

Competencies for Teaching—Classroom Instruction

Incidental Intervention

1. Student Teacher	Last Name	First		Initial	File Number	ASSESSMENT
Lesson Number	Subject or Activity		Number of Pupils	Tape Recorded ☐	Duration	PRACTICUM TEACHER Direct ☐ Recorded ☐ SUPERVISOR Direct ☐ Recorded ☐

2. OBSERVATION	
	S N S N

3. INTERVENTION	
	S N S N

4. RESPONSE	
	S N S N

5. RECOMMENDATIONS	
	S N S N

6. Signature	STUDENT TEACHER	PRACTICUM TEACHER	SUPERVISOR	DATE	H P I F

Competencies for Teaching—Classroom Instruction

Incidental Intervention

1. Student Teacher	Last Name	First	Initial	File Number
Lesson Number	Subject or Activity	Number of Pupils	Tape Recorded ☐	Duration

ASSESSMENT

PRACTICUM TEACHER ☐ Direct ☐ Recorded   SUPERVISOR ☐ Direct ☐ Recorded

2. OBSERVATION	S N S N
3. INTERVENTION	S N S N
4. RESPONSE	S N S N
5. RECOMMENDATIONS	S N S N

6. Signature	STUDENT TEACHER	PRACTICUM TEACHER	SUPERVISOR	DATE	H P I F

Competencies for Teaching—Classroom Instruction

Incidental Intervention

1. Student Teacher	Last Name	First	Initial	File Number	ASSESSMENT
Lesson Number	Subject or Activity	Number of Pupils	Tape Recorded ☐	Duration	

		PRACTICUM TEACHER ☐ Direct ☐ Recorded	SUPERVISOR ☐ Direct ☐ Recorded

2. OBSERVATION

S N   S N

3. INTERVENTION

S N   S N

4. RESPONSE

S N   S N

5. RECOMMENDATIONS

S N   S N

6. Signature	STUDENT TEACHER	PRACTICUM TEACHER	SUPERVISOR	DATE	H P I F

Directions for Incidental Intervention

An incidental intervention is an unplanned event in which the student teacher helps a pupil or pupils solve an immediate behavior or learning problem.

When you observe pupils needing help, or when requested by your practicum teacher to provide help, intervene by employing the following procedure.

a. Turn on your tape recorder.

b. Intervene by asking questions, explaining solutions, demonstrating a correct procedure, suggesting references, resolving a dispute or fight, reinforcing appropriate behavior, and so forth.

c. Replay the tape and complete the Incidental Observation Record. If the intervention was not recorded, complete the form from memory.

1. Identifying Information. Each incidental intervention will be assigned a consecutive *Lesson Number* (1 to 6). The *Subject or Activity* identifies the nature of the program at the time of the intervention (for example, recess, reading, physical education, or lunch). *Number of Pupils* refers only to those involved in the intervention. If you taped the intervention, place a check in the box labeled *Tape Recorded*. Enter the approximate *Duration* (in minutes) of the intervention. *Note*: This type of indentifying information will be completed for each instructional form whether it is Incidental Intervention, Questions, Single Task, or Lesson Plan.

2. Observation. Describe what you observed before you intervened, such as, "Alice asked for help with an addition problem," or "Mike pushed his way through the lunch line."

3. Intervention. Describe what you did to help solve the problem. Listen to the replay of your tape and write a condensed report of your actions.

4. Response. From your memory of the event or from replaying your tape, describe briefly the response of the pupil or pupils to your intervention.

5. Recommendations. Evaluate the effectiveness of your intervention according to the pupils' response. Based on this evaluation, state your recommendations for future interventions. Indicate whether you consider your intervention to have been satisfactory, or describe the modifications you would make in similar situations in the future.

6. <u>Assessment</u>. When you have completed the form to your satisfaction, initial or sign your name in the space provided.

Obtain an evaluation of your intervention by either your practicum teacher or your teacher education supervisor.

a. At a convenient time for your practicum teacher, request an evaluation of your intervention. If the assessment is based on the practicum teacher's direct observation, check the box labeled *Direct*. If it is based on replay of a tape, check *Recorded*. Both may be checked when applicable. As each section is assessed, request that the practicum teacher circle either "S" for satisfactory or "N" for needs improvement. Your practicum teacher will then sign or initial the form in the space provided.

b. If the assessment is to be made by your teacher education supervisor, follow the same procedure as above. In either case, show the form to your supervisor, who will read the entries and will circle "H" for honors, "P" for pass, or "I" for incomplete. "I" indicates that the form requires more information before it is submitted. "F" indicates failure. Your supervisor will then initial or sign the form. You may make brief notes regarding suggestions for improvement in the space opposite each section. Enter the date and distribute the copies of the forms as indicated at the top of each form.

Competencies for Teaching—Classroom Instruction

Incidental Intervention

1. Student Teacher	Last Name		First		Initial	File Number	ASSESSMENT
Lesson Number	Subject or Activity			Number of Pupils	Tape Recorded ☐	Duration	PRACTICUM TEACHER Direct ☐ Recorded ☐ SUPERVISOR Direct ☐ Recorded ☐

2. OBSERVATION

S N   S N

3. INTERVENTION

S N   S N

4. RESPONSE

S N   S N

5. RECOMMENDATIONS

S N   S N

6. Signature	STUDENT TEACHER	PRACTICUM TEACHER	SUPERVISOR	DATE	H P I F

Distribution: Forward this form to the *Classroom Teacher*

Competencies for Teaching—Classroom Instruction

Incidental Intervention

1. Student Teacher	Last Name	First	Initial	File Number	ASSESSMENT
Lesson Number	Subject or Activity	Number of Pupils	Tape Recorded ☐	Duration	PRACTICUM TEACHER ☐Direct ☐Recorded / SUPERVISOR ☐Direct ☐Recorded

2. OBSERVATION

S N   S N

3. INTERVENTION

S N   S N

4. RESPONSE

S N   S N

5. RECOMMENDATIONS

S N   S N

6. Signature	STUDENT TEACHER	PRACTICUM TEACHER	SUPERVISOR	DATE	H P I F

Competencies for Teaching—Classroom Instruction

Incidental Intervention

1. Student Teacher	Last Name	First	Initial	File Number	ASSESSMENT
Lesson Number	Subject or Activity	Number of Pupils	Tape Recorded ☐	Duration	

ASSESSMENT

PRACTICUM TEACHER ☐ Direct ☐ Recorded
SUPERVISOR ☐ Direct ☐ Recorded

2. OBSERVATION

S N   S N

3. INTERVENTION

S N   S N

4. RESPONSE

S N   S N

5. RECOMMENDATIONS

S N   S N

6. Signature	STUDENT TEACHER	PRACTICUM TEACHER	SUPERVISOR	DATE	
					H P I F

Directions for Incidental Intervention

An incidental intervention is an unplanned event in which the student teacher helps a pupil or pupils solve an immediate behavior or learning problem.

When you observe pupils needing help, or when requested by your practicum teacher to provide help, intervene by employing the following procedure.

   a. Turn on your tape recorder.

   b. Intervene by asking questions, explaining solutions, demonstrating a correct procedure, suggesting references, resolving a dispute or fight, reinforcing appropriate behavior, and so forth.

   c. Replay the tape and complete the Incidental Observation Record. If the intervention was not recorded, complete the form from memory.

1. <u>Identifying Information</u>. Each incidental intervention will be assigned a consecutive *Lesson Number* (1 to 6). The *Subject or Activity* identifies the nature of the program at the time of the intervention (for example, recess, reading, physical education, or lunch). *Number of Pupils* refers only to those involved in the intervention. If you taped the intervention, place a check in the box labeled *Tape Recorded*. Enter the approximate *Duration* (in minutes) of the intervention. *Note*: This type of indentifying information will be completed for each instructional form whether it is Incidental Intervention, Questions, Single Task, or Lesson Plan.

2. <u>Observation</u>. Describe what you observed before you intervened, such as, "Alice asked for help with an addition problem," or "Mike pushed his way through the lunch line."

3. <u>Intervention</u>. Describe what you did to help solve the problem. Listen to the replay of your tape and write a condensed report of your actions.

4. <u>Response</u>. From your memory of the event or from replaying your tape, describe briefly the response of the pupil or pupils to your intervention.

5. <u>Recommendations</u>. Evaluate the effectiveness of your intervention according to the pupils' response. Based on this evaluation, state your recommendations for future interventions. Indicate whether you consider your intervention to have been satisfactory, or describe the modifications you would make in similar situations in the future.

6. <u>Assessment</u>. When you have completed the form to your satisfaction, initial or sign your name in the space provided.

Obtain an evaluation of your intervention by either your practicum teacher or your teacher education supervisor.

a. At a convenient time for your practicum teacher, request an evaluation of your intervention. If the assessment is based on the practicum teacher's direct observation, check the box labeled *Direct*. If it is based on replay of a tape, check *Recorded*. Both may be checked when applicable. As each section is assessed, request that the practicum teacher circle either "S" for satisfactory or "N" for needs improvement. Your practicum teacher will then sign or initial the form in the space provided.

b. If the assessment is to be made by your teacher education supervisor, follow the same procedure as above. In either case, show the form to your supervisor, who will read the entries and will circle "H" for honors, "P" for pass, or "I" for incomplete. "I" indicates that the form requires more information before it is submitted. "F" indicates failure. Your supervisor will then initial or sign the form. You may make brief notes regarding suggestions for improvement in the space opposite each section. Enter the date and distribute the copies of the forms as indicated at the top of each form.

Competencies for Teaching—Classroom Instruction

Incidental Intervention

1. Student Teacher	Last Name	First	Initial	File Number	ASSESSMENT
Lesson Number	Subject or Activity	Number of Pupils	Tape Recorded ☐	Duration	PRACTICUM TEACHER ☐ Direct ☐ Recorded SUPERVISOR ☐ Direct ☐ Recorded

2. OBSERVATION

S N   S N

3. INTERVENTION

S N   S N

4. RESPONSE

S N   S N

5. RECOMMENDATIONS

S N   S N

6. Signature	STUDENT TEACHER	PRACTICUM TEACHER	SUPERVISOR	DATE	H P I F

Competencies for Teaching—Classroom Instruction

Incidental Intervention

1. Student Teacher	Last Name	First	Initial	File Number
Lesson Number	Subject or Activity	Number of Pupils	Tape Recorded ☐	Duration

ASSESSMENT

PRACTICUM TEACHER ☐ Direct ☐ Recorded   SUPERVISOR ☐ Direct ☐ Recorded

2. OBSERVATION

S N   S N

3. INTERVENTION

S N   S N

4. RESPONSE

S N   S N

5. RECOMMENDATIONS

S N   S N

6. Signature	STUDENT TEACHER	PRACTICUM TEACHER	SUPERVISOR	DATE

H P I F

Competencies for Teaching—Classroom Instruction

Incidental Intervention

1. Student Teacher	Last Name	First	Initial	File Number	ASSESSMENT	
Lesson Number	Subject or Activity	Number of Pupils	Tape Recorded ☐	Duration	PRACTICUM TEACHER ☐☐ Direct ☐☐ Recorded	SUPERVISOR ☐☐ Direct ☐☐ Recorded

2. OBSERVATION		S N	S N

3. INTERVENTION		S N	S N

4. RESPONSE		S N	S N

5. RECOMMENDATIONS		S N	S N

6. Signature	STUDENT TEACHER	PRACTICUM TEACHER	SUPERVISOR	DATE	H P I F

Directions for Questions

This lesson is an exercise to develop your skill in questioning. Ask your practicum teacher for a group of from two to six pupils for the purpose of questioning on a specific topic.

 1. _Identifying Information_. Enter the required information. These forms will be assigned consecutive numbers (1 to 6). The _Duration_ of the lesson will be entered after the questioning sequence has been completed.

 2. _Questions_. Construct four questions in a developmental sequence related to the specific topic. Follow the instructions, "Developing Questioning Skills," in Chapter Six of _Classroom Instruction_, in writing the questions and carrying out the following procedure.

 a. _Question_: Write your questions in the four _Question_ spaces.

 b. Turn on your tape recorder and begin your questioning procedure. After pupil response, you may wish to redirect, rephrase, prompt, or ask for pupil clarification.

 c. _Process_: After completing your presentation of the _four questions_ of this lesson, replay your tape and analyze the _Process_ for the first question. Tally the number of times a particular process was used.

PROCESS	CORRECT	REDIRECT	REPHRASE	PROMPT	PUPIL CLARIFICATION
			/	////	/

 d. _Evaluation_: Evaluate the question according to pupil responses. Check the box indicating that the question was _Adequate_, or that it should have been _Easier, Harder, More Specific, Open-Ended_, or _Clearer_.

 e. _Recommendation_: Write your _Recommendation_ regarding the future use of this question. If the question was adequate, indicate that you would "repeat" its use. If inadequate, rewrite the question in the space provided.

 f. Repeat the procedures described in (c), (d), and (e) for the other three questions.

3. <u>Presentation</u>. After you have assessed the questions, evaluate your overall *Presentation*. Circle "S" for satisfactory or "N" for needs improvement—for *Attention, Voice, Pause, Approval, Participation,* and *Distribution*.

4. <u>Assessment</u>. Obtain assessment from either your practicum teacher or your supervisor. Follow the procedure described in the *Assessment* instructions for Incidental Intervention.

Show the completed form to your teacher education supervisor for an evaluation, H, P, I, or F. Enter the date and distribute the copies of this form as indicated.

Competencies for Teaching—Classroom Instruction

Questions

1. Student Teacher	Last Name	First	Initial	File Number	ASSESSMENT

Lesson Number	Subject or Activity	Number of Pupils	Tape Recorded ☐	Duration	

ASSESSMENT column: PRACTICUM TEACHER — Direct ☐ Recorder ☐; SUPERVISOR — Direct ☐ Recorder ☐

2. QUESTIONS

Q1

Question:

PROCESS	CORRECT	REDIRECT	REPHRASE	PROMPT	PUPIL CLARIFICATION

EVALUATION	ADEQUATE ☐	EASIER ☐	HARDER ☐	MORE SPECIFIC ☐	OPEN-ENDED ☐	CLEARER ☐

Recommendation:

S N   S N

Q2

Question:

PROCESS	CORRECT	REDIRECT	REPHRASE	PROMPT	PUPIL CLARIFICATION

EVALUATION	ADEQUATE ☐	EASIER ☐	HARDER ☐	MORE SPECIFIC ☐	OPEN-ENDED ☐	CLEARER ☐

Recommendation:

S N   S N

Q3

Question:

PROCESS	CORRECT	REDIRECT	REPHRASE	PROMPT	PUPIL CLARIFICATION

EVALUATION	ADEQUATE ☐	EASIER ☐	HARDER ☐	MORE SPECIFIC ☐	OPEN-ENDED ☐	CLEARER ☐

Recommendation:

S N   S N

Q4

Question:

PROCESS	CORRECT	REDIRECT	REPHRASE	PROMPT	PUPIL CLARIFICATION

EVALUATION	ADEQUATE ☐	EASIER ☐	HARDER ☐	MORE SPECIFIC ☐	OPEN-ENDED ☐	CLEARER ☐

Recommendation

S N   S N

3. PRESENTATION

ATTENTION: prerequisite to questioning.	S N
VOICE: tone pleasant, enunciation clear.	S N
PAUSE: precedes calling on pupil.	S N
APPROVAL: acceptable responses reinforced.	S N
PARTICIPATION: all pupils encouraged.	S N
DISTRIBUTION: questions directed to volunteers and nonvolunteers.	S N

S N   S N

4. Signature

STUDENT TEACHER	PRACTICUM TEACHER	SUPERVISOR	DATE	H P I F

Competencies for Teaching—Classroom Instruction

Questions

1. Student Teacher	Last Name	First	Initial	File Number	ASSESSMENT
Lesson Number	Subject or Activity	Number of Pupils	Tape Recorded ☐	Duration	PRACTICUM TEACHER ☐ Direct ☐ Recorder / SUPERVISOR ☐ Direct ☐ Recorder

2. QUESTIONS

Q1

Question:

PROCESS

CORRECT	REDIRECT	REPHRASE	PROMPT	PUPIL CLARIFICATION

EVALUATION

| ADEQUATE ☐ | EASIER ☐ | HARDER ☐ | MORE SPECIFIC ☐ | OPEN-ENDED ☐ | CLEARER ☐ |

Recommendation:

S N   S N

Q2

Question:

PROCESS

CORRECT	REDIRECT	REPHRASE	PROMPT	PUPIL CLARIFICATION

EVALUATION

| ADEQUATE ☐ | EASIER ☐ | HARDER ☐ | MORE SPECIFIC ☐ | OPEN-ENDED ☐ | CLEARER ☐ |

Recommendation:

S N   S N

Q3

Question:

PROCESS

CORRECT	REDIRECT	REPHRASE	PROMPT	PUPIL CLARIFICATION

EVALUATION

| ADEQUATE ☐ | EASIER ☐ | HARDER ☐ | MORE SPECIFIC ☐ | OPEN-ENDED ☐ | CLEARER ☐ |

Recommendation:

S N   S N

Q4

Question:

PROCESS

CORRECT	REDIRECT	REPHRASE	PROMPT	PUPIL CLARIFICATION

EVALUATION

| ADEQUATE ☐ | EASIER ☐ | HARDER ☐ | MORE SPECIFIC ☐ | OPEN-ENDED ☐ | CLEARER ☐ |

Recommendation

S N   S N

3. PRESENTATION

ATTENTION: prerequisite to questioning.	S N
VOICE: tone pleasant, enunciation clear.	S N
PAUSE: precedes calling on pupil.	S N
APPROVAL: acceptable responses reinforced.	S N
PARTICIPATION: all pupils encouraged.	S N
DISTRIBUTION: questions directed to volunteers and nonvolunteers.	S N

S N   S N

4. Signature	STUDENT TEACHER	PRACTICUM TEACHER	SUPERVISOR	DATE	H P I F

Competencies for Teaching—Classroom Instruction

Questions

1. Student Teacher	Last Name	First		Initial	File Number	ASSESSMENT
Lesson Number	Subject or Activity		Number of Pupils	Tape Recorded ☐	Duration	

ASSESSMENT: PRACTICUM TEACHER ☐ Direct ☐ Recorder SUPERVISOR ☐ Direct ☐ Recorder

2. QUESTIONS

Q1

Question:

PROCESS	CORRECT	REDIRECT	REPHRASE	PROMPT	PUPIL CLARIFICATION

EVALUATION	ADEQUATE ☐	EASIER ☐	HARDER ☐	MORE SPECIFIC ☐	OPEN-ENDED ☐	CLEARER ☐

Recommendation:

S N   S N

Q2

Question:

PROCESS	CORRECT	REDIRECT	REPHRASE	PROMPT	PUPIL CLARIFICATION

EVALUATION	ADEQUATE ☐	EASIER ☐	HARDER ☐	MORE SPECIFIC ☐	OPEN-ENDED ☐	CLEARER ☐

Recommendation:

S N   S N

Q3

Question:

PROCESS	CORRECT	REDIRECT	REPHRASE	PROMPT	PUPIL CLARIFICATION

EVALUATION	ADEQUATE ☐	EASIER ☐	HARDER ☐	MORE SPECIFIC ☐	OPEN-ENDED ☐	CLEARER ☐

Recommendation:

S N   S N

Q4

Question:

PROCESS	CORRECT	REDIRECT	REPHRASE	PROMPT	PUPIL CLARIFICATION

EVALUATION	ADEQUATE ☐	EASIER ☐	HARDER ☐	MORE SPECIFIC ☐	OPEN-ENDED ☐	CLEARER ☐

Recommendation

S N   S N

3. PRESENTATION

ATTENTION: prerequisite to questioning.	S N	
VOICE: tone pleasant, enunciation clear.	S N	
PAUSE: precedes calling on pupil.	S N	
APPROVAL: acceptable responses reinforced.	S N	
PARTICIPATION: all pupils encouraged.	S N	
DISTRIBUTION: questions directed to volunteers and nonvolunteers.	S N	S N S N

4. Signature	STUDENT TEACHER	PRACTICUM TEACHER	SUPERVISOR	DATE	H P I F

Directions for Questions

This lesson is an exercise to develop your skill in questioning. Ask your practicum teacher for a group of from two to six pupils for the purpose of questioning on a specific topic.

1. Identifying Information. Enter the required information. These forms will be assigned consecutive numbers (1 to 6). The *Duration* of the lesson will be entered after the questioning sequence has been completed.

2. Questions. Construct four questions in a developmental sequence related to the specific topic. Follow the instructions, "Developing Questioning Skills," in Chapter Six of *Classroom Instruction*, in writing the questions and carrying out the following procedure.

    a. Question: Write your questions in the four *Question* spaces.

    b. Turn on your tape recorder and begin your questioning procedure. After pupil response, you may wish to redirect, rephrase, prompt, or ask for pupil clarification.

    c. Process: After completing your presentation of the *four questions* of this lesson, replay your tape and analyze the *Process* for the first question. Tally the number of times a particular process was used.

PROCESS	CORRECT	REDIRECT	REPHRASE	PROMPT	PUPIL CLARIFICATION
			/	////	/

    d. Evaluation: Evaluate the question according to pupil responses. Check the box indicating that the question was *Adequate*, or that it should have been *Easier, Harder, More Specific, Open-Ended,* or *Clearer*.

    e. Recommendation: Write your *Recommendation* regarding the future use of this question. If the question was adequate, indicate that you would "repeat" its use. If inadequate, rewrite the question in the space provided.

    f. Repeat the procedures described in (c), (d), and (e) for the other three questions.

3. Presentation. After you have assessed the questions, evaluate your overall *Presentation*. Circle "S" for satisfactory or "N" for needs improvement—for *Attention*, *Voice*, *Pause*, *Approval*, *Participation*, and *Distribution*.

4. Assessment. Obtain assessment from either your practicum teacher or your supervisor. Follow the procedure described in the *Assessment* instructions for Incidental Intervention.

Show the completed form to your teacher education supervisor for an evaluation, H, P, I, or F. Enter the date and distribute the copies of this form as indicated.

Competencies for Teaching—Classroom Instruction

Questions

1. Student Teacher	Last Name		First		Initial	File Number	ASSESSMENT
Lesson Number	Subject or Activity			Number of Pupils	Tape Recorded ☐	Duration	PRACTICUM TEACHER ☐☐ Direct ☐☐ Recorder / SUPERVISOR ☐☐ Direct ☐☐ Recorder

2. QUESTIONS

Q1

Question:

PROCESS

CORRECT	REDIRECT	REPHRASE	PROMPT	PUPIL CLARIFICATION

EVALUATION

ADEQUATE ☐   EASIER ☐   HARDER ☐   MORE SPECIFIC ☐   OPEN-ENDED ☐   CLEARER ☐

Recommendation:

S N   S N

Q2

Question:

CORRECT	REDIRECT	REPHRASE	PROMPT	PUPIL CLARIFICATION

ADEQUATE ☐   EASIER ☐   HARDER ☐   MORE SPECIFIC ☐   OPEN-ENDED ☐   CLEARER ☐

Recommendation:

S N   S N

Q3

Question:

CORRECT	REDIRECT	REPHRASE	PROMPT	PUPIL CLARIFICATION

ADEQUATE ☐   EASIER ☐   HARDER ☐   MORE SPECIFIC ☐   OPEN-ENDED ☐   CLEARER ☐

Recommendation:

S N   S N

Q4

Question:

CORRECT	REDIRECT	REPHRASE	PROMPT	PUPIL CLARIFICATION

ADEQUATE ☐   EASIER ☐   HARDER ☐   MORE SPECIFIC ☐   OPEN-ENDED ☐   CLEARER ☐

Recommendation

S N   S N

3. PRESENTATION

ATTENTION: prerequisite to questioning.	S N
VOICE: tone pleasant, enunciation clear.	S N
PAUSE: precedes calling on pupil.	S N
APPROVAL: acceptable responses reinforced.	S N
PARTICIPATION: all pupils encouraged.	S N
DISTRIBUTION: questions directed to volunteers and nonvolunteers.	S N

S N   S N

4. Signature

STUDENT TEACHER	PRACTICUM TEACHER	SUPERVISOR	DATE	H P I F

Competencies for Teaching—Classroom Instruction

Questions

1. Student Teacher	Last Name	First	Initial	File Number	ASSESSMENT
Lesson Number	Subject or Activity	Number of Pupils	Tape Recorded ☐	Duration	PRACTICUM TEACHER Direct ☐ Recorder ☐ / SUPERVISOR Direct ☐ Recorder ☐

QUESTIONS

2.

Q1

Question:

PROCESS	CORRECT	REDIRECT	REPHRASE	PROMPT	PUPIL CLARIFICATION

EVALUATION	ADEQUATE ☐	EASIER ☐	HARDER ☐	MORE SPECIFIC ☐	OPEN-ENDED ☐	CLEARER ☐

Recommendation:

S N S N

Q2

Question:

PROCESS	CORRECT	REDIRECT	REPHRASE	PROMPT	PUPIL CLARIFICATION

EVALUATION	ADEQUATE ☐	EASIER ☐	HARDER ☐	MORE SPECIFIC ☐	OPEN-ENDED ☐	CLEARER ☐

Recommendation:

S N S N

Q3

Question:

PROCESS	CORRECT	REDIRECT	REPHRASE	PROMPT	PUPIL CLARIFICATION

EVALUATION	ADEQUATE ☐	EASIER ☐	HARDER ☐	MORE SPECIFIC ☐	OPEN-ENDED ☐	CLEARER ☐

Recommendation:

S N S N

Q4

Question:

PROCESS	CORRECT	REDIRECT	REPHRASE	PROMPT	PUPIL CLARIFICATION

EVALUATION	ADEQUATE ☐	EASIER ☐	HARDER ☐	MORE SPECIFIC ☐	OPEN-ENDED ☐	CLEARER ☐

Recommendation

S N S N

3. PRESENTATION

ATTENTION: prerequisite to questioning.	S N	
VOICE: tone pleasant, enunciation clear.	S N	
PAUSE: precedes calling on pupil.	S N	
APPROVAL: acceptable responses reinforced.	S N	
PARTICIPATION: all pupils encouraged.	S N	
DISTRIBUTION: questions directed to volunteers and nonvolunteers.	S N	S N S N

4. Signature	STUDENT TEACHER	PRACTICUM TEACHER	SUPERVISOR	DATE	H P I F

Competencies for Teaching—Classroom Instruction

Questions

1. Student Teacher	Last Name		First		Initial	File Number	ASSESSMENT
Lesson Number	Subject or Activity		Number of Pupils	Tape Recorded ☐	Duration		

ASSESSMENT: PRACTICUM TEACHER (Direct ☐ Recorder ☐), SUPERVISOR (Direct ☐ Recorder ☐)

2. QUESTIONS

Q1
Question:

PROCESS:

CORRECT	REDIRECT	REPHRASE	PROMPT	PUPIL CLARIFICATION

EVALUATION:

ADEQUATE ☐	EASIER ☐	HARDER ☐	MORE SPECIFIC ☐	OPEN-ENDED ☐	CLEARER ☐

Recommendation:

S N   S N

Q2
Question:

PROCESS:

CORRECT	REDIRECT	REPHRASE	PROMPT	PUPIL CLARIFICATION

EVALUATION:

ADEQUATE ☐	EASIER ☐	HARDER ☐	MORE SPECIFIC ☐	OPEN-ENDED ☐	CLEARER ☐

Recommendation:

S N   S N

Q3
Question:

PROCESS:

CORRECT	REDIRECT	REPHRASE	PROMPT	PUPIL CLARIFICATION

EVALUATION:

ADEQUATE ☐	EASIER ☐	HARDER ☐	MORE SPECIFIC ☐	OPEN-ENDED ☐	CLEARER ☐

Recommendation:

S N   S N

Q4
Question:

PROCESS:

CORRECT	REDIRECT	REPHRASE	PROMPT	PUPIL CLARIFICATION

EVALUATION:

ADEQUATE ☐	EASIER ☐	HARDER ☐	MORE SPECIFIC ☐	OPEN-ENDED ☐	CLEARER ☐

Recommendation

S N   S N

3. PRESENTATION

ATTENTION: prerequisite to questioning.	S N
VOICE: tone pleasant, enunciation clear.	S N
PAUSE: precedes calling on pupil.	S N
APPROVAL: acceptable responses reinforced.	S N
PARTICIPATION: all pupils encouraged.	S N
DISTRIBUTION: questions directed to volunteers and nonvolunteers.	S N

S N   S N

4. Signature

STUDENT TEACHER	PRACTICUM TEACHER	SUPERVISOR	DATE	H P I F

Directions for Questions

This lesson is an exercise to develop your skill in questioning. Ask your practicum teacher for a group of from two to six pupils for the purpose of questioning on a specific topic.

1. <u>Identifying Information</u>. Enter the required information. These forms will be assigned consecutive numbers (1 to 6). The *Duration* of the lesson will be entered after the questioning sequence has been completed.

2. <u>Questions</u>. Construct four questions in a developmental sequence related to the specific topic. Follow the instructions, "Developing Questioning Skills," in Chapter Six of *Classroom Instruction*, in writing the questions and carrying out the following procedure.

    a. <u>Question</u>: Write your questions in the four *Question* spaces.

    b. Turn on your tape recorder and begin your questioning procedure. After pupil response, you may wish to redirect, rephrase, prompt, or ask for pupil clarification.

    c. <u>Process</u>: After completing your presentation of the *four questions* of this lesson, replay your tape and analyze the *Process* for the first question. Tally the number of times a particular process was used.

PROCESS	CORRECT	REDIRECT	REPHRASE	PROMPT	PUPIL CLARIFICATION
			/	////	/

    d. <u>Evaluation</u>: Evaluate the question according to pupil responses. Check the box indicating that the question was *Adequate*, or that it should have been *Easier, Harder, More Specific, Open-Ended,* or *Clearer*.

    e. <u>Recommendation</u>: Write your *Recommendation* regarding the future use of this question. If the question was adequate, indicate that you would "repeat" its use. If inadequate, rewrite the question in the space provided.

    f. Repeat the procedures described in (c), (d), and (e) for the other three questions.

3. <u>Presentation</u>. After you have assessed the questions, evaluate your overall *Presentation*. Circle "S" for satisfactory or "N" for needs improvement—for *Attention, Voice, Pause, Approval, Participation,* and *Distribution.*

4. <u>Assessment</u>. Obtain assessment from either your practicum teacher or your supervisor. Follow the procedure described in the *Assessment* instructions for Incidental Intervention.

Show the completed form to your teacher education supervisor for an evaluation, H, P, I, or F. Enter the date and distribute the copies of this form as indicated.

Competencies for Teaching—Classroom Instruction

Questions

1. Student Teacher	Last Name	First	Initial	File Number		ASSESSMENT
Lesson Number	Subject or Activity	Number of Pupils	Tape Recorded ☐	Duration		PRACTICUM TEACHER: Direct ☐ Recorder ☐ SUPERVISOR: Direct ☐ Recorder ☐

2.

Q 1

Question:

PROCESS	CORRECT	REDIRECT	REPHRASE	PROMPT	PUPIL CLARIFICATION

EVALUATION	ADEQUATE ☐	EASIER ☐	HARDER ☐	MORE SPECIFIC ☐	OPEN-ENDED ☐	CLEARER ☐

Recommendation:

S N   S N

Q 2

Question:

PROCESS	CORRECT	REDIRECT	REPHRASE	PROMPT	PUPIL CLARIFICATION

EVALUATION	ADEQUATE ☐	EASIER ☐	HARDER ☐	MORE SPECIFIC ☐	OPEN-ENDED ☐	CLEARER ☐

Recommendation:

S N   S N

Q 3

Question:

PROCESS	CORRECT	REDIRECT	REPHRASE	PROMPT	PUPIL CLARIFICATION

EVALUATION	ADEQUATE ☐	EASIER ☐	HARDER ☐	MORE SPECIFIC ☐	OPEN-ENDED ☐	CLEARER ☐

Recommendation:

S N   S N

Q 4

Question:

PROCESS	CORRECT	REDIRECT	REPHRASE	PROMPT	PUPIL CLARIFICATION

EVALUATION	ADEQUATE ☐	EASIER ☐	HARDER ☐	MORE SPECIFIC ☐	OPEN-ENDED ☐	CLEARER ☐

Recommendation

S N   S N

3. PRESENTATION

ATTENTION: prerequisite to questioning.	S N	
VOICE: tone pleasant, enunciation clear.	S N	
PAUSE: precedes calling on pupil.	S N	
APPROVAL: acceptable responses reinforced.	S N	
PARTICIPATION: all pupils encouraged.	S N	
DISTRIBUTION: questions directed to volunteers and nonvolunteers.	S N	S N S N

4. Signature	STUDENT TEACHER	PRACTICUM TEACHER	SUPERVISOR	DATE	H P I F

Competencies for Teaching—Classroom Instruction

Questions

1. Student Teacher	Last Name		First		Initial	File Number	ASSESSMENT

Lesson Number	Subject or Activity		Number of Pupils	Tape Recorded	☐	Duration	PRACTICUM TEACHER ☐ Direct ☐ Recorder SUPERVISOR ☐ Direct ☐ Recorder

2.   QUESTIONS

Q 1

Question:

PROCESS

CORRECT	REDIRECT	REPHRASE	PROMPT	PUPIL CLARIFICATION

EVALUATION

ADEQUATE ☐	EASIER ☐	HARDER ☐	MORE SPECIFIC ☐	OPEN-ENDED ☐	CLEARER ☐

Recommendation:

S N | S N

Q 2

Question:

PROCESS

CORRECT	REDIRECT	REPHRASE	PROMPT	PUPIL CLARIFICATION

EVALUATION

ADEQUATE ☐	EASIER ☐	HARDER ☐	MORE SPECIFIC ☐	OPEN-ENDED ☐	CLEARER ☐

Recommendation:

S N | S N

Q 3

Question:

PROCESS

CORRECT	REDIRECT	REPHRASE	PROMPT	PUPIL CLARIFICATION

EVALUATION

ADEQUATE ☐	EASIER ☐	HARDER ☐	MORE SPECIFIC ☐	OPEN-ENDED ☐	CLEARER ☐

Recommendation:

S N | S N

Q 4

Question:

PROCESS

CORRECT	REDIRECT	REPHRASE	PROMPT	PUPIL CLARIFICATION

EVALUATION

ADEQUATE ☐	EASIER ☐	HARDER ☐	MORE SPECIFIC ☐	OPEN-ENDED ☐	CLEARER ☐

Recommendation

S N | S N

3.   PRESENTATION

ATTENTION: prerequisite to questioning.	S N
VOICE: tone pleasant, enunciation clear.	S N
PAUSE: precedes calling on pupil.	S N
APPROVAL: acceptable responses reinforced..	S N
PARTICIPATION: all pupils encouraged.	S N
DISTRIBUTION: questions directed to volunteers and nonvolunteers.	S N

S N | S N

4. Signature	STUDENT TEACHER	PRACTICUM TEACHER	SUPERVISOR	DATE	H P I F

Competencies for Teaching—Classroom Instruction

Questions

1. Student Teacher	Last Name	First	Initial	File Number	ASSESSMENT

Lesson Number	Subject or Activity	Number of Pupils	Tape Recorded ☐	Duration	PRACTICUM TEACHER ☐ Direct ☐ Recorder SUPERVISOR ☐ Direct ☐ Recorder

2.

QUESTIONS

Q1

Question:

PROCESS

CORRECT	REDIRECT	REPHRASE	PROMPT	PUPIL CLARIFICATION

EVALUATION

ADEQUATE ☐	EASIER ☐	HARDER ☐	MORE SPECIFIC ☐	OPEN-ENDED ☐	CLEARER ☐

Recommendation:

S N   S N

Q2

Question:

PROCESS

CORRECT	REDIRECT	REPHRASE	PROMPT	PUPIL CLARIFICATION

EVALUATION

ADEQUATE ☐	EASIER ☐	HARDER ☐	MORE SPECIFIC ☐	OPEN-ENDED ☐	CLEARER ☐

Recommendation:

S N   S N

Q3

Question:

PROCESS

CORRECT	REDIRECT	REPHRASE	PROMPT	PUPIL CLARIFICATION

EVALUATION

ADEQUATE ☐	EASIER ☐	HARDER ☐	MORE SPECIFIC ☐	OPEN-ENDED ☐	CLEARER ☐

Recommendation:

S N   S N

Q4

Question:

PROCESS

CORRECT	REDIRECT	REPHRASE	PROMPT	PUPIL CLARIFICATION

EVALUATION

ADEQUATE ☐	EASIER ☐	HARDER ☐	MORE SPECIFIC ☐	OPEN-ENDED ☐	CLEARER ☐

Recommendation

S N   S N

3.

PRESENTATION

ATTENTION: prerequisite to questioning.	S N
VOICE: tone pleasant, enunciation clear.	S N
PAUSE: precedes calling on pupil.	S N
APPROVAL: acceptable responses reinforced.	S N
PARTICIPATION: all pupils encouraged.	S N
DISTRIBUTION: questions directed to volunteers and nonvolunteers.	S N

S N   S N

4. Signature	STUDENT TEACHER	PRACTICUM TEACHER	SUPERVISOR	DATE	H P I F

Directions for Questions

This lesson is an exercise to develop your skill in questioning. Ask your practicum teacher for a group of from two to six pupils for the purpose of questioning on a specific topic.

1. <u>Identifying Information</u>. Enter the required information. These forms will be assigned consecutive numbers (1 to 6). The *Duration* of the lesson will be entered after the questioning sequence has been completed.

2. <u>Questions</u>. Construct four questions in a developmental sequence related to the specific topic. Follow the instructions, "Developing Questioning Skills," in Chapter Six of *Classroom Instruction*, in writing the questions and carrying out the following procedure.

  a. <u>Question</u>: Write your questions in the four *Question* spaces.

  b. Turn on your tape recorder and begin your questioning procedure. After pupil response, you may wish to redirect, rephrase, prompt, or ask for pupil clarification.

  c. <u>Process</u>: After completing your presentation of the *four questions* of this lesson, replay your tape and analyze the *Process* for the first question. Tally the number of times a particular process was used.

PROCESS	CORRECT	REDIRECT	REPHRASE	PROMPT	PUPIL CLARIFICATION
			/	////	/

  d. <u>Evaluation</u>: Evaluate the question according to pupil responses. Check the box indicating that the question was *Adequate*, or that it should have been *Easier*, *Harder*, *More Specific*, *Open-Ended*, or *Clearer*.

  e. <u>Recommendation</u>: Write your *Recommendation* regarding the future use of this question. If the question was adequate, indicate that you would "repeat" its use. If inadequate, rewrite the question in the space provided.

  f. Repeat the procedures described in (c), (d), and (e) for the other three questions.

3. <u>Presentation</u>. After you have assessed the questions, evaluate your overall *Presentation*. Circle "S" for satisfactory or "N" for needs improvement—for *Attention*, *Voice*, *Pause*, *Approval*, *Participation*, and *Distribution*.

4. <u>Assessment</u>. Obtain assessment from either your practicum teacher or your supervisor. Follow the procedure described in the *Assessment* instructions for Incidental Intervention.

Show the completed form to your teacher education supervisor for an evaluation, H, P, I, or F. Enter the date and distribute the copies of this form as indicated.

Competencies for Teaching—Classroom Instruction

Questions

1. Student Teacher	Last Name	First	Initial	File Number	ASSESSMENT
Lesson Number	Subject or Activity	Number of Pupils	Tape Recorded ☐	Duration	PRACTICUM TEACHER ☐ Direct ☐ Recorder / SUPERVISOR ☐ Direct ☐ Recorder

2.

QUESTIONS

Q1

Question:

PROCESS

CORRECT	REDIRECT	REPHRASE	PROMPT	PUPIL CLARIFICATION

EVALUATION

ADEQUATE ☐	EASIER ☐	HARDER ☐	MORE SPECIFIC ☐	OPEN-ENDED ☐	CLEARER ☐

Recommendation:

S N   S N

Q2

Question:

PROCESS

CORRECT	REDIRECT	REPHRASE	PROMPT	PUPIL CLARIFICATION

EVALUATION

ADEQUATE ☐	EASIER ☐	HARDER ☐	MORE SPECIFIC ☐	OPEN-ENDED ☐	CLEARER ☐

Recommendation:

S N   S N

Q3

Question:

PROCESS

CORRECT	REDIRECT	REPHRASE	PROMPT	PUPIL CLARIFICATION

EVALUATION

ADEQUATE ☐	EASIER ☐	HARDER ☐	MORE SPECIFIC ☐	OPEN-ENDED ☐	CLEARER ☐

Recommendation:

S N   S N

Q4

Question:

PROCESS

CORRECT	REDIRECT	REPHRASE	PROMPT	PUPIL CLARIFICATION

EVALUATION

ADEQUATE ☐	EASIER ☐	HARDER ☐	MORE SPECIFIC ☐	OPEN-ENDED ☐	CLEARER ☐

Recommendation

S N   S N

3.

PRESENTATION

ATTENTION: prerequisite to questioning.	S N
VOICE: tone pleasant, enunciation clear.	S N
PAUSE: precedes calling on pupil.	S N
APPROVAL: acceptable responses reinforced.	S N
PARTICIPATION: all pupils encouraged.	S N
DISTRIBUTION: questions directed to volunteers and nonvolunteers.	S N

S N   S N

4. Signature	STUDENT TEACHER	PRACTICUM TEACHER	SUPERVISOR	DATE	H P I F

Distribution: Forward this form to the *Classroom Teacher*

Competencies for Teaching—Classroom Instruction

Questions

1. Student Teacher	Last Name	First	Initial	File Number
Lesson Number	Subject or Activity	Number of Pupils	Tape Recorded ☐	Duration

ASSESSMENT: PRACTICUM TEACHER ☐ Direct ☐ Recorder; SUPERVISOR ☐ Direct ☐ Recorder

2. QUESTIONS

Q 1 Question:

PROCESS	CORRECT	REDIRECT	REPHRASE	PROMPT	PUPIL CLARIFICATION

EVALUATION: ADEQUATE ☐ EASIER ☐ HARDER ☐ MORE SPECIFIC ☐ OPEN-ENDED ☐ CLEARER ☐

Recommendation:

S N | S N

Q 2 Question:

PROCESS	CORRECT	REDIRECT	REPHRASE	PROMPT	PUPIL CLARIFICATION

EVALUATION: ADEQUATE ☐ EASIER ☐ HARDER ☐ MORE SPECIFIC ☐ OPEN-ENDED ☐ CLEARER ☐

Recommendation:

S N | S N

Q 3 Question:

PROCESS	CORRECT	REDIRECT	REPHRASE	PROMPT	PUPIL CLARIFICATION

EVALUATION: ADEQUATE ☐ EASIER ☐ HARDER ☐ MORE SPECIFIC ☐ OPEN-ENDED ☐ CLEARER ☐

Recommendation:

S N | S N

Q 4 Question:

PROCESS	CORRECT	REDIRECT	REPHRASE	PROMPT	PUPIL CLARIFICATION

EVALUATION: ADEQUATE ☐ EASIER ☐ HARDER ☐ MORE SPECIFIC ☐ OPEN-ENDED ☐ CLEARER ☐

Recommendation

S N | S N

3. PRESENTATION

ATTENTION: prerequisite to questioning.	S N
VOICE: tone pleasant, enunciation clear.	S N
PAUSE: precedes calling on pupil.	S N
APPROVAL: acceptable responses reinforced.	S N
PARTICIPATION: all pupils encouraged.	S N
DISTRIBUTION: questions directed to volunteers and nonvolunteers.	S N

S N | S N

4. Signature	STUDENT TEACHER	PRACTICUM TEACHER	SUPERVISOR	DATE	H P I F

Competencies for Teaching—Classroom Instruction

Questions

1. Student Teacher	Last Name	First	Initial	File Number	ASSESSMENT

| Lesson Number | Subject or Activity | Number of Pupils | Tape Recorded ☐ | Duration |

ASSESSMENT: PRACTICUM TEACHER ☐ Direct ☐ Recorder | SUPERVISOR ☐ Direct ☐ Recorder

2.

Q1
Question:

PROCESS	CORRECT	REDIRECT	REPHRASE	PROMPT	PUPIL CLARIFICATION

| EVALUATION | ADEQUATE ☐ | EASIER ☐ | HARDER ☐ | MORE SPECIFIC ☐ | OPEN-ENDED ☐ | CLEARER ☐ |

Recommendation:

S N | S N

Q2
Question:

PROCESS	CORRECT	REDIRECT	REPHRASE	PROMPT	PUPIL CLARIFICATION

| EVALUATION | ADEQUATE ☐ | EASIER ☐ | HARDER ☐ | MORE SPECIFIC ☐ | OPEN-ENDED ☐ | CLEARER ☐ |

Recommendation:

S N | S N

Q3
Question:

PROCESS	CORRECT	REDIRECT	REPHRASE	PROMPT	PUPIL CLARIFICATION

| EVALUATION | ADEQUATE ☐ | EASIER ☐ | HARDER ☐ | MORE SPECIFIC ☐ | OPEN-ENDED ☐ | CLEARER ☐ |

Recommendation:

S N | S N

Q4
Question:

PROCESS	CORRECT	REDIRECT	REPHRASE	PROMPT	PUPIL CLARIFICATION

| EVALUATION | ADEQUATE ☐ | EASIER ☐ | HARDER ☐ | MORE SPECIFIC ☐ | OPEN-ENDED ☐ | CLEARER ☐ |

Recommendation

S N | S N

3. PRESENTATION

	S N
ATTENTION: prerequisite to questioning.	S N
VOICE: tone pleasant, enunciation clear.	S N
PAUSE: precedes calling on pupil.	S N
APPROVAL: acceptable responses reinforced.	S N
PARTICIPATION: all pupils encouraged.	S N
DISTRIBUTION: questions directed to volunteers and nonvolunteers.	S N	S N	S N

4. Signature	STUDENT TEACHER	PRACTICUM TEACHER	SUPERVISOR	DATE	H P I F

Directions for Questions

This lesson is an exercise to develop your skill in questioning. Ask your practicum teacher for a group of from two to six pupils for the purpose of questioning on a specific topic.

1. Identifying Information. Enter the required information. These forms will be assigned consecutive numbers (1 to 6). The *Duration* of the lesson will be entered after the questioning sequence has been completed.

2. Questions. Construct four questions in a developmental sequence related to the specific topic. Follow the instructions, "Developing Questioning Skills," in Chapter Six of *Classroom Instruction*, in writing the questions and carrying out the following procedure.

   a. Question: Write your questions in the four *Question* spaces.

   b. Turn on your tape recorder and begin your questioning procedure. After pupil response, you may wish to redirect, rephrase, prompt, or ask for pupil clarification.

   c. Process: After completing your presentation of the *four questions* of this lesson, replay your tape and analyze the *Process* for the first question. Tally the number of times a particular process was used.

PROCESS	CORRECT	REDIRECT	REPHRASE	PROMPT	PUPIL CLARIFICATION
			/	////	/

   d. Evaluation: Evaluate the question according to pupil responses. Check the box indicating that the question was *Adequate*, or that it should have been *Easier*, *Harder*, *More Specific*, *Open-Ended*, or *Clearer*.

   e. Recommendation: Write your *Recommendation* regarding the future use of this question. If the question was adequate, indicate that you would "repeat" its use. If inadequate, rewrite the question in the space provided.

   f. Repeat the procedures described in (c), (d), and (e) for the other three questions.

3. <u>Presentation</u>. After you have assessed the questions, evaluate your overall *Presentation*. Circle "S" for satisfactory or "N" for needs improvement—for *Attention, Voice, Pause, Approval, Participation,* and *Distribution.*

4. <u>Assessment</u>. Obtain assessment from either your practicum teacher or your supervisor. Follow the procedure described in the *Assessment* instructions for Incidental Intervention.

Show the completed form to your teacher education supervisor for an evaluation, H, P, I, or F. Enter the date and distribute the copies of this form as indicated.

Competencies for Teaching—Classroom Instruction

Questions

1. Student Teacher	Last Name		First		Initial	File Number	ASSESSMENT
Lesson Number	Subject or Activity			Number of Pupils	Tape Recorded ☐	Duration	PRACTICUM TEACHER ☐ Direct ☐ Recorder / SUPERVISOR ☐ Direct ☐ Recorder

2. QUESTIONS

Q 1

Question:

PROCESS	CORRECT	REDIRECT	REPHRASE	PROMPT	PUPIL CLARIFICATION

EVALUATION	ADEQUATE ☐	EASIER ☐	HARDER ☐	MORE SPECIFIC ☐	OPEN-ENDED ☐	CLEARER ☐

Recommendation:

S N | S N

Q 2

Question:

PROCESS	CORRECT	REDIRECT	REPHRASE	PROMPT	PUPIL CLARIFICATION

EVALUATION	ADEQUATE ☐	EASIER ☐	HARDER ☐	MORE SPECIFIC ☐	OPEN-ENDED ☐	CLEARER ☐

Recommendation:

S N | S N

Q 3

Question:

PROCESS	CORRECT	REDIRECT	REPHRASE	PROMPT	PUPIL CLARIFICATION

EVALUATION	ADEQUATE ☐	EASIER ☐	HARDER ☐	MORE SPECIFIC ☐	OPEN-ENDED ☐	CLEARER ☐

Recommendation:

S N | S N

Q 4

Question:

PROCESS	CORRECT	REDIRECT	REPHRASE	PROMPT	PUPIL CLARIFICATION

EVALUATION	ADEQUATE ☐	EASIER ☐	HARDER ☐	MORE SPECIFIC ☐	OPEN-ENDED ☐	CLEARER ☐

Recommendation

S N | S N

3. PRESENTATION

ATTENTION: prerequisite to questioning.	S N	
VOICE: tone pleasant, enunciation clear.	S N	
PAUSE: precedes calling on pupil.	S N	
APPROVAL: acceptable responses reinforced.	S N	
PARTICIPATION: all pupils encouraged.	S N	
DISTRIBUTION: questions directed to volunteers and nonvolunteers.	S N	S N S N

4. Signature	STUDENT TEACHER	PRACTICUM TEACHER	SUPERVISOR	DATE	H P I F

Competencies for Teaching—Classroom Instruction

Questions

1. Student Teacher	Last Name	First		Initial	File Number	ASSESSMENT
Lesson Number	Subject or Activity		Number of Pupils	Tape Recorded ☐	Duration	PRACTICUM TEACHER ☐ Direct ☐ Recorder SUPERVISOR ☐ Direct ☐ Recorder

2. / **QUESTIONS**

Q1

Question:

PROCESS	CORRECT	REDIRECT	REPHRASE	PROMPT	PUPIL CLARIFICATION

EVALUATION	ADEQUATE ☐	EASIER ☐	HARDER ☐	MORE SPECIFIC ☐	OPEN-ENDED ☐	CLEARER ☐

Recommendation:

S N   S N

Q2

Question:

PROCESS	CORRECT	REDIRECT	REPHRASE	PROMPT	PUPIL CLARIFICATION

EVALUATION	ADEQUATE ☐	EASIER ☐	HARDER ☐	MORE SPECIFIC ☐	OPEN-ENDED ☐	CLEARER ☐

Recommendation:

S N   S N

Q3

Question:

PROCESS	CORRECT	REDIRECT	REPHRASE	PROMPT	PUPIL CLARIFICATION

EVALUATION	ADEQUATE ☐	EASIER ☐	HARDER ☐	MORE SPECIFIC ☐	OPEN-ENDED ☐	CLEARER ☐

Recommendation:

S N   S N

Q4

Question:

PROCESS	CORRECT	REDIRECT	REPHRASE	PROMPT	PUPIL CLARIFICATION

EVALUATION	ADEQUATE ☐	EASIER ☐	HARDER ☐	MORE SPECIFIC ☐	OPEN-ENDED ☐	CLEARER ☐

Recommendation

S N   S N

3. / **PRESENTATION**

ATTENTION: prerequisite to questioning.	S N
VOICE: tone pleasant, enunciation clear.	S N
PAUSE: precedes calling on pupil.	S N
APPROVAL: acceptable responses reinforced.	S N
PARTICIPATION: all pupils encouraged.	S N
DISTRIBUTION: questions directed to volunteers and nonvolunteers.	S N

S N   S N

4. Signature	STUDENT TEACHER	PRACTICUM TEACHER	SUPERVISOR	DATE	H P I F

Competencies for Teaching—Classroom Instruction

Questions

1. Student Teacher	Last Name		First		Initial	File Number	ASSESSMENT
Lesson Number	Subject or Activity			Number of Pupils	Tape Recorded ☐	Duration	PRACTICUM TEACHER ☐ Direct ☐ Recorder / SUPERVISOR ☐ Direct ☐ Recorder

2. **QUESTIONS**

Q1

Question:

PROCESS	CORRECT	REDIRECT	REPHRASE	PROMPT	PUPIL CLARIFICATION

| EVALUATION | ADEQUATE ☐ | EASIER ☐ | HARDER ☐ | MORE SPECIFIC ☐ | OPEN-ENDED ☐ | CLEARER ☐ |

Recommendation:

S N | S N

Q2

Question:

PROCESS	CORRECT	REDIRECT	REPHRASE	PROMPT	PUPIL CLARIFICATION

| EVALUATION | ADEQUATE ☐ | EASIER ☐ | HARDER ☐ | MORE SPECIFIC ☐ | OPEN-ENDED ☐ | CLEARER ☐ |

Recommendation:

S N | S N

Q3

Question:

PROCESS	CORRECT	REDIRECT	REPHRASE	PROMPT	PUPIL CLARIFICATION

| EVALUATION | ADEQUATE ☐ | EASIER ☐ | HARDER ☐ | MORE SPECIFIC ☐ | OPEN-ENDED ☐ | CLEARER ☐ |

Recommendation:

S N | S N

Q4

Question:

PROCESS	CORRECT	REDIRECT	REPHRASE	PROMPT	PUPIL CLARIFICATION

| EVALUATION | ADEQUATE ☐ | EASIER ☐ | HARDER ☐ | MORE SPECIFIC ☐ | OPEN-ENDED ☐ | CLEARER ☐ |

Recommendation

S N | S N

3. **PRESENTATION**

ATTENTION: prerequisite to questioning.	S N	
VOICE: tone pleasant, enunciation clear.	S N	
PAUSE: precedes calling on pupil.	S N	
APPROVAL: acceptable responses reinforced.	S N	
PARTICIPATION: all pupils encouraged.	S N	
DISTRIBUTION: questions directed to volunteers and nonvolunteers.	S N	S N	S N

4. Signature	STUDENT TEACHER	PRACTICUM TEACHER	SUPERVISOR	DATE	H P I F

Directions for Questions

This lesson is an exercise to develop your skill in questioning. Ask your practicum teacher for a group of from two to six pupils for the purpose of questioning on a specific topic.

1. <u>Identifying Information</u>. Enter the required information. These forms will be assigned consecutive numbers (1 to 6). The *Duration* of the lesson will be entered after the questioning sequence has been completed.

2. <u>Questions</u>. Construct four questions in a developmental sequence related to the specific topic. Follow the instructions, "Developing Questioning Skills," in Chapter Six of *Classroom Instruction*, in writing the questions and carrying out the following procedure.

    a. <u>Question</u>: Write your questions in the four *Question* spaces.

    b. Turn on your tape recorder and begin your questioning procedure. After pupil response, you may wish to redirect, rephrase, prompt, or ask for pupil clarification.

    c. <u>Process</u>: After completing your presentation of the *four questions* of this lesson, replay your tape and analyze the *Process* for the first question. Tally the number of times a particular process was used.

PROCESS	CORRECT	REDIRECT	REPHRASE	PROMPT	PUPIL CLARIFICATION
			/	////	/

    d. <u>Evaluation</u>: Evaluate the question according to pupil responses. Check the box indicating that the question was *Adequate*, or that it should have been *Easier, Harder, More Specific, Open-Ended,* or *Clearer*.

    e. <u>Recommendation</u>: Write your *Recommendation* regarding the future use of this question. If the question was adequate, indicate that you would "repeat" its use. If inadequate, rewrite the question in the space provided.

    f. Repeat the procedures described in (c), (d), and (e) for the other three questions.

3. <u>Presentation</u>. After you have assessed the questions, evaluate your overall *Presentation*. Circle "S" for satisfactory or "N" for needs improvement—for *Attention, Voice, Pause, Approval, Participation,* and *Distribution*.

4. <u>Assessment</u>. Obtain assessment from either your practicum teacher or your supervisor. Follow the procedure described in the *Assessment* instructions for Incidental Intervention.

Show the completed form to your teacher education supervisor for an evaluation, H, P, I, or F. Enter the date and distribute the copies of this form as indicated.

Competencies for Teaching—Classroom Instruction

Questions

1. Student Teacher	Last Name	First	Initial	File Number	ASSESSMENT
Lesson Number	Subject or Activity	Number of Pupils	Tape Recorded ☐	Duration	PRACTICUM TEACHER Direct ☐ Recorder ☐ / SUPERVISOR Direct ☐ Recorder ☐

QUESTIONS

2.

Q 1

Question:

PROCESS	CORRECT	REDIRECT	REPHRASE	PROMPT	PUPIL CLARIFICATION

EVALUATION	ADEQUATE ☐	EASIER ☐	HARDER ☐	MORE SPECIFIC ☐	OPEN-ENDED ☐	CLEARER ☐

Recommendation:

S N | S N

Q 2

Question:

PROCESS	CORRECT	REDIRECT	REPHRASE	PROMPT	PUPIL CLARIFICATION

EVALUATION	ADEQUATE ☐	EASIER ☐	HARDER ☐	MORE SPECIFIC ☐	OPEN-ENDED ☐	CLEARER ☐

Recommendation:

S N | S N

Q 3

Question:

PROCESS	CORRECT	REDIRECT	REPHRASE	PROMPT	PUPIL CLARIFICATION

EVALUATION	ADEQUATE ☐	EASIER ☐	HARDER ☐	MORE SPECIFIC ☐	OPEN-ENDED ☐	CLEARER ☐

Recommendation:

S N | S N

Q 4

Question:

PROCESS	CORRECT	REDIRECT	REPHRASE	PROMPT	PUPIL CLARIFICATION

EVALUATION	ADEQUATE ☐	EASIER ☐	HARDER ☐	MORE SPECIFIC ☐	OPEN-ENDED ☐	CLEARER ☐

Recommendation

S N | S N

3. PRESENTATION

ATTENTION: prerequisite to questioning.	S N
VOICE: tone pleasant, enunciation clear.	S N
PAUSE: precedes calling on pupil.	S N
APPROVAL: acceptable responses reinforced.	S N
PARTICIPATION: all pupils encouraged.	S N
DISTRIBUTION: questions directed to volunteers and nonvolunteers.	S N

S N | S N

4. Signature

STUDENT TEACHER	PRACTICUM TEACHER	SUPERVISOR	DATE	H P I F

Competencies for Teaching—Classroom Instruction

Questions

1. Student Teacher	Last Name		First		Initial	File Number	ASSESSMENT

Lesson Number	Subject or Activity		Number of Pupils	Tape Recorded ☐	Duration	

PRACTICUM TEACHER — Direct ☐ Recorder ☐
SUPERVISOR — Direct ☐ Recorder ☐

2.

Q 1

Question:

PROCESS	CORRECT	REDIRECT	REPHRASE	PROMPT	PUPIL CLARIFICATION

EVALUATION	ADEQUATE ☐	EASIER ☐	HARDER ☐	MORE SPECIFIC ☐	OPEN-ENDED ☐	CLEARER ☐

Recommendation:

S N   S N

Q 2

Question:

PROCESS	CORRECT	REDIRECT	REPHRASE	PROMPT	PUPIL CLARIFICATION

EVALUATION	ADEQUATE ☐	EASIER ☐	HARDER ☐	MORE SPECIFIC ☐	OPEN-ENDED ☐	CLEARER ☐

Recommendation:

S N   S N

Q 3

Question:

PROCESS	CORRECT	REDIRECT	REPHRASE	PROMPT	PUPIL CLARIFICATION

EVALUATION	ADEQUATE ☐	EASIER ☐	HARDER ☐	MORE SPECIFIC ☐	OPEN-ENDED ☐	CLEARER ☐

Recommendation:

S N   S N

Q 4

Question:

PROCESS	CORRECT	REDIRECT	REPHRASE	PROMPT	PUPIL CLARIFICATION

EVALUATION	ADEQUATE ☐	EASIER ☐	HARDER ☐	MORE SPECIFIC ☐	OPEN-ENDED ☐	CLEARER ☐

Recommendation

S N   S N

QUESTIONS

3. PRESENTATION

ATTENTION: prerequisite to questioning.	S N	
VOICE: tone pleasant, enunciation clear.	S N	
PAUSE: precedes calling on pupil.	S N	
APPROVAL: acceptable responses reinforced.	S N	
PARTICIPATION: all pupils encouraged.	S N	
DISTRIBUTION: questions directed to volunteers and nonvolunteers.	S N	S N S N

4. Signature	STUDENT TEACHER	PRACTICUM TEACHER	SUPERVISOR	DATE	H P I F

Competencies for Teaching—Classroom Instruction

Questions

1. Student Teacher	Last Name		First		Initial	File Number
Lesson Number	Subject or Activity			Number of Pupils	Tape Recorded ☐	Duration

ASSESSMENT

PRACTICUM TEACHER ☐ Direct ☐ Recorder SUPERVISOR ☐ Direct ☐ Recorder

2. QUESTIONS

Q1

Question:

PROCESS

CORRECT	REDIRECT	REPHRASE	PROMPT	PUPIL CLARIFICATION

EVALUATION

ADEQUATE ☐	EASIER ☐	HARDER ☐	MORE SPECIFIC ☐	OPEN-ENDED ☐	CLEARER ☐

Recommendation:

S N   S N

Q2

Question:

PROCESS

CORRECT	REDIRECT	REPHRASE	PROMPT	PUPIL CLARIFICATION

EVALUATION

ADEQUATE ☐	EASIER ☐	HARDER ☐	MORE SPECIFIC ☐	OPEN-ENDED ☐	CLEARER ☐

Recommendation:

S N   S N

Q3

Question:

PROCESS

CORRECT	REDIRECT	REPHRASE	PROMPT	PUPIL CLARIFICATION

EVALUATION

ADEQUATE ☐	EASIER ☐	HARDER ☐	MORE SPECIFIC ☐	OPEN-ENDED ☐	CLEARER ☐

Recommendation:

S N   S N

Q4

Question:

PROCESS

CORRECT	REDIRECT	REPHRASE	PROMPT	PUPIL CLARIFICATION

EVALUATION

ADEQUATE ☐	EASIER ☐	HARDER ☐	MORE SPECIFIC ☐	OPEN-ENDED ☐	CLEARER ☐

Recommendation

S N   S N

3. PRESENTATION

ATTENTION: prerequisite to questioning.	S N
VOICE: tone pleasant, enunciation clear.	S N
PAUSE: precedes calling on pupil.	S N
APPROVAL: acceptable responses reinforced.	S N
PARTICIPATION: all pupils encouraged.	S N
DISTRIBUTION: questions directed to volunteers and nonvolunteers.	S N

S N   S N

4. Signature	STUDENT TEACHER	PRACTICUM TEACHER	SUPERVISOR	DATE

H P I F

Directions for Single Task

A single-task lesson is a brief instructional session designed to achieve a single objective. In teaching single-task lessons, it is advisable to repeat the same lesson one or more times using different groups of pupils, making improvements based on your experience. Request an assignment to teach a single-task lesson to a group of up to six pupils.

1. Identifying Information. Enter the required information. Each single-task lesson will be assigned a consecutive *Lesson Number* (1 to 6). Enter the *Duration* of the lesson after its completion.

2. Objectives. Write a specific objective, such as, "Solve two-digit multiplication problems," "From photographs, identify and name three types of plants," "Add the prefix *in* to four root words."

3. Materials. List the instructional materials, such as, "worksheet of multiplication problems," "slides and reference books illustrating types of plants," or "Kenworth Educational Prefix Game."

4. Presentation. Describe the methods of presentation you intend to use, such as, "*Demonstrate* procedure for multiplying two-digit numbers and *provide* worksheet," "*Present* slides and *command* pupils to look up the plants in reference books," or "*Demonstrate* Kenworth Educational Prefix Game."

5. Key Questions. Write two to four questions that you will use during the lesson.

6. Assignment. Describe the pupil activity, such as, "Complete five problems on this worksheet," "Write the names of the plants," or "Write words having the prefix *in*."

7. Evaluation. After taping the presentation of the lesson, and after the pupils have completed the assignment, evaluate the results. Write the names of each *Pupil* and draw a line or bar graph from *Entering* toward *Terminal*, indicating the degree of achievement of the lesson's objective for each pupil.

8. Recommendations. Write suggestions for improving your instruction in future presentations of this lesson, such as, "Ask questions to ensure attention before demonstrating multiplication," "Provide sample of real foliage," or "Provide more praise for correct use of prefixes."

9. Assessment. Obtain assessment from either your practicum teacher or your supervisor. Follow the proce-

dure described in the *Assessment* instructions for Incidental Intervention. Show the completed form to your teacher education supervisor for an evaluation, H, P, I, or F. Date and distribute the forms as indicated.

Competencies for Teaching—Classroom Instruction

Single Task

1. Student Teacher	Last Name		First		Initial	File Number	ASSESSMENT

Lesson Number	Subject or Activity			Number of Pupils	Tape Recorded ☐	Duration	

ASSESSMENT: PRACTICUM TEACHER — Direct ☐ Recorded ☐ | SUPERVISOR — Direct ☐ Recorded ☐

Section	Content	Practicum Teacher	Supervisor
2. OBJECTIVE		S N	S N
3. MATERIALS		S N	S N
4. PRESENTATION		S N	S N
5. KEY QUESTIONS		S N	S N
6. ASSIGNMENT		S N	S N

7. EVALUATION

PUPIL	ENTERING		TERMINAL
1.			
2.			
3.			
4.			
5.			
6.			

PROGRESS NOT SIGNIFICANT	PROGRESS TOWARD OBJECTIVE	PROGRESS WITHIN RANGE OF OBJECTIVE	S N	S N

8. RECOMMENDATIONS

	S N	S N

9. Signature	STUDENT TEACHER	PRACTICUM TEACHER	SUPERVISOR	DATE	H P I F

Competencies for Teaching—Classroom Instruction

Single Task

1. Student Teacher	Last Name	First	Initial	File Number	ASSESSMENT

Lesson Number	Subject or Activity	Number of Pupils	Tape Recorded	Duration	PRACTICUM TEACHER — Direct □ Recorded □	SUPERVISOR — Direct □ Recorded □

2. OBJECTIVE

S N — S N

3. MATERIALS

S N — S N

4. PRESENTATION

S N — S N

5. KEY QUESTIONS

S N — S N

6. ASSIGNMENT

S N — S N

7. EVALUATION

PUPIL	ENTERING		TERMINAL
1.			
2.			
3.			
4.			
5.			
6.			
	PROGRESS NOT SIGNIFICANT	PROGRESS TOWARD OBJECTIVE	PROGRESS WITHIN RANGE OF OBJECTIVE

S N — S N

8. RECOMMENDATIONS

S N — S N

9. Signature	STUDENT TEACHER	PRACTICUM TEACHER	SUPERVISOR	DATE	H P I F

Competencies for Teaching—Classroom Instruction

Single Task

1. Student Teacher	Last Name	First	Initial	File Number	ASSESSMENT

Lesson Number	Subject or Activity	Number of Pupils	Tape Recorded ☐	Duration	PRACTICUM TEACHER Direct ☐ Recorded ☐	SUPERVISOR Direct ☐ Recorded ☐

2. OBJECTIVE

S N   S N

3. MATERIALS

S N   S N

4. PRESENTATION

S N   S N

5. KEY QUESTIONS

S N   S N

6. ASSIGNMENT

S N   S N

7. EVALUATION

PUPIL	ENTERING		TERMINAL
1.			
2.			
3.			
4.			
5.			
6.			
	PROGRESS NOT SIGNIFICANT	PROGRESS TOWARD OBJECTIVE	PROGRESS WITHIN RANGE OF OBJECTIVE

S N   S N

8. RECOMMENDATIONS

S N   S N

9. Signature	STUDENT TEACHER	PRACTICUM TEACHER	SUPERVISOR	DATE	H P I F

Directions for Single Task

A single-task lesson is a brief instructional session designed to achieve a single objective. In teaching single-task lessons, it is advisable to repeat the same lesson one or more times using different groups of pupils, making improvements based on your experience. Request an assignment to teach a single-task lesson to a group of up to six pupils.

1. <u>Identifying Information</u>. Enter the required information. Each single-task lesson will be assigned a consecutive *Lesson Number* (1 to 6). Enter the *Duration* of the lesson after its completion.

2. <u>Objectives</u>. Write a specific objective, such as, "Solve two-digit multiplication problems," "From photographs, identify and name three types of plants," "Add the prefix *in* to four root words."

3. <u>Materials</u>. List the instructional materials, such as, "worksheet of multiplication problems," "slides and reference books illustrating types of plants," or "Kenworth Educational Prefix Game."

4. <u>Presentation</u>. Describe the methods of presentation you intend to use, such as, "*Demonstrate* procedure for multiplying two-digit numbers and *provide* worksheet," "*Present* slides and *command* pupils to look up the plants in reference books," or "*Demonstrate* Kenworth Educational Prefix Game."

5. <u>Key Questions</u>. Write two to four questions that you will use during the lesson.

6. <u>Assignment</u>. Describe the pupil activity, such as, "Complete five problems on this worksheet," "Write the names of the plants," or "Write words having the prefix *in*."

7. <u>Evaluation</u>. After taping the presentation of the lesson, and after the pupils have completed the assignment, evaluate the results. Write the names of each *Pupil* and draw a line or bar graph from *Entering* toward *Terminal*, indicating the degree of achievement of the lesson's objective for each pupil.

8. <u>Recommendations</u>. Write suggestions for improving your instruction in future presentations of this lesson, such as, "Ask questions to ensure attention before demonstrating multiplication," "Provide sample of real foliage," or "Provide more praise for correct use of prefixes."

9. <u>Assessment</u>. Obtain assessment from either your practicum teacher or your supervisor. Follow the proce-

dure described in the *Assessment* instructions for Incidental Intervention. Show the completed form to your teacher education supervisor for an evaluation, H, P, I, or F. Date and distribute the forms as indicated.

Competencies for Teaching—Classroom Instruction

Single Task

1. Student Teacher	Last Name		First		Initial	File Number	ASSESSMENT

Lesson Number	Subject or Activity	Number of Pupils	Tape Recorded ☐	Duration	PRACTICUM TEACHER / SUPERVISOR

Section		Assessment
2. OBJECTIVE		S N S N
3. MATERIALS		S N S N
4. PRESENTATION		S N S N
5. KEY QUESTIONS		S N S N
6. ASSIGNMENT		S N S N

7.

EVALUATION	PUPIL	ENTERING	TERMINAL
	1.		
	2.		
	3.		
	4.		
	5.		
	6.		

PROGRESS NOT SIGNIFICANT	PROGRESS TOWARD OBJECTIVE	PROGRESS WITHIN RANGE OF OBJECTIVE	S N S N

8. RECOMMENDATIONS		S N S N

9. Signature	STUDENT TEACHER	PRACTICUM TEACHER	SUPERVISOR	DATE	H P I F

Distribution: Forward this form to the *Classroom Teacher*

Competencies for Teaching—Classroom Instruction

Single Task

1. Student Teacher	Last Name	First	Initial	File Number	ASSESSMENT

Lesson Number	Subject or Activity	Number of Pupils	Tape Recorded	Duration	PRACTICUM TEACHER / SUPERVISOR

2. OBJECTIVE — S N   S N

3. MATERIALS — S N   S N

4. PRESENTATION — S N   S N

5. KEY QUESTIONS — S N   S N

6. ASSIGNMENT — S N   S N

7. EVALUATION

PUPIL	ENTERING	TERMINAL
1.		
2.		
3.		
4.		
5.		
6.		
	PROGRESS NOT SIGNIFICANT	PROGRESS TOWARD OBJECTIVE	PROGRESS WITHIN RANGE OF OBJECTIVE

S N   S N

8. RECOMMENDATIONS — S N   S N

9. Signature	STUDENT TEACHER	PRACTICUM TEACHER	SUPERVISOR	DATE	H P I F

Competencies for Teaching—Classroom Instruction

Single Task

1. Student Teacher	Last Name	First	Initial	File Number	ASSESSMENT	

Lesson Number	Subject or Activity		Number of Pupils	Tape Recorded ☐	Duration	PRACTICUM TEACHER — Direct ☐ Recorded ☐	SUPERVISOR — Direct ☐ Recorded ☐

2. OBJECTIVE						S N	S N

3. MATERIALS						S N	S N

4. PRESENTATION						S N	S N

5. KEY QUESTIONS						S N	S N

6. ASSIGNMENT						S N	S N

7. EVALUATION		PUPIL	ENTERING	TERMINAL		
	1.					
	2.					
	3.					
	4.					
	5.					
	6.					
			PROGRESS NOT SIGNIFICANT	PROGRESS TOWARD OBJECTIVE	PROGRESS WITHIN RANGE OF OBJECTIVE	S N S N

8. RECOMMENDATIONS						S N	S N

9. Signature	STUDENT TEACHER	PRACTICUM TEACHER	SUPERVISOR	DATE	H P I F

Directions for Single Task

A single-task lesson is a brief instructional session designed to achieve a single objective. In teaching single-task lessons, it is advisable to repeat the same lesson one or more times using different groups of pupils, making improvements based on your experience. Request an assignment to teach a single-task lesson to a group of up to six pupils.

1. Identifying Information. Enter the required information. Each single-task lesson will be assigned a consecutive *Lesson Number* (1 to 6). Enter the *Duration* of the lesson after its completion.

2. Objectives. Write a specific objective, such as, "Solve two-digit multiplication problems," "From photographs, identify and name three types of plants," "Add the prefix *in* to four root words."

3. Materials. List the instructional materials, such as, "worksheet of multiplication problems," "slides and reference books illustrating types of plants," or "Kenworth Educational Prefix Game."

4. Presentation. Describe the methods of presentation you intend to use, such as, "*Demonstrate* procedure for multiplying two-digit numbers and *provide* worksheet," "*Present* slides and *command* pupils to look up the plants in reference books," or "*Demonstrate* Kenworth Educational Prefix Game."

5. Key Questions. Write two to four questions that you will use during the lesson.

6. Assignment. Describe the pupil activity, such as, "Complete five problems on this worksheet," "Write the names of the plants," or "Write words having the prefix *in*."

7. Evaluation. After taping the presentation of the lesson, and after the pupils have completed the assignment, evaluate the results. Write the names of each *Pupil* and draw a line or bar graph from *Entering* toward *Terminal*, indicating the degree of achievement of the lesson's objective for each pupil.

8. Recommendations. Write suggestions for improving your instruction in future presentations of this lesson, such as, "Ask questions to ensure attention before demonstrating multiplication," "Provide sample of real foliage," or "Provide more praise for correct use of prefixes."

9. Assessment. Obtain assessment from either your practicum teacher or your supervisor. Follow the proce-

dure described in the *Assessment* instructions for Incidental Intervention. Show the completed form to your teacher education supervisor for an evaluation, H, P, I, or F. Date and distribute the forms as indicated.

Competencies for Teaching—Classroom Instruction

Single Task

1. Student Teacher	Last Name	First	Initial	File Number	ASSESSMENT

Lesson Number	Subject or Activity	Number of Pupils	Tape Recorded ☐	Duration	PRACTICUM TEACHER — Direct ☐ Recorded ☐	SUPERVISOR — Direct ☐ Recorded ☐

2. OBJECTIVE		S N	S N

3. MATERIALS		S N	S N

4. PRESENTATION		S N	S N

5. KEY QUESTIONS		S N	S N

6. ASSIGNMENT		S N	S N

7. EVALUATION	PUPIL	ENTERING	TERMINAL
	1.		
	2.		
	3.		
	4.		
	5.		
	6.		

PROGRESS NOT SIGNIFICANT	PROGRESS TOWARD OBJECTIVE	PROGRESS WITHIN RANGE OF OBJECTIVE	S N	S N

8. RECOMMENDATIONS		S N	S N

9. Signature	STUDENT TEACHER	PRACTICUM TEACHER	SUPERVISOR	DATE	H P I F

Competencies for Teaching—Classroom Instruction

Single Task

1. Student Teacher	Last Name		First		Initial	File Number	ASSESSMENT	
Lesson Number	Subject or Activity		Number of Pupils	Tape Recorded ☐		Duration	PRACTICUM TEACHER — Direct ☐ Recorded ☐	SUPERVISOR — Direct ☐ Recorded ☐

2. OBJECTIVE

S N | S N

3. MATERIALS

S N | S N

4. PRESENTATION

S N | S N

5. KEY QUESTIONS

S N | S N

6. ASSIGNMENT

S N | S N

7. EVALUATION

PUPIL	ENTERING		TERMINAL
1.			
2.			
3.			
4.			
5.			
6.			
	PROGRESS NOT SIGNIFICANT	PROGRESS TOWARD OBJECTIVE	PROGRESS WITHIN RANGE OF OBJECTIVE

S N | S N

8. RECOMMENDATIONS

S N | S N

9. Signature	STUDENT TEACHER	PRACTICUM TEACHER	SUPERVISOR	DATE	H P I F

Competencies for Teaching—Classroom Instruction

Single Task

1. Student Teacher	Last Name	First	Initial	File Number	ASSESSMENT

Lesson Number	Subject or Activity	Number of Pupils	Tape Recorded ☐	Duration	PRACTICUM TEACHER Direct ☐ Recorded ☐	SUPERVISOR Direct ☐ Recorded ☐

2. OBJECTIVE

S N   S N

3. MATERIALS

S N   S N

4. PRESENTATION

S N   S N

5. KEY QUESTIONS

S N   S N

6. ASSIGNMENT

S N   S N

7. EVALUATION

PUPIL	ENTERING	TERMINAL
1.		
2.		
3.		
4.		
5.		
6.		

PROGRESS NOT SIGNIFICANT	PROGRESS TOWARD OBJECTIVE	PROGRESS WITHIN RANGE OF OBJECTIVE

S N   S N

8. RECOMMENDATIONS

S N   S N

9. Signature	STUDENT TEACHER	PRACTICUM TEACHER	SUPERVISOR	DATE	H P I F

Directions for Single Task

A single-task lesson is a brief instructional session designed to achieve a single objective. In teaching single-task lessons, it is advisable to repeat the same lesson one or more times using different groups of pupils, making improvements based on your experience. Request an assignment to teach a single-task lesson to a group of up to six pupils.

1. <u>Identifying Information</u>. Enter the required information. Each single-task lesson will be assigned a consecutive *Lesson Number* (1 to 6). Enter the *Duration* of the lesson after its completion.

2. <u>Objectives</u>. Write a specific objective, such as, "Solve two-digit multiplication problems," "From photographs, identify and name three types of plants," "Add the prefix *in* to four root words."

3. <u>Materials</u>. List the instructional materials, such as, "worksheet of multiplication problems," "slides and reference books illustrating types of plants," or "Kenworth Educational Prefix Game."

4. <u>Presentation</u>. Describe the methods of presentation you intend to use, such as, "*Demonstrate* procedure for multiplying two-digit numbers and *provide* worksheet," "*Present* slides and *command* pupils to look up the plants in reference books," or "*Demonstrate* Kenworth Educational Prefix Game."

5. <u>Key Questions</u>. Write two to four questions that you will use during the lesson.

6. <u>Assignment</u>. Describe the pupil activity, such as, "Complete five problems on this worksheet," "Write the names of the plants," or "Write words having the prefix *in*."

7. <u>Evaluation</u>. After taping the presentation of the lesson, and after the pupils have completed the assignment, evaluate the results. Write the names of each *Pupil* and draw a line or bar graph from *Entering* toward *Terminal*, indicating the degree of achievement of the lesson's objective for each pupil.

8. <u>Recommendations</u>. Write suggestions for improving your instruction in future presentations of this lesson, such as, "Ask questions to ensure attention before demonstrating multiplication," "Provide sample of real foliage," or "Provide more praise for correct use of prefixes."

9. <u>Assessment</u>. Obtain assessment from either your practicum teacher or your supervisor. Follow the proce-

dure described in the *Assessment* instructions for Incidental Intervention. Show the completed form to your teacher education supervisor for an evaluation, H, P, I, or F. Date and distribute the forms as indicated.

Competencies for Teaching—Classroom Instruction

Single Task

1. Student Teacher	Last Name		First		Initial	File Number	ASSESSMENT	
Lesson Number	Subject or Activity			Number of Pupils	Tape Recorded ☐	Duration	PRACTICUM TEACHER — Direct ☐ Recorded ☐	SUPERVISOR — Direct ☐ Recorded ☐

2. OBJECTIVE		S N	S N

3. MATERIALS		S N	S N

4. PRESENTATION		S N	S N

5. KEY QUESTIONS		S N	S N

6. ASSIGNMENT		S N	S N

7. EVALUATION

PUPIL	ENTERING	TERMINAL
1.		
2.		
3.		
4.		
5.		
6.		

PROGRESS NOT SIGNIFICANT	PROGRESS TOWARD OBJECTIVE	PROGRESS WITHIN RANGE OF OBJECTIVE	S N	S N

8. RECOMMENDATIONS		S N	S N

9. Signature	STUDENT TEACHER	PRACTICUM TEACHER	SUPERVISOR	DATE	H P I F

Competencies for Teaching—Classroom Instruction

Single Task

1. Student Teacher	Last Name	First	Initial	File Number	ASSESSMENT

Lesson Number	Subject or Activity	Number of Pupils	Tape Recorded ☐	Duration	PRACTICUM TEACHER Direct ☐ Recorded ☐	SUPERVISOR Direct ☐ Recorded ☐

2. OBJECTIVE

S N | S N

3. MATERIALS

S N | S N

4. PRESENTATION

S N | S N

5. KEY QUESTIONS

S N | S N

6. ASSIGNMENT

S N | S N

7. EVALUATION

PUPIL	ENTERING		TERMINAL
1.			
2.			
3.			
4.			
5.			
6.			
	PROGRESS NOT SIGNIFICANT	PROGRESS TOWARD OBJECTIVE	PROGRESS WITHIN RANGE OF OBJECTIVE

S N | S N

8. RECOMMENDATIONS

S N | S N

9. Signature	STUDENT TEACHER	PRACTICUM TEACHER	SUPERVISOR	DATE	H P I F

Competencies for Teaching—Classroom Instruction

Single Task

1. Student Teacher	Last Name		First		Initial	File Number	ASSESSMENT
Lesson Number	Subject or Activity			Number of Pupils	Tape Recorded ☐	Duration	PRACTICUM TEACHER ☐ Direct ☐ Recorded / SUPERVISOR ☐ Direct ☐ Recorded

2. OBJECTIVE		S N	S N

3. MATERIALS		S N	S N

4. PRESENTATION		S N	S N

5. KEY QUESTIONS		S N	S N

6. ASSIGNMENT		S N	S N

7. EVALUATION

PUPIL	ENTERING	TERMINAL
1.		
2.		
3.		
4.		
5.		
6.		
	PROGRESS NOT SIGNIFICANT	PROGRESS TOWARD OBJECTIVE	PROGRESS WITHIN RANGE OF OBJECTIVE

S N   S N

8. RECOMMENDATIONS		S N	S N

9. Signature	STUDENT TEACHER	PRACTICUM TEACHER	SUPERVISOR	DATE	H P I F

Directions for Single Task

A single-task lesson is a brief instructional session designed to achieve a single objective. In teaching single-task lessons, it is advisable to repeat the same lesson one or more times using different groups of pupils, making improvements based on your experience. Request an assignment to teach a single-task lesson to a group of up to six pupils.

1. <u>Identifying Information</u>. Enter the required information. Each single-task lesson will be assigned a consecutive *Lesson Number* (1 to 6). Enter the *Duration* of the lesson after its completion.

2. <u>Objectives</u>. Write a specific objective, such as, "Solve two-digit multiplication problems," "From photographs, identify and name three types of plants," "Add the prefix *in* to four root words."

3. <u>Materials</u>. List the instructional materials, such as, "worksheet of multiplication problems," "slides and reference books illustrating types of plants," or "Kenworth Educational Prefix Game."

4. <u>Presentation</u>. Describe the methods of presentation you intend to use, such as, "*Demonstrate* procedure for multiplying two-digit numbers and *provide* worksheet," "*Present* slides and *command* pupils to look up the plants in reference books," or "*Demonstrate* Kenworth Educational Prefix Game."

5. <u>Key Questions</u>. Write two to four questions that you will use during the lesson.

6. <u>Assignment</u>. Describe the pupil activity, such as, "Complete five problems on this worksheet," "Write the names of the plants," or "Write words having the prefix *in*."

7. <u>Evaluation</u>. After taping the presentation of the lesson, and after the pupils have completed the assignment, evaluate the results. Write the names of each *Pupil* and draw a line or bar graph from *Entering* toward *Terminal*, indicating the degree of achievement of the lesson's objective for each pupil.

8. <u>Recommendations</u>. Write suggestions for improving your instruction in future presentations of this lesson, such as, "Ask questions to ensure attention before demonstrating multiplication," "Provide sample of real foliage," or "Provide more praise for correct use of prefixes."

9. <u>Assessment</u>. Obtain assessment from either your practicum teacher or your supervisor. Follow the proce-

dure described in the *Assessment* instructions for Incidental Intervention. Show the completed form to your teacher education supervisor for an evaluation, H, P, I, or F. Date and distribute the forms as indicated.

Competencies for Teaching—Classroom Instruction

Single Task

1. Student Teacher	Last Name	First	Initial	File Number	ASSESSMENT
Lesson Number	Subject or Activity	Number of Pupils	Tape Recorded ☐	Duration	PRACTICUM TEACHER Direct ☐ Recorded ☐	SUPERVISOR Direct ☐ Recorded ☐

2. OBJECTIVE		S N	S N

3. MATERIALS		S N	S N

4. PRESENTATION		S N	S N

5. KEY QUESTIONS		S N	S N

6. ASSIGNMENT		S N	S N

7. EVALUATION	PUPIL	ENTERING	TERMINAL
	1.		
	2.		
	3.		
	4.		
	5.		
	6.		
		PROGRESS NOT SIGNIFICANT	PROGRESS TOWARD OBJECTIVE	PROGRESS WITHIN RANGE OF OBJECTIVE	S N	S N

8. RECOMMENDATIONS		S N	S N

9. Signature	STUDENT TEACHER	PRACTICUM TEACHER	SUPERVISOR	DATE	H P I F

Competencies for Teaching—Classroom Instruction

Single Task

1. Student Teacher	Last Name		First		Initial	File Number	ASSESSMENT
Lesson Number	Subject or Activity		Number of Pupils	Tape Recorded ☐	Duration		

		PRACTICUM TEACHER Direct ☐ Recorded ☐	SUPERVISOR Direct ☐ Recorded ☐

2. OBJECTIVE		S N	S N

3. MATERIALS		S N	S N

4. PRESENTATION		S N	S N

5. KEY QUESTIONS		S N	S N

6. ASSIGNMENT		S N	S N

7. EVALUATION

PUPIL	ENTERING	TERMINAL
1.		
2.		
3.		
4.		
5.		
6.		

PROGRESS NOT SIGNIFICANT	PROGRESS TOWARD OBJECTIVE	PROGRESS WITHIN RANGE OF OBJECTIVE	S N	S N

8. RECOMMENDATIONS		S N	S N

9. Signature	STUDENT TEACHER	PRACTICUM TEACHER	SUPERVISOR	DATE	H P I F

Competencies for Teaching—Classroom Instruction

Single Task

1. Student Teacher	Last Name		First		Initial	File Number	ASSESSMENT	

Lesson Number	Subject or Activity		Number of Pupils	Tape Recorded ☐	Duration		PRACTICUM TEACHER	SUPERVISOR
							Direct ☐ Recorded ☐	Direct ☐ Recorded ☐

2. OBJECTIVE				
				S N	S N

3. MATERIALS				
				S N	S N

4. PRESENTATION				
				S N	S N

5. KEY QUESTIONS				
				S N	S N

6. ASSIGNMENT				
				S N	S N

7. EVALUATION

PUPIL	ENTERING	TERMINAL
1.		
2.		
3.		
4.		
5.		
6.		

PROGRESS NOT SIGNIFICANT	PROGRESS TOWARD OBJECTIVE	PROGRESS WITHIN RANGE OF OBJECTIVE	S N	S N

8. RECOMMENDATIONS				
				S N	S N

9. Signature	STUDENT TEACHER	PRACTICUM TEACHER	SUPERVISOR	DATE	H P I F

Directions for Single Task

A single-task lesson is a brief instructional session designed to achieve a single objective. In teaching single-task lessons, it is advisable to repeat the same lesson one or more times using different groups of pupils, making improvements based on your experience. Request an assignment to teach a single-task lesson to a group of up to six pupils.

1. <u>Identifying Information</u>. Enter the required information. Each single-task lesson will be assigned a consecutive *Lesson Number* (1 to 6). Enter the *Duration* of the lesson after its completion.

2. <u>Objectives</u>. Write a specific objective, such as, "Solve two-digit multiplication problems," "From photographs, identify and name three types of plants," "Add the prefix *in* to four root words."

3. <u>Materials</u>. List the instructional materials, such as, "worksheet of multiplication problems," "slides and reference books illustrating types of plants," or "Kenworth Educational Prefix Game."

4. <u>Presentation</u>. Describe the methods of presentation you intend to use, such as, "*Demonstrate* procedure for multiplying two-digit numbers and *provide* worksheet," "*Present* slides and *command* pupils to look up the plants in reference books," or "*Demonstrate* Kenworth Educational Prefix Game."

5. <u>Key Questions</u>. Write two to four questions that you will use during the lesson.

6. <u>Assignment</u>. Describe the pupil activity, such as, "Complete five problems on this worksheet," "Write the names of the plants," or "Write words having the prefix *in*."

7. <u>Evaluation</u>. After taping the presentation of the lesson, and after the pupils have completed the assignment, evaluate the results. Write the names of each *Pupil* and draw a line or bar graph from *Entering* toward *Terminal*, indicating the degree of achievement of the lesson's objective for each pupil.

8. <u>Recommendations</u>. Write suggestions for improving your instruction in future presentations of this lesson, such as, "Ask questions to ensure attention before demonstrating multiplication," "Provide sample of real foliage," or "Provide more praise for correct use of prefixes."

9. <u>Assessment</u>. Obtain assessment from either your practicum teacher or your supervisor. Follow the proce-

dure described in the *Assessment* instructions for Incidental Intervention. Show the completed form to your
teacher education supervisor for an evaluation, H, P, I,
or F. Date and distribute the forms as indicated.

Distribution: Forward this form to your *Teacher Education Supervisor*

Competencies for Teaching—Classroom Instruction

Single Task

1. Student Teacher	Last Name	First	Initial	File Number	ASSESSMENT

| Lesson Number | . | Subject or Activity | Number of Pupils | Tape Recorded ☐ | Duration | |

2. OBJECTIVE

S N | S N

3. MATERIALS

S N | S N

4. PRESENTATION

S N | S N

5. KEY QUESTIONS

S N | S N

6. ASSIGNMENT

S N | S N

7. EVALUATION

PUPIL	ENTERING	TERMINAL
1.		
2.		
3.		
4.		
5.		
6.		

PROGRESS NOT SIGNIFICANT | PROGRESS TOWARD OBJECTIVE | PROGRESS WITHIN RANGE OF OBJECTIVE

S N | S N

8. RECOMMENDATIONS

S N | S N

9. Signature | STUDENT TEACHER | PRACTICUM TEACHER | SUPERVISOR | DATE

H P I F

PRACTICUM TEACHER Direct ☐ Recorded ☐   SUPERVISOR Direct ☐ Recorded ☐

Competencies for Teaching—Classroom Instruction

Single Task

1. Student Teacher	Last Name	First	Initial	File Number		ASSESSMENT
Lesson Number	Subject or Activity	Number of Pupils	Tape Recorded ☐	Duration		

ASSESSMENT

PRACTICUM TEACHER — Direct ☐ Recorded ☐
SUPERVISOR — Direct ☐ Recorded ☐

Section		Practicum Teacher	Supervisor
2. OBJECTIVE		S N	S N
3. MATERIALS		S N	S N
4. PRESENTATION		S N	S N
5. KEY QUESTIONS		S N	S N
6. ASSIGNMENT		S N	S N

7. EVALUATION

PUPIL	ENTERING		TERMINAL
1.			
2.			
3.			
4.			
5.			
6.			
	PROGRESS NOT SIGNIFICANT	PROGRESS TOWARD OBJECTIVE	PROGRESS WITHIN RANGE OF OBJECTIVE

S N   S N

8. RECOMMENDATIONS

S N   S N

9. Signature	STUDENT TEACHER	PRACTICUM TEACHER	SUPERVISOR	DATE	H P I F

Competencies for Teaching—Classroom Instruction

Single Task

1. Student Teacher	Last Name		First		Initial	File Number	ASSESSMENT
Lesson Number	Subject or Activity		Number of Pupils	Tape Recorded ☐		Duration	PRACTICUM TEACHER ☐☐ Direct Recorded / SUPERVISOR ☐☐ Direct Recorded

2. OBJECTIVE

S N   S N

3. MATERIALS

S N   S N

4. PRESENTATION

S N   S N

5. KEY QUESTIONS

S N   S N

6. ASSIGNMENT

S N   S N

7. EVALUATION

PUPIL	ENTERING		TERMINAL
1.			
2.			
3.			
4.			
5.			
6.			
	PROGRESS NOT SIGNIFICANT	PROGRESS TOWARD OBJECTIVE	PROGRESS WITHIN RANGE OF OBJECTIVE

S N   S N

8. RECOMMENDATIONS

S N   S N

9. Signature	STUDENT TEACHER	PRACTICUM TEACHER	SUPERVISOR	DATE	H P I F

Competencies for Teaching—Classroom Instruction

Directions for Lesson Plan

This lesson plan outline provides guidance in preparing, presenting, and evaluating phases of a lesson. Request from your practicum teacher an assignment of lessons to be taught. A lesson may require one or several periods for its complete presentation.

1. <u>Identifying Information</u>. Enter the required information. Each lesson plan will be assigned a consecutive number (1 to 6). The duration will be entered after completion, for example, "45 minutes," "3, 30-minute periods," "2 periods, total 82 minutes."

2. <u>Objectives</u>. Write the lesson's terminal objective. For example, "Know Roman numerals I to XII." Follow "Lesson Planning" in Chapter Nine of *Classroom Instruction* to complete the assignment. Write the enroute objectives. For example, "Identify uses of Roman numerals," "Recall the letters in Roman numerals I to XII," and "Write Arabic and Roman numerals from 1 to 12 and I to XII."

3. <u>Introduction</u>. Describe briefly how you will stimulate interest in the topic. For example, "Show pictures of clocks, monuments, and other examples of Roman numerals," "Ask questions regarding pupils' experiences with Roman numerals."

4. <u>Materials</u>. List special instructional materials, such as "clock face, pictures of monuments, and Grade III sign."

5. <u>Presentation</u>. Describe the methods of presentation you intend to use, such as, "*Explain* equivalence of Arabic and Roman numerals," "*Demonstrate* writing Roman numerals."

6. <u>Key Questions</u>. Write several key questions. For example, "Where have you seen Roman numerals?" and "What time does this clock show?"

7. <u>Assignment</u>. Describe the activity assigned to pupils. For example, "Complete exercises on mimeographed sheet." *Note*: If assignment is a test or worksheet, include a sample when submitting your lesson plan to your supervisor.

8. <u>Evaluation</u>. After taping the presentation of the lesson, and after the pupils have completed the assignment, evaluate pupil achievement in relation to the lesson's objectives. If the assignment was a test or a task that yielded a score, report the range and mean of the scores. If the assignment was an activity that was evaluated subjectively, estimate how well the objective was

achieved, such as, "Some progress toward objective, but objective not achieved," or "Progress within range of objective."

9. <u>Recommendations</u>. Write your recommendations for improving your instructions for presenting this lesson in the future.

10. <u>Assessment</u>. Obtain assessment from either your practicum teacher or supervisor. Follow the procedure described in the *Assessment* instructions for Incidental Intervention. Show the completed form to your teacher education supervisor for an evaluation, H, P, I, or F. Date and distribute the forms as indicated.

Competencies for Teaching—Classroom Instruction

Lesson Plan

1. Student Teacher	Last Name	First	Initial	File Number	ASSESSMENT
Lesson Number	Subject or Activity	Number of Pupils	Tape Recorded ☐	Duration	PRACTICUM TEACHER ☐ Direct ☐ Recorded SUPERVISOR ☐ Direct ☐ Recorded

2. OBJECTIVES	LESSON			
	ENROUTE			S N	S N

3. INTRODUCTION		

4. MATERIALS		S N	S N

5. PRESENTATION		S N	S N

6. KEY QUESTIONS		S N	S N

7. ASSIGNMENT		S N	S N

8. EVALUATION		S N	S N

9. RECOMMENDATIONS		S N	S N

10. Signature	STUDENT TEACHER	PRACTICUM TEACHER	SUPERVISOR	DATE	H P I F

Distribution: Forward this form to the *Classroom Teacher*

Competencies for Teaching—Classroom Instruction

Lesson Plan

1. Student Teacher	Last Name	First	Initial	File Number	ASSESSMENT

| Lesson Number | Subject or Activity | Number of Pupils | Tape Recorded ☐ | Duration | |

2. OBJECTIVES — LESSON / ENROUTE

PRACTICUM TEACHER ☐ Direct ☐ Recorded — SUPERVISOR ☐ Direct ☐ Recorded

S N | S N

3. INTRODUCTION

4. MATERIALS — S N | S N

5. PRESENTATION — S N | S N

6. KEY QUESTIONS — S N | S N

7. ASSIGNMENT — S N | S N

8. EVALUATION — S N | S N

9. RECOMMENDATIONS — S N | S N

10. Signature	STUDENT TEACHER	PRACTICUM TEACHER	SUPERVISOR	DATE	H P I F

Competencies for Teaching—Classroom Instruction

Lesson Plan

1. Student Teacher	Last Name		First		Initial	File Number	ASSESSMENT

Lesson Number	Subject or Activity	Number of Pupils	Tape Recorded	Duration	PRACTICUM TEACHER □ Direct □ Recorded	SUPERVISOR □ Direct □ Recorded

2. OBJECTIVES — LESSON / ENROUTE

S N | S N

3. INTRODUCTION

4. MATERIALS

S N | S N

5. PRESENTATION

S N | S N

6. KEY QUESTIONS

S N | S N

7. ASSIGNMENT

S N | S N

8. EVALUATION

S N | S N

9. RECOMMENDATIONS

S N | S N

10. Signature	STUDENT TEACHER	PRACTICUM TEACHER	SUPERVISOR	DATE	H P I F

Directions for Lesson Plan

This lesson plan outline provides guidance in preparing, presenting, and evaluating phases of a lesson. Request from your practicum teacher an assignment of lessons to be taught. A lesson may require one or several periods for its complete presentation.

1. <u>Identifying Information</u>. Enter the required information. Each lesson plan will be assigned a consecutive number (1 to 6). The duration will be entered after completion, for example, "45 minutes," "3, 30-minute periods," "2 periods, total 82 minutes."

2. <u>Objectives</u>. Write the lesson's terminal objective. For example, "Know Roman numerals I to XII." Follow "Lesson Planning" in Chapter Nine of *Classroom Instruction* to complete the assignment. Write the enroute objectives. For example, "Identify uses of Roman numerals," "Recall the letters in Roman numerals I to XII," and "Write Arabic and Roman numerals from 1 to 12 and I to XII."

3. <u>Introduction</u>. Describe briefly how you will stimulate interest in the topic. For example, "Show pictures of clocks, monuments, and other examples of Roman numerals," "Ask questions regarding pupils' experiences with Roman numerals."

4. <u>Materials</u>. List special instructional materials, such as "clock face, pictures of monuments, and Grade III sign."

5. <u>Presentation</u>. Describe the methods of presentation you intend to use, such as, "*Explain* equivalence of Arabic and Roman numerals," "*Demonstrate* writing Roman numerals."

6. <u>Key Questions</u>. Write several key questions. For example, "Where have you seen Roman numerals?" and "What time does this clock show?"

7. <u>Assignment</u>. Describe the activity assigned to pupils. For example, "Complete exercises on mimeographed sheet." *Note*: If assignment is a test or worksheet, include a sample when submitting your lesson plan to your supervisor.

8. <u>Evaluation</u>. After taping the presentation of the lesson, and after the pupils have completed the assignment, evaluate pupil achievement in relation to the lesson's objectives. If the assignment was a test or a task that yielded a score, report the range and mean of the scores. If the assignment was an activity that was evaluated subjectively, estimate how well the objective was

achieved, such as, "Some progress toward objective, but objective not achieved," or "Progress within range of objective."

9. _Recommendations_. Write your recommendations for improving your instructions for presenting this lesson in the future.

10. _Assessment_. Obtain assessment from either your practicum teacher or supervisor. Follow the procedure described in the _Assessment_ instructions for Incidental Intervention. Show the completed form to your teacher education supervisor for an evaluation, H, P, I, or F. Date and distribute the forms as indicated.

Competencies for Teaching—Classroom Instruction

Lesson Plan

1. Student Teacher	Last Name	First	Initial	File Number	ASSESSMENT
Lesson Number	Subject or Activity	Number of Pupils	Tape Recorded ☐	Duration	PRACTICUM TEACHER ☐☐ Direct ☐☐ Recorded / SUPERVISOR ☐☐ Direct ☐☐ Recorded

2. OBJECTIVES		
	LESSON	
	ENROUTE	
		S N	S N

3. INTRODUCTION	

4. MATERIALS	
	S N	S N

5. PRESENTATION	
	S N	S N

6. KEY QUESTIONS	
	S N	S N

7. ASSIGNMENT	
	S N	S N

8. EVALUATION	
	S N	S N

9. RECOMMENDATIONS	
	S N	S N

10. Signature	STUDENT TEACHER	PRACTICUM TEACHER	SUPERVISOR	DATE	H P I F

Distribution: Forward this form to the *Classroom Teacher*

Competencies for Teaching—Classroom Instruction

Lesson Plan

1. Student Teacher	Last Name	First	Initial	File Number	ASSESSMENT

| Lesson Number | Subject or Activity | Number of Pupils | Tape Recorded ☐ | Duration | PRACTICUM TEACHER ☐ Direct ☐ Recorded | SUPERVISOR ☐ Direct ☐ Recorded |

2. OBJECTIVES

LESSON

ENROUTE

S N | S N

3. INTRODUCTION

4. MATERIALS

S N | S N

5. PRESENTATION

S N | S N

6. KEY QUESTIONS

S N | S N

7. ASSIGNMENT

S N | S N

8. EVALUATION

S N | S N

9. RECOMMENDATIONS

S N | S N

| 10. Signature | STUDENT TEACHER | PRACTICUM TEACHER | SUPERVISOR | DATE | H P I F |

Distribution: Retain this Copy

Competencies for Teaching—Classroom Instruction

Lesson Plan

1. Student Teacher	Last Name	First	Initial	File Number	ASSESSMENT
Lesson Number	Subject or Activity	Number of Pupils	Tape Recorded ☐	Duration	PRACTICUM TEACHER ☐ Direct ☐ Recorded / SUPERVISOR ☐ Direct ☐ Recorded

2. OBJECTIVES
- LESSON
- ENROUTE

S N | S N

3. INTRODUCTION

4. MATERIALS

S N | S N

5. PRESENTATION

S N | S N

6. KEY QUESTIONS

S N | S N

7. ASSIGNMENT

S N | S N

8. EVALUATION

S N | S N

9. RECOMMENDATIONS

S N | S N

| 10. Signature | STUDENT TEACHER | PRACTICUM TEACHER | SUPERVISOR | DATE | H P I F |

Directions for Lesson Plan

This lesson plan outline provides guidance in preparing, presenting, and evaluating phases of a lesson. Request from your practicum teacher an assignment of lessons to be taught. A lesson may require one or several periods for its complete presentation.

1. <u>Identifying Information</u>. Enter the required information. Each lesson plan will be assigned a consecutive number (1 to 6). The duration will be entered after completion, for example, "45 minutes," "3, 30-minute periods," "2 periods, total 82 minutes."

2. <u>Objectives</u>. Write the lesson's terminal objective. For example, "Know Roman numerals I to XII." Follow "Lesson Planning" in Chapter Nine of *Classroom Instruction* to complete the assignment. Write the enroute objectives. For example, "Identify uses of Roman numerals," "Recall the letters in Roman numerals I to XII," and "Write Arabic and Roman numerals from 1 to 12 and I to XII."

3. <u>Introduction</u>. Describe briefly how you will stimulate interest in the topic. For example, "Show pictures of clocks, monuments, and other examples of Roman numerals," "Ask questions regarding pupils' experiences with Roman numerals."

4. <u>Materials</u>. List special instructional materials, such as "clock face, pictures of monuments, and Grade III sign."

5. <u>Presentation</u>. Describe the methods of presentation you intend to use, such as, "*Explain* equivalence of Arabic and Roman numerals," "*Demonstrate* writing Roman numerals."

6. <u>Key Questions</u>. Write several key questions. For example, "Where have you seen Roman numerals?" and "What time does this clock show?"

7. <u>Assignment</u>. Describe the activity assigned to pupils. For example, "Complete exercises on mimeographed sheet." *Note*: If assignment is a test or worksheet, include a sample when submitting your lesson plan to your supervisor.

8. <u>Evaluation</u>. After taping the presentation of the lesson, and after the pupils have completed the assignment, evaluate pupil achievement in relation to the lesson's objectives. If the assignment was a test or a task that yielded a score, report the range and mean of the scores. If the assignment was an activity that was evaluated subjectively, estimate how well the objective was

achieved, such as, "Some progress toward objective, but objective not achieved," or "Progress within range of objective."

9. <u>Recommendations</u>. Write your recommendations for improving your instructions for presenting this lesson in the future.

10. <u>Assessment</u>. Obtain assessment from either your practicum teacher or supervisor. Follow the procedure described in the *Assessment* instructions for Incidental Intervention. Show the completed form to your teacher education supervisor for an evaluation, H, P, I, or F. Date and distribute the forms as indicated.

Competencies for Teaching—Classroom Instruction

Lesson Plan

1. Student Teacher	Last Name	First		Initial	File Number	ASSESSMENT

Lesson Number	Subject or Activity		Number of Pupils	Tape Recorded ☐	Duration	PRACTICUM TEACHER ☐ Direct ☐ Recorded SUPERVISOR ☐ Direct ☐ Recorded

2. OBJECTIVES

LESSON

ENROUTE

S N | S N

3. INTRODUCTION

4. MATERIALS

S N | S N

5. PRESENTATION

S N | S N

6. KEY QUESTIONS

S N | S N

7. ASSIGNMENT

S N | S N

8. EVALUATION

S N | S N

9. RECOMMENDATIONS

S N | S N

10. Signature	STUDENT TEACHER	PRACTICUM TEACHER	SUPERVISOR	DATE	H P I F

Competencies for Teaching—Classroom Instruction

Lesson Plan

1. Student Teacher	Last Name		First		Initial	File Number		ASSESSMENT	
Lesson Number	Subject or Activity			Number of Pupils	Tape Recorded ☐	Duration		PRACTICUM TEACHER Direct ☐ Recorded ☐	SUPERVISOR Direct ☐ Recorded ☐

2. OBJECTIVES	LESSON			
	ENROUTE		S N	S N

3. INTRODUCTION		

4. MATERIALS		S N	S N

5. PRESEN-TATION		S N	S N

6. KEY QUESTIONS		S N	S N

7. ASSIGNMENT		S N	S N

8. EVALUATION		S N	S N

9. RECOMMENDATIONS		S N	S N

10. Signature	STUDENT TEACHER	PRACTICUM TEACHER	SUPERVISOR	DATE	H P I F

Competencies for Teaching—Classroom Instruction

Lesson Plan

1. Student Teacher	Last Name	First	Initial	File Number	ASSESSMENT

Lesson Number | Subject or Activity | Number of Pupils | Tape Recorded ☐ | Duration

ASSESSMENT — PRACTICUM TEACHER ☐ Direct ☐ Recorded — SUPERVISOR ☐ Direct ☐ Recorded

2. OBJECTIVES — LESSON / ENROUTE		S N	S N
3. INTRODUCTION			
4. MATERIALS		S N	S N
5. PRESENTATION		S N	S N
6. KEY QUESTIONS		S N	S N
7. ASSIGNMENT		S N	S N
8. EVALUATION		S N	S N
9. RECOMMENDATIONS		S N	S N

| 10. Signature | STUDENT TEACHER | PRACTICUM TEACHER | SUPERVISOR | DATE | H P I F |

Directions for Lesson Plan

This lesson plan outline provides guidance in preparing, presenting, and evaluating phases of a lesson. Request from your practicum teacher an assignment of lessons to be taught. A lesson may require one or several periods for its complete presentation.

1. Identifying Information. Enter the required information. Each lesson plan will be assigned a consecutive number (1 to 6). The duration will be entered after completion, for example, "45 minutes," "3, 30-minute periods," "2 periods, total 82 minutes."

2. Objectives. Write the lesson's terminal objective. For example, "Know Roman numerals I to XII." Follow "Lesson Planning" in Chapter Nine of *Classroom Instruction* to complete the assignment. Write the enroute objectives. For example, "Identify uses of Roman numerals," "Recall the letters in Roman numerals I to XII," and "Write Arabic and Roman numerals from 1 to 12 and I to XII."

3. Introduction. Describe briefly how you will stimulate interest in the topic. For example, "Show pictures of clocks, monuments, and other examples of Roman numerals," "Ask questions regarding pupils' experiences with Roman numerals."

4. Materials. List special instructional materials, such as "clock face, pictures of monuments, and Grade III sign."

5. Presentation. Describe the methods of presentation you intend to use, such as, "*Explain* equivalence of Arabic and Roman numerals," "*Demonstrate* writing Roman numerals."

6. Key Questions. Write several key questions. For example, "Where have you seen Roman numerals?" and "What time does this clock show?"

7. Assignment. Describe the activity assigned to pupils. For example, "Complete exercises on mimeographed sheet." *Note*: If assignment is a test or worksheet, include a sample when submitting your lesson plan to your supervisor.

8. Evaluation. After taping the presentation of the lesson, and after the pupils have completed the assignment, evaluate pupil achievement in relation to the lesson's objectives. If the assignment was a test or a task that yielded a score, report the range and mean of the scores. If the assignment was an activity that was evaluated subjectively, estimate how well the objective was

achieved, such as, "Some progress toward objective, but objective not achieved," or "Progress within range of objective."

9. Recommendations. Write your recommendations for improving your instructions for presenting this lesson in the future.

10. Assessment. Obtain assessment from either your practicum teacher or supervisor. Follow the procedure described in the *Assessment* instructions for Incidental Intervention. Show the completed form to your teacher education supervisor for an evaluation, H, P, I, or F. Date and distribute the forms as indicated.

Competencies for Teaching—Classroom Instruction

Lesson Plan

1. Student Teacher	Last Name		First		Initial	File Number	ASSESSMENT

Lesson Number	Subject or Activity			Number of Pupils	Tape Recorded ☐	Duration	PRACTICUM TEACHER / SUPERVISOR — Direct / Recorded

2. OBJECTIVES

LESSON

ENROUTE

S N S N

3. INTRODUCTION

4. MATERIALS

S N S N

5. PRESENTATION

S N S N

6. KEY QUESTIONS

S N S N

7. ASSIGNMENT

S N S N

8. EVALUATION

S N S N

9. RECOMMENDATIONS

S N S N

10. Signature	STUDENT TEACHER	PRACTICUM TEACHER	SUPERVISOR	DATE	H P I F

Competencies for Teaching—Classroom Instruction

Lesson Plan

1. Student Teacher	Last Name		First		Initial	File Number	ASSESSMENT
Lesson Number	Subject or Activity		Number of Pupils	Tape Recorded ☐		Duration	PRACTICUM TEACHER ☐ Direct ☐ Recorded / SUPERVISOR ☐ Direct ☐ Recorded

2. OBJECTIVES
- LESSON
- ENROUTE

Assessment: S N   S N

3. INTRODUCTION

4. MATERIALS

Assessment: S N   S N

5. PRESENTATION

Assessment: S N   S N

6. KEY QUESTIONS

Assessment: S N   S N

7. ASSIGNMENT

Assessment: S N   S N

8. EVALUATION

Assessment: S N   S N

9. RECOMMENDATIONS

Assessment: S N   S N

10. Signature	STUDENT TEACHER	PRACTICUM TEACHER	SUPERVISOR	DATE	H P I F

Competencies for Teaching—Classroom Instruction

Lesson Plan

1. Student Teacher	Last Name	First	Initial	File Number		ASSESSMENT
Lesson Number	Subject or Activity		Number of Pupils	Tape Recorded	Duration	PRACTICUM TEACHER □ Direct □ Recorded / SUPERVISOR □ Direct □ Recorded

2. OBJECTIVES	LESSON		
	ENROUTE		S N / S N

3. INTRODUCTION		

4. MATERIALS		S N / S N

5. PRESEN-TATION		S N / S N

6. KEY QUESTIONS		S N / S N

7. ASSIGNMENT		S N / S N

8. EVALUATION		S N / S N

9. RECOMMENDATIONS		S N / S N

10. Signature	STUDENT TEACHER	PRACTICUM TEACHER	SUPERVISOR	DATE	H P I F

Directions for Lesson Plan

This lesson plan outline provides guidance in preparing, presenting, and evaluating phases of a lesson. Request from your practicum teacher an assignment of lessons to be taught. A lesson may require one or several periods for its complete presentation.

1. <u>Identifying Information</u>. Enter the required information. Each lesson plan will be assigned a consecutive number (1 to 6). The duration will be entered after completion, for example, "45 minutes," "3, 30-minute periods," "2 periods, total 82 minutes."

2. <u>Objectives</u>. Write the lesson's terminal objective. For example, "Know Roman numerals I to XII." Follow "Lesson Planning" in Chapter Nine of *Classroom Instruction* to complete the assignment. Write the enroute objectives. For example, "Identify uses of Roman numerals," "Recall the letters in Roman numerals I to XII," and "Write Arabic and Roman numerals from 1 to 12 and I to XII."

3. <u>Introduction</u>. Describe briefly how you will stimulate interest in the topic. For example, "Show pictures of clocks, monuments, and other examples of Roman numerals," "Ask questions regarding pupils' experiences with Roman numerals."

4. <u>Materials</u>. List special instructional materials, such as "clock face, pictures of monuments, and Grade III sign."

5. <u>Presentation</u>. Describe the methods of presentation you intend to use, such as, "*Explain* equivalence of Arabic and Roman numerals," "*Demonstrate* writing Roman numerals."

6. <u>Key Questions</u>. Write several key questions. For example, "Where have you seen Roman numerals?" and "What time does this clock show?"

7. <u>Assignment</u>. Describe the activity assigned to pupils. For example, "Complete exercises on mimeographed sheet." *Note*: If assignment is a test or worksheet, include a sample when submitting your lesson plan to your supervisor.

8. <u>Evaluation</u>. After taping the presentation of the lesson, and after the pupils have completed the assignment, evaluate pupil achievement in relation to the lesson's objectives. If the assignment was a test or a task that yielded a score, report the range and mean of the scores. If the assignment was an activity that was evaluated subjectively, estimate how well the objective was

achieved, such as, "Some progress toward objective,
but objective not achieved," or "Progress within range
of objective."

    9. Recommendations. Write your recommendations
for improving your instructions for presenting this
lesson in the future.

    10. Assessment. Obtain assessment from either
your practicum teacher or supervisor. Follow the procedure described in the *Assessment* instructions for Incidental Intervention. Show the completed form to your
teacher education supervisor for an evaluation, H, P, I,
or F. Date and distribute the forms as indicated.

Competencies for Teaching—Classroom Instruction

Lesson Plan

1. Student Teacher	Last Name	First	Initial	File Number	ASSESSMENT
Lesson Number	Subject or Activity	Number of Pupils	Tape Recorded ☐	Duration	PRACTICUM TEACHER Direct ☐ Recorded ☐ / SUPERVISOR Direct ☐ Recorded ☐

| 2. OBJECTIVES | LESSON | | | S N | S N |
| | ENROUTE | | | | |

| 3. INTRODUCTION | | | | |

| 4. MATERIALS | | | S N | S N |

| 5. PRESENTATION | | | S N | S N |

| 6. KEY QUESTIONS | | | S N | S N |

| 7. ASSIGNMENT | | | S N | S N |

| 8. EVALUATION | | | S N | S N |

| 9. RECOMMENDATIONS | | | S N | S N |

| 10. Signature | STUDENT TEACHER | PRACTICUM TEACHER | SUPERVISOR | DATE | H P I F |

Competencies for Teaching—Classroom Instruction

Lesson Plan

1. Student Teacher	Last Name	First	Initial	File Number	ASSESSMENT

Lesson Number	Subject or Activity	Number of Pupils	Tape Recorded	Duration	PRACTICUM TEACHER Direct Recorded / SUPERVISOR Direct Recorded

2. OBJECTIVES	LESSON			
	ENROUTE			S N	S N

3. INTRODUCTION			

4. MATERIALS		S N	S N

5. PRESENTATION		S N	S N

6. KEY QUESTIONS		S N	S N

7. ASSIGNMENT		S N	S N

8. EVALUATION		S N	S N

9. RECOMMENDATIONS		S N	S N

10. Signature	STUDENT TEACHER	PRACTICUM TEACHER	SUPERVISOR	DATE	H P I F

Competencies for Teaching—Classroom Instruction

Lesson Plan

1. Student Teacher	Last Name	First		Initial	File Number	ASSESSMENT
Lesson Number	Subject or Activity		Number of Pupils	Tape Recorded ☐	Duration	PRACTICUM TEACHER ☐ Direct ☐ Recorded / SUPERVISOR ☐ Direct ☐ Recorded

2. OBJECTIVES	LESSON			
	ENROUTE			S N	S N

3. INTRODUCTION		

4. MATERIALS		S N	S N

5. PRESENTATION		S N	S N

6. KEY QUESTIONS		S N	S N

7. ASSIGNMENT		S N	S N

8. EVALUATION		S N	S N

9. RECOMMENDATIONS		S N	S N

10. Signature	STUDENT TEACHER	PRACTICUM TEACHER	SUPERVISOR	DATE	H P I F

Directions for Lesson Plan

This lesson plan outline provides guidance in preparing, presenting, and evaluating phases of a lesson. Request from your practicum teacher an assignment of lessons to be taught. A lesson may require one or several periods for its complete presentation.

1. <u>Identifying Information</u>. Enter the required information. Each lesson plan will be assigned a consecutive number (1 to 6). The duration will be entered after completion, for example, "45 minutes," "3, 30-minute periods," "2 periods, total 82 minutes."

2. <u>Objectives</u>. Write the lesson's terminal objective. For example, "Know Roman numerals I to XII." Follow "Lesson Planning" in Chapter Nine of *Classroom Instruction* to complete the assignment. Write the enroute objectives. For example, "Identify uses of Roman numerals," "Recall the letters in Roman numerals I to XII," and "Write Arabic and Roman numerals from 1 to 12 and I to XII."

3. <u>Introduction</u>. Describe briefly how you will stimulate interest in the topic. For example, "Show pictures of clocks, monuments, and other examples of Roman numerals," "Ask questions regarding pupils' experiences with Roman numerals."

4. <u>Materials</u>. List special instructional materials, such as "clock face, pictures of monuments, and Grade III sign."

5. <u>Presentation</u>. Describe the methods of presentation you intend to use, such as, "*Explain* equivalence of Arabic and Roman numerals," "*Demonstrate* writing Roman numerals."

6. <u>Key Questions</u>. Write several key questions. For example, "Where have you seen Roman numerals?" and "What time does this clock show?"

7. <u>Assignment</u>. Describe the activity assigned to pupils. For example, "Complete exercises on mimeographed sheet." *Note*: If assignment is a test or worksheet, include a sample when submitting your lesson plan to your supervisor.

8. <u>Evaluation</u>. After taping the presentation of the lesson, and after the pupils have completed the assignment, evaluate pupil achievement in relation to the lesson's objectives. If the assignment was a test or a task that yielded a score, report the range and mean of the scores. If the assignment was an activity that was evaluated subjectively, estimate how well the objective was

achieved, such as, "Some progress toward objective, but objective not achieved," or "Progress within range of objective."

9. Recommendations. Write your recommendations for improving your instructions for presenting this lesson in the future.

10. Assessment. Obtain assessment from either your practicum teacher or supervisor. Follow the procedure described in the *Assessment* instructions for Incidental Intervention. Show the completed form to your teacher education supervisor for an evaluation, H, P, I, or F. Date and distribute the forms as indicated.

Competencies for Teaching—Classroom Instruction

Lesson Plan

1. Student Teacher	Last Name		First		Initial	File Number	ASSESSMENT
Lesson Number	Subject or Activity		Number of Pupils	Tape Recorded ☐		Duration	PRACTICUM TEACHER ☐ Direct ☐ Recorded / SUPERVISOR ☐ Direct ☐ Recorded

2. OBJECTIVES	LESSON		
	ENROUTE		
			S N S N

3. INTRODUCTION		

4. MATERIALS		S N S N

5. PRESENTATION		S N S N

6. KEY QUESTIONS		S N S N

7. ASSIGNMENT		S N S N

8. EVALUATION		S N S N

9. RECOMMENDATIONS		S N S N

10. Signature	STUDENT TEACHER	PRACTICUM TEACHER	SUPERVISOR	DATE	H P I F

Competencies for Teaching—Classroom Instruction

Lesson Plan

1. Student Teacher	Last Name	First	Initial	File Number	ASSESSMENT
Lesson Number	Subject or Activity	Number of Pupils	Tape Recorded ☐	Duration	PRACTICUM TEACHER ☐ Direct ☐ Recorded / SUPERVISOR ☐ Direct ☐ Recorded

2. OBJECTIVES — LESSON / ENROUTE

S N   S N

3. INTRODUCTION

4. MATERIALS

S N   S N

5. PRESENTATION

S N   S N

6. KEY QUESTIONS

S N   S N

7. ASSIGNMENT

S N   S N

8. EVALUATION

S N   S N

9. RECOMMENDATIONS

S N   S N

10. Signature	STUDENT TEACHER	PRACTICUM TEACHER	SUPERVISOR	DATE	H P I F

Competencies for Teaching—Classroom Instruction

Lesson Plan

1. Student Teacher	Last Name	First	Initial	File Number	ASSESSMENT
Lesson Number	Subject or Activity	Number of Pupils	Tape Recorded ☐	Duration	PRACTICUM TEACHER ☐ Direct ☐ Recorded / SUPERVISOR ☐ Direct ☐ Recorded

2. OBJECTIVES		ASSESSMENT
LESSON		
ENROUTE		S N S N

3. INTRODUCTION		

4. MATERIALS		S N S N

5. PRESENTATION		S N S N

6. KEY QUESTIONS		S N S N

7. ASSIGNMENT		S N S N

8. EVALUATION		S N S N

9. RECOMMENDATIONS		S N S N

10. Signature	STUDENT TEACHER	PRACTICUM TEACHER	SUPERVISOR	DATE	H P I F

Directions for Concomitant Experience

As you progress through your practicum, you will have many opportunities to acquire valuable supplementary experiences. These experiences include observing, operating, constructing, participating, reviewing, attending or visiting items listed on this form. Obviously not all items can be included, so you should add those experiences that you consider to be of most value.

Monitor your progress by recording the date on which you completed a particular project or experience. Attempt to include some items in each category.

1. Identifying Information. Enter your name.

2. Material Used. Identify the major instructional materials you used.

3. Materials Made. Identify teaching aids and materials that you made for teaching this class.

4. Equipment. Learn to operate the equipment listed. If needed, seek help from your practicum teacher, college instructor, or other responsible individual. List other equipment you have operated.

5. Support Services. Obtain permission to review the cumulative folders and other records of the pupils in your practicum class. If the opportunity arises, attend conferences concerning pupil welfare. The knowledge derived from these experiences must be handled as privileged, confidential information.

6. Special Education. Obtain information regarding the policies governing visitations to special classes and then visit and observe some of those available.

7. Special Events. Participate in or observe special activities, including your practicum teacher's preplanning and follow-up of field trips and other events.

8. Professional Activities. Request permission to accompany your practicum teacher to some of the meetings or other professional activities listed.

9. Community Resources. Through knowing the community resources, your teaching can be more realistic and acquaint pupils with more effective utilization of their community.

10. Supplementary Experience. Use this list for additional activities, such as using a language lab, administering a standardized test, or meeting with administrative or special services staff, curriculum specialists,

counselors, psychologists, speech therapists, remedial teachers, and so forth.

   11. Signature. At the conclusion of your practicum, check and sign this form. Enter the date on the form and distribute the copies as indicated.

Competencies for Teaching—Classroom Instruction

Concomitant Experience

1. Student Teacher	Last Name	First	Initial	File Number

2. MATERIALS USED

	Date
Basic Texts	
Course of Study	
Initial Teaching Alphabet	
Programed Instruction	

3. MATERIALS MADE

	Date
Bulletin Board Charts	
Filmstrip/Slides	
Murals	
Overhead Transparencies	
Tape Recordings	

4. EQUIPMENT

	Date
Copy Machine	
Filmstrip/Slide Projector	
Fluid Duplicator	
Motion Picture Projector	
Overhead Projector	
Tape Recorder	

5. SUPPORT SERVICES

Cumulative Folder	
Guidance Conference	
Guidance Folder	
Health Record	
Parent Conference	

6. SPECIAL EDUCATION

EH/NH Class	
EMR Class	
Gifted	
Remedial Reading	
Speech Therapy	

7. SPECIAL EVENTS

Assembly	
Field Trip	
School Club	
Sports Event	

8. PROFESSIONAL ACTIVITIES

Department Meeting	
Faculty Meeting	
P.T.A.	
Teacher Association	

9. COMMUNITY RESOURCES

Art Exhibits	
Business District	
Civic Center	
Library	
Museum	
Parks	
Public Utilities	

10. SUPPLEMENTARY EXPERIENCES

Language Lab	
Reading Lab	
Standardized Testing	

Signature	STUDENT TEACHER	DATE

Competencies for Teaching—Classroom Instruction

Concomitant Experience

1. Student Teacher	Last Name	First	Initial	File Number

2. MATERIALS USED	Date
Basic Texts	
Course of Study	
Initial Teaching Alphabet	
Programed Instruction	

3. MATERIALS MADE	Date
Bulletin Board Charts	
Filmstrip/Slides	
Murals	
Overhead Transparencies	
Tape Recordings	

4. EQUIPMENT	Date
Copy Machine	
Filmstrip/Slide Projector	
Fluid Duplicator	
Motion Picture Projector	
Overhead Projector	
Tape Recorder	

5. SUPPORT SERVICES	
Cumulative Folder	
Guidance Conference	
Guidance Folder	
Health Record	
Parent Conference	

6. SPECIAL EDUCATION	
EH/NH Class	
EMR Class	
Gifted	
Remedial Reading	
Speech Therapy	

7. SPECIAL EVENTS	
Assembly	
Field Trip	
School Club	
Sports Event	

8. PROFESSIONAL ACTIVITIES	
Department Meeting	
Faculty Meeting	
P.T.A.	
Teacher Association	

9. COMMUNITY RESOURCES	
Art Exhibits	
Business District	
Civic Center	
Library	
Museum	
Parks	
Public Utilities	

10. SUPPLEMENTARY EXPERIENCES	
Language Lab	
Reading Lab	
Standardized Testing	

Signature	STUDENT TEACHER	DATE

Competencies for Teaching—Classroom Instruction

Concomitant Experience

1. Student Teacher	Last Name	First	Initial	File Number

2. MATERIALS USED

	Date
Basic Texts	
Course of Study	
Initial Teaching Alphabet	
Programed Instruction	

3. MATERIALS MADE

	Date
Bulletin Board Charts	
Filmstrip/Slides	
Murals	
Overhead Transparencies	
Tape Recordings	

4. EQUIPMENT

	Date
Copy Machine	
Filmstrip/Slide Projector	
Fluid Duplicator	
Motion Picture Projector	
Overhead Projector	
Tape Recorder	

5. SUPPORT SERVICES

Cumulative Folder	
Guidance Conference	
Guidance Folder	
Health Record	
Parent Conference	

6. SPECIAL EDUCATION

EH/NH Class	
EMR Class	
Gifted	
Remedial Reading	
Speech Therapy	

7. SPECIAL EVENTS

Assembly	
Field Trip	
School Club	
Sports Event	

8. PROFESSIONAL ACTIVITIES

Department Meeting	
Faculty Meeting	
P.T.A.	
Teacher Association	

9. COMMUNITY RESOURCES

Art Exhibits	
Business District	
Civic Center	
Library	
Museum	
Parks	
Public Utilities	

10. SUPPLEMENTARY EXPERIENCES

Language Lab	
Reading Lab	
Standardized Testing	

Signature	STUDENT TEACHER	DATE

Index